Colección Támesis

SERIE A: MONOGRAFÍAS, 218

A COMPANION TO CERVANTES'S *NOVELAS EJEMPLARES*

This edited volume of fourteen specially commissioned essays written from a variety of critical perspectives by leading Cervantine scholars seeks to provide an overview of Cervantes's *Novelas ejemplares* which will be of interest to a broad academic readership. An extensive general Introduction places the *Novelas* in the context of Cervantes's life and work; provides basic information about their content, composition, internal ordering, publication, and critical reception, gives detailed consideration to the contemporary literary-theoretical issues implicit in the title, and outlines and contributes to the key critical debates on their variety, unity, exemplarity, and supposed 'hidden mystery'. Studies of the individual *novelas* follow and the volume concludes with two survey essays devoted, respectively, to the understanding of *eutrapelia* implicit in the *Novelas*, and to the dynamics of the character pairing that is one of their salient features. Detailed plot summaries of each of the stories, and a Guide to Further Reading are supplied as appendices.

Stephen Boyd is a lecturer in the Department of Hispanic Studies at University College, Cork.

A COMPANION TO CERVANTES'S *NOVELAS EJEMPLARES*

Edited by

Stephen Boyd

TAMESIS

First published 2005 by Tamesis, Woodbridge

ISBN 1 85566 118 7

Tamesis is an imprint of Boydell & Brewer Ltd
PO Box 9, Woodbridge, Suffolk IP12 3DF, UK
and of Boydell & Brewer Inc.
668 Mt Hope Avenue, Rochester, NY 14620, USA
website: www.boydellandbrewer.com

A CIP catalogue record for this book is available
from the British Library

This publication is printed on acid-free paper

Printed in Great Britain by
Antony Rowe Ltd., Chippenham, Wiltshire

CONTENTS

PREFACE

This *Companion to Cervantes's 'Novelas ejemplares'* has its origins in a colloquium entitled '*Artificio e Invención*: Cervantes's *Novelas ejemplares*' held at University College, Cork from 6 to 7 April 2001 at which earlier versions of Chapters 3, 4, 8, 9 and 14 were read as papers. These have been adapted for this volume and are accompanied by a further nine specially commissioned essays, so that with the exceptions of *El amante liberal* (The Generous Lover), *Las dos doncellas* (The Two Damsels) and *La señora Cornelia* (Lady Cornelia), each of the twelve stories that comprise the *Novelas ejemplares* has a whole chapter devoted to it. One of them, *La fuerza de la sangre* (The Power of Blood) is considered from different points of view in two separate chapters (7 and 8). The first chapter looks at the *Prólogo al lector* (Prologue to the Reader), Cervantes's preface to the *Novelas*, while each of the two final chapters (13 and 14) examines an important aspect of the collection as a whole. The chapters are arranged to reflect the original ordering of the stories. The intention has been to provide students and non-specialist readers with a general overview of the *Novelas ejemplares* (a function primarily, although not exclusively fulfilled by the Introduction, Chapters 13 and 14, the Synopses, and the Guide to Further Reading), and to complement this by offering detailed analyses of individual stories, or of particular aspects of them, by specialists whose work represents something of the variety of critical approaches to be found in contemporary Cervantine scholarship.

English translations for quotations from the *Novelas ejemplares*, and for other citations in Spanish or other languages, have been provided. Where these translations have been taken from published sources, or are the work of individual contributors, this is acknowledged in footnotes. All other translations are by the editor.

The editor gratefully acknowledges the receipt of generous grants towards the publication of this book from the Research Publication Fund of the Faculty of Arts at University College, Cork, and from the Research Publication Fund of the National University of Ireland.

Special thanks are due to those who have assisted in different ways in the preparation of this book: to Pernilla Vizard who performed the task of editorial assistant with exemplary care and patience; to Jo Mackenzie for valuable editorial help in the early stages of the project; to Professor Edwin Williamson (University of Oxford) for his kind assistance with grant applications; to my colleagues, Professor David Mackenzie and Professor Terence O'Reilly for their advice and encouragement; to Elspeth Ferguson, Managing Editor at Támesis, for her patient forbearance; and to my wife, Marjorie, for her unfailing help and support.

LIST OF ABBREVIATIONS

AC	*Anales Cervantinos*
BHS	*Bulletin of Hispanic Studies (Liverpool)*
BRAE	*Boletín de la Real Academia Española*
FMLS	*Forum for Modern Language Studies*
HR	*Hispanic Review*
KRQ	*Kentucky Romance Quarterly*
MLN	*Modern Language Notes*
MLR	*Modern Language Review*
NRFH	*Nueva Revista de Filología Hispánica*
RCEH	*Revista Canadiense de Estudios Hispánicos*

Introduction

Cervantes's most famous work is undoubtedly *Don Quijote*, which was published in two parts in 1605 and 1615. Next to the *Quijote* his *Novelas ejemplares* (Exemplary Tales), which appeared in 1613, have attracted most critical attention, but, except in the case of professional academic scholars and their students, they have always remained relatively little known outside the Spanish-speaking world.[1] It is the aim of this Companion volume to introduce them to a wider English-speaking audience. This Introduction will attempt to give a general overview of the *Novelas ejemplares* – their dating, sources and generic affiliations – as well as of the Spanish and broader European literary-historical environments in which Cervantes wrote them, with special attention being devoted to the related and much-discussed questions of the coherence of the stories as a collection and their exemplary nature.

Cervantes and His Work

Cervantes was born in 1547 in Alcalá de Henares, a small university town close to Madrid. His family seems to have moved around Spain during his childhood, and it is known that his father, a surgeon, was living in Seville in 1564. The praise of the education offered in the Jesuit college in Seville in the last of the *Novelas ejemplares*, *El casamiento engañoso y El coloquio de los perros* (The Deceitful Marriage and The Dialogue of the Dogs) has been used to support speculation that he may have received a Jesuit education there. The family moved to Madrid in 1566, and in 1568 Cervantes published his first work, a poem in praise of the newly-born Princess Catalina, the second daughter of Philip II. In 1569 he contributed four poems to an anthology compiled by Juan López de Hoyos to commemorate the death in October 1568 of the King's third wife, Isabel de Valois. In this volume, López de Hoyos, the rector of an academy called the Estudio de la Villa, refers to him as 'nuestro caro y amado discípulo' (our dear and beloved pupil),[2] showing that although Cervantes never received a university education, he did, even for a short period, pursue the equivalent of third-level studies. It has been suggested that his teacher was an admirer of the work of Erasmus, the

[1] For a list of translations, see Appendix II.

[2] Juan López de Hoyos, *Historia y relación verdadera de la enfermedad, felicísimo tránsito, y sumptuosas exequias fúnebres de la serenísima Reina de España Doña Isabel de Valois nuestra Señora* (Madrid: Pierres Cosin, 1569), fol. 147 (misprinted as 138) v.

Dutch humanist scholar and church reformer whose writings, which had been enormously popular in Spain in the earlier sixteenth century, had been placed on the 1559 Spanish Index of Prohibited Books. It is tempting to imagine that Cervantes's own ironic and sceptical cast of mind may owe something to a possible exposure in these formative years to Erasmus's writings.[3] For reasons that remain unclear, Cervantes moved to Rome in 1569 and spent a period working in the household of one of the great Roman prelates, Monsignor (later Cardinal) Giulio Acquaviva. The following year, still in Italy, he enlisted in the Spanish army (much of Italy was ruled by Spain in this period) and for the next five years fought in various campaigns against the Turks around the Mediterranean, most notably at the Battle of Lepanto on 7 October 1571 when a combined Christian fleet (put together by Spain, the Republic of Venice and the Pope) inflicted a severe defeat on a larger Turkish naval force in the Eastern Mediterranean. Cervantes suffered permanent damage to his left hand from an arquebus (an early form of rifle) shot and contemporary accounts attest his bravery in battle. It is clear that he took great pride in his participation in this action, mentioning it a number of times in his work, most notably in the Prologue to *Don Quijote*, Part II and, not without irony, in the Prologue to the *Novelas ejemplares* (see Chapter 1, pp. 65–6). In September 1575, having resigned his commission, he was returning to Spain with his brother, Rodrigo (also a soldier), when their ship, the *Sol*, was attacked by Turkish pirates. Cervantes spent the next five years in captivity in Algiers, leading several daring but unsuccessful escape bids, before being ransomed with money raised by his family and the Trinitarian religious order (founded to ransom Christian captives), and returned to Spain on 24 October 1580. This experience is also briefly mentioned in the Prologue to the *Novelas ejemplares*, while Cervantes's acquaintance with Italy, with Spanish military campaigns in the Mediterranean and with the life of Christian captives in Algiers are clearly reflected in *El licenciado Vidriera* (The Glass Graduate) and (indirectly) in *El amante liberal* (The Generous Lover). Back in Spain, Cervantes attempted, unsuccessfully, to establish himself as a dramatist in Madrid. He had greater success with the publication in 1585 of Book I of *La Galatea*, a pastoral romance of the kind very much in fashion at the time. In the previous year he had married doña Catalina Palacios Salazar from Esquivias in the province of Toledo. For the rest of the 1580s and all of the 1590s he struggled to make a living in minor government posts, firstly as a commissioner of supplies for the Armada that King Philip II of Spain was planning to send against England, and then, from 1597, as a tax collector. In the meantime, his application in 1590 for an administrative post in the New World had been rejected. He was mostly based in Seville during this period, and was imprisoned on two (perhaps three)

[3] Among the best accounts of the possible influence of Erasmus on Cervantes are Marcel Bataillon's 'El erasmismo de Cervantes' in his magisterial *Erasmo y España*, tr. Antonio Altatorre, 2nd edn rev. (Mexico City: Fondo de Cultura Económica, 1966), pp. 777–801, and Antonio Vilanova, *Erasmo y Cervantes* (Barcelona: Lumen, 1989).

occasions for professional and financial irregularities. His knowledge of Seville, and especially of its infamous *hampa* (criminal underworld) is evidenced in *Rinconete y Cortadillo* (Rinconete and Cortadillo), *El celoso extremeño* (The Jealous Old Man from Extremadura) and *El casamiento engañoso y el coloquio de los perros* (The Deceitful Marriage and The Dialogue of the Dogs). By 1602 he was living in Valladolid (it provides the setting for *El casamiento engañoso*) and must have been completing *Don Quijote*, Part I, which was published in Madrid in 1605. He spent the last eleven years of his life, a period of intense literary activity, in Madrid. He had secured a patron in the person of Pedro Fernández de Castro, Count of Lemos, one of the most powerful men in Spain (he was viceroy of Naples from 1611 to 1616) and also a supporter of other major literary figures such as the dramatist Lope de Vega and the poet Luis de Góngora; he attended literary 'academies' (regular gatherings of writers and intellectuals at which work was read aloud and set topics debated), and he published a whole series of works in all the major genres: the *Novelas ejemplares* in 1613, the *Viaje del Parnaso* (Voyage to Parnassus) (a review of contemporary Spanish poetry in the form of a long poem) in 1614, *Don Quijote*, Part II in 1615, and *Ocho comedias y ocho entremeses* (Eight Plays and Eight Interludes) also in 1615. Cervantes died on 22 April 1616 (within a week of Shakespeare) and was buried clothed in the habit of a Franciscan tertiary. His Byzantine romance in imitation of Heliodorus's *Aethiopica* (Ethiopian History; third century AD), *Los trabajos de Persiles y Sigismunda* (The Trials of Persiles and Sigismunda), was published posthumously in 1617.

Cervantes's especially broad experience of life within Spain and outside it probably helped him to write about such a variety of places and human personalities, and may also have helped to foster that acute awareness of the diversity of mental worlds that human beings can inhabit which permeates much of his work.

The 'Novelas ejemplares'

Although the title *Novelas ejemplares* is often translated into English as 'Exemplary Novels', they are not 'novels' as that term is generally understood and, indeed, were written before the novel as a literary genre came into existence. A more adequate translation might be 'tales' or 'stories'. If each of the final pair of interconnected *novelas* is counted separately, there are twelve of them. In order of appearance within the collection they are: *La gitanilla* (The Little Gypsy Girl); *El amante liberal* (The Generous Lover); *Rinconete y Cortadillo* (Rinconete and Cortadillo); *La española inglesa* (The English Spanish Girl); *El licenciado Vidriera* (The Glass Graduate); *La fuerza de la sangre* (The Power of Blood); *El celoso extremeño* (The Jealous Old Man from Extremadura); *La ilustre fregona* (The Illustrious Kitchen Maid); *Las dos doncellas* (The Two Damsels); *La señora Cornelia* (Lady Cornelia); and *El casamiento engañoso y El coloquio de los perros* (The Deceitful Marriage and The Dialogue of the

Dogs). They are supposedly *exemplary*, meaning, ostensibly, that they are intended to have a morally beneficial effect on their readers. In his introductory *Prólogo al lector* (Prologue to the Reader), Cervantes claims that 'no hay ninguna de quien no se pueda sacar algún ejemplo provechoso' ('there is not one from which you cannot extract some profitable example'), adding that the 'sabroso y honesto fruto' ('delicious and wholesome fruit') which they offer may be gleaned 'así de todas juntas como de cada una de por sí' ('from the collection as a whole and from each one alone').[4] These and other claims he makes about the *ejemplaridad* (exemplarity) of his stories, an issue which has aroused intense critical debate, will be explored in pages 27–31 of this Introduction.

Publication

The first edition of the *Novelas ejemplares* was published by Juan de la Cuesta in Madrid in 1613. It was followed by another in 1614, and by the end of the seventeenth century twenty-two editions in Spanish had been published, indicating a considerable degree of popular success.

Composition

Although attempts have been made to establish approximate datings, the dates of composition of individual *novelas* are uncertain. In addition, there is no guarantee that the order of the *novelas* as they appear in the first and in most subsequent editions reflects the order in which they were written.[5] However, as Peter Dunn has said, 'lo más que se puede decir sin riesgo de error es que las *Novelas* se escribieron, probablemente, entre 1590 y 1612' (the most that can be said without running the risk of error is that the *Novelas* were probably written between 1590 and 1612).[6] What is certain is that earlier and significantly different versions of *Rinconete y Cortadillo* and *El celoso extremeño* appeared in a manuscript literary anthology compiled around 1605 by the prebendary Francisco Porras de la Cámara to provide leisure reading for the Archbishop of Seville.[7] It also contained a third *novela*, entitled *La tía fingida* (The False Aunt)

[4] Miguel de Cervantes, *Novelas ejemplares*, ed. Harry Sieber, 2 vols (Madrid: Cátedra, 1986), I, p. 52. The English translation is from Miguel de Cervantes, *Exemplary Novels / Novelas ejemplares*, ed. B. W. Ife, 4 vols (Warminster: Aris & Phillips, 1992), I, pp. 3, 5. Subsequent references are to these editions.

[5] One of the most serious (and controversial) attempts to establish which *novelas* might be 'late' or 'earlier' works on the grounds of style is Ruth El Saffar's *Novel to Romance: A Study of Cervantes's 'Novelas ejemplares'* (Baltimore, MD: Johns Hopkins University Press, 1974).

[6] See Peter N. Dunn, 'Las *Novelas ejemplares*', in *Suma cervantina*, ed. J. B. Avalle-Arce and E. C. Riley (London: Támesis, 1973), pp. 81–118 (p. 82).

[7] The Porras versions of *Rinconete y Cortadillo* and *El celoso extremeño*, as transcribed by Isidoro Bosarte in the eigthteenth century, can be found in Miguel de Cervantes, *Novelas*

whose authorship by Cervantes has been much debated, with the majority of scholarly opinion being against its acceptance as authentic.[8] The only other indisputable piece of evidence about dating is a reference to *Rinconete y Cortadillo* in Chapter 47 of *Don Quijote*, Part I. Clearly, then, at least two stories were written before 1605.

Ordering

To add to this uncertainty, it is not even clear to what extent, if any, the sequence in which the *novelas* appear in the first and in most subsequent editions was dictated by Cervantes. Nevertheless, because they appear to form a complementary, contrasting pair, it does seem likely that at least the first and last stories (*La gitanilla* and *El casamiento engañoso* y *El coloquio de los perros*) were intended to occupy those positions. *La gitanilla* shines with the beauty, virtue, and grace of its protagonist, but there are some stains upon this radiant surface (as there are flaws on Preciosa's almost perfect body – the mole under her left breast and her webbed toe): her fiancé, don Juan/Andrés, has deceived his parents to be with the young gypsy girl; he has killed the nephew of the mayor of a small town near Murcia, and only his good social connections and his family's money secure his release from prison, persuade the relatives of the dead man to drop court proceedings, encourage the Archbishop of Murcia to waive the normal rules about banns, and so make his happy-ever-after marriage to Preciosa possible. If the brilliance of *La gitanilla* is mottled with traces of darkness, the almost total moral darkness of *El casamiento engañoso y El coloquio de los perros* is relieved by faint pinpricks of light; these include the remnants of reason and conscience present in the witch, la Cañizares and symbolized by the little lamps illuminating her room and its innermost recess, the lamp carried by Mahudes to guide him and the dogs through the night-time streets of Valladolid as he raises funds for the Hospital of the Resurrection, the incipient physical and moral recovery of the Ensign Campuzano, and the friendship between Campuzano and Peralta. In addition, this last story incorporates direct and indirect references to characters and situations from other *novelas*: for example, to Monipodio (*Rinconete y Cortadillo*) (II, pp. 329–330) (IV, p.119) and (in the form of an allusive echo) to the principal protagonists of *La gitanilla* (II, p. 348) (IV, p. 141). These references, taken in

ejemplares, ed. J. B. Avalle-Arce, 2 vols (Madrid: Castalia, 1982), I (pp. 273–317) and II (pp. 223–63) respectively. On the similarities and differences between these versions and the published ones, see E. T. Aylward, *Cervantes: Pioneer and Plagiarist* (London: Támesis, 1982), and Geoffrey Stagg, 'The Refracted Image: Porras and Cervantes', *Cervantes*, 4.1 (1984), 139–53.

[8] On this issue, see E. T. Aylward, 'Significant Disparities in the Text of *La tía fingida* vis-à-vis Cervantes's *El casamiento engañoso*', *Cervantes*, 19.1 (1999), 40–65, and Francisco Márquez Villanueva, '*La tía fingida*: literatura universitaria', in *On Cervantes: Essays for L. A. Murillo*, ed. James A. Parr (Newark, DE: Juan de la Cuesta, 1991), pp. 119–48.

conjuction with of a number of other indications (the final section, for example, is clearly valedictory), make it virtually certain that it was intended to come at the end of the collection. Despite the lack of definite proof, the likelihood is that Cervantes did indeed specify the order of the stories in the first edition, for, as Mary Malcolm Gaylord has observed, 'this author who explores so many other signifying possibilities of form, especially one who insists that the secret fruit of his book belongs to his whole book as well as to its parts, would certainly have taken some care with arrangement'.[9]

Early Reception of the 'Novelas ejemplares'

The first indications we have of how the *Novelas ejemplares* were received come from the four *aprobaciones* (censor's reports) that were issued prior to their publication and included, as the law required, with the other preliminary matter (in particular the Prologue and Dedication) in the printed text. The three censors who read the manuscript personally warmly praise both the artistic merit and moral worth of the *novelas*. Thus, for example, Fray Diego de Hortigosa says:

> [. . .] hallo en él [el libro] cosas de mucho entretenimiento para los curiosos lectores, y avisos y sentencias de mucho provecho, y que preceden de la fecundidad del ingenio de su autor, que no lo muestra en éste menos que en los demás que ha sacado a luz. (I, p.46)
>
> [. . .] I find in it [the book] things that will greatly entertain curious readers, and very beneficial pieces of advice and maxims, all springing from the fertility of the author's wit, which he displays no less in this book than in the others that he has published [. . .].

The four prefatory poems (three of which are sonnets) written by friends of Cervantes are, not surprisingly, also enthusiastic in their praise. In what is probably one of the most suggestive tributes to Cervantes's complex inventiveness in these stories, Fernando Bermúdez y Carvajal, calls them 'doce laberintos' (twelve labyrinths) that display 'mayor ingenio' (greater ingenuity) than that shown by 'aquel Dédalo ingenioso' (that ingenious Daedalus) who created the Cretan labyrinth ('obra peregrina y rara' [I, p. 55] [a rare and extraordinary work]). In his *Viaje del Parnaso* of 1614, Cervantes himself offered this intriguing assessment:

> Yo he abierto en mis *Novelas* un camino,
por do la lengua castellana puede
mostrar con propiedad un desatino.[10]

[9] Mary Malcolm Gaylord, 'Cervantes' Other Fiction', in *The Cambridge Companion to Cervantes*, ed. Anthony J. Cascardi (Cambridge: Cambridge University Press, 2002), pp. 100–130 (p. 112).

[10] Miguel de Cervantes, *Viaje del Parnaso*, ed. Vicente Gaos (Madrid: Castalia, 1973), IV, 25–7 (p. 103).

(In my *Novelas* I have opened up a path
Whereby the Castilian language may
Display a piece of nonsense with propriety.)

The *Novelas* were paid the compliment of imitation by Cervantes's literary rival, Lope de Vega, in his *Filomena* (1621) and *La Circe* (1624). The four *novelas* collected in these works were, Lope claimed, written at the behest of his lover Marta de Nevares. Addressing her as 'Marcia Leonarda' at the start of the *Filomena*, he says:

> En España también se intenta, por no dejar de intentarlo todo, también hay libros de novelas, dellas traducidas de italianos, y dellas propias, en que no faltó gracia y estilo a Miguel de Cervantes. Confieso que son libros de grande entretenimiento, y podrían ser ejemplares, como algunas de las historias trágicas del Bandello [. . .].[11]
>
> (In Spain too, just so as not to fail to attempt everything, attempts have been made [to write *novelas*], so that there are also collections of *novelas*, some of them translated from Italian originals, others native productions, an undertaking in which grace and style were not wanting in Miguel de Cervantes. I must confess that they are very entertaining books, and they could be exemplary, like some of Bandello's tragic tales [. . .])

In his miscellany of three plays and four stories, *Los cigarrales de Toledo* (The Country Houses of Toledo; 1624) Tirso de Molina, famously, although probably not flatteringly, hailed Cervantes as 'nuestro español Bocacio' (our Spanish Boccaccio). Other early seventeenth-century Spanish collections of *novelas* that show a clear debt to Cervantes include Diego de Agredo y Vargas's *Novelas morales: útiles por sus documentos* (Moral Tales: Useful for their Teachings; 1620) and María de Zayas y Sotomayor's *Novelas amorosas y ejemplares* (Amorous and Exemplary Tales; 1637) and *Desengaños amorosos* (The Disenchantments of Love; 1647).[12] The *Novelas ejemplares* were also well received outside Spain. Translations into French, English and Italian appeared in 1614/15, 1626 and 1640 respectively.[13] In his *aprobación* (censor's report) for

[11] Lope de Vega, *Novelas a Marcia Leonarda*, ed. Francisco Rico (Madrid: Alianza, 1968), p. 28.

[12] Diego de Agredo y Vargas, *Novelas morales: útiles por sus documentos* (Valencia: A Costa de Felipe Pincinali Mercader de Libros, 1620); María de Zayas y Sotomayor, *Novelas amorosas y ejemplares*, ed. Agustín G. de Amezúa y Mayo (Madrid: Aldús, 1948); and *Desengaños amorosos*, ed. Alicia Yllera (Madrid: Cátedra, 1983).

[13] *Les nouvelles de Miguel de Cervantes Saavedra*, tr. François de Rosset and Vital d'Audiguier, Sieur de la Ménor, 2 vols (Paris: J. Richer, 1614–15); *Il Novelliere Castigliano*, tr. Gugliemo Alessandro de Novilieri Clavelli (Venice: Presso il Barezzi, 1626); *Exemplarie Novells in Sixe Books*, tr. James Mabbe alias 'Don Diego Puede-Ser' (London: John Dawson, 1640). For the latter, see also *Exemplary Novels by Cervantes*, tr. James Mabbe, ed. S. W. Orson, 2 vols (London: Gibbings; Philadelphia: J. B. Lippincott, 1900). For a detailed account

Don Quijote, Part II (1615) the Licentiate Francisco Márquez Torres recounts how in February 1615 he had heard the French ambassador and his retinue praise Cervantes's work:

> [. . .] apenas oyeron el nombre de Miguel de Cervantes, cuando se comenzaron a hacer lenguas, encareciendo la estimación en que, así en Francia como en los reinos sus confinantes, se tenían sus obras: la *Galatea*, que alguno dellos tiene casi de memoria la primera parte désta, y las *Novelas.*[14]
>
> ([. . .] scarely had they heard Miguel de Cervantes's name when they began to sing his praises, stressing the high esteem in which his works – the *Galatea*, the first part of which a certain one of them knows almost by heart, and the *Novelas* – were held both in France and in the neighbouring kingdoms.)

The Title 'Novelas ejemplares'

The title *Novelas ejemplares* would probably have struck the original readers as something of an oxymoron, rather (*pace* some exaggeration) as if one were to talk today of '*Art* Soap Operas'. In order to understand this it is necessary to know something about the meaning and connotations of the words '*novelas*' and '*ejemplares*'.

In the Prologue to the *Novelas ejemplares* Cervantes claims, essentially correctly, that he is 'el primero que [ha] novelado en lengua castellana' ('the first to write novels in Castilian'), adding that, although many such stories are in print in Spain, 'todas son traducidas de lenguas estranjeras, y éstas son mías propias, no imitadas ni hurtadas' (I, p. 52) ('[they] are all translated from foreign tongues, and these are my very own, neither imitated nor stolen' [I, p. 5]). The *novella* as a genre originated in Italy. Giovanni Boccaccio's *Decameron* (1348–58) is the first great collection of such stories – one hundred of them divided into ten *decades* of ten. Its framing narrative (a device which became a standard feature of the genre) recounts how ten young people who have fled to the hills surrounding Florence in order to escape the plague ravaging the city pass the time (ten days) by telling each other stories, some of which are supposedly 'true' accounts of events that have happened in their own times. The stories are called *novelle* since the original meaning of the word *novella* was 'something new' or 'a piece of news', 'a novelty'. The *novella* as a genre was 'novel' because it reflected the imagined everyday life of remoter times, but especially that of fourteenth-century Italy, in a new, convincing, approximately realistic way. Boccaccio also set the standard for the style of such stories: they were relatively brief, concentrated narratives in which plot

of the reception of the *Novelas* from the eighteenth to the late twentieth centuries, see Michael Nerlich, 'Juan Andrés to Alban Forcione. On the Critical Reception of the *Novelas ejemplares*', in *Cervantes's 'Exemplary Novels' and the Adventure of Writing*, ed. Michael Nerlich and Nicholas Spadaccini (Minneapolis: The Prisma Institute, 1989), pp. 9–47.

[14] *Don Quijote*, ed. John Jay Allen, 2 vols (Madrid: Cátedra, 1992), II, p. 20.

predominated over characterization and in which every detail was subordinate to the working out of the 'point'. In addition, as we have said, they were often given unity and coherence as a collection by being circumscribed within an overall framing narrative.[15] The *Decameron* and other collections of *novelle* it inspired within Italy were eagerly translated and imitated in other European countries. In France, for example, Marguerite de Navarre produced the *Heptameron* (1559), a collection of seventy-two (extant) tales, so-called because in terms of the framing narrative they are recounted over seven days. One of the most voluminous and popular collections was Matteo Bandello's volume of two hundred and fourteen *Novelle* (1554, 1573), which were published in Spanish translation in 1589 and again in 1603. Another was Giambattista Giraldi Cinthio's *Gli Ecatommiti* (*Hecatommithi*; 1565), which appeared in Spanish in 1590. The *Decameron* itself had been translated into Spanish in 1496 as *Las cien novelas*, and by 1559 there were four editions, but the first person to introduce versions of the Italian stories to Spain was Juan de Timoneda in his *El patrañuelo* (1567), a collection of twenty-two *patrañas* (tales, fables), thirteen of which are directly based on original Italian *novelle*.[16] One of the characteristics of the *novelle* that may have accounted for their popularity was their relatively direct and unfettered presentation of the love lives and sexual conduct (or, more often, misconduct) of young Italian townspeople of comfortable means. For this reason, and also because of their often unsympathetic portrayal of the clergy (as, for example, in one of the best known of all such stories, Bandello's 'Romeo et Giulietta' [II, 9]) they became the object of church censorship in Italy, France and Spain (for example, only the 1573 Italian expurgated version of the *Decameron* was allowed to circulate in the latter half of the sixteenth century, after the original full text was placed on the 1559 Spanish Index of Prohibited Books). Spanish translators and adapters of these stories attempted to accommodate their more 'trangressive' features to the tastes of their own more conservative society. For example, as Carmen Rabell has shown, in the version of Bandello's 'Romeo et Giulietta' included in his *Novelas morales: útiles por sus documentos*, Diego de Agreda y Vargas removes all hints of criticism of the nature of Friar Lorenzo's involvement with the young couple.[17] In Catholic countries the official attitude of Church and State towards these stories hardened even further after the Council of Trent (1545–63).

15 For a brief but very useful summary of the characteristics of Boccaccio's stories, see Alban K. Forcione, *Cervantes and the Humanist Vision: A Study of Four 'Exemplary Novels'* (Princeton, NJ: Princeton University Press, 1982), pp. 31–41.

16 On the development of the *novela* in Spain in the Golden Age period, see Jean-Michel Lásperas, *La nouvelle en Espagne au Siècle d'Or* (Montpellier: Editions du Castillet, 1987); Yvonne Yarbro-Bejarano, *The Tradition of the Novela in Spain from Pero Mexía (1540) to Lope de Vega's 'Novelas a Marcia Leonarda'* (1621, 1624) (New York: Garland, 1991); and Carmen R. Rabell, *Rewriting the Italian Novella in Counter-Reformation Spain* (London: Támesis, 2003). Specifically in relation to Cervantes, the fundamental study is Agustín G. de Amezúa y Mayo's *Cervantes creador de la novela corta española*, 2 vols (Madrid: Consejo Superior de Investigaciones Científicas, 1956–58).

17 See Rabell, pp. 48–68.

The Council had been summoned to define the doctrine and reform the practice of the Catholic Church in response to the Protestant Reformation. The Council had underlined the moral responsibilities of Catholic writers, artists and musicians, whose primary aim should be to promote the truths of the Catholic faith. Thus, it seems, a new, more earnest moral climate had already begun to prevail in the Spain in which Cervantes grew up. In this climate, works of fiction, like the *novelle*, with dubious moral (and sometimes anti-clerical) content, and which seemed intended primarily to entertain rather than 'instruct' their readers, were regarded with growing suspicion, although relatively few of them appeared on the Spanish Indices of prohibited books, which were more concerned with removing from circulation books that appeared to question Catholic doctrine.[18] The demand, frequently voiced by Spanish commentators on literature (most of them clerics, religious, humanist scholars, and academics), that works of secular literature should seek to instruct their readers rather than merely entertain them was conditioned not only (to a probably limited extent) by the Council of Trent, but also by the Renaissance debate – mostly conducted by Italian theorists, some of whom (like Torquato Tasso) were also distinguished poets and writers – about the value and function of literature. Two of the key areas of discussion were the questions of the 'truthfulness' of literature and of whether its primary purpose should be to teach or to entertain. Crucial to the discussion of the first question was the 'rediscovery' of Aristotle's *Poetics* when a revised Latin transcription was made by Alessandro de' Pazzi in 1536. Coming as it did from the mouth of the most respected philosopher of classical antiquity, Aristotle's argument that Poetic Truth was superior to Historical Truth because it was more 'philosophical' (since it dealt with 'universals' rather than 'particulars') provided welcome ammunition – especially in the wake of the Council of Trent – for those who were eager to defend the worth of secular literature.[19] The key text around which debate on the second question revolved was a few lines from Horace's *De arte poetica* (On the Art of Poetry): 'Aut prodesse volunt aut delectare poetae | aut simul et iucunda et idonea dicere vitae' (333–34) ('Poets aim either to benefit, or to amuse, or to utter words

[18] For a detailed discussion of these issues, see Peter E. Russell, 'El Concilio de Trento y la literatura profana: reconsideración de una teoría', in his *Temas de 'La Celestina' y otros estudios* (Barcelona: Ariel, 1978), pp. 442–78. Here, he warns against exaggerating the effects of the Council, concluding that 'muy complejo es el problema, al discutir sobre todo en la literatura, distinguir lo que pertenece al ideario y el gusto tridentino y postridentino de lo que paraece originarse en el espíritu europeo de la época sin tener alineamiento con particulares dogmas religiosos' (p. 475) (the problem, especially when it comes to discussing literature, of distinguishing what pertains to Tridentine and post-Tridentine ideology and taste from what appears to originate in the European spirit of the age and is without alignment to particuar religious dogmas, is a very complex one). I am grateful to my colleague, Professor Terence O'Reilly, for drawing my attention to this essay.

[19] 'For this reason poetry is something more philosophical and more worthy of serious attention than history; for while poetry is concerned with universal truths, history treats of particular facts' (Chapter 9). See *Aristotle, Horace, Longinus: Classical Literary Criticism*, tr. T. S. Dorsch (Harmondsworth: Penguin, 1965; repr.1974), pp. 29–75 (pp. 43–4).

at once both pleasing and helpful to life').[20] Some theorists, although a minority (including, for example, Ludovico Castelvetro in his *Poetica* of 1570), defended the view that the primary function of literature was to entertain. Others, notably Julius Caesar Scaliger in his *Poetices libri septem* (Poetics in Seven Books; 1561), advocated a compromise position, believing that works of literature should both entertain and instruct. This belief is reflected in the formula that proliferates to the point of cliché in the prologues to Golden-Age Spanish works of poetry and fiction proclaiming that the author has sought to 'deleitar enseñando' (entertain *while* teaching). Although the most distinguished contributions to these discussions came from Italian theorists, the debate was eagerly taken up in other European countries. In Spain, the most extensive and original work of literary theory was Alonso López Pinciano's *Philosophía antigua poética* (Ancient Poetic Philosophy), published in 1596. In it, El Pinciano advanced the standard neo-Aristotelian view that literature should aim at *verismilitude*, or 'likeness to truth'. It is highly likely that Cervantes knew this work, and there is certainly abundant evidence in his work (not least in the Prologue to the *Novelas ejemplares*, for example) that he was intensely interested in literary-theoretical questions.[21] The point of this discussion is to underscore the fact that, especially in the climate prevailing in Spain in the later sixteenth and early seventeenth centuries, stories of the *novella* kind would have been regarded in some sectors with a certain suspicion, as being, at best, frivolous, and, at worst, a source of serious moral and spiritual damage. This is the primary reason why the title *Novelas ejemplares* would have seemed improbable to the Spanish reading public in 1613.

Let us now look more closely at the second element of the title, the adjective '*ejemplares*'. The fundamental meaning coincides with English 'exemplary', meaning something or someone offering a model or pattern of excellence worthy of imitation. In the moral sense, which, ostensibly, is the primary sense in which Cervantes uses it, it refers to the kind of good conduct that is worthy of imitation. However, it is important to recognize that an *ejemplo* (derived from the Latin *exemplum*) could also be used to refer to the opposite: 'an example of conduct to be avoided'.[22] In Latin and in Spanish the word referred not just to a morally beneficial 'teaching' or 'lesson' but also to the proverb, anecdote or story that conveyed that lesson. Thus, collections of short tales called *exempla* designed to

20 Horace, *Satires, Epistles, 'Ars Poetica'*, tr. H. Rushton Fairclough, Loeb Classical Library (London: Heinemann; New York: G. P. Putnam's Sons, 1929), pp. 478–79.

21 The seminal work on Cervantes's engagement with Italian literary theory is E. C. Riley's *Cervantes's Theory of the Novel* (Oxford: Clarendon Press, 1962). See also Alban K. Forcione, *Cervantes, Aristotle, and the 'Persiles'* (Princeton, NJ: Princeton University Press, 1970). For a brief but very useful summary of Renaissance views on literature, see *The Continental Renaissance 1500–1600*, ed. A. J. Krailsheimer (Harmondsworth: Penguin, 1971), pp. 21–44.

22 Covarrubias, for example, says: 'Absolutamente exemplo se toma en buena parte, pero dezimos dar mal exemplo' (In the absolute sense an example is taken to be a good one, but we also speak of giving bad example). Sebastián de Covarrubias Orozco, *Tesoro de la lengua castellana o española* (Madrid, 1611; repr. Madrid: Turner, 1970), p. 575.

teach a moral lesson, and often specifically to assist the clergy in the preparation of their homilies, proliferate in Europe throughout the medieval period and beyond. One might cite, as an example, the fourteenth-century Spanish collection of short exemplary tales known as *El conde Lucanor* (The Count Lucanor) compiled by the nobleman, don Juan Manuel between 1330 and 1335, and still very popular in sixteenth-century Spain. The Count Lucanor asks his fictional counsellor Patronio's advice on a whole series of practical problems. On each occasion, to illustrate his recommended solution, Patronio tells a story which concludes with a two-line verse summary of its moral. The term *exemplo* (a medieval spelling of *ejemplo*) is used both of the tales told by Patronio and of the couplets that point up the lesson to be learned.[23] In the Prologue to his *Novelas ejemplares*, Cervantes is using the word in the senses of 'example of good or bad moral conduct' and of 'lesson' when, as we have seen, he says of his stories: 'no hay ninguna de quien no se pueda sacar algún ejemplo provechoso' (I, p. 52) ('there is not one from which you cannot extract some profitable example' [I, pp. 3, 5]). However, many critics have argued that he may have called his *Novelas* '*ejemplares*' to indicate not only their moral worth, but also (and perhaps primarily) their aesthetic excellence as 'examples' of good story-telling.[24] This is a question that we shall consider when we come to examine the critical debate about their *ejemplaridad* (exemplarity).

Variety

Variety is a key characteristic of the *Novelas ejemplares*: they explore and interweave many imaginative and historically specific worlds and are filled with characters of all ages, social classes and temperaments. Thus, for example, the collection opens with the fairy-tale-like *La gitanilla* which tells of how a young girl of the aristocratic class, stolen as a baby by a gypsy woman and brought up by her among the gypsies, is eventually restored to her family and marries the young nobleman who had agreed to live with her community for two years in order to prove his love for her; it includes a story (*El licenciado Vidriera* [The Glass Graduate]) about a brilliant young scholar who goes mad, imagining that he is made of glass, and who, after his restoration to sanity, joins the army and dies fighting in battle in Flanders; several of the stories (in particular, *Rinconete y Cortadillo* and *El coloquio de los perros* [The Dialogue of the Dogs]) offer

[23] For example, 'Exemplo VI' concludes with the words: 'Et porque entendió don Iohan que este enxiemplo era muy bueno, fízole poner en este libro et fizo estos viessos que dizen assí: *En [el]comienço deve omne partir | el daño que non le pueda venir*' (And because don Juan realised that this example was a very good one, he had it put into this book and composed the following verses: *A man must remove himself from harm at the start | so that it may not come to him*). See Don Juan Manuel, *El conde Lucanor*, ed. José Manuel Blecua, 2nd edn (Madrid: Castalia, 1971), p. 83.

[24] Avalle-Arce, for example, puts forward this argument in his edition of the *Novelas* (I, pp. 16–18). See also Ife (ed.), I, pp. xii–xiv.

glimpses of Spain's criminal underworld, while others (*El amante liberal* [The Generous Lover], *La española inglesa* [The English Spanish Girl], *Las dos doncellas* [The Two Damsels], *La señora Cornelia* [Lady Cornelia]) are concerned with the love-entanglements of young people of the upper class. The collection concludes with *El coloquio de los perros*, supposedly the transcript of a midnight conversation between two dogs overheard by the protagonist of the framing story, *El casamiento engañoso* (The Deceitful Marriage), while recovering in hospital from syphilis. Although the majority of the stories are set in the Spain of Cervantes's time, or of the not-too-distant past, they also feature other European and non-European places. Thus, for example, *El amante liberal* is largely set in Nicosia and partially in Sicily; the action of much of *La española inglesa* transpires in Elizabethan London; the protagonist of *El licenciado Vidriera* undertakes a long trip around Italy, which is described in some detail, and returns to Spain after passing through Antwerp, Ghent and Brussels. Those stories set in Spain also employ a great variety of locations: the gypsies in *La gitanilla* move down from Madrid to Murcia; the protagonists of *Rinconete y Cortadillo* meet each other at the (historically real) *Molinillo* inn halfway between Toledo and Córdoba and journey down to Seville where most of the story is set; the two young gentlemen disguised as *pícaros* (delinquents) in *La ilustre fregona* leave their families in Burgos and make their way to Toledo via Valladolid and Madrid. Not surprisingly, since Cervantes spent so much time there, Seville, in particular, features strongly as a location (in *Rinconete y Cortadillo*, *El celoso extremeño* [The Jealous Old Man from Extremadura], and *El casamiento engañoso y El coloquio de los perros*).

However, it is with respect to genre, narrative structure and technique that the *Novelas*'s diversity is most original and striking. Cervantes has drawn not just on the Italian *novella* for inspiration (its influence is perhaps most directly seen in *La fuerza de la sangre* and *El celoso extremeño*) but also on wide variety of other literary and non-literary genres. Among the most significant are: the folktale and popular anecdote (as, for example, the story of Domingo ('Sunday'), an Old Christian, being urged to give precedence in entering a church to 'Sábado' ('Saturday'/'Sabbath'), a New Christian of Jewish descent, in *El licenciado Vidriera* [II, p. 56] [II, p.75]); classical mythology, which is especially important in *El celoso extremeño*; classical prose literature, particularly Lucianic dialogue, the Milesian fable and Apuleius's *Golden Ass*, all of which subtend *El coloquio de los perros*;[25] classical Latin poetry (for example, the passages from Ovid cited in *El licenciado Vidriera* [II, pp. 58–9][II, p.79]); Byzantine romance

[25] Specifically, Lucian of Samosata's (born *c.*120 AD) imaginary dialogue (called *The Dream, or The Cock*) between a shoemaker called Micyllus and Pythagoras in the form of a cock. Milesian fables are stories of roguery often with erotic content written by, or in the style of, the second-century (BC) Greek author, Aristides of Miletus. They provided the inspiration for *The Golden Ass*, a satire by the Roman writer, Apuleius (*c.*124–*c.*170 AD) whose protagonist, Lucius, is transformed into an ass. See Frank Pierce, 'Cervantes' Animal Fable', *Atlante*, 3.3 (1955), pp. 103–15.

(*El amante liberal*; *La española inglesa*; *Las dos doncellas*; *La señora Cornelia*); pastoral romance (*La gitanilla*; *La ilustre fregona*); the picaresque novel (*Rinconete y Cortadillo; La ilustre fregona; El casamiento engañoso y El coloquio de los perros*);[26] the Bible (throughout, but especially in *El celoso extremeño*, in which the parable of the Prodigal Son functions as an important sub-text); and popular secular and devotional verse (*La gitanilla*). *El licenciado Vidriera* and *El casamiento engañoso y El coloquio de los perros* show his experimentation with narration at its most radical. It is not, however, the variety of sources *per se* that makes the *Novelas ejemplares* so original, but rather the innovative way in which Cervantes blends elements of their content, structure and language, blurring and breaking down traditionally well-defined generic boundaries. Thus, for example, among other genres, *La gitanilla* draws simultaneously on the folktale motif of the 'Lost Child Found',[27] pastoral and chivalresque romance, the picaresque novel, the Bible, and popular secular and religious verse. While some stories (such as *La gitanilla, El amante liberal, La española inglesa, La fuerza de la sangre, Las dos doncellas* and *La señora Cornelia*) appear to offer themselves as examples of well-rounded stories that succeed in integrating their sub-plots and flashbacks in the smooth, harmonious manner that is especially typical of Byzantine romance, two stories in particular, *El licenciado Vidriera* and, above all, *El casamiento engañoso y El coloquio de los perros*, seem to experiment with a very different kind of aesthetic, one that makes

[26] Byzantine romances are stories of love and adventure modelled on the *Ethiopian History* (also known as the *History of Theogenes and Chariclea*) by Heliodorus (3rd century AD) and *Leucippe and Cleitophon* by Achilles Tatius (2nd century AD), both late-Greek writers. These works were popular in translation in sixteenth- and seventeenth-century Europe. Both the prototypes and the works inspired by them are characterized by their elaborate interweaving of (often improbable) adventures. See Alban K. Forcione, 'Heliodorus and Literary Theory', in *Cervantes, Aristotle and the 'Persiles'*, pp 49–87. Pastoral romances (or Pastoral novels) are a Renaissance invention. They are intricate stories of unrequited love set in an idealized, Arcadian landscape, protagonized by aristocratic pseudo-shepherds and shepherdesses (sometimes identifiable under their Latinate pseudonyms as members of the author's social circle) and interspersed with neo-Platonic love poems. Essentially, they provided a vehicle for the exploration of the psychology of love. The most famous Spanish example is Jorge de Montemayor's *La Diana* (1559). Cervantes's first published work of prose fiction *La Galatea* (1585) was a 'novela pastoril'. For a general survey, see Amadeu Solé-Leris, *The Spanish Pastoral Novel* (Boston: Twayne, 1980). The picaresque novel (*La novela picaresca*) originated in Spain with the publication in 1554 of the anonymous *Lazarillo de Tormes*, the short fictional autobiography of the eponymous *pícaro* (rogue, or delinquent) who recounts his experiences with a series of cruel masters, and his rise through 'fuerza y maña' (force and guile) to the 'pinnacle of all good fortune' as a towncrier and complaisant husband of an archpriest's mistress. The picaresque novel *par excellence* for Cervantes's contemporaries was Mateo Alemán's two-volume *Guzmán de Alfarache* (1599, 1604). See Peter N. Dunn, *Spanish Picaresque Fiction: A New Literary History* (Ithaca, NY: Cornell University Press, 1993).

[27] See R. M. Price, 'Cervantes and the Topic of the "Lost Child Found" in the *Novelas ejemplares*', *AC*, 27 (1989), 203–14.

a virtue out of what looks like fragmentation and even shapelessness.[28] The first of these is notable for its markedly disproportionate correlation between 'real' and narrated time: the reader is told almost nothing about the background of the protagonist, Tomás Rodaja, who is about eleven years old at the start of the story, very little about his eight years of study at Salamanca, a lot (relatively) about his short tour of Italy and his two-year period of mental illness back in Spain, and almost nothing about the final period of his life as a soldier in the Netherlands where he dies in battle. But perhaps the most unusual feature of the story, especially in light of the lack of information about the protagonist himself, is its incorporation of lengthy lists of Spanish and Italian wines, of the sights of Italy and, above all, of Tomás's acidly critical comments on almost every sector of society in Spain. The comparatively angular and seemingly disjointed rhythms and texture of this *novela* led many critics before Casalduero to consider it an artistic failure.[29] It is possible, however, to see this fragmentation of structure in a very different way: as a carefully calculated and singularly appropriate correlative of the mental imbalance, and subsequent madness, of the protagonist.[30] The final story in the collection, *El Casamiento engañoso y El coloquio de los perros* is even more unconventional. As its title indicates, it falls into two seemingly independent parts: in the first, the Ensign Campuzano tells his friend, the Licentiate Peralta, the story of his 'deceitful marriage' for money to a woman whom he thought to be wealthy but who turned out to be as poor as himself and, in fact, to have married him for what she thought was his wealth. He contracted syphilis as a result and had to spend a period being treated in hospital. He hands his friend what he claims to be the transcript of a nocturnal conversation he overheard between the two hospital guard dogs. This 'Dialogue of the Dogs', which at first sight appears to be only circumstantially related to the story of Campuzano's marriage, is in fact closely linked to it in theme: one dog tells the other of his life with a series of masters from all walks of life, unfolding as he does so a depressing picture of human greed and egotism that forms the second and materially most substantial part of the story. In a brief coda, the two friends

[28] This is the view advanced by Alban K. Forcione in his *Cervantes and the Mystery of Lawlessness: A Study of 'El casamiento engañoso y El coloquio de los perros'* (Princeton, NJ: Princeton University Press, 1984), pp. 36–58.

[29] For example, William C. Atkinson believed that 'its artistic value as a short story is nil', 'Cervantes, El Pinciano and the *Novelas ejemplares*', *HR*, 16 (1948), 189–208 (p. 203). See Joaquín Casalduero, *Sentido y forma de las 'Novelas ejemplares'* (Madrid: Gredos, 1962) pp. 137–49.

[30] Compare, for example, the way in which the greatest painter of the Spanish Golden Age, Velázquez (1599–1660), breaks the rules of decorum governing portraiture by using deliberately ill-defined spacial settings, angular drawing and 'distressed' brushwork in his portraits of the *bufones* (court jesters), Pablo de Valladolid (*c.*1635–40, Madrid, Museo del Prado) and Calabazas (*c.*1639, Madrid, Museo del Prado). As Jonathan Brown observes, 'Velázquez's official portraits provided no opportunity to examine the inner life of the sitters; what mattered was their status, not their state of mind. But when he painted portraits of jesters and dwarfs, who were on the margins of court society, he was free to experiment'. See his *The Golden Age of Painting in Spain* (New Haven; London: Yale University Press, 1991), p. 152.

discuss the truthfulness of the dialogue, agree to disagree, and then set off for a walk. Not only has Cervantes combined different literary genres, the tale and the dialogue – and the dialogue in turn with some of the conventions of picaresque fiction and of classical satire – in a most original way, but he has also created an elaborate 'Russian doll'-like structure of narrators and narratees and told his tale so that it moves backwards from the fictional present of the opening conversation between Campuzano and Peralta to the story of the deceitful marriage, and then forward again to the start of the *Coloquio*. In the *Coloquio* itself, one of the dogs, Berganza, tells the other (Cipión) the story of his life, going back in the middle of his account to the moment of their birth and then forward again to their present. At the end of the *Coloquio* (as a text within a text) this present coincides not only with that of the fictional author (Campuzano) and reader (Peralta) of the dogs' conversation, but also with that of the real reader. Thus, the narrative pattern of the two stories taken together has a double, overlapping, chiastic structure: in each part (the *Casamiento* and the *Coloquio*) the narrator takes the narratee back in time, and then forward again to their shared present, but the point furthest back in fictional time – the birth of the dogs – lies in the middle of the *Coloquio* so that, although as a narrative the *Coloquio* is enveloped in and subordinate to the *Casamiento*, in terms of temporal evolution, material size and theme (the human capacity for deceit) it precedes and takes precedence over the *Casamiento*.[31] It is, perhaps, not surprising, then, that at one point the nature of narrative itself should become the subject of the dogs' discussion. Indeed, Cipión's image of the octopus for the amorphousness (as he sees it) of Berganza's story (' – Quiero decir que la sigas [tu historia] de golpe, sin que la hagas que parezca pulpo, según la vas añadiendo colas' [II, p. 319]) ('I mean that you should carry on [your story] straightaway, without adding tails to it which makes itseem like an octopus' [IV, p. 107]) might be seen as being applicable to the whole *novela* which radiates outwards, temporally and thematically, from the central point of the witch, la Cañizares's account of the birth of the dogs. It would not be surprising if Cervantes had *El casamiento engañoso y El coloquio de los perros* – the seond part is, after all, a conversation between two dogs – specifically in mind when he made the remark [see pp. 6–7 above] about finding a way to 'display a piece of nonsense with propriety'. Evidently, in the *Novelas ejemplares* as, *par excellence*, in *Don Quijote*, he was interested in conducting experiments in narration, with the aim of offering the widest possible sample of ways in which a story might be told, and so compiling a kind of exemplary *ars narrandi*. As Antonio Rey Hazas puts it:

> Tan portentoso esfuerzo de reflexión, meditación, asimilación y, sobre todo, de innovación novelesca no puede deberse, obvio es decirlo, a la casualidad. Se trata, sin duda, del resultado, magistral por otra parte, de un plan total de renovación de la novela quinientista. De un proyecto consciente, bien concebido

[31] See Edward Aylward's detailed discussion of the narrative structure of the *Casamiento/Coloquio* in Chapter 12 of the present volume.

> y mejor acabado, de remozamiento de todas las formas narrativas existentes, cuyo fruto general y, desde luego, en los mejores casos, es, simplemente, la novela, sin más adjetivos, o la novela moderna, si se quiere.[32]
>
> (It hardly needs pointing out that such an extraordinary effort of reflection, meditation, assimilation, and, above all, of narrative innovation, cannot be put down to chance. There can be no doubt that what we are actually looking at are, on the contrary, the magisterial results of a coherent plan to renew sixteenth-century fiction, a conscious, well-conceived and even better executed project to rejuvenate all existing narrative forms, the overall result of which – in the best cases, of course – is simply, and without further qualification, the novel, or, if you will, the modern novel.)

Unifying Patterns

In the Prologue to the *Cigarrales de Toledo*, Tirso de Molina spoke of his stories as '*Doce Novelas* ni hurtadas de las toscanas, ni ensartadas unas tras otras como procesión de disciplinantes, sino con su argumento que lo comprehende todo' (*Twelve Novels* neither filched from the Tuscan [Italian] examples, nor strung together one after another like a procession of penitents, but with an argument that embraces all of them). As Anthony Close has observed, this is almost certainly a slighting reference to what Tirso saw as a lack of coherence (principally due to the lack of a narrative frame) in Cervantes's *Novelas*.[33] Indeed, the sheer variety of Cervantes's collection does raise the question of unity: are these simply quite different stories, written independently of each other, at different times from the 1590s onwards, and finally put together for publication by Cervantes in 1612 under a convenient and eye-catching title, but with no particular coherence as a collection other than the fact that they are written by the same author and therefore bound, almost inevitably, to betray the common imprint of his style and his preoccupations? Cervantes's claim in the *Prologue* that the reader may extract their 'sabroso y honesto fruto [. . .] así de todas juntas, como de cada una de por sí' (I, p. 52) ('delicious and wholesome fruit [. . .] from the collection as a whole and from each one alone' [I, pp. 3, 5]) certainly seems to imply that his stories are intended to form a single body of work. Many attempts have been made to discern a unifying principle or pattern (thematic, structural, autobiographical, and so on) underlying the seemingly random variety of subject matter, generic codes and narrative techniques to be found in the *Novelas*. Leaving aside, for the moment, attempts to categorize them in terms of genre typology

32 Antonio Rey Hazas, '*Novelas ejemplares*', in *Cervantes*, ed. Anthony Close and others (Alcalá de Henares: Centro de Estudios Cervantinos, 1995), pp. 173–209 (p. 182).

33 *Obras Completas de Tirso de Molina*, ed. Pilar Palomo and Isabel Prieto, 3 vols (Madrid: Turner, 1994), I (Prosa y verso), p. 11; and see Anthony Close, *Cervantes and the Comic Mind of his Age* (Oxford: Oxford University Press, 2000), p. 244.

(these will be considered at pp. 19–20 below), one can cite, for example, Werner Krauss's belief that the stories are unified by their autobiographical background, a belief that led him to suggest an alternative ordering;[34] Joaquín Casalduero's thesis, outlined in his extremely influential *Sentido y forma de las 'Novelas ejemplares'* (1962), that the central theme of love gave the collection its coherence and precise shape;[35] and Walter Pabst's argument that the collection has a maze-like structure, that the final stories (the *Casamiento* and the *Coloquio*) constitute a 'retroactive', but removable frame, and that unity consists in the kind of synthesizing effort of interpretation Cervantes requires of the reader.[36] More recently, William H. Clamurro, while stating his conviction that the *Novelas* 'cannot be reduced into a unifying framework' has argued that 'each of [them] embodies a vision of the interlocking problems of individual identity and social order';[37] and Edward Aylward has tried to demonstrate that what he terms the 'crucible concept' (the representation of 'life as a sentimental crucible in which the protagonists' inflated egos undergo a process of psychological dissolution and coagulation in a series of harrowing and sometimes near miraculous occurences') is 'the overriding thematic element that manages to hold together an otherwise curious and incongruous collection'.[38] An important trend in criticism of the *Novelas*, which emerges even in the work of those who (like Clamurro) seek to discover in them the maximum possible unity, is the maintenance of a sceptical attitude towards the possibility, or indeed the value, of uncovering any kind of interpretative 'master key' that would unlock the 'misterio escondido' (hidden mystery) of these texts.[39] Without making any claims to comprehensiveness or to having discovered any such 'master key', one can nonetheless identify some recurring motifs, patterns and themes that do give a sense of unity to the *Novelas* as a whole. We shall now identity and selectively discuss some of them.

[34] See Werner Krauss, 'Cervantes und der Spanische Weg der Novelle', in *Studien und Aufsätze* (Berlin: PUB, 1959), pp. 93–138.

[35] 'Cada una de las once novelas nos cuenta una historia de amor, la cual ocupa un plano distinto en cada obra y, por lo tanto, da lugar a una perspectiva diferente en cada novela, con la consiguiente ordenación de valores' (p. 12) (Each of the eleven [he counts the last two stories as one story] *novelas* tells us a story of love, which occupies a different plane in each work and, therefore, gives rise to a different perspective in each *novela*, along with a corresponding ordering of values).

[36] See Walter Pabst, *La novela corta en la teoría y en la creación literaria*, tr. Rafael de la Vega (Madrid: Gredos, 1972).

[37] See William H. Clamurro, *Beneath the Fiction: The Contrary Worlds of Cervantes's 'Novelas ejemplares'* (New York: Peter Lang, 1997), p. xi.

[38] See E. T. Aylward, *The Crucible Concept: Thematic and Narrative Patterns in Cervantes's 'Novelas ejemplares'* (Madison, NJ: Associated University Press, 1999), p. 11.

[39] See, for example, Peter Dunn's remarks in Chapter 3 (pp. 86–9). In the Prologue, Cervantes claims that, since he has dedicated his novelas to the Count of Lemos, they contain 'algún misterio escondido [. . .] que las levanta' (I, p. 53) ('some hidden mystery which elevates them to that level' [I, p. 5]). For a general overview of *Novelas ejemplares* interpretation, see Nerlich, 'Juan Andrés', and Aylward, *The Crucible Concept*, pp. 19–29.

One of the ways in which scholars have tried to find a pattern in the *Novelas ejemplares* is through typological classification. This has usually meant dividing them dualistically into 'romance' versus 'satirical', 'open' versus 'closed', 'idealistic' versus 'realistic, 'romance' versus 'novelistic', and so on.[40] Probably one of the most useful and influential attempts to classify them in terms of genre is by the distinguished Cervantine scholar, E.C. Riley.[41] He considered that they might be divided into three basic types: 1. 'Predominantly Romance' 2. 'Predominantly Novelistic' and 3. 'Mixed' (or 'Hybrid') (pp. 77–8). According to Riley, those in the first group are characterized by some or all of the features traditionally associated with 'romance-style' narratives. That is, they are stories of 'adventure or love, usually both' (p. 76) involving idealized, stereotypical characters (often outstandingly good-looking young people of the higher social classes); 'exotic', remote, or unfamiliar settings; complex plot patterns characterised by coincidence, recognition scenes and reversals of fortune; and happy endings, often featuring the marriage of young lovers whose fidelity to each other has been tested by their overcoming of such obstacles as disapproving parents, jealous rivals, or their own (usually the male partner's) moral shortcomings. As Riley sees it, the *novelas* in this group are: *El amante liberal*, *La fuerza de la sangre*, *La española inglesa*, *Las dos doncellas,* and *La señora Cornelia.* The 'predominantly novelistic' stories are fundamentally more realistic (in a strictly relative sense) – so that the characters are of all ages and social classes and may well be old and physically and/or morally unattractive (like the protagonist of *El celoso extremeño*); the plots unfold in a less 'artificial' way, often in real places in Spain, and in clearly identified historical periods (as, for example, in *El licenciado Vidriera*), and there is a greater variety of theme.[42] The stories he includes in this group are: *Rinconete y Cortadillo*, *El licenciado Vidriera*, *El celoso extremeño*, *El casamiento engañoso*, and *El coloquio de los perros*. His third group comprises two stories, *La gitanilla* and *La ilustre fregona*, in which he sees 'romance' and 'novelistic' elements blended in a highly original and experimental way. As Riley points out, it is the 'novelistic' stories that proved most popular with twentieth-century readers and critics, whereas seventeenth-century readers seem to have shown a marked preference for the 'romance' kind. He cites in evidence (pp. 78–9) James Mabbe's selection of *Las dos doncellas*, *La señora Cornelia*, *El amante liberal*, *La fuerza de la sangre*, *La española inglesa*, and *El celoso extremeño* for his 1640 English version, which one might

40 For good summaries of these attempts, see again Nerlich, 'Juan Andrés', especially pp. 21–4 and 34–8; and Aylward, *The Crucible Concept*, pp. 19–29.

41 E. C. Riley, 'Cervantes: A Question of Genre', in *Medieval and Renaissance Studies on Spain and Portugal in Honour of P. E. Russell*, ed. F. W. Hodcroft and others (Oxford: Society for the Study of Mediaeval Languages and Literature, 1981), pp. 69–85.

42 Riley explains that he uses the term 'novelistic' 'to refer to prose narrative of the kind generally associated with modern realistic fiction, without distinguishing types of realism' (p. 71). On the issue of 'realism' in the *Novelas*, see Frank Pierce, 'Reality and Realism in the *Exemplary Novels*', *BHS*, 30 (1953), 134–42.

compare with C.A. Jones's choice of *La gitanilla*, *Rinconete y Cortadillo*, *El licenciado Vidriera*, *El celoso extremeño*, and *El casamiento engañoso y El coloquio de los perros* for the Penguin *Exemplary Stories* (1972).[43] Since Riley wrote his article, and especially in recent years, this trend has become less dominant and there has been renewed critical interest in and appreciation of all of Cervantes's romance-type fictions, including the 'idealistic' *novelas* and, above all, the *Persiles*.[44]

Another possible patterning, that could suggest that the *Novelas* do form some kind of whole, has to do with their titles. These almost always refer to their protagonists and often involve a combination of generic noun and qualifying adjective, as, for example, *El amante liberal*, or *El celoso extremeño*. In many cases the combination of noun and adjective is intriguing and sometimes oxymoronic (like the title of the collection itself): *La gitanilla* (The Little Gypsy Girl) (because of the softness of attitude it implies, the use of the diminutive ending is unusual, since gypsies were a then much despised social group); *La española inglesa* (The English Spanish Girl); *El licenciado Vidriera* (The Glass Graduate); *La ilustre fregona* (The Illustrious Kitchenmaid). In three cases the titles refer to the protagonists in a more neutral way: *Rinconete y Cortadillo* (these nicknames are nonetheless intriguing), *Las dos doncellas* (The Two Damsels), and *La señora Cornelia* (Lady Cornelia). Only in two cases do the titles not refer to the protagonists but to the content of the story, and these titles are also clearly calculated to arouse curiosity: *La fuerza de la sangre* (The Power of Blood) and *El casamiento engañoso y El coloquio de los perros* (The Deceitful Marriage and The Dialogue of the Dogs). The latter is particularly intriguing because of its two inbuilt contradictions: a marriage that involves deceit, and dogs that can talk. These unusual, paradoxical, sometimes oxymoronic, titles – although perhaps designed, on one level, to encourage people to read (and buy) the collection – also provide pointers towards one of Cervantes's most serious and central concerns: the contradictory patterns of life itself (see pp. 27–31 and 31–40 below).

Yet another pattern which seems to point towards the unity of the collection is that formed by what look like internal echoes between some of the stories. In a number of them, for example, the names of characters are markedly similar: thus, we have a series of male protagonists whose names begin with 'R': Ricardo (*El amante liberal*); Ricaredo (*La española inglesa*); Rodolfo (*La fuerza de la sangre*); and another series of female protagonists whose names begin with 'Leo . . .': Leonisa (*El amante liberal*), Leocadia (*La fuerza de la sangre*), Leonora (*El celoso extremeño*), and Leocadia (again) in *Las dos doncellas*. In *La*

43 Miguel de Cervantes, *Exemplary Stories*, tr. C. A. Jones (Harmondsworth: Penguin, 1972). Harriet de Onís's selection for translation is almost exactly the same as Jones's, except that she also includes *El amante liberal*; see *Cervantes: Six Exemplary Tales* (Woodbury, NY: Barron's, 1961).

44 As Mary Malcolm Gaylord observes, 'the grid-resistant diversity of the motley "hybrids" has pointed the way beyond preconceptions and pigeonholing towards more probing readings of all of the *Exemplary Novels*' ('Cervantes' other fiction', p. 112).

gitanilla and *La ilustre fregona*, the two *novelas* which feature young aristocratic women who have been brought up in humble circumstances before being restored to their rightful place in society, the protagonists, names are the same: Costanza (although Preciosa [*La gitanilla*] is also referred to as Constanza). Many of the principal male characters have surnames beginning in 'Ca . . .': don Juan de Cárcamo (*La gitanilla*); Felipo de Carrizales (*El celoso extremeño*); don Diego de Carriazo (Junior and Senior) (*La ilustre fregona*); and Ensign Campuzano (*El casamiento engañoso y El coloquio de los perros*). We have already mentioned (p. 5) a number of ways in which the final story alludes to some of the other, preceding ones, but there is at least one other example of such internal cross-referencing. In *La ilustre fregona*, the two young aristocratic protagonists, Diego de Carriazo and Tomás de Avendaño, are making their way to Seville dressed as *pícaros*. At Illescas they encounter two other young men, both muleteers (a profession often associated with criminality), one of whom is coming up from Seville and the other going down to it. As Carriazo and Avendaño continue on their way they mimic the accents and gestures of the muleteers (II, p. 149) (III, p.71). Apart from the irony of the fact that they are already playing at being *pícaros* in a much more thoroughgoing way, one may also discern here a double inverted echo of the other pair of *pícaros* who feature in the *Novelas ejemplares*: the eponymous protagonists of *Rinconete y Cortadillo*, who also make their way down from the centre of Spain to Seville, and who are shown in their first conversation to imitate the language of young gentlemen (I, pp. 193–98) (I, pp. 175, 177, 179). However, it is probably wise not to take such patterns too seriously. Indeed, the case of the deranged mathematician in the *Coloquio* who has spent twenty-two years trying to find the fixed point and to square the circle (II, p. 356) (IV, p. 153) seems to send out a strong warning signal to those tempted to mistake neat pattern-making for truth.

The most alluring key to the possible unity of the *Novelas ejemplares*, however, seems to lie in the area of theme. Love, marriage, friendship, freedom, identity, desire, sin, the problems of knowing the truth (about anything), and the workings of Divine Providence are certainly identifiable as recurrent themes. With respect to the first two of these, virtually all of the stories, with the exception of *Rinconete y Cortadillo* and *El licenciado Vidiera* (in which, however, ideas about friendship are important), centrally concern a relationship between a man and a woman which ends in marriage. In many cases (*La gitanilla*, *El amante liberal*, *La española inglesa*, *La fuerza de la sangre*, *La ilustre fregona*, *Las dos doncellas*, *La señora Cornelia*) it is a happy and fruitful one, but in others (*El celoso extremeño* and *El casamiento engañoso*), it is inappropriate or abusive. In the first group (with the exception of *La ilustre fregona*), the male characters must overcome their sensuality or irresponsibility, or begin to control their jealousy and possessiveness. However, young Diego de Carriazo in *La ilustre fregona* is never shown to acknowledge his misdemeanours (some of which – causing considerable injury to a water-seller and almost beating a young boy to death – are serious) or to receive any proportionate punishment for them; on the contrary, he appears to to be rewarded with a happy marriage and, we are told, is only occasionally troubled by the apprehension that some day someone who remembers his wild exploits in Toledo may turn up and momentarily ruffle the respectability he has acquired in middle life.

In many of the stories an exceptionally beautiful and virtuous female character is the victim of an injustice (often a displacement from the world or social class into which she was born) that is eventually put right: for example, Preciosa (*La gitanilla*); Leonisa (*El amante liberal*); Isabel (*La española inglesa*); Leocadia (*La fuerza de la sangre*); Costanza (*La ilustre fregona*); Teodosia (*Las dos doncellas*); and Cornelia Bentibolli (*La señora Cornelia*). In contrast, however, a few important female characters are 'demonic' figures, driven by lust and greed: Juana Carducha (*La gitanilla*); doña Estefanía (*El casamiento engañoso*); and the witch, la Cañizares (*El casamiento engañoso*).

Freedom, especially inner freedom, is a central theme, which will be explored in greater detail in pp. 32–3 below. It emerges especially strongly in *La gitanilla*, *El amante liberal*, *El celoso extremeño*, and *El coloquio de los perros*. In the person of its protagonist (Preciosa), the first story, *La gitanilla*, offers a vision of what perfect inner freedom looks like. She is someone who combines goodness with spontaneity and wit, neither lapsing into the licence typical of the gypsy community in which she has been brought up, nor becoming a prisoner of the hypocritical concern with respectability that is seen to characterize the upper-class milieu into which she was born, and to which she is eventually restored. In contrast, both parts of the final story, *El casamiento engañoso y El coloquio de los perros*, are replete with characters whose freedom is constrained by their attachment to their selfish desires. The Ensign Campuzano confesses to his friend Peralta that at the time of his marriage he paid no attention to '[otros] discursos de aquellos a que daba lugar el gusto, que me tenía echados grillos al entendimiento' (II, p. 285) ('arguments other than those dictated by my pleasure, which had my powers of reasoning in its grip' [IV, p. 71]). In the *Coloquio*, the beauty, singing and dancing of Preciosa – external expressions of her freedom – find their complementary opposite in the physical degradation of the old witch, la Cañizares, withdrawn into 'su aposento, que era escuro, estrecho y bajo' (II, p. 336) ('her room, which was dark, narrow and with a low ceiling' [IV, p. 127]) – the perfect image of her servitude – and acknowledging, like Campuzano, that 'como el deleite me tiene echados grillos a la voluntad, siempre he sido y seré mala' (II, p. 342) ('as pleasure has gripped my will, I am and will always be evil' [IV, p. 135]).

The theme of identity, linked with that of transformation, is also fundamental. As we have already observed, many of the *Novelas ejemplares* feature characters who undergo some kind of transformation, whether outward or inward, or both. These changes may be very marked, or, more often, partial, incipient or merely aspirational. Cervantes uses them as vehicles for exploring some of the determinants of individual identity and some of the coordinates between which it may move or fluctuate: nature and nurture; male and female; higher and lower social rank; Christian and Muslim; Catholic and Protestant; Spanish and English; vice and virtue; the human and the demonic; the human and the animal; and the human and the divine. In *La gitanilla*, Preciosa the gypsy eventually becomes who (in a social sense) she has been all along, the aristocratic doña Constanza de Azevedo y de Meneses. In *El amante liberal*, as a captive of the Turks in Cyprus, Ricardo learns, like don Juan/Andrés (*La qitanilla*), to be less possessive of the woman he loves, while his friend and compatriot, Mahamut, and Halima, the wife of the cadi, who had both become renegades, are finally reconciled to the Church. In *Rinconete y Cortadillo*, on the other hand, apart from their adoption of various linguistic disguises for the purposes of deception, the two picaresque protagonists appear not to change at all. In *La española inglesa*, Isabel, a Spanish Catholic, is captured by an English Catholic and brought up in England as an outward Protestant. For a period, as a result of poisoning, she finds her beauty transformed into hideous ugliness, before she is able to return to her country and the open practice of her faith. Her suitor, Ricaredo, the son of her captor, is another young man who must learn to control his presumptuous possessiveness. In *El licenciado Vidriera*, the humbly born Tomás Rodaja becomes a distinguished graduate of the University of Salamanca; then, during a two-year period, the deranged Licenciado Vidriera; then, having recovered his sanity, the failed lawyer, Rueda; and, finally, a soldier who dies in battle in Flanders. In *La fuerza de la sangre*, Leocadia, the dishonoured daughter of impoverished but noble parents, a girl who has had to lead a life of concealment after bearing a child as the result of a rape, ends by marrying her rapist, Rodolfo, the son of one of the wealthiest and most illustrious families in Toledo. Although he is not said to express any regret for his assault, it may be that his eventual, more spiritual appreciation of Leocadia's beauty (se le iba entrando por los ojos a tomar posesión de *su alma* la hermosura de Leocadia' [II, pp. 92–3]) ('the beautiful image of Leocadia entered, by his eyes, into *his soul* and took possession of it' [II, p. 123]; emphases added), and his concern for her when she faints, may indicate that he has just begun to move away from his habitual, selfish sensuality towards love. In *El celoso extremeño*, Felipo de Carrizales, the son of a noble family from Extremadura, spends his inheritance recklessly and ends up destitute in Seville. He takes a ship to Peru (at the other extreme of the known world) and after a twenty-year absence returns to Seville, having amassed a fortune. Once a young spendthrift, he has become a miserly old man of sixty-eight who proceeds to marry a girl of thirteen going on fourteen in order to beget an heir. As he lies dying, believing his wife to have committed adultery, he admits that he should never have married someone so much younger. However, even in the midst of his repentance, it is clear that his habits of self-deception and manipulation remain largely intact. In *La ilustre fregona*, two young aristocrats adopt false names and take a moral holiday as *pícaros*, while a young serving girl in a Toledo inn is revealed to be the illegitimate daughter of noble parents. The two female protagonists of *Las dos doncellas* disguise themselves as men in order to pursue the man who has promised marriage to both of them. The most dramatic transformations of all, however, take place in the final *novela*, *El casamiento engañoso y El coloquio de los perros*: at the start of the *Casamiento* the once dashing Ensign Campuzano who had been so confident that he could 'matarlas en el aire'

(II, p. 284) ('have any woman [he] wanted' [IV, p. 69]) has been reduced by the effects of syphilis to a pathetically enfeebled figure, only able to walk with the support of his sword; at the start of the *Coloquio*, the dogs Berganza and Cipión are amazed to find that they have been suddenly and inexplicably endowed with the human gift of speech, and, later, Cipión is even more surprised to learn from Berganza that they had both been born as human babies to a witch and immediately transformed into dogs by their mother's jealous colleague, but with the possibility of becoming human once again. Although the witch, la Cañizares, who reveals this to Berganza, is a self-confessed and self-despairing devotee of the Devil, she believes that there may ultimately be some hope for her: 'con todo esto sé que Dios es bueno y misericordioso y que Él sabe lo que ha de ser de mí, y basta' (II, p. 343) ('Despite all this, I am aware that God is good and merciful and He knows what is to become of me, and that is enough for me' [IV, p. 135]). It is not surprising, then, that the issue of transformation should arise explicitly in the *Novelas*, and that it should do so both in this story and in *La ilustre fregona*. When, in the *Coloquio*, la Cañizares describes the supposed powers of her colleague, la Camacha, to Berganza she distinguishes between imaginary, or mythical, outward changes of form and the real changes that can take place in the inner self:

> Tuvo fama que convertía los hombres en animales, y que se había servido de un sacristán seis años, en forma de asno, real y verdaderamente, lo que yo nunca he podido alcanzar cómo se haga, porque lo que se dice de aquellas antiguas magas, que convertían los hombres en bestias, dicen los que más saben que no era otra cosa sino que ellas, con su mucha hermosura y con sus halagos, atraían los hombres de manera a que las quisiesen bien, y los sujetaban de suerte, sirviéndose dellos en todo cuanto querían, que parecían bestias. (II, p. 337)
>
> (She had the reputation of being able to change men into animals, and that she had used a sacristan as an ass, really and truly, for six years, and I have never found out how it was done, for it is said of those old magicians who turn men into beasts by those who know about these things that they simply attract men by their great beauty and charm and make them fall in love with them and keep them so subjugated, doing whatever is asked of them, that they appear to be animals. [IV, p. 127])

In *La ilustre fregona* the narrator makes a humorously ironic, but pointed, comparison between the new low-life social identities adopted by Carriazo and Avendaño, the two well-born protagonists, and the myths of transformation recounted in Ovid's *Metamorphoses*:

> He aquí tenemos ya – en buena hora se cuente – a Avendaño hecho mozo del mesón, con nombre de Tomás Pedro, que así dijo que se llamaba, y a Carriazo, con el de Lope Asturiano, hecho aguador: transformaciones dignas de anteponerse a las del narigudo poeta. (II, p.159)

> (So at this point we have Avendaño, who has become an ostler, by the name of Tomás Pedro, for that was the name he gave, and Carriazo, alias Lope Asturiano, transformed into a water-carrier: metamorphoses which compare favourably with those related by the long-nosed poet. [III, p. 83])

Although, of course, the humour here stems from the sense that there is really no comparison at all, in the midst of its festive panache *La ilustre fregona* explores the question of social and personal identity with considerable depth. A remarkable example of this is the story's interrogation of a pair of coördinates (of outer and inward identity), *caballerosidad* (gentlemanliness) and virtue, whose relationship in practice was particularly problematic in the Spain of Cervantes's time, a Spain which saw itself as supremely Christian but which also espoused an aristocratic cult of honour. Even in the midst of his 'picaresque' life, Diego de Carriazo is said to retain all the marks of his good breeding: 'En fin en Carriazo vio el mundo un pícaro virtuoso, limpio, bien criado y más que medianamente discreto' (II, p. 140) ('In short, to the world Carriazo was a virtuous *pícaro*, unsullied by that life, well bred and with more than his fair share of wisdom' [III, p. 63]). When he loses his temper playing cards with the water-sellers of Toledo, the narrator leaves it deliberately unclear as to whether the others (as mere 'riff-raff' are bound to do) unconsciously recognize and respect the noble indignation of a gentleman, or whether, judging him by their own standards, they can tell that he is someone even more dangerously thuggish than they are, or whether they are duped by what is purely theatrical posturing on his part:

> [. . .] les pareció no ser bien llevar aquel negocio por fuerza, porque juzgaron ser de tal brío el Asturiano [Carriazo] que no consentiría que se la hiciesen; el cual, como estaba hecho al trato de las almadrabas, donde se ejercita todo género de rumbo y jácara y de extraordinarios juramentos y boatos, voleó allí el capelo y empuñó un puñal que debajo del capotillo traía, y púsose en tal postura, que infundió temor y respeto en toda aquella aguadora compañía. (II, p. 182)
>
> ([. . .] [they] did not think it wise to settle the matter by force, for they reckoned Asturiano's [Carriazo's] determination was such that he would not allow them to so. Lope, since he was used to making deals in the tunny fisheries where every kind of danger is met and threatening behaviour, as well as outrageous swearing and bragging is practised, threw his hat well away from him and took a dagger which he carried under his cloak. He took up such a stance that he instilled fear and respect into the whole company of water-carriers. [III, p.113])

The passage is typical of this *novela* as a whole (indeed of the *Novelas* as a whole in their treatment of questions of identity) because of the way in which its ironic shifts of perspective are orchestrated to suggest that 'gentlemanly' violence may be indistinguishable from thuggish violence, or that any difference is purely cosmetic, merely a matter of culturally conditioned perception. More importantly, of course, it suggests that gentlemanliness itself, and by extension aristocratic identity, and by further extension, any social identity, may be merely a construct, a role with associated words and gestures that can be so thoroughly learned as to become a kind of second nature that passes itself off as an essential reality. A further irony here is that if readers are still amused by the reference to 'toda aquella aguadora compañía' (the whole aquiferous company) they are still, even to a minor extent, tacitly accepting the categories they think that they have just seen through. This is a good example of how Cervantes invokes and then blurs the boundaries between the conceptual terms in which fundamental questions like that of identity are normally framed; how, in other words, he deploys his own version of the Socratic method to disorientate his readers, forcing them to wonder at and question what they may previously have taken for granted. Indeed, the very 'geography' of *La ilustre fregona* appears to offer a paradigm of this process. Avendaño and Carriazo set out from Burgos in northern Spain, ostensibly on their way to Salamanca, although actually headed for Seville, almost at the other end of the peninsula. In fact they never get beyond Toledo, which is roughly halfway between Burgos and Seville, having passed through Illescas, which is roughly halfway between Madrid and Toledo, and before that through Valladolid, which is roughly halfway between Burgos and Madrid. Of course the dimensions are not exact, and Cervantes seems to deliberately disrupt what, nevertheless, seems to be a deliberately established pattern by having the boys spend a night at Mojados, which lies only about twenty-one kilometres south of Valladolid on the road to Madrid. As has already been mentioned, it is at Illescas that the two boys overhear the conversation between the other two boys – one going down to Seville and the other coming up from it – that leads to them ending up at the Inn of the Sevillano *in* Toledo. At the inn they are given a room 'que ni era de caballeros ni de criados, sino de gente que podía hacer medio entre los dos extremos' (II, pp. 150–51) ('which was for neither gentleman nor servant, but for people whose station was between the two' [III, p. 73]). The relevance of this pseudo-geometrical patterning to the central theme of the story – the difficulty in practice of pinpointing the boundaries between upper- and lower-class people, between lust and love, between good and bad taste, between virtue and vice, between good breeding and goodness – is not far to seek: the boys are aristocrats dressed as inn servants, so that, 'logically', splitting the difference, they *must* be what we would call 'middle class'. Of course, the point, sardonically implied, is that although questions of identity and morality may be subject to rational analysis, they can never be resolved with that kind of mathematical precision. On their journey from Burgos to Toledo the boys will have crossed certain empirically determinable halfway marks, but they will not have been aware of the *exact* moment when they were nearer to Madrid than to Valladolid, or nearer to Toledo than Illescas, although they will, of course, at some stage have become aware of being nearer to one place than to another. Similarly, it is implied, that at some stages in Diego de Carriazo's career as a *pícaro*, and to some indeterminable extent, his activities will have marked a shift in his character, an actual coarsening, moving him further and further away from at least the moral ideal of *caballerosidad*. Thus, the vision of individual identity that informs this *novela* (and the others), is one of something that is complex and multidimensional, something that can be relatively stable or relatively fluctuating and unstable, and which is always on the move between the many oppositional forces that shape it, often, but by no means always, recognizably closer to some boundaries than others. Cervantes's vision of these problems, and most specifically, of the mysteriously close interaction of good and evil, brings to mind the well-known Gospel parable of the wheat and the tares (Matthew 13: 24–30), one of whose purposes was to point out that only God can ultimately judge where the boundaries between them lie. What his concept of the 'mystery' of human, volition and action may have been will be considered in more detail below (pp. 31–3), as will another consistent feature of the *Novelas* – the many references scattered throughout them to the great Christian mysteries of the Incarnation, the Death and Resurrection of Christ, and to the intercessory powers of the Virgin Mary.

'Ejemplaridad'

The question of the coherence of the collection goes hand in hand with the much-discussed issue of *ejemplaridad.* In the Prologue, as we have seen, Cervantes claims that the benefit to be got from reading his *novelas* may be obtained not only from each one individually, but also from the whole collection. So far, no attempt to find and explicate such a 'meta-exemplum' has proved definitive, or even convincing, for most Cervantes scholars. It has been pointed out (for example by Ife [I, p. x]) that Cervantes's repeated and apparently sincere claims about the moral exemplarity of the collection in the Prologue are not so obviously fulfilled by the stories themselves. Only two of the *novelas* (*El celoso extremeño* and *La española inglesa*) contain an explicit concluding statement about their didactic purpose, and, at least in the first case, this is couched in such a heavily ironic tone that it is difficult to take it seriously. Also, the content of the stories (there is no shortage of sex and violence) does not, apparently, accord with his claim that the 'requiebros amorosos que *en algunas* hallarás son [. . .] honestos y [. . .] medidos con la razón y discurso cristiano' (I, pp. 51–2) ('the sweet nothings you will find *in some of them* are [. . .] proper and [. . .] seasoned with reason and Christian discourse' [I, p. 3]; emphases added). Even Cervantes's remark about preferring to cut off the hand with which he wrote them rather than be responsible for causing the slightest moral damage to his readers (could there be a clearer guarantee of his sincerity about their exemplary content?)[45] is not as straightforward as it appears, since (as Anthony Lappin points out [pp. 166–68,

[45] '[. . .] que si por algún modo alcanzara que la lección destas novelas pudiera inducir a quien las leyera a algún mal deseo o pensamiento, antes me cortara la mano con que las escribí, que sacarlas en público' (I, p. 52) ('if by any chance it should happen that the reading of these novels might lead my readers into evil thoughts or desires, I would rather cut off the hand with which I wrote them than have them published' [I, p. 5]).

below]) it disconcertingly mixes references to the Gospel warning about offending the conscience of others and to his own physical handicap (his paralysed left hand) with a, probably, initially imperceptible joke about this injury: what would he use to cut off his uninjured hand?

The crucial questions, therefore, are: 'are the *novelas* morally exemplary?'; 'were they intended to be so?'; and 'what is the nature of this exemplarity, if it exists?' Assuming the claims in the Prologue to be at least partially serious, we shall begin by considering the last of these questions. As we have seen, most of the stories do not contain an explicit statement setting forth the lessons that they seek to teach. Cervantes seems to prepare his readers for this absence in the Prologue by making, and then immediately withdrawing, a tantalizing offer to tell them plainly what they can learn: '[. . .] y si no fuera por no alargar este sujeto, quizá te mostrara el sabroso y honesto fruto que se podría sacar, así de todas juntas, como de cada una de por sí' (I, p. 52) ('[. . .] and if it were not for the fact that it would make this over-long, perhaps I would show you the delicious and wholesome fruit which could be pulled both from the collection as a whole and from each one alone' [I, pp. 3, 5]). In fact, the offer is being withdrawn even as (or before) it is made, and is in any case an extremely tentative one: 'si no fuera [. . .] *quizá* te mostrara' ('if it were not for [. . .] *perhaps* I would show you'; emphases added). It is quite likely, in fact, that Cervantes is parodying the traditional, clichéd language associated with assertions of exemplarity.[46] In traditional exemplary tales, from Aesop's *Fables* onwards, the vehicle (the story) is conditioned by and subordinate to the explicitly stated lesson it is designed to illustrate.[47] In the Prologue to *Don Quijote*, Part I, Cervantes makes deprecating reference to the kind of moralizing literature in which there seems to be a glaring disjunction between the often prurient content of the story itself and the piously trite 'sermoncico cristiano' (little Christian sermon [I, p. 80]) appended to it.[48] What he seems to have objected to was the lack of artistic integrity implied in this divorce between the medium and the message – the story told and the lesson taught. Apart from the considerations advanced above, this makes it all the more likely that, when in the Prologue to the *Novelas ejemplares* he speaks of how it is possible to '*sacar* algún ejemplo provechoso' (I, p. 52) ('*extract* some profitable example' [I, p. 3]), and of the 'sabroso y honesto fruto que se podría *sacar*' (I, p. 52) ('delicious and wholesome fruit which could be *pulled*' [I, pp. 3, 5]; emphases added), he is more likely to be drawing attention to the inadequacy of this model of how literature can be morally exemplary than (as he might appear to be doing) earnestly proffering a helping hand to the struggling reader. No wonder, then, that the offer to reveal what meaning and profit one can

46 For a discussion of this, see Chapter 1, pp. 53–4.

47 *El conde Lucanor* is representative (see p. 12 above).

48 Almost undoubtedly, this criticism was specifically aimed Mateo Alemán's large-scale picaresque novel, *Guzmán de Alfarache* (1599, 1604), the fictional autobiography of a reformed sinner, whose pages are filled with just this kind of didactic running commentary.

pluck from his *novelas* (as one might pluck fruit from a bush) is withdrawn, and equally no wonder that most of the stories do not come with a statement of their *ejemplaridad* appended. The first conclusion must be that if the *Novelas*, individually and collectively, are exemplary, it is not in *this* way.

An important concomitant of Cervantes's original approach to exemplarity is that the characters in his stories do not simply exist as 'illustrations' of good and bad qualities and behaviours. What he does is to readjust and even reverse the focus of traditional tales, by exploring vice and virtue, or, more accurately, the dynamics of their subtle coexistence, *in* his characters rather than *through* them.[49] These characters are indeed fundamentally generic, and yet complex and contradictory, constantly revealing themselves in different and unexpected ways, and most interesting when, as often happens, they act rightly for the wrong reasons or wrongly for the right reasons. The protagonist of *El licenciado Vidriera* provides an excellent example. In the opening pages his acute intellect and powerful memory are repeatedly underscored: 'y tenía tan felice memoria, que era cosa de espanto; e ilustrábala tanto con su buen entendimiento, que no era menos famoso por él que por ella' (II, p. 44) ('and his memory was so brilliant that it was alarming, and he so illuminated it with his good understanding that he was equally famous for both' [II, p. 63]). Nothing is said initially of his will ('voluntad'), the third of what were considered to be the three constituent powers, or 'faculties' of the soul. On the other hand, it is the goodwill of the two 'caballeros estudiantes' (II, p. 43) ('gentleman students' [I, p. 63]) who adopt Tomás as their servant and companion that makes it possible for him to study at the University of Salamanca. Here, he is 'de todo género de gentes [. . .] estimado y querido' (II, p. 44) ('loved and esteemed by all sorts of people' [II, p. 63]), but there is little mention of his returning this warmth of feeling. Indeed, when he decides that he would like to return to Salamanca for further study, his masters give him everything he will need to support himself for a further three years, and we are told that: 'Despidióse dellos, *mostrando en sus palabras* su agradecimiento [. . .]' (II, p. 44) ('He took his leave of them with *many expressions of gratitude* [. . .]' [II, p. 65]; emphases added). It is difficult not to detect an implied frigidity, a coldly polite detachment, if not actual *ingratitude* in these words. It is not that Tomás lacks 'will' in the sense of determination – he certainly has an obsessive will to study, and considerable ambition. On first meeting his aristocratic patrons he shows no signs of being intimidated by their superior social status, but actually a certain defiant pride, as he informs them that he intends to bring honour to his parents and his home region 'con mis estudios [. . .] siendo famoso por ellos' (II, p. 43) ('by being famous for my learning' [II, p. 63]). However, he is also impressionable and emotionally vulnerable. On his way back to Salamanca he meets up with a captain who is recruiting soldiers for the Spanish army. Like most others, Captain Valdivia is much taken by Tomás – 'contentísimo de [su]

49 For a similar view, although expressed in different terms, see Anthony J. Cascardi, 'Cervantes's Exemplary Subjects' in Nerlich and Spadaccini (ed.), *Cervantes and the Adventure of Writing*, pp. 49–71.

buena presencia, ingenio y desenvoltura' (II, p. 45) ('very pleased with [his] good appearance, intelligence, and free manners' [II, p. 65]) – and tries to tempt him to come to Italy with the army but with no obligation to actually become a soldier. Tomás's response displays that intriguing mixture of engagement and detachment, softness and hardness of will, which characterizes him in the first part of the story. Having heard Valdivia's description of the visual and culinary delights of Italy, 'la discreción de nuestro Tomás Rodaja comenzó a titubear y la voluntad a aficionarse a aquella vida, que tan cerca tiene la muerte' (II, p. 45) ('the good sense of our friend Tomás Rodaja began to waver, and his will began to fancy that way of life, which is so close to death' [I, p. 65]). For the first time, will, in the sense of the desire for pleasure, seems about to assert itself and supplant the desire for knowledge. He accepts the Captain's offer to travel to Italy, but at the same time insists that he will only go on his own terms ('más quiero ir suelto que obligado' (I, p. 46) ('I would prefer to go as a free man rather than under obligation' [II, p. 65]), thus maintaining that determined attitude of noncommittal to others or to things outside his own control that the text has begun to establish as the hallmark of his personality. As El Saffar (p. 54) and Forcione (*Cervantes and the Humanist Vision*, p. 229) have so well observed, the description of Tomás's tour of Italy (with its listings of sights seen and its repeated use of the verb *ver* [to see]) underlines his status as an observer of life rather than a participant in it. Only once is this pattern almost broken: 'Por poco fueran los de Calipso los regalos y pasatiempos que halló nuestro curioso en Venecia, pues casi le hacían olvidar de su primer intento' (II, p. 51) ('The delights and activities our curious traveller found in Venice were little short of Calypsan, since they almost made him forget his original intention' [II, p. 68]). This clearly means that Tomás has only just succeeded in resisting the sexual allurements of Venice, probably the first time his will has been seriously drawn in the direction of a sexual encounter with a woman. Yet, he *has* resisted. Obviously, any orthodox Catholic reader of Cervantes's time would be bound to applaud this rejection of temptation, but Cervantes has so configured the incident (through his emphasis on Tomás's habitual detachment) that a tension is provoked between the approval conditioned by faith and a more human doubt about the real moral status of this resistance. Later, having returned to his studies in Salamanca, Tomás is confronted with sexual temptation for a second time. Egged on by his fellow students, he visits a courtesan, a 'dama de todo rumbo y manejo' (II, p. 52) ('a lady full of craft and guile' [II, p. 71]), who has taken up residence in Salamanca after plying her trade in Italy and Flanders. She falls in love with him and openly declares her feelings, but is firmly told that he will have nothing more to do with her. Once again, it would have been difficult for Cervantes's original readers not to approve, in the abstract, of the rightness and practical wisdom of Tomás's rejection of this woman's advances. At the same time, the prim righteousness of his attitude impinges inescapably in the tone of: 'Pero como él atendía más a sus libros que a otros pasatiempos, en ninguna manera respondía al gusto de la señora' (II, p. 52) ('But since he attached more importance to his books than to other pastimes, he did not respond to the desire of the lady' [II, p. 71]). Then comes a phrase which not only perfectly epitomizes Tomás's doubtful 'virtue', but also Cervantes's moral and artistic tact: the woman, we are told, decides to resort to using a love potion since 'por medios ordinarios y corrientes no podía conquistar *la roca* de la voluntad de Tomás' (II, p. 52) (she was unable by ordinary means to conquer the *rock* of Tomás's will; emphasis added). Applied to another character in another context, the metaphor of the rock might denote an admirable firmness of will, an unwavering pursuit of virtue, but here, it suggests equally or primarily (it is ultimately up to the reader to decide) that somewhat unpleasant unyieldingness of heart, that rigid guardedness which is so much a part of Tomás's *condición* (nature), and which is therefore, arguably, almost as close to being a vice as it is to being a virtue. There are many such examples of Cervantes's moral sensitivity to be found throughout the *Novelas ejemplares*: in *El celoso extremeño*, for example, we are invited to see the young layabout, Loaysa's penetration of the protagonist, Carrizales's fortress-like home (where his young wife lives as a virtual prisoner) as, by turns, a heroic enterprise of liberation, like Orpheus's descent into the Underworld to rescue Eurydice, and as an act of malicious destruction, like Satan's attempt to ruin the paradisiacal happiness of Adam and Eve. In *La ilustre fregona* the adventures of the two young aristocratic characters who have absconded from their homes are written to be seen as either the pardonable (even, necessary and laudable) excesses of two high-spirited young men from 'good' backgrounds, or, as the unworthy irresponsibility of two over-indulged delinquents who only escape the punishment due to them because of the wealth and social contacts of their parents, or, as occupying some undetermined point on the moral spectrum between these extremes. By creating these kinds of puzzle in the *Novelas ejemplares*, Cervantes offers his readers the opportunity to refine their moral judgement 'sin daño de barras' (I, p. 52) ('without snookering anyone else' [I, p. 5]) – without incurring the penalties that mistaken judgements are likely to incur in real life.

'Misterio escondido'

The foregoing considerations may help us to approach the question of what Cervantes meant by another much-discussed statement in the *Prólogo al lector*: 'Sólo esto quieres que consideres, que pues yo he tenido osadía de dirigir estas novelas al gran Conde de Lemos, algún misterio tienen escondido que las levanta' (I, p. 53) ('I would only wish you to consider this: that since I have been bold enough to dedicate these novels to the Count of Lemos, they must contain some hidden mystery which elevates them to that level' [I, p. 5]). We would like to suggest that, among other things, it may signal at least three closely interrelated aspects of life which Cervantes was clearly interested in exploring: the mystery of individual human identity; the mystery of the human will; the mystery of the interaction of the human and metaphysical worlds. Since the first of these has already been examined in pp. 22–7, we shall consider only the last two here.

Cervantes's work as a whole testifies to his fascination with the operations of the will. Again and again, his characters and narrators defend the orthodox Catholic belief that the will is always ultimately free however much it may be constrained by circumstance or bad habit.[50] Yet many of the *Novelas* seem to indicate that, even if the will is indeed ultimately free, it is very difficult in life as we experience it to distinguish where the boundary between the domain of its free operation and that of its constrained operation actually lies. We have already looked at the case of Tomás Rodaja (*El licenciado Vidriera*), but another interesting exemplification of this problem occurs in *El celoso extremeño*. In this story, the principal female character is Leonora, the barely fourteen-year-old wife of the sixty-eight-year-old protagonist, Felipo de Carrizales, a wealthy, miserly, pathologically jealous *indiano* (wealthy returned emigrant). He has only married her because he hopes that she will give him an heir to whom to pass on his immense fortune and because her extreme youth and lack of worldly experience seem to guarantee that he will never have reason to be jealous. He sets up a home for her that is as closed off from the outside world as he can make it. There, she leads a life that is totally regulated and policed by him. Loaysa, a young layabout on the make, hears a rumour that this fortress-like house, which he has often seen and wondered about, contains a very beautiful young woman. He decides that he will see if he can get inside the house and come into contact with her. Eventually, after using a series of clever stratagems that take him past one locked door after another, he makes an agreement with Leonora's duenna, Marialonso, that he will sleep with her if she will persuade her mistress to sleep with him. Leonora has seen and liked the look of the handsome Loaysa, but only agrees to get into bed with him after very forceful persuasion by the duenna: 'Tomó Marialonso por la mano a su señora, y *casi por fuerza*, preñados de lágrimas los ojos, la llevó donde Loaysa estaba [. . .]' (II, p. 129) ('Marialonso took her mistress by the hand, the girl's eyes brimming with tears, and led her, *almost by force*, to where Loaysa was waiting [. . .]' [III, p. 47]; emphases added). In the version of this story collected in the Porras manuscript, Leonora enjoys full sexual contact with Loaysa, but in the published version she determinedly resists his advances. There has been much critical debate about this fundamental change in the *novela*'s plot, but it seems likely that Cervantes made this change for good artistic reasons rather than out of moral caution: Leonora has always been manipulated by others (her parents, her husband, her servants, Marisalonso, Loaysa) and so this refusal may be seen as the first important assertion of her free will, the beginning of a transition from artificially prolonged infancy to adulthood.[51] Yet, it is difficult not to think of other

[50] For example, the narrator in *El licenciado Vidrera* is at pains to point out that no witchcraft or charm or spell can interfere with the freedom of the will: 'como si hubiese en el mundo yerbas, encantos ni palabras suficientes a forzar el libre albedrío' (II, p. 52) ('as if there could be in the world herbs, charms, or words sufficient to overcome free-will' [II, p. 71]).

[51] For a full discussion of this issue, see Forcione, *Cervantes and the Humanist Vision,* pp. 72–84 (especially p. 77).

factors which may condition this apparently free decision: fear of her husband; fear of public disgrace; fear of Loaysa who is an almost total stranger to her; and, perhaps, fear of the unfamiliar feelings of sexual desire which she may be experiencing for the first time. We are left to guess what the real springs of Leonora's refusal of Loaysa are, as later we are left to guess why she decides to enter a strictly enclosed convent after Carrizales dies believing that she has betrayed him, but forgiving her and stipulating in his will that she should marry Loaysa. Is it because she has seen enough of the ugliness and deceit of life in the world to make her want to devote herself wholly to what is reliably – and eternally – true? Is it because she knows (since her servants will inevitably talk) that, as a dishonoured woman, she has no alternative? Is it because, traumatized and afraid, she is looking for refuge in another version of the only life with which she is familiar – one led behind protective walls and in which all the important decisions are made for her? Is she motivated by a combination of all of these things? At the end of the *novela*, as if to confirm that its exemplary force lies in such questions, and not in any facile illustration of the freedom of the will, Cervantes has his narrator, who is clearly not a man to leave a mystery unsolved, wearily but confidently proffer this resoundingly trite summary of its lesson: 'Y yo quedé con el deseo de llegar al fin deste suceso, ejemplo y espejo de lo poco que hay que fiar de llaves, tornos y paredes *cuando queda la volundad libre* [. . .]' (II, p. 135) ('And I was left wishing to come to the end of this affair, an example and image of how little faith one should have in keys, revolving doors and walls *when the will remains free*' [III, p. 55]; emphases added). Immediately after this, he finds himself forced to admit that, in this particular case, he does not know why Leonora did not put more effort into making it clear that she was innocent. Finally, in the very same breath, and as if suddenly and slightly desperately aware that he is duty-bound to come up with something (a moral teacher cannot *not* know), he quickly improvises two plausible but almost equally banal explanations, throws them at the reader and, duty done, lays down his pen: 'pero la turbación le ató la lengua, y la priesa que se dio a morir su marido no dio lugar a su disculpa' (II, p. 135) ('but bewilderment made her tongue-tied, and the speed with which her husband died gave her no chance to absolve herself from guilt' [III, p. 55]). The ironies generated by the transparent inadequacy of this attempted summary could not point more eloquently to Cervantes's sensitivity to and respect for the final inscrutability of the individual will.

The third mystery that seems to surface time and time again in the *Novelas ejemplares* is that of the coexistence of the visible and invisible worlds, and more specifically the relationship between the individual human will and the will of God. Many *novelas* contain coherent but unobtrusive religious allusions that allow them to be read in providentialist terms. In many cases, these allusions are to the Virgin Mary or to the devotion that particular characters have to her. Thus, in *La gitanilla*, Preciosa is imaginatively associated with the Virgin because one of her first actions is to dance in front of a statue of St Anne in the church of Santa María in Madrid while singing an improvised ballad about the Holy Family. The ballad recounts the story of how Saints Joachim and Anne, the parents of the

Virgin, had to wait for many years before their one child was born. St Anne is addressed as 'Árbol preciosísimo' (I. p. 64) ('Most precious tree' [I, p. 15]), the adjective obviously linking her with Preciosa, while the mention of St Joachim's fruitful patience suggests a parallel with Andrés /don Juan, who must prove the sincerity of his love for Preciosa by going through the test of living as a gypsy for two years. In *Rinconete y Cortadillo* we are told that a cheap image of the Virgin – 'una imagen de Nuestra Señora, destas de mala estampa' (I, p. 209) ('an Image of Our Lady [. . .] one of those poor quality ones' [I, p. 193]) – hangs in a small room leading off the inner courtyard of the house of Monipodio, the director of crime in Seville. While the image is the focus of the amusingly hypocritical religious devotions of the criminal community who gather there, it also, arguably, serves as a reminder that even in the midst of great moral darkness the light of what, in Cervantes's culture, would have been considered ultimate truth still persists. In *El licenciado Vidriera* the religious allusions are woven into a more elaborate pattern. Tomás Rodaja, the protagonist, is found sleeping under a tree at the start of the story. Bearing in mind his over-zealous pursuit of knowledge and the strong element of pride and ambition motivating that pursuit, this is clearly an allusion to the Tree of Knowledge in the Garden of Eden.[52] Later, Tomás is poisoned and is plunged into a two-year period of madness after eating a quince jelly spiked with a love potion. Since he has resisted the advances of the woman who gave it to him, the incident obviously cannot be read as a direct reworking of the story of Eve's temptation of Adam, but rather as a displaced image of the damage done to him by his own unbalanced desire to know. It is significant that the symptoms of his madness – the belief that he is made of glass and his bitter criticism of society – clearly represent the pathological externalization of tendencies (emotional vulnerability and wariness of others, for example) that are already present in his character. He is eventually cured by 'un religioso de la Orden de San Jerónimo, que tenía gracia y ciencia particular en hacer que los mudos entendiesen y en cierta manera hablasen, y en curar locos [. . .]' (II, p. 73) ('a friar of the Hieronymite order, who had a particular gift for making the deaf and dumb understand and even speak to some extent, and for curing insanity [. . .]' [II, p. 95]). But this individual experience of recovery through 'gracia y ciencia' (literally: grace and knowledge) is anticipated by a remarkable passage earlier on in the story where Tomás's visit to the shrine of Loreto is described. The basilica at Loreto contains what was (and is) believed to be the *Sancta Domus* (Holy House), the house in which the Virgin Mary received the Annunciation. Tomás cannot see the walls of the shrine 'porque todas estaban cubiertas de muletas, de mortajas, de cadenas, de grillos, de esposas, de cabelleras, de medios bultos de cera y de pinturas y retablos' (I, p. 50) ('because they were all covered with crutches, shrouds, chains, shackles, handcuffs, wigs, half-bodies made of wax, and paintings and retables' [II, p. 69]), the *ex-votos* left behind by those who believed that they had been cured through the

52 As noted by Forcione, *Cervantes and the Humanist Vision*, p. 240.

intercession of the Virgin. The description of the shrine, which comes in the middle of a breathless account of Tomás's sight-seeing tour of Italy, draws attention to itself because of its detail (only the description of Rome, as one might expect, is more extensive), and because the sudden and very marked solemnity of the language slows the hitherto rapid narrative pace to a virtual standstill: 'Vio el mismo aposento y estancia donde se relató la más alta embajada y de más importancia que vieron, y no entendieron, todos los cielos, y todos los ángeles, y todos los moradores de las moradas sempiternas' (II, p. 50) ('He saw the very place and room where the highest and most important message was delivered and witnessed but not understood by the angels, the heavens, and all the dwellers of the celestial places' [II, p. 69]). Tomás had brought only two books with him on his journey to Italy 'unas *Horas de Nuestra Señora* y un *Garcilaso* sin comento' (II, p.47) ('an *Hours of Our Lady*, and a Garcilaso without notes' [II, p. 67]). He clearly has a devotion to the Virgin and it is difficult not to see all these details in conjunction as suggesting that his own recovery from madness is one more example of the 'innumerables mercedes que muchos habían recibido de la mano de Dios por intercesión de su divina Madre' (II, p. 50) ('the innumerable mercies which many people had received from the hand of God, by intercession of his divine Mother' [II, p. 69]). Yet, the *novela* itself is not an obvious (and certainly not a spectacular) miracle story. If a miracle has occurred, it has been wrought by 'ciencia' (knowledge) as well as 'gracia' (grace) and, although Tomás is cured of his madness, it is hard to know how much he has fundamentally changed, or whether, after he is forced to abandon his career in the Law, the ambiguous description of his death as a soldier points more in the direction of ultimate, lonely failure rather than final success in committing himself to the world and to others:

> [. . .] y se fue a Flandes, donde la vida que había comenzado a eternizar por las letras la acabó de eternizar por las armas, en compañía de su buen amigo el capitán Valdivia, dejando fama en su muerte de prudente y valentísimo soldado. (II, p. 74)
>
> ([. . .]Tomás went off to Flanders, where, in the company of his good friend Captain Valdivia, the life which he had begun to make famous by learning he ended by fame in arms, leaving behind him, when de died, the reputation of having been a wise and most valiant soldier. [II, p. 97])

La fuerza de la sangre seems to exemplify the truth of the Spanish saying (cited by the principal female protagonist, Leocadia): 'cuando Dios da la llaga da la medecina' (II, p. 88) ('when God sends the wound he also sends the medicine' [II, p. 117]). She has been abducted and raped in a darkened room by an unknown assailant. Before being blindfolded and put back out onto the street, she takes a crucifix from the room 'no por devoción ni por hurto, sino llevada de un discreto designio suyo' (II, p. 82) ('not for devotion, or as theft, but inspired by a clever plan she had' [II, p. 109]). Eventually, she is able to use the crucifix to prove to the parents of Rodolfo, the man who raped her, that he is the father of the child to whom she later gave birth. (The child is accidentally trampled by a horseman in the street and is picked up by Rodolfo's father, brought to his house, and laid on the very bed where his mother was raped.) Rodolfo's mother, who has promised to find him a beautiful wife, then arranges for Leocadia to appear, splendidly dressed, at a meal that she has organized to celebrate his return from Italy. Leocadia enters leading her son by the hand, 'y delante della venían dos doncellas alumbrándola con dos velas de cera en dos candeleros de plata' (II, p. 92) ('and two maids preceded her, lighting her way with candles in silver candlesticks' [II, p. 123]). As Ray Calcraft has observed, Leocadia is described in a way that evokes typical devotional images of the Virgin set between votive candles.[53] The reaction of the dinner guests reinforces this interpretation: 'Levantáronse todos a hacerle reverencia, como si fuera alguna cosa del cielo que allí milagrosamente se había aparecido' (II, p. 92) ('Everyone rose to do her honour, as if she were something divine which had miraculously come among them' [II, p. 123]). Rodolfo is so overwhelmed by Leocadia's beauty that is he led to say to himself that 'si la mitad de esta hermosura tuviera la que mi madre me tiene escogida por esposa, tuviérame por el más dichoso hombre del mundo' (II, p. 92) ('if the lady my mother has chosen for me to marry had even half of this beauty, I should think myself the happiest man on earth' [II, p. 123]). When he discovers her identity, he is happy to accept Leocadia as his wife, which is exactly what she and his mother wanted. All ends happily; a great injustice is put right; Leocadia's honour has been restored and her son will be brought up by both of his parents. Has a kind of miracle happened; have grace and Providence intervened to bring justice and happiness out of sin and suffering? Or, bearing in mind that Rodolfo shows no sign of sorrow or repentance for his terrible act, are we to understand that coincidence and discreet human, and specifically feminine, calculation have conspired to produce a socially and personally satisfactory solution to a very awkward situation? Or, have all these forces cooperated in some mysterious way to do so? As usual, Cervantes leaves the answers to these questions to the discretion (and beliefs) of his readers, but, crucially, he makes sure, because of the way in which the story is written, that they become conscious of the processes of reasoning, and of the (perhaps previously unquestioned) beliefs, that lead them to those answers.

The other stories which incorporate patterns of religious allusion are similarly ambiguous. Like the Prodigal Son, to whom he is explicitly compared, Felipo de Carrizales, the protagonist of *El celoso extremeño*, has spent his inheritance recklessly. Unlike the Prodigal Son, he does not literally return to the home of his father, but on board the ship that takes him to the New World he does decide to reform his life: 'se iba tomando una firme resolución de mudar manera de vida, y de tener otro estilo en guardar la hacienda que Dios fuese servido de darle, y de proceder con más recato que hasta allí con las mujeres' (II, p. 100) ('[he set

[53] See R. P. Calcraft, 'Structure, Symbol and Meaning in Cervantes's *La fuerza de la sangre*', *BHS*, 58.3 (1981), 197–204 (pp. 202–3).

about making] a firm resolution to change his ways and to behave differently with any possessions that it might please God to bestow upon him, and to be more restrained than hitherto in his dealings with women' [III, p. 9]) . It is clear, when he returns as a very rich man to Spain twenty years later, that he has kept at least one part of this resolution. But, if he was prodigal with money in his youth, he has become mean and miserly in old age, so that it seems that his repentance has merely involved exchanging one form of selfishness for its opposite extreme. On his death-bed, after his marriage to Leonora has gone disastrously wrong, it appears that he does at last come home to himself. He has summoned his wife's parents to give them an account of what he believes to be their daughter's adultery and to hear the terms of his will. When they arrive, they are surprised to find the house, which had always been so closed off to the outside world, lying wide open: 'hallaron la puerta de la calle y la del patio abiertas y la casa sepultada en silencio y sola' (II, p. 132) ('they found the street door and the patio door open, and the house entombed in silence and unattended' [III, p. 51]). The language here, which evokes the description in the Gospels (particularly, Mark 16: 1–4) of the finding of the empty tomb on the first Easter Sunday, seems to set the scene for an ending which will show us an inwardly resurrected Carrizales. The expectation appears to be fulfilled when he acknowledges his own primary guilt for the ruin of his marriage: 'fui estremado en lo que hice [. . .] debiera considerar que mal podían estar ni compadecerse en uno los quince años desta muchacha con los casi ochenta míos' (II, p. 133) ('my behaviour was [out of the ordinary] [. . .] I should have taken into consideration that this girl's fifteen years and my eighty could ill live or blend together' [III, p. 53]). It is not only this open admission of wrong-doing that appears to indicate that Carrizales has undergone some kind of transformation or regeneration, but also the language in which it is couched, and especially one image that he applies to himself: 'Yo fui el que como el gusano de seda, me fabriqué la casa donde muriese [. . .]' (II, p. 133) ('It was I, who like the silk worm, built the house where I would die [. . .]' [III, p. 53]). Even so, when other aspects of this death-bed confession are taken into account, it is less clear that the Prodigal has returned. He still insists that he had treated his wife generously ('[t]ambién sabéis con cuánta liberalidad la doté [. . .]' (II, p. 132) ('[y]ou are also aware of what a generous dowry I gave her [. . .]' [III, p. 51]), and that he did not deserve such a betrayal. Even his act of forgiveness seems (at least partially) calculated to allow him to enjoy the thought of how generous it will make him seem in the eyes of others ('que quede en el mundo por ejemplo, si no de bondad, al menos de simplicidad jamás oída ni vista' (II, p. 134) ('so that it remains alive as an example, if not of goodness, then of unheard-of and unparalleled sincerity' [III, p. 53]), and the request in his will that Leonora should marry the young man with whom she has supposedly committed adultery sounds very like an attempt to extend his control over her even beyond the grave. Yet, he does publicly acknowledge responsibility for his own wrong-doing (or, at least, folly) for the first time in the story, and he does leave money in his will for 'obras pías' (II, p. 134) ('worthy causes' [III, p. 53]), something he had only fantasized about doing when he returned to Spain from Peru. This too, of course, could be interpreted as more manipulation of his posthumous image, or, even worse, of the Judge whom he knows he is about to face. His final inner state remains, appropriately – since this is the real point of the story – inscrutable.

In *La ilustre fregona*, Costanza, the eponymous protagonist, is a child conceived as the result of an act of rape and born in a Toledo hostelry where her aristocratic mother paused on her discreetly undertaken pilgrimage to the shrine of Our Lady of Guadalupe. Because her mother died before she was able to send for her, Costanza is raised as their own daughter by the innkeeper and his wife. Like her mother, she has great devotion to the Virgin, a virtue that her putative father puts at the head of a list of her good qualities when he is describing her to the Corregidor (whose son is infatuated with her): 'Ella, lo primero y principal, es devotísima de Nuestra Señora; confiesa y comulga cada mes [. . .]' (II, p. 189) ('First and most important, she is very devoted to Our Lady; she confesses and takes communion every month [. . .] [III, p. 123]). Indeed, after the first detailed description of her in the story, we are given a glimpse of what, no doubt, is her daily morning routine: 'Cuando salió de la sala se persignó y santiguó, y con mucha devoción y sosiego hizo una profunda reverencia a una imagen de Nuestra Señora que en una de las paredes del patio estaba colgada [. . .]' (II, p. 156) ('When she came out of the room she made the sign of the cross and in a composed, devout fashion she genuflected deeply before a statue of Our Lady which was hanging on one of the walls of the courtyard' [III, p. 79]). Eventually, through an extraordinary series of coincidences – or providentially ordained events – her true identity is revealed and she marries Tomás de Avendaño, the young nobleman disguised as a stable-boy who had courted her in the inn. This young man's best friend, Diego de Carriazo, who has assumed the identity of a water-carrier, is revealed to be Constanza's half-brother when both boys' fathers come to the inn in search, not of their sons, but of Costanza herself. Diego de Carriazo (Senior), her real father, has only recently been told of her existence and her whereabouts by an old servant of her mother's who has made a death-bed confession, revealing how his desire to keep the money that should have been sent on to Constanza as a dowry led him to keep the story secret. Thus, as the pattern of events suggests, through the intercession of the Virgin Mary, a last-minute act of repentance helps to put right some of the wrongs created by an act of serious sin. Yet, although the logic of providential intervention is less contested in this *novela* than in the ones we have just been considering, Cervantes allows some troubling shadows to cloud what otherwise could be an all-too-neat pattern of loss and restoration: Costanza's father never expresses contrition for his 'original' sin; his son never expresses any regret over his deception of his parents (both boys have absconded with money given to them to study at Salamanca), and, because of his social status, wealth and family connections, he is never held to account for almost beating a young boy to death in Toledo; Costanza is taken away from the only life and the only parents she has known to lead a completely different life in Burgos. It will be an incomparably more comfortable one with a husband whom she appears to genuinely love. Nevertheless, the wrench with her previous existence, and especially the pain of her departure from the innkeeper's wife, is movingly emphasized: 'Pero cuando dijo el Corregidor a Costanza que entrase también en el coche, se anubló el corazón, y ella y la huéspeda se asieron una a otra y comenzaron a hacer tan amargo llanto, que quebraba los corazones de cuantos le escuchaban' (II, p. 197) ('But when the Corregidor told Costanza to enter the carriage as well, she became dejected and she and the innkeeper's wife clasped one another tight and began to weep so bitterly that it grieved the hearts of all those present' [III, p. 133]). We must imagine, too, that the innkeeper and his wife, because of the new physical and social distance between them, will rarely, if ever again, see the girl they brought up as their daughter.

In the final 'double' *novela, El casamiento engañoso y El coloquio de los perros*, the Ensign Campuzano, tells his friend, the Licentiate Perlata, that after his abandonment by his wife doña Estefanía, he was on the verge of despair when he heard what he believed to be the voice of his guardian angel 'acudiendo a decirme en el corazón que mirase que era cristiano y que el mayor pecado de los hombres era el de la desesperación, por ser pecado de demonios' (II, pp. 289–90) ('[who] interceded to help me by reminding me that I was a Christian and that the greatest sin is despair' [IV, p. 77]). In his account of the dogs' conversation which he claims to have overheard in the Hosptial of the Resurrection, he includes la Cañizares's prophecy about the recovery of their human identity being dependent on 'seeing with their own eyes' a text that parodies the Magnificat:[54]

> Volverán a su forma verdadera
> cuando vieren con presta diligencia
> derribar los soberbios levantados
> y alzar a los humildes abatidos
> por mano poderosa para hacello. (II, p. 346)
>
> (they will return to their true form
> when they see how quickly and surely
> the haughty are brought down
> and the meek exalted
> by the hand with the power to do it. [IV, p. 139])

As we have already seen (p. 22), her words about the paralysis of her will ('todo lo veo y todo lo entiendo, y como el deleite me tiene echados grillos a la voluntad, siempre he sido y seré mala' [II, p. 342] ('as pleasure has gripped my will, I am and will always be evil' [IV, p. 135]) are very closely echoed in Campuzano's description of his own addiction to pleasure, a fact which makes it difficult not to conclude that it is his dream that has enabled him to reach a deeper, transformative understanding of his own experience and of himself. Thus, he appears to emerge from the Hospital of the Resurrection not only partially restored physically

[54] As pointed out by Pamela Waley, 'The Unity of the *Casamiento engañoso* and the *Coloquio de los perros*', *BHS*, 34 (1957), 201–12 (p. 211).

(he still has to use crutches and stumbles as he walks) but also inwardly renewed. His dream, then, invites interpretation as kind of revelation having, perhaps, an ultimately divine source (like the voice of the guardian angel he claims he heard in his head earlier), and intended to produce this restorative effect. But, just as the dogs have difficulty understanding the text that is the key to their liberation, it is not clear that Campuzano fully understands, or has been fully transformed by the 'text' of his dream. It does seem, however, that he is on the way to such understanding and that – as the logic of this dual *novela*'s structure suggests – to the extent to which their experience and their willingness to engage with its content allow, similar *re-creación* (re-creation) is being offered to its real and fictional readers. The last of the *Novelas*, then, points clearly towards what, as one reads them, one sees emerging as the fundamental feature of their exemplarity: their offer not of solutions to the problems and mysteries of life, but of subtle, convincing, and always varied reconstructions of the dynamic, fluid relationship between particular situations in life and the matrix of forces, natural and metaphysical, that frames them, and in terms of which they are to be ultimately understood. To invoke the metaphor of the 'mesa de trucos' (I, p. 52) ('billiard table' [I, p. 5]) which Cervantes uses in the Prologue, the *Novelas* involve an ever-changing interaction between the balls on the table (the particulars of each story), the rules of the game (the great, stable principles which, in Cervantes's culture, were believed to underpin life) and the players (the writer and the reader).

Conclusion

In conclusion, and in the light for the foregoing discussion, one may say that Cervantes has written *novelas*, entertaining stories, which are artistically and morally exemplary in a variety of ways. The entertainment the stories offer is of course dependent on their artistic originality, specifically the originality of their plots; their judicious treatment of extreme and/or unusual cases (for example, *El celoso extremeño*; *El licenciado Vidirera*; *El casamiento engañoso y El coloquio de los perros*) that make a powerful appeal to the imagination and yet just fall within the bounds of possibility; their experimental form (*El coloquio de los perros*; *El Licenciado Vidriera*); their subversion of traditional generic boundaries and conventions (*La gitanilla*; *El casamiento engañoso y El coloquio de los perros*; *El celoso extremeño*); their stylistic variety, and their lively use of dialogue. This sustained originality makes them not only entertaining, but also artistically exemplary because they provide samples of the great variety of ways in which a story can be told. The nature of their moral exemplarity is equally original and various. At the very least (or most) they may be seen as examples of what Cervantes's contemporaries called *eutrapelia*, the kind of pleasure which is automatically morally beneficial.[55] They are exemplary in a direct and obvious sense

[55] Thus, one of the original censors, Fray Juan Bautista, wrote: 'y supuesto que es sentencia llana del angélico doctor Sancto Tomás, que la eutropelia es virtud, la que consiste en un

because each one is full of moral observations, apothegms, proverbs and adages that offer useful, if limited, advice about how to live life. For those readers who want to consider them more deeply, they provide puzzles that problematize the relationship between many of the then available conceptual frameworks that seek to explain life and the often very confused and shifting truths at play in particular experiences of it. Finally, for those readers who want to look deeper still, they point toward the mysteries of the human heart itself; of individual identity; of volition; and of the interpenetration of the natural and metaphysical worlds. Essentially, of course, their artistic originality and the subtle moral vision they offer are completely interdependent. Thus, as we have seen, although they do also offer moral instruction of a traditional kind, the *Novelas* are principally characterized by their use of all kinds of strategies aimed at engaging readers in an active process of effort towards understanding, not just of the stories themselves, but of themselves and their own lives. Their self-conscious fictionality, their drawing attention to the fact that they are not life, but only a representation of it, is perhaps the most effective of these strategies. A clear example of this comes, fittingly, at the very end of the collection. As we have already seen, the last double *novela* is structured around a complex, concentric, layered pattern of narrators and listeners/readers (la Cañizares – Berganza – Cipión – Campuzano – Peralta). All of these readers/listeners have the opportunity to learn something from those who precede them in the chain. At the end of the *Coloquio*, having finished reading his friend, Campuzano's account of the conversation of the dogs, Peralta lays the manuscript aside, briefly comments on it, and then suggests that they both take a walk to the square of the Espolón in Valladolid: 'Vámonos al Espolón a recrear los ojos del cuerpo, pues ya he recreado los del entendimiento' ('Let's repair to the Espolón to entertain our eyes for we have already entertained our minds'). Campuzano agrees: '—Vamos —dijo el Alférez' ('"Let's go," the Ensign said'), and both disappear out of the page and into the rest of their fictional lives: 'Y con esto, se fueron' (II, p. 359) ('And with this, they left' [IV, p. 157]). Thus, at the end of this *novela*, and of the collection, the worlds of the real writer (Cervantes), of the fictional author and reader of the *Coloquio* (Campuzano and Peralta), and of the real reader of the *Novelas ejemplares* momentarily coincide, and then immediately diverge as all re-enter their separate modes of existence. For a strangely moving and, one could say, most completely exemplary moment, the real reader is offered a direct awareness of the strangeness of consciousness, of the many places the mind can inhabit, and of the various kinds of time it can experience. What is meant by calling this carefully induced experience 'most completely exemplary' is that it represents the summation of the entire moral thrust of the *Novelas*, which do not so much

entretenimiento honesto, juzgo que la verdadera eutropelia está en estas *Novelas*' (I, p. 45) (For since it is the clear teaching of the Angelic Doctor, Saint Thomas [Aquinas] that eutrapelia is a virtue which consists in virtuous entertainment, it is my opinion that true eutrapelia is present in these *Novelas*). For a full discussion of *eutrapelia* in the *Novelas ejemplares*, see Chapter 13 of the present volume.

attempt to provide readers with lessons about life, as to stimulate awareness of how their own lives are mirrored by, and how they are different from, those of the characters they read about, and of how those lives are both representatively human and unique. Above all, though, it is 'complete' because, besides offering an attractive image of life at its best – of reading, writing, conversation, friendship, the needs of mind and body being met in due order – it acknowledges and exemplifies incompletion: the Ensign saying that he intends to write down the second conversation of the dogs; the two friends setting off to take a walk to the Espolón, a place which in turn offered 'una vista bella, de alamedas, huertas, fuentes y monasterios [. . .]' (a beautiful view of poplar groves, *huertas*, fountains and monasteries).[56] The summation of this completeness in incompleteness is the sense of presence and absence that radiates around the final words, 'Y con esto, se fueron' (II, p. 359) ('And with this, they left' [IV, p. 157]). It implies a conscious opening up to all that lies beyond the text and an implicit, humble acknowledgement of its vastness and unknowability.

One of the most original features of the *Novelas ejemplares* is their questioning of the possibility of exemplarity itself: to be more precise, they probe the gap between the knowledge of what is morally true and right and the putting into practice of that knowledge. For a writer who is so very conscious of the prevalence of that gap (as his creation of a character like the witch, la Cañizares, in the *Coloquio* clearly indicates) effective exemplarity must mean something more than the straightforward reiteration or illustration of familiar truths (although it is clear that Cervantes respects the value of all formulations of truth – proverbs and adages included); it must take account of the fact, for instance, that in real life people are often forced to choose between competing truths, to decide which is the greater of two goods or the lesser of two evils. The *Novelas* not only show characters struggling with such decisions (for example), but they also force their readers to face them and to be aware that they may make what might be considered objectively accurate judgements for the wrong reasons. One of the techniques that Cervantes uses to induce this awareness is to place a judgement in the mouth of a character or narrator that is designed to reflect back opinions associated with a certain mentality to a reader of (or in) a similar frame of mind. One of the clearest examples of this comes at the end of *Rinconete y Cortadillo* when Rinconete condemns the criminal community (which he has just joined and perhaps never leaves) in language that mimics the rhetoric of an offended 'law and

[56] This is how the view from the Espolón is described by A. González de Amezúa y Mayo in his critical edition of *El casamiento engañoso y El Coloquio de los perros* (Madrid: Bailly-Baillière, 1912), p. 42 (as cited in Sieber, II, p. 359, n.136). It seems singularly appropriate that Cervantes's linking of 'Horas [. . .] de recreación' ('time for recreation') with the provision of 'alamedas [. . .] fuentes [. . .] jardines' (I, p. 52) ('poplar groves [. . .] fountains [. . .] gardens' [I, p. 5] in the Prologue should find not only a direct echo in the two friends' final words about giving recreation to 'los ojos del cuerpo' (II, p. 359) (the eyes of the body), but also an indirect one in what (according to Amezúa's description) their eyes would have seen from the Espolón.

order' sensibility: it is a community formed, in his opinion, of 'gente tan perniciosa y tan contraria a la misma naturaleza, [que] propuso en sí de aconsejar a su compañero no durasen mucho en aquella vida tan perdida y tan mala, tan inquieta, y tan libre y disoluta' (I, p. 240) ('people who were so obnoxious and whose behaviour so contradicted the laws of nature [that] [. . .] he made up his mind that he would advise his companion that they should not stay long living that God-forsaken way of life, which was so evil, so precarious, so libertine and so corrupt' [I, p. 229]).

Does this very intelligent openness to the complexity of life and of the processes of representing and judging it indicate that Cervantes was a moral relativist, a thoroughgoing sceptic? The evidence of his work in general (especially the *Persiles*) and of what is known about his religious commitment in life, along with the statement made by Cipión at the end of the *Coloquio* – one that impresses with its benignly authoritative tone – would seem to indicate that this is not the case: 'La virtud y el buen entendimiento siempre es una y siempre es uno: desnudo o vestido, solo o acompañado. Bien es verdad que puede padecer acerca de la estimación de la gentes, mas no en la realidad verdadera de lo que merece y vale' (II, p. 359) ('Virtue and understanding are always one and the same, naked or dressed up, alone or accompanied. It may well be that they might suffer a loss of esteem by the people but not of their true worth and merit' [IV, p. 157]). This seems to mean at least two things: first, and most obviously, that goodness and right understanding always retain their positive value whether they exist in their pure form, or whether they are accompanied or mixed with what is less than good (or even bad) and with ignorance; second, that they have an objective identity and value independent of changing opinions about what they are, or about how pleasant or unpleasant they may seem to be. If we do accept this as a statement of Cervantes's own view, it would indicate that, if he is sceptical, it is not about the existence of truth as his culture defined it (that he is not a nominalist), but about the ability and willingness of human beings to apprehend and act upon it.

Another (and perhaps primary) reason for the apparent indeterminacy of these stories (and of much of Cervantes's writing) has got to do not so much with even this kind of scepticism but with what appears to be his profound respect for the mystery and unfathomability of reality itself. Mystery, by definition, involves the coexistence of things which on the level of discursive reason are contradictory and incompatible: the great Christian mysteries of death and resurrection, of wholeness emerging from error and suffering, of the 'Felix Culpa', as we have seen, subtend many of the *Novelas*. As is stated with emphatic solemnity in the passage in *El licenciado Vidriera* about Tomás's visit to Loreto, these are things that even beings endowed with purely spiritual intelligence cannot understand: 'Vio el mismo aposento y estancia donde se relató la más alta embajada y de más importancia que vieron, y no entendieron, todos los cielos, y todos los ángeles, y todos los moradores de las moradores sempiternas' (II, p. 50) ('He saw the very place and room where the highest and most important message was delivered and witnessed but not understood by the angels, the heavens, and all the dwellers of the celestial places' [II, p. 69]).

It is most important to point out, though, that there are other *Novelas* in which there are relatively few allusions to the spiritual world or its mysteries. *El amante liberal*, *Las dos doncellas*, and *La señora Cornelia*, for example, trace patterns of cause and effect in which the emphasis is primarily (although, even here, not quite exclusively) on natural forces. Their inclusion may point to a desire on Cervantes's part to encompass, and exemplify, all the worlds of life and of fiction from the Romance heaven-on-earth of *La gitanilla* to the picaresque underworld of the *Coloquio* (and all that lies between), by not reducing them, like the deranged mathematician of the *Coloquio*, to facile patterns and false symmetries, but by leaving what is irregular and immeasurable in place. It is precisely this acceptance of not knowing permeating the *Novelas ejemplares*, and their corresponding openness to the reader, that make them such attractive and, paradoxically, such genuinely instructive, stories.

Works cited

Agredo y Vargas, Diego de, *Novelas morales: útiles por sus documentos* (Valencia: a costa de Felipe Pincinali Mercader de Libros, 1620).

Amezúa y Mayo, Agustín G. de, *Cervantes creador de la novela corta española*, 2 vols (Madrid: Consejo Superior de Investigaciones Científicas, 1956–58).

Aristotle, *Poetics*, in *Aristotle, Horace, Longinus: Classical Literary Criticism*, tr. T. S. Dorsch (Harmondsworth: Penguin, 1965; repr. 1974).

Atkinson, William C., 'Cervantes, El Pinciano and the *Novelas ejemplares*', *HR*, 16 (1948), 189–208.

Aylward, E. T., *Cervantes: Pioneer and Plagiarist* (London: Támesis, 1982).

———, 'Significant Disparities in the Text of *La tía fingida* vis-à-vis Cervantes's *El casamiento engañoso*', *Cervantes*, 19.1 (1999), 40–65.

———, *The Crucible Concept: Thematic and Narrative Patterns in Cervantes's 'Novelas ejemplares'* (Madison, NJ: Associated University Press, 1999).

Bataillon, Marcel, 'El erasmismo de Cervantes', in *Erasmo y España*, tr. Antonio Altatorre, 2nd edn rev. (Mexico City: Fondo de Cultura Económica, 1966), pp. 777–801.

Brown, Jonathan, *The Golden Age of Painting in Spain* (New Haven; London: Yale University Press, 1991).

Calcraft, R. P., 'Structure, Symbol and Meaning in Cervantes's *La fuerza de la sangre*', *BHS*, 58.3 (1981), 197–204.

Casalduero, Joaquín, *Sentido y forma de las 'Novelas ejemplares'* (Madrid: Gredos, 1962).

Cascardi, Anthony J., 'Cervantes's Exemplary Subjects', in *Cervantes and the Adventure of Writing*, ed. Michael Nerlich and Nicholas Spadaccini (Minneapolis: The Prisma Institute, 1989), pp. 49–71.

Cervantes Saavedra, Miguel de, *Don Quijote*, ed. John Jay Allen, 2 vols (Madrid: Cátedra, 1992).

———, *El casamiento engañoso y El Coloquio de los perros*, ed. A. González de Amezúa y Mayo (Madrid: Bailly-Baillière, 1912).

———, *Exemplarie Novells in Sixe Books*, tr. James Mabbe alias 'Don Diego Puede-Ser' (London: John Dawson, 1640).

Cervantes Saavedra, *Exemplary Novels by Cervantes*, tr. James Mabbe, ed. S. W. Orson, 2 vols (London: Gibbings; Philadelphia: J. B. Lippincott, 1900).
———, *Il Novelliere Castigliano*, tr. Gugliemo Alessandro de Novilieri Clavelli (Venice: Presso il Barezzi, 1626).
———, *Les nouvelles de Miguel de Cervantes Saavedra*, tr. François de Rosset and Vital d'Audiguier, Sieur de la Ménor, 2 vols (Paris: J. Richer, 1614–15).
———, *Novelas ejemplares*, ed. J. B. Avalle-Arce, 2 vols (Madrid: Castalia, 1982).
———, *Novelas ejemplares*, ed. Harry Sieber, 2 vols (Madrid: Cátedra, 1986).
———, *Exemplary Novels / Novelas ejemplares*, ed. B. W. Ife, 4 vols (Warminster: Aris & Phillips, 1992).
———, *Six Exemplary Tales*, tr. Harriet de Onís (Woodbury, NY: Barron's, 1961).
———, *Exemplary Stories*, tr. C. A. Jones (Harmondsworth: Penguin, 1972).
———, *Viaje del Parnaso*, ed. Vicente Gaos (Madrid: Castalia, 1973).
Clamurro, William H., *Beneath the Fiction: The Contrary Worlds of Cervantes's 'Novelas ejemplares'* (New York: Peter Lang, 1997).
Close, Anthony, *Cervantes and the Comic Mind of his Age* (Oxford: Oxford University Press, 2000).
Covarrubias Orozco, Sebastián de, *Tesoro de la lengua castellana o española* (Madrid, 1611; repr. Madrid: Turner, 1970).
Dunn, Peter N., 'Las *Novelas ejemplares*', in *Suma cervantina*, ed. J. B. Avalle-Arce and E. C. Riley (London: Támesis, 1973), pp. 81–118.
———, *Spanish Picaresque Fiction: A New Literary History* (Ithaca, NY: Cornell University Press, 1993).
El Saffar, Ruth, *Novel to Romance: A Study of Cervantes's 'Novelas ejemplares'* (Baltimore, MD: Johns Hopkins University Press, 1974).
Forcione, Alban K., *Cervantes, Aristotle, and the 'Persiles'* (Princeton, NJ: Princeton University Press, 1970).
———, *Cervantes and the Humanist Vision: A Study of Four 'Exemplary Novels'* (Princeton, NJ: Princeton University Press, 1982).
———, *Cervantes and the Mystery of Lawlessness: A Study of 'El casamiento engañoso y El coloquio de los perros'* (Princeton, NJ: Princeton University Press, 1984).
Gaylord, Mary Malcolm, 'Cervantes' Other Fiction', in *The Cambridge Companion to Cervantes*, ed. Anthony J. Cascardi (Cambridge: Cambridge University Press, 2002), pp. 100–130.
Horace, *Satires, Epistles, 'Ars Poetica'*, tr. H. Rushton Fairclough, Loeb Classical Library (London: Heinemann; New York: G. P. Putnam's Sons, 1929).
Juan Manuel, Don, *El conde Lucanor*, ed. José Manuel Blecua, 2nd edn (Madrid: Castalia, 1971).
Krailsheimer, A. J. (ed.), *The Continental Renaissance 1500–1600* (Harmondsworth: Penguin, 1971).
Krauss, Werner, 'Cervantes und der Spanische Weg der Novelle', in *Studien und Aufsätze* (Berlin: PUB, 1959), pp. 93–138.
Láspcras, Jean-Michel, *La nouvelle en Espagne au Siècle d'Or* (Montpellier: Editions du Castillet, 1987).
López de Hoyos, Juan, *Historia y relación verdadera de la enfermedad, felicísimo tránsito, y sumptuosas exequias fúnebres de la serenísima Reina de España Doña Isabel de Valois nuestra Señora* (Madrid: Pierres Cosin, 1569).

Mancing, Howard, 'Prototypes of Genre in Cervantes's *Novelas ejemplares*', *Cervantes*, 20.1 (2000), 127–50.

Márquez Villanueva, Francisco, '*La tía fingida*: literatura universitaria', in *On Cervantes: Essays for L. A. Murillo*, ed. James A. Parr (Newark, DE: Juan de la Cuesta, 1991), pp. 119–48.

Molina, Tirso de, *Obras Completas*, ed. Pilar Palomo and Isabel Prieto, 3 vols (Madrid: Turner, 1994).

Nerlich, Michael, 'Juan Andrés to Alban Forcione. On the Critical Reception of the *Novelas ejemplares*', in *Cervantes's 'Exemplary Novels' and the Adventure of Writing*, ed. Michael Nerlich and Nicholas Spadaccini (Minneapolis: The Prisma Institute, 1989), pp. 9–47.

Pabst, Walter, *La novela corta en la teoría y en la creación literaria*, tr. Rafael de la Vega (Madrid: Gredos, 1972).

Pierce, Frank, 'Reality and Realism in the *Exemplary Novels*', *BHS*, 30 (1953), 134–42.

———, 'Cervantes' Animal Fable', *Atlante*, 3.3 (1955), 103–15.

Price, R. M., 'Cervantes and the Topic of the "Lost Child Found" in the *Novelas ejemplares*', *AC*, 27 (1989), 203–214.

Rabell, Carmen R., *Rewriting the Italian Novella in Counter-Reformation Spain* (London: Támesis, 2003).

Rey Hazas, Antonio, '*Novelas ejemplares*', in *Cervantes*, ed. Anthony Close and others (Alcalá de Henares: Centro de Estudios Cervantinos, 1995), pp. 173–209.

Riley, E. C., *Cervantes's Theory of the Novel* (Oxford: Clarendon Press, 1962).

———, 'Cervantes: A Question of Genre', in *Medieval and Renaissance Studies on Spain and Portugal in Honour of P. E. Russell*, ed. F. W. Hodcroft and others (Oxford: Society for the Study of Mediaeval Languages and Literature, 1981), pp. 69–85.

Russell, Peter E., 'El Concilio de Trento y la literatura profana: reconsideración de una teoría', in his *Temas de 'La Celestina' y otros estudios* (Barcelona: Ariel, 1978), pp. 442–78.

Solé-Leris, Amadeu, *The Spanish Pastoral Novel* (Boston: Twayne, 1980).

Stagg, Geoffrey, 'The Refracted Image: Porras and Cervantes', *Cervantes*, 4.1 (1984), 139–53.

Vega, Lope de, *Novelas a Marcia Leonarda*, ed. Francisco Rico (Madrid: Alianza, 1968).

Vilanova, Antonio, *Erasmo y Cervantes* (Barcelona: Lumen, 1989).

Waley, Pamela, 'The Unity of the *Casamiento engañoso* and the *Coloquio de los perros*', *BHS*, 34 (1957), 201–12.

Yarbro-Bejarano, Yvonne, *The Tradition of the Novela in Spain from Pero Mexía (1540) to Lope de Vega's 'Novelas a Marcia Leonarda'* (1621, 1624) (New York: Garland, 1991).

Zayas y Sotomayor, María de, *Novelas amorosas y ejemplares*, ed. Agustín G. de Amezúa y Mayo (Madrid: Aldús, 1948).

———, *Desengaños amorosos*, ed. Alicia Yllera (Madrid: Cátedra, 1983).

1

Cervantes's Exemplary Prologue

Stephen Boyd
University College, Cork

This essay will try to show that the 'Prólogo al lector' (Prologue to the Reader) that prefaces the *Novelas ejemplares* is exemplary in its appropriateness to the stories it introduces. As one would expect from the introduction to any book, it serves the purely functional purpose of providing readers with general information about what they are about to read, but beyond that, and more unusually, for those who do not refuse its challenges, it also offers an induction into the reading skills, or habits of mind, that they will require if they are to properly understand and enjoy the *novelas*. In other words, the readerly expertise required to understand the enigmas of the Prologue is closely analogous to that demanded by the stories themselves. It is commonplace to observe that Cervantes liked to experiment with the conventions associated with the various literary genres of his time. The *Novelas ejemplares* are a prime example of this love of literary experimentation, and the first sense in which the Prologue is exemplary as an introduction to them is in its artful exploitation of the conventions of the genre. Therefore, before considering the content and structure of this prologue, and the other ways in which it is exemplary, it is appropriate to begin by briefly describing those conventions and outlining Cervantes's approach to them as evidenced in the introductions he provided for some of his other works.

Cervantes and the Prologue Tradition

As George McSpadden has made clear, Spanish readers in Cervantes's time (and before it) had come to expect much more from a prologue than mere information:

> Spanish authors, especially through the Golden Age, wrote their prefaces with merriment, wit, energy and imagination. They would take a difficult situation which confronts authors in general, namely that of introducing their books to their readers, and make of it an opportunity for playful, humorous, literary art, and they thus created an original little literary genre, the *prólogo*.[1]

[1] George E. McSpadden, *'Don Quijote' and the Spanish Prologues: Glimpses of the Genius of Cervantes at Work*, Vol. I (Potomac, MD: Porrúa Turanzas, 1979), p. 1. On the Spanish

Traditionally, the primary purpose of the prologue, from the author's point of view, was the *captatio benevolentiae*: the 'capturing' of the goodwill of the reader. To that end it was customary for the writer to address the reader directly and with exaggerated deference as, for example: 'Discreto lector' (Wise Reader), 'Curioso lector' (Curious Reader), 'Amantísimo lector' (Most Beloved Reader). Often he would then go on to beg forgiveness for his book's shortcomings, speaking of it metaphorically as a son or daughter, sometimes launching into an attack on the times he lived in and on the intellectual shortcomings and pretensions of other authors.[2] As Elias Rivers (pp. 167–68) has pointed out, Cervantes's first prologue, to *La Galatea* (1585), is courteous and conventional to the point of timidity, and so quite unlike the famously mould-breaking preface he was to write for *Don Quijote*, Part I (1605) twenty years later. Here the reader is addressed as 'Desocupado lector' (Idle Reader) and, although this is not the first time this kind of salutation had been used in Spain, its ironically familiar tone (just falling short of insolence) prepares the way for the most unconventional attitude of defensive pride, mixed with good humour, which the author maintains throughout the preamble.[3] The other original features of this remarkable introduction are well known: the *topos* of the book as child, for example, is expanded and developed into a virtual mini-narrative, but most of all it is Cervantes's skilful dramatization of his inability to write the prologue itself (involving the story of the 'friend' who gives him advice about what he should say) that makes this a genuine *tour de force*.[4] It is little wonder (and ironically appropriate), then, that Cervantes should invoke it and the criticism it aroused to explain his reluctance to write the Prologue to the *Novelas ejemplares*: 'Quisiera yo si fuera posible, lector amantísimo, excusarme de escribir este prólogo, por que no me fue tan bien con el que puse en mi *Don Quijote*, que quedase con gana de segundar con éste' ('I would have preferred, had it been possible, Dearest Reader, not to write

Golden-Age Prologue in general, see Alberto Porqueras Mayo, *El prólogo como género literario: Su estudio en el siglo de oro español* (Madrid: Consejo Superior de Investigaciones Científicas, 1957). On Cervantes's prologues, see Elias L. Rivers, 'Cervantes' Art of the Prologue', in *Estudios literarios de hispanistas norteamericanos dedicados a Helmut Hatzfeld con motivo de su 80 aniversario*, ed. J. M. Sola-Solé and others (Barcelona: Hispam, 1975), pp. 167–71; and also Alberto Porqueras Mayo, 'En torno a los prólogos de Cervantes', in *Cervantes: Su obra y su mundo: Actas del I congreso internacional sobre Cervantes*, ed. Manuel Criado del Val (Madrid: EDI-6, 1981), pp. 75–83.

2 'The Prologue is basically an apology by the author for the work [. . .], an ingenious piece of literary criticism which justifies its writer [. . .], gives his main purposes, and, in order to do so, parodies [. . .] and ridicules [. . .] the vices of the time and the preliminaries to other authors' works' (McSpadden, p. 16).

3 McSpadden (p. 9) notes that in the Chivalric Romance, *Palmerín de Inglaterra* of 1547 (often mentioned in *Don Quijote*), the readers are addressed as 'Ociosos lectores' (Idle Readers).

4 For a good discussion of these and other features (with a useful bibliography), see Charles Presberg, '"This is not a Prologue": Paradoxes of Historical and Poetic Discourse in the Prologue of *Don Quijote*, Part I', *MLN*, 110 (1995), 215–39.

this Prologue: the one I put in my *Don Quijote* was not such a success that I am anxious to follow it with another').[5] For the purposes of the discussion which follows, there are four points (two general, and two of especial relevance to the prologues of Cervantes) that are worth bearing in mind. First, although they appeared at the start of a book, prologues, as would normally be the case at any time, were written after the main text had been completed, a fact which has an obvious bearing on the second point: that, especially in the late sixteenth and early seventeenth centuries, the prologue tends to be much more closely integrated artistically with the work it prefaces. Porqueras-Mayo uses the term *permeabilidad* to describe the way in which introduction and text interpenetrate each other: '[el] prólogo individual, según la obra que acompañe (novela, teatro, ensayo, etc.) puede estar sometido a unas sacudidas y relaciones de contagio con la obra, fenómeno que ya he designado *permeabilidad*, en otro lugar' ('En torno . . .', p. 76) (according to the work it accompanies [novel, play, essay, etc.] [the] individual prologue can be subject to some disturbance and 'contamination' from the work itself, a phenomenon which, elsewhere, I have termed *permeability*). Third, and with reference to the same period, prologues become, increasingly, self-conscious works of meta-fiction. As Porqueras-Mayo, again, put it: 'Los prologuistas empiezan también a ensayar y reflexionar sobre los prólogos, y rompen antiguos moldes' ('En torno . . .', p. 77) (Writers of prologues also start to discourse and reflect on their prologues, breaking long-established moulds), and with specific reference to the Prologue to *Don Quijote*, Part I, he goes on to say: 'Y es entonces cuando inventa al amigo que le visita en su estudio de escritor. El lector (nosotros) a través de este mecanismo penetramos más íntimamente en la inmediata cotidianidad del *escritor escribiendo*' (p. 78) (And it is then that he invents the friend who visits him in his writer's study. By means of this device, we, the readers, enter into more intimate contact with the immediate daily experience of the *writer writing*). Fourth, and finally, although the prologue writer's presence in the prologue is generally especially strongly felt in this period, Cervantes writes himself into his prefatory texts (including, as Elias Rivers notes [p. 169], the Dedicatory Letter to the Count of Lemos in the *Novelas*) with a reflective depth unsurpassed by any of his contemporaries.

The structure of the 'Prológo al lector'

The *Prólogo al lector* that prefaces the *Novelas ejemplares*, written in epistolary form, and addressed, using the familiar second person singular pronoun 'tú', to the 'lector amantísimo' (I, p. 50) ('Dearest Reader' [I, p. 3]), may be divided into

[5] Miguel de Cervantes, *Novelas ejemplares*, ed. Harry Sieber, 2 vols (Madrid: Cátedra, 1986), I, p. 50. The English translation is from Miguel de Cervantes, *Exemplary Novels / Novelas ejemplares*, ed. B. W. Ife, 4 vols (Warminster: Aris & Phillips, 1992), I, p. 3. Subsequent references are to these editions.

roughly three parts. In the first, which occupies about half of the whole, Cervantes explains, very much tongue-in-cheek, that he had hoped to evade the obligation to write a prologue by having a friend substitute an engraving of him based on an already existing portrait by Juan de Jáuregui, a famous poet and painter of the time.[6] (The fact of Jáuregui's double vocation may well be thematically significant, as we shall see). He imagines the kind of explanatory text – consisting of a physical description and a condensed biography – that this friend might have written and appended to the engraving. But the friend has failed to perform this service and he is now forced to 'valerme por mi pico' (I, p. 51) ('make do with my tongue' [I, p. 3]). In the second section, Cervantes makes a series of statements which are all designed to underline the moral wholesomeness of his *novelas*: their love-scenes (and these are, supposedly, only to be found in a few) are so chaste and 'tan medidos con la razón y el discurso cristiano'(I, pp. 51–2) ('so proper and so seasoned with reason and Christian discourse') that they will not 'mover a mal pensamiento al descuidado o cuidadoso que las leyere' ('provoke anyone who might read them, careless or otherwise, into evil thoughts' [I, p. 3]); they have been called 'ejemplares' because useful lessons may be extracted 'así de todas juntas, como de cada una de por sí' (I, p. 52) ('both from the collection as a whole and from each one alone' [I, p. 5]); if not positively morally beneficial, they are at least as unlikely to harm the reader as indulgence in any other innocent pastime, such as the 'mesa de trucos' (I, p. 52) ('a billiard table' [I, p. 5]); in offering rest to the 'afligido espíritu' (I, p. 52) ('tormented spirit' [I, p. 5]) they fulfil a re-creative and therapeutic function comparable to that associated with public walkways, fountains, and gardens. Then, in order that there should be no doubt about how seriously he takes his responsibilities as a writer, Cervantes states emphatically that he would rather cut off the hand with which he wrote these stories than that their publication should provide an occasion of sin for any reader. In the third and final section he claims, fundamentally correctly, that he is the first writer to produce original *novelas* in Spanish. He then goes on to provide a list of his forthcoming publications, and before finally bidding farewell to the reader (hoping that he will be granted patience to endure the nit-picking attentions of his critics), he adds, enigmatically, and in a suddenly solemn tone, that, since he has dedicated these stories to his patron, the Count of Lemos, they contain 'algún misterio [. . .] escondido que las levanta' (I, p. 53) ('some hidden mystery which elevates them to that level' [I, p. 5]). This statement has occasioned a great deal of critical debate, as has the claim earlier in the Prologue that moral teaching may be gleaned not only from each individual story but also from the collection as a

[6] Juan de Jáuregui (1583–1641) was a poet and painter for whose work as a poet Cervantes professed great admiration. The portrait of Cervantes that hangs in the headquarters of the Real Academia Española (Spanish Royal Academy) in Madrid, and which was once accepted as being by Jáuregui, is no longer regarded as authentic. See Enrique Lafuente Ferrari, *La 'Novela ejemplar' de los retratos de Cervantes* (Madrid: Dossat, 1948).

whole. We shall briefly consider both of these claims and the debates surrounding them in the course of this essay, but since they have been extensively discussed in the Introduction (pp. 27–40), we shall pay special attention to another central feature of this Prologue: the remarkable predominance of Cervantes himself (or the contrived persona of Cervantes) in it. We have already observed that about half of the text is devoted to the transparently fictitious story of the missing engraving of the author that ought to have replaced it on the first page of the book. Why does Cervantes devote such apparently disproportionate space to speaking about himself rather than about the *novelas*, which, one would imagine, ought to be the main focus of attention? And, if Cervantes does wish to supply information about his appearance and his personal history, why does he not do so directly, rather than having recourse to the convoluted fiction of a 'friend' who 'could have' supplied an engraving based on a portrait that Cervantes 'would have' given to him? Before trying to answer these questions, we shall first examine the second part of the Prologue which, especially because of the claims made about exemplarity, does seem more obviously pertinent as an introduction to the *Novelas*.

The Assertions of Exemplarity

We shall consider in turn each of the claims that Cervantes makes about the exemplarity of his stories, including the first, which has not been mentioned so far, a statement, both startling and puzzling, about what they are not: 'Y así te digo otra vez, lector amable, que destas novelas que te ofrezco, en ningún modo podrás hacer pepitoria' (I. p. 51) ('And so I say again, Gentle Reader, that you cannot make a fricassée with these novels' [I, p. 3]). Most editions provide a footnote citing Covarrubias's definition of *pepitoria* as 'un guisado que se hace de los pescuezos y alones del ave [. . .]' (a stew made from the necks and wings of fowl).[7] The first explanation that Cervantes proffers of this enigmatic metaphor is hardly less impenetrable than the metaphor itself: the stories cannot be made into a stew 'porque no tienen pies, ni cabeza, ni entrañas, ni cosa que les parezca' (I, p. 51) ('for they have no feet, nor head, nor entrails, or anything of that kind' [I, p. 3]). Obviously anticipating the reader's mystification, he then spells out what he does mean: 'quiero decir que los requiebros amorosos que en algunas hallarás, son tan honestos y tan medidos con la razón y discurso cristiano, que no podrán mover a mal pensamiento al descuidado o cuidadoso que las leyere' (I, pp. 51–2) ('I mean that the sweet nothings you will find in some of them are so proper and so seasoned with reason and Christian discourse, that they could not provoke anyone who might read them, careless or otherwise, into evil thoughts' [I, p. 3]). Even then, the reader probably has to struggle a little to

[7] See Sebastián de Covarrubias Orozco, *Tesoro de la lengua castellana o española* (Madrid, 1611; repr. Madrid: Turner, 1970), p. 862.

understand the point of comparison, rather as he has to do when confronted with a *concepto* (conceit) in the poetry of the period.[8] The principal meaning appears to be that, with regard to their content, the stories that follow are not what we might term 'pornographic': they do not contain 'spicy' descriptions of bodily parts, and are therefore not like a *pepitoria*. A secondary, implied meaning – despite the jocular pun about their not having 'pies, ni cabeza' (either head or tail to them) – is that, individually and collectively, the stories have the ordered, rational integrity of a complete body: they are works of art written in accordance with reason and Christian principles, not an incoherent mishmash of titillating sex scenes. Considered in the context of the Prologue as a whole, several features of this first statement about the *novelas* are worth remarking upon. First, the choice of the unusual but richly significant metaphor of the *pepitoria* (comparable in these respects to that of the *mesa de trucos* [billiard table] which appears later) and the interpretative effort it requires of the reader. (The role and responsibility of the reader in 'making something' of the stories is also implied when Cervantes says, not that they are *not* like a *pepitoria*, but that the reader cannot reasonably *turn them into* one). Second, the use of the image of the body and of bodily parts (bearing in mind that the reader has just been offered an 'anatomy' of Cervantes's body in the opening section which is taken up with the story of the missing engraving) and the implied contrast between a structure which is harmoniously ordered (the use of the adjective 'medidos' ['aligned with'] in close proximity to the noun *razón* ['reason'] whose etymological root, *ratio*, also implies ordered proportionality helps to underline this concept) and one which is fragmentary or formless. Third, there is Cervantes's acknowledgement that a reader may be 'descuidado o cuidadoso' ('careless or otherwise'), implying acceptance of the view that the meaning and subjective worth of a work of literature may be partly determined by the quality of the individual act of reading. Fourth, there is the ascent through different levels of being implicit in the sequence: 'pepitoria' ('fricassée') – inanimate object; 'pies [. . .] cabeza [. . .] entrañas' ('feet [. . .] head [. . .] entrails') – the body parts of animals and of human beings; 'requiebros amorosos [. . .] honestos y medidios con la razón' ('sweet nothings [. . .] so proper and so seasoned with reason and Christian discourse') – human sexual love, in which body and soul participate, described

[8] A *concepto* (conceit) is a kind of metaphor which depends on an abstract (or not immediately discernable) point of comparison between things normally perceived to be dissimilar or opposite to each other. For example, in his first *Soledad* the poet Luis de Góngora (1561–1627), whose work was much admired by Cervantes, refers to the trunk of an ilex tree burning in a bonfire as 'mariposa en cenizas desatada' (l. 89) ('a moth into ash dissolving'). See, Luis de Góngora, *Soledades*, ed. and tr. Philip Polack (Bristol: Bristol Classical Press, 1997), p. 10–11. The tree, renowned for the hardness of its wood, is now like a moth (one of the most fragile things in nature) because the colours of the flames that consume it recall the patterns on the insect's wings, and because the ashes with their powdery texture are reminiscent of the dust-like coating on those wings. In addition, moths are attracted by candle flames and die in them, as the tree 'dies' in the fire.

in accordance with virtue and reason; and, finally, 'discurso cristiano' (human reason assisted by divine grace). We shall see later how these considerations resurface in other parts of the Prologue.

In his second statement Cervantes explains why he has called his stories 'ejemplares' (exemplary): 'Heles dado nombre de ejemplares, y si bien lo miras, no hay ninguna de quien no se pueda sacar algún ejemplo provechoso [. . .]' (I, p. 52) ('I have called them *Exemplary*, and if you look closely, you will see that there is not one from which you cannot extract some profitable example' [I, p. 3]). There is nothing surprising here; we would expect that exemplary tales would contain some beneficial moral teaching that we could extract from them. The formulaic banality of the language here lulls the reader into momentary inattention, ensuring that the impact of the quite unexpected remarks that follow is all the greater: 'y si no fuera por no alargar este sujeto, quizá te mostrara el sabroso y honesto fruto que se podría sacar, así de todas juntas, como de cada una de por sí' (I, p. 52) ('and if it were not for the fact that it would make this over-long, perhaps I might show you the delicious and wholesome fruit which could be pulled both from the collection as a whole and from each one alone' (I, pp. 3, 5]). Cervantes tantalizingly proffers, and simultaneously withdraws, the possibility that he *might* reveal the nature of the moral teaching his stories contain, frustrating the curiosity that he has deliberately aroused with his assertion that the 'delicious and wholesome fruit' can be gleaned from the collection as a whole, not just from each individual *novela*. In retrospect, this piece of very conscious game playing may prompt the reader to re-evaluate the apparent innocuousness of the language in which it is framed: plucking fruit from a tree is a commonplace metaphor for extracting a moral lesson from a moral tale, but the sheer heavy-handedness of the repetition of the verb *sacar* (to extract) now appears quite deliberate. It seems that Cervantes is actually parodying the cliché, rather than indulging in it. Similarly, we may also be led to consider more carefully how his stories manage to reconcile pleasure with virtue, not an easy matter despite the glib reference to their 'sabroso y honesto fruto' ('delicious and wholesome fruit'), a variant of the more usual 'deleitar enseñando' ('entertain and instruct') formula.[9] We may reflect further on the fact that, although it might well be possible to encapsulate the moral lesson of an individual *novela* in some brief statement, this would be much more difficult to do in the case of an entire collection of stories, especially one in which there is so much variety. Particularly after we have read the *Novelas ejemplares* and observed that only two of them – *La española inglesa* (The English Spanish Girl) and *El celoso extremeño* (The Jealous Old Man from Extremadura) – contain any explicit statement of their exemplary content, we may begin to appreciate that Cervantes's withholding of such summaries is exemplary in itself, a device to make us reflect on our assumptions about how moral literature functions. If the teaching that the stories contain can be summed up ('sacado' ['extracted']) and conveniently

[9] For a discussion of this, see the Introduction, pp. 10–11.

summarized for us in advance, why bother reading them at all? If the fruit can be offered to us on a plate without us having to pluck it from the tree, why approach the tree? The fact that Cervantes does not offer us any such clear statements here or in the stories suggests that this is because what they teach is not expressible in those terms.

If the second statement begins innocuously, the third opens with a pointedly enigmatic metaphor:

> Mi intento ha sido poner en la plaza de nuestra república una mesa de trucos, donde cada uno pueda llegar a entretenerse, sin daño de barras; digo sin daño del alma ni del cuerpo, porque los ejercicios honestos y agradables, antes aprovechan que dañan. (I, p. 52)
>
> (My intention was to set up in the main square of our society a billiard table, where anyone could come and have fun without snookering anyone else; that is, without harming body or soul, for honest and agreeable exercise is of benefit rather than harm. [I, p.5])

As in the case of the first statement, involving an initially puzzling, negative comparison of the *novelas* with a 'spicy stew', Cervantes obliges the reader with an explanation of his metaphor of the billiard table, and of what he means by providing entertainment without 'daño de barras' (penalties). The claim being made in this highly unusual way is, in the abstract, quite clear and simple in the light of the explanation: the *Novelas ejemplares*, like any other innocent leisure pursuit, will not harm the reader physically (obviously), or spiritually, and are, in fact, more likely to benefit him. But the image of the 'billiard table' (along with the mention of one of its unique features, the 'daño de barras') as a representation of recreation in general is so original and specific, and implants itself so vividly in the imagination, that it actually distracts attention from the simple truth it is meant to represent. In fact (like the *pepitoria*), it can be identified as a *concepto* (a conceit). Reading is a solitary activity, but billiards involves two or more players pitting their skills against one another. The text of a *novela*, like any other piece of writing, is fixed; the possible configurations of the balls on a billiard table, once the game starts, are infinite, and different in every game; there are no rules for reading a story in the sense that there are rules governing the play at the *mesa de trucos*. The aptness of the *mesa de trucos* as a metaphor for the *Novelas ejemplares* probably only begins to reveal itself after they have been read and pondered a good many times. Then one may become conscious that, in the sense that they present complex intellectual challenges to their readers, they are 'interactive', like the game played at the table; the words of the text are fixed on the page (like the number of balls in the game) but often they are the vehicle for fluid, shifting patterns of meaning and plays of irony that seem designed to make the stories reveal themselves to different readers in different ways in different successive acts of reading. Like the player at the *mesa de trucos*, the readers of these stories are required to be active and to constantly refine their skills in order to derive the greatest benefit and enjoyment from them; although each game played at the table is different, the rules governing the game, and the space within which it is played (the table itself) are, respectively, unchanging and clearly delimited, perhaps suggesting that, although the stories do not have fixed, 'stable' meanings but do evince discernable, finite configurations of, for example, irony and contradiction, they may ultimately have a stability of meaning that depends on and subsumes this calculated indeterminacy. Thus, because it is eccentric – even, at first sight, bizarre – the metaphor of the *mesa de trucos* offers readers the opportunity of discovering for themselves why it may be especially appropriate as an analogue of the *novelas*.

The fourth statement falls into three parts: Cervantes points out to his readers that, while it is very important to attend to the duties of religion and work, these cannot occupy the whole life of any individual; he reminds them that the need for periods of leisure 'donde el afligido espíritu descanse' (I, p. 52) ('when the tormented spirit can rest' [I, p. 5]) is generally recognized; finally, he substantiates this claim by pointing to examples of how this need is catered for by the creation of public avenues, fountains and landscaped gardens. This is a persuasive argument for the necessity and value of recreation, and one that Cervantes clearly felt the need to make in a religiously based society that tended (officially) to be suspicious of leisure, or at least of the pleasure attendant upon it. Obviously, this is a defence of the reading of his *novelas* as a worthwhile leisure activity, and therefore an amplification of his earlier comparison of them to the *mesa de trucos* as 'ejercicios honestos y agradables' (I, p. 52) ('honest and agreeable exercise' [I, p. 5]). But there is a different emphasis here, encapsulated in the differing connotations of *ejercicios* (exercise) and *recreación* (recreation). As an *ejercicio*, the game played at the *mesa de trucos* is a physical activity that benefits primarily the body but also the mind, as part of the soul. In contrast, the *recreación* (undoubtedly used with its etymological root in mind, as Colin Thompson [Chapter 13, p. 264] points out) afforded by walking in a garden, or by sitting next to a fountain, is associated with quiet places, is passively received, and benefits the 'afligido espíritu' ('tormented spirit'), the deepest part of the self. Cervantes suggests, therefore, that the exemplary force of his *Novelas ejemplares* can operate subliminally upon the reader at an unconscious level to produce a recreative and transformative effect analogous to that wrought upon the 'tormented spirit' by simply being in a garden and enjoying the presence of nature ordered by human art.[10] Essentially, having pointed out that his stories feed the mind and are harmless (if not positively beneficial) to body and soul, and by now saying that they also offer rest and restoration to the troubled spirit, Cervantes is claiming a therapeutic value for them. To use current terminology, this amounts to saying

[10] The metaphorical use of the garden in the titles of books designed to provide pleasure or spiritual refreshment was common throughout Europe in the sixteenth and seventeenth centuries; for example, Pedro de Padilla's *Jardín espiritual* (Spiritual Garden) (Madrid: Querino Gerardo, 1585), and Cervantes's own lost work *Semanas del jardín* (Weeks in the Garden), announced as forthcoming towards the end of the *Prólogo al lector* (I, p. 53) (I, p. 5).

that their exemplarity is 'holistic', operating upon the readers at all levels of their being.

The final statement in defence of the moral soundness of the stories is the most personal and passionate:

> Una cosa me atreveré a decirte, que si por algún modo alcanzara que la lección destas novelas pudiera inducir a quien las leyera a algún mal deseo o pensamiento, antes me cortara la mano con que las ecribí, que sacarlas en público. Mi edad no está ya para burlarse con la otra vida, que al cincuenta y cinco de los años gano por nueve más y por la mano. (I, p. 52)
>
> (One thing I will venture to say, and that is that if by any chance it should happen that the reading of these novels might lead my readers into evil thoughts or desires, I would rather cut off the hand with which I wrote them than have them published. [I, p. 5])

The argument here, unlike the previous ones, is based not on the character of the stories themselves but on the age and implied moral integrity of the author: he is sixty-four (a considerable age in the seventeenth century), probably nearing the end of his life, and presents himself as conscious that he will soon face the judgement of his Maker, and thus is in no position to 'burlarse con la otra vida' (I, p. 52) ('mess around with the hereafter' [I, p. 5]), imperilling the eternal well-being of his own soul by damaging the souls of others. In the context of Cervantes's time and culture this is an extremely powerful argument and, as we have seen, it is put forward with what looks like impassioned sincerity. If, however, we look more closely, we see that it is shot through with what, in the light of the statement taken at face value, seems to be an incongruous, punning humour that completely undermines this impression of deep seriousness. The humour is not immediately obvious, and the readers may only begin to glimpse its presence when they ask themselves (as they are bound to do) why Cervantes refers to his age in such a round-about fashion: 'al cincuenta y cinco de los años gano por nueve más y por la mano' (I, p. 52) (literally: at fifty-five years of age I am earning for nine more and for my hand). Any reader, informed or not about the author's true age at the time of the publication of the *Novelas ejemplares*, is likely to understand the phrase 'gano [. . .] por la mano' to mean that his need to make money from writing is all the more pressing because of his handicap, and that he would therefore be unlikely to approach his task with anything less than a fully responsible attitude. Because readers are forced to wonder about the meaning of this whole sentence, they are then more likely to notice that it incorporates a colloquial idiom 'ganar por la mano' which means something like 'to steal a march on others'. It appears now that Cervantes is referring to his need to keep one step ahead of his rivals by getting a successful book into print. The humour may seem all the more inappropriate because in the previous sentence Cervantes has referred to his willingness to cut off the hand with which he wrote the *novelas* as the greatest guarantee of his sense of moral responsibility as a writer. But even here, as Anthony Lappin points out (Chapter 7, pp. 166–68), there is a joke. The humour may appear inappropriate, or even tasteless, but it need not imply insincerity. The very fact that Cervantes makes himself the butt of these jokes suggests that we should discern a different, more subtle kind of authenticity in what is said – not the over-earnest protestations of a morally anxious puritan, but the good humoured self-acceptance of true wisdom.

The Fiction of the Missing Engraving and the 'Misterio escondido'

The kind of humour we have just been discussing is in evidence throughout the Prologue, from the very first line, in which Cervantes expresses his reluctance to write it in the first place: 'Quisiera yo, si fuera posible lector amantísimo, excusarme de escribir este prólogo, porque no me fue tan bien con el que puse en mi *Don Quijote*, que quedase con gana de segundar con éste' (I, p. 50) ('I would have preferred, had it been possible, Dearest Reader, not to write this Prologue: the one I put in my *Don Quijote* was not such a success that I am anxious to follow it with another' [I, p. 3]). Of course, the irony is that, if the first part of the present Prologue is shaped by Cervantes's feigned reluctance to write it, the Prologue to *Don Quijote*, Part I (1605) may well have drawn the criticism he mentions because it is spun out of his professed inability to do so. As we have already outlined, Cervantes pretends that he has been forced to write this Prologue because a friend whom he hoped would supply an engraving of him, based on a portrait by Juan de Jáuregui, has let him down. He describes the friend as 'algún amigo de los muchos que en el discurso de mi vida he granjeado, antes con mi condición que con mi ingenio' (I, p. 50) (one of the many friends I have acquired in the course of my life, more because of my nature than my intelligence). The distinction made between 'condición' (nature) and 'ingenio' (intelligence) is interesting and significant, and we shall return to it later in this essay (p. 59). If the reader wonders why Cervantes should have wanted an engraved image of himself to appear on the frontispiece of the book, two answers are supplied: first, that it is the 'uso y costumbre' (I, p. 50) (the custom), as indeed it was, and, second, that 'con esto quedara mi ambición satisfecha, y el deseo de algunos que querían saber qué rostro y talle tiene quien se atreve a salir con tantas invenciones en la plaza del mundo, a los ojos de las gentes' (I, pp. 50–1) ('With that, my ambition would have been satisfied, as too would be the desire of anyone keen to know what he looks like, this man who dares to display his inventions and submit them to public gaze in the market-place of the world' [I, p. 3]).[11] But it was unusual for an engraving of the author or – in the case of a work of biography, autobiography or hagiography – of the subject, to appear, un[accompanied] by some form of preface. It might, indeed, be more justifiable if this were to happen in these cases, but the *Novelas ejemplares* are not

[11] On the relationship between prefatory poems and their accompanying engravings in the Golden Age, see Pierre Civil, '*Ut pictura poesis* en los preliminaries del libro español del siglo de oro: el poema al retrato grabado', in *Actas del IV Congreso Internacional de la Asociación*

about Cervantes, and therefore an engraving of him could hardly be an adequate substitute for a proper introduction to them. Cervantes claims, however, that some of his readers are anxious to know what he looks like, and that he would have been happy enough to satisfy that curiosity and not to bother writing the usual prologue. There can be little doubt that this indulgent attitude towards what might be called vulgar curiosity is not assumed without irony. Even so, by putting down the kind of verbal description and condensed biography that he imagines that his unreliable friend might have appended to the engraving, he does give these readers what they want, and more. This elaborate, patently concocted tale of an absent engraving that should have substituted for a prologue, and the speculative but actually present text that could have been appended to it, occupies almost half of the entire space of the Prologue that we do have. It raises a number of questions: why is it there at all, and, assuming (as seems likely) that Cervantes's reference to public curiosity is ironic, why does he in fact devote so much space to satisfying it? Why, even if he did want to give some account of himself, did he not do so directly without recourse to this convoluted piece of whimsy? Cervantes's assessment of his 'friend's' pen-portrait of him may provide a useful starting point for answering these questions. He professes to be annoyed with him – 'de quien me quejo' (I, p. 51) ('of whom I complain' [I, p. 3]) – for producing a description which is too flattering: 'Porque pensar que dicen puntualmente la verdad los tales elogios, es disparate, por no tener punto preciso ni determinado las alabanzas ni los vituperios' (I, p. 51) ('For it is foolish to imagine that such eulogies tell the exact truth, as praise and vituperation have no fixed abode' [I, p. 3]). That is, an over-flattering portrayal falls as far short of truth on the one hand as vituperation does on the other. The words 'puntualmente' (literally: exactly) and 'punto preciso' (literally: precise point) imply that the truth exists in this case (as perhaps in others) and that, if it does, it must of necessity be something absolutely precise, so precise that it is easier to miss it than to hit upon it. These words also imply that any inaccuracy in truth telling, however minimal or involuntary, is a departure from truth itself. Interestingly, the word 'verdades' (truths) occurs in the next sentence, although here Cervantes has moved on to speaking about the lost opportunity represented by the missing engraving:

> En fin, pues ya esta occasion se pasó, y yo he quedado en blanco y sin figura, será forzoso valerme por mi pico, que aunque tartamudo, no lo será para decir verdades, que, dichas por señas, suelen ser entendidas. (I, p. 51)
>
> (In the event, for that opportunity was lost and I have been left blank and unillustrated, I shall have to make do with my tongue, which, although tied, will be quick enough to tell home truths, which are wont to be understood even in the language of signs. [I, p. 3])

Internacional Siglo de Oro (AISO), ed. María Cruz García de Enterría and Alicia Cordón Mesa, 2 vols (Alcalá: Universidad, 1998), I, pp. 419–32. I am grateful to Barry Taylor of the British Library for bringing this article to my attention.

Although the 'truths' spoken of here are apparently of a different kind – so big and obvious that they can, for example, be communicated by visual signing in the form of gestures – what is important for the purposes of this argument is that the issue of truth and truths surfaces in such a concentrated way in this central part of the Prologue. Since this is the Prologue to a collection of *Novelas ejemplares*, tales whose purpose, presumably, is to teach their readers something about moral truth, it is probably not surprising that this is the case. We have seen that Cervantes judges his friend's supposed description of himself according to the criterion of truthfulness and finds it wanting. We cannot know how objectively accurate or inaccurate it is, but it may be helpful to think about the whole fiction of Cervantes's friend and the absent engraving with the word 'truth' in mind. At least four complementary questions about, specifically, art and truth seem to be implied by this fiction: first, the ability of art in general to faithfully represent reality; second, the relative strengths and weaknesses of poetry and painting (or, more broadly, verbal and visual media) as modes of mimesis; third, the ability of the artist to apprehend and communicate truth; fourth, the nature of truth itself. We shall look at each of these questions in turn.

The account of Cervantes that we read in the Prologue is, supposedly, Cervantes's speculative version of the verbal account that one of his friend's *could have* ('bien *pudiera*' [I, p. 50]; emphasis added) appended as a supplement to an engraved image of him that was never supplied in the end. The engraving would have been based on a portrait of Cervantes by Juan de Jáuregui that might well have existed in reality. If it did, it would, presumably, have been painted from the life. Therefore, we are asked to imagine that the verbal portrait that we read as part of the Prologue is at least five removes from the 'real' Cervantes: it represents what Cervantes, as he presents himself in the Prologue, imagines that his friend might have written about him to supplement an engraving that was never made, which would in turn have been based on a portrait of him by Juan de Jáuregui, painted presumably from the life, and so based on the real Cervantes. As if this were not enough, the reliability of the 'friend' as a source of knowledge about Cervantes has already been called into question by the remark (averted to above) that he is 'algún amigo, de los muchos que en el discurso de mi vida he granjeado, antes con mi condición que con mi ingenio' (I, p. 50) (one of the many friends I have acquired in the course of my life, more because of my nature than my intelligence). It appears, then, that he is not so much a friend as one of many acquaintances who have been attracted by Cervantes's social persona, or personality, but who know very little about the workings of his mind and imagination, that is to say, about his inner, essential self. Any account of Cervantes by such a person would necessarily be relatively superficial. He could tell us what Cervantes looked like, and offer some snippets of information about his life, and perhaps throw in some generalizations about his character, but he could tell us very little about what Cervantes was 'really' like. The description of Cervantes that we do have in the Prologue (written by Cervantes himself, of course) appears to be of this kind. If Cervantes did, for whatever reason, want to offer the reader some account of himself, why does he do it in this complicated way? The answer is not difficult to find. Cervantes's intense interest in the problems of artistic representation, in questions of literary theory, is in evidence everywhere in his work and has been much studied.[12] It seems likely that the primary purpose of the fiction of the missing engraving is to encourage the reader to ponder these problems as a preparation for reading a collection of stories in which questions about human nature, individual identity, and moral truth – and their artistic representation – are explored in a very profound and subtle way. The multi-layered structure of this opening fiction in the Prologue is typically Cervantine, and is to be found most fully developed in *Don Quijote* and in the last of the *Novelas ejemplares*, *El casamiento engañoso y El coloquio de los perros* (The Deceitful Marriage and The Dialogue of the Dogs), a point to which we shall shortly return.[13] In this case it may have been designed to remind Cervantes's better-educated original readers of Plato's famous critique of artistic representation in Book 10 of his *Republic*. Plato considers allowing no place for lyric and, more particularly, dramatic, poets in his ideal society because of his belief that art (in all its forms), as an imitation of the world apprehended by the senses which is in turn an imperfect imitation of an invisible, eternal Reality, is at least two removes from truth, and therefore unworthy of attention, if not positively harmful.[14] Cervantes's purpose in alluding to Plato's negative view of artistic mimesis is probably not to indicate that he concurs with it, but to remind the reader, by indicating that he is aware of it, of the inevitable 'truth deficit' inherent in any work of art, his own *novelas* included. It is very likely too that he wanted the reader to remember the defence of poetry advanced in his *Poetics* by Plato's pupil, Aristotle, who famously distinguished between the kind of truth that historians deal with, the 'particular truth' concerning specific persons living in a particular time and place, and 'poetic truth', the revelation of the workings of universal human nature, irrespective of time or place, offered by writers in poems and plays that represent, not things that did happen, but things that could have happened. Aristotle not only defended the value of 'poetic truth', but preferred it to

[12] The classic study is E. C. Riley's *Cervantes's Theory of the Novel* (Oxford: Clarendon Press, 1962). See also Alban K. Forcione, *Cervantes, Aristotle and the 'Persiles'* (Princeton, NJ: Princeton University Press, 1970), and, specifically in relation to portraiture, Mary Gaylord Randel, 'Cervantes' Portraits and Literary Theory in the Text of Fiction', *Cervantes* 6.1 (1986), 57–80.

[13] For a detailed discussion of the structure of the *Casamiento / Coloquio*, see Chapter 12 of the present volume.

[14] Specifically discussing artists who imitate other products of human skill, Plato says: ' "So the tragic poet, if his art is representation, is by nature at third remove from the throne of truth; and the same is true of all other representative artists" ' (597e). Although his attitude to both kinds of poetry is ambiguous (' "for we know their fascination only too well ourselves" ' [607c]), his provisional conclusion is that ' "poetry has no serious value or claim to truth, and we shall warn its hearers to fear its effects on the constitution of their own inner selves" ' (608ab). See Plato, *The Republic*, tr. Desmond Lee, 2nd edn rev. (Harmondsworth: Penguin, 1974), pp. 425, 438, 439.

'historical truth' because it was more 'philosophical'.[15] To a certain extent, although not totally or systematically, the two parts of Cervantes's self-portrait, the first a physical description, the second a condensed biography, correspond to the Aristotelian categories of 'poetry' and 'history', a point that we shall further explore later in this essay. It is interesting that the issue of 'poetic truth' which is broached in these opening pages of the *Novelas ejemplares* should resurface at the very end of the last double-*novela*, *El casamiento engañoso y El coloquio de los perros*. As we noted above, this *novela* provides an extended example of the kind of multi-layered narrative structure that we find in the fiction of the missing engraving: at the end of the first part, the *Casamiento engañoso*, the Ensign Campuzano asks his friend, the Licenciate Peralta, to read his transcript of the nocturnal conversation between two guard-dogs that he claims he heard in hospital in Valladolid. The text of this conversation is the second part of the *novela*, the *Coloquio de los perros*, which consists of one dog, Berganza, telling the story of his life to his companion, Cipión. The real reader, then, in the company of the fictional reader, Peralta, reads Campuzano's transcript of Berganza's oral autobiography, which is listened to and commented upon by Cipión. When he has finished reading his friend's manuscript, Peralta no longer wishes to pursue the issue of its literal or historical truth, as he had originally done: 'Señor Alférez, no volvamos más a esa disputa. Yo alcanzo el artifico del *Coloquio* y la invención, y basta.' (II, p. 359) ('Ensign, sir, let's not get involved in that again. I see the art of the Colloquy and its invention, and that is enough' [IV, p. 157].) He is content now to accept the artistic truth of its 'artificio e invención' ('art [. . .] and [. . .] invention'). In this way, then, the fiction of the missing engraving can be seen to constitute an 'announcement' of issues that, to a greater or lesser extent, are explored in all of the stories, but with special concentration and profundity in the final two. Whether or not the verbal portrait of Cervantes in the Prologue is historically accurate is inevitably of interest, but (maybe) not as significant as the broader question of what kind of truth art, and specifically fiction, can communicate.

In order to consider that 'broader question' we shall need to look closely at the pen-portrait that Cervantes imagines that his friend might have supplied. It falls, as already noted, into two parts. The first consists of a minutely detailed description of Cervantes's appearance, especially of his face. The second gives a very brief outline of his life, concentrating especially on his military career and most particularly on his participation in the Battle of Lepanto (1571). The physical description reads as follows:

> Éste que veis aquí, de rostro aguileño, de cabello castaño, frente lisa y desembarazada, de alegres ojos y de nariz corva, aunque bien proporcionada; las

[15] 'For this reason poetry is something more philosophical and more worthy of serious attention than history; for while poetry is concerned with universal truths, history treats of particular facts' (Chapter 9). See *Aristotle, Horace, Longinus: Classical Literary Criticism*, tr. T. S. Dorsch (Harmondsworth: Penguin, 1965; repr. 1974), pp. 43–4.

> barbas de plata, que no ha veinte años que fueron de oro, los bigotes grandes, la boca pequeña, los dientes ni menudos ni crecidos, porque no tiene sino seis, y ésos mal acondicionados y peor puestos, porque o tienen correspondencia los unos con los otros; el cuerpo entre dos extremos, ni grande, ni pequeño, la color viva, antes blanca que morena; algo cargado de espaldas y no muy ligero de pies; éste digo que es el rostro del autor de *La Galatea* y de *Don Quijote de la Mancha*.' (I, p. 51)
>
> ('This man you see here, with aquiline face, chestnut hair, smooth, unwrinkled brow, joyful eyes and curved though well-proportioned nose; silvery beard which not twenty years ago was golden, large moustache, small mouth, teeth neither small nor large, since he has only six, and those are in poor condition and worse alignment; of middling height, neither tall nor short, fresh-faced, rather fair than dark; somewhat stooping and none too light on his feet; this, I say, is the likeness of the author of *La Galatea* and *Don Quijote de la Mancha*.' [I, p. 3])

After suggesting a general impression – 'de rostro aguileño' ('with aquiline face') – every feature of the face is individually described in descending order in accordance with the conventions of the classical *descriptio pulchritudinis* (description of beauty) or *descriptio puellae* (description of a girl), starting with the hair of the head, and moving downwards from the forehead, eyes, nose, beard, moustaches, mouth and teeth, to a briefer, less-detailed account of the rest of the body, which is described as being of medium size, the skin colour rather more pale than dark, with the mention of the sloping shoulders and the reference to being 'no muy ligero de pies' ('none too light on his feet') suggesting the restricted mobility of old age.[16] Paradoxically, despite the wealth of detail (it would be difficult to find any of Cervantes's fictional characters so minutely anatomized), this description offers only the most generalized impression of Cervantes's appearance to the imagination. This could be any elderly man of the same physical type. Even the mention of the 'alegres ojos' ('joyful eyes') only provides the illusion of bringing us closer to a sense of Cervantes as an individual. The rest of the text supplies a list of his published works and a condensed account of his life that concentrates virtually exclusively on his military career. In terms of the debate about painting and 'poetry' (which may be understood to mean 'literature' in general), one can observe that the first part of the text shows words acting as an imagined supplement to a work of visual portraiture, an

[16] For an excellent account of the theory of portraiture in the period (including a useful summary of classical *descriptio*), see Gareth Alban Davies, '"Pintura": Background and Sketch of a Spanish Seventeenth-Century Court Genre', *Journal of the Warburg and Cortauld Institutes*, 38 (1975), 288–313 (pp. 293–94). Summarizing the theory of *descriptio* elaborated in the thirteenth century by Matthew of Vendôme, Davies writes: 'And since Art imitates Nature the poet must imitate God the artist: description therefore, like Creation, must begin with the head, proceed via hair, brow and eyebrows, to nose, eyes and cheeks, and thence to lips and chin' (p. 293).

engraving of Cervantes, but in actual fact as an inadequate substitute for that absent work. The second part of the text, however, provides information that the engraving could not have supplied, and which it would be very difficult for any work of visual art to supply: it tells us what Cervantes has achieved as a writer and as a soldier. Implicitly, then, the text suggests that painting is more accurate when it comes to representing the appearance of things, but that verbal art has the advantage when it comes to the representation of events in time and of invisible, inner realities such as thoughts or the moral character of a person – Cervantes's exasperation over unlicensed editions of his works, or the patience he claims he has acquired through adversity, for example. If we look more carefully, though, at the first part of the text, we can see that it too supplies information that we would not be able to get from an engraving: most obviously, but least important (since a painting could show this), it tells us about the colour of Cervantes's hair, beard and complexion; less obviously, but also less important (and for the same reason), it tells us that Cervantes is of medium stature and no longer able to move about very quickly: it would be difficult to make a judgement about the relative stature of a sitter from an engraved portrait (even if it represented a full-length view, which was extremely rare), or a painting, and impossible to know (although one might speculate about it) how agile he or she was. But no visual representation could tell us that twenty years previously Cervantes's now silver-coloured beard had been (specifically) golden, and it would be highly unusual for any portrait to offer the kind of dentist's eye view of the inside of the sitter's mouth that would allow us to know that his teeth were 'ni menudos ni crecidos, porque no tiene sino seis, y ésos mal acondicionados y peor puestos, porque no tienen correspondencia los unos con los otros' ('neither small nor large, since he has only six, and those are in poor condition and worse alignment'). In terms of the 'ut pictura poesis' *topos*, which was fundamental to Renaissance debates about the comparative merits of the sister arts of poetry and painting, the implication of this passage, once again, is that visual art is relatively restricted when it comes to the representation of more than what the eye can see at any one time.[17] Nevertheless, the humorously detailed reference to his bad teeth may well indicate that, although Cervantes was interested in this debate, he was impatient with the pedantic approach to artistic truthfulness that characterized all too many contributions to it: is this information about the exact number, condition and faulty alignment of Cervantes's teeth really worthy of inclusion in a description of his 'rostro y talle' (face and build)?[18] In another sense, though, notwithstanding its inadequacies as a physical evocation, this

[17] The phrase, 'ut pictura poesis' (poetry is like painting) comes from Horace's *Ars poetica* (361–65). For good account of this debate, see Rensellaer W. Lee, *'Ut pictura poesis': The Humanistic Theory of Painting* (New York: W. W. Norton, 1967), and also, Davies (pp. 288–89).

[18] The belief of some Renaissance literary theorists (such as Torquato Tasso), that the 'poet' should base his plots as closely as possible on historical events, using the minimum

portrait, precisely because it is a verbal one, gives a very lively impression of what Cervantes might have been like: that is, of what he might have been like as a person. It is not what we see with the eyes of the imagination that counts here, but rather what we apprehend from the rhythm and tone of the passage, from what might be termed its stylistic trace. Apart from enumeration, its most prominent stylistic feature, one which is very consciously foregrounded (to the point of distracting from the content), is the systematic deployment of oppositional and contrastive terms: 'nariz *corva*, aunque *bien proporcionada* [. . .]' ('*curved* though *well-proportioned* nose'); ' las barbas de *plata* [. . .] que fueron de *oro*' ('*silvery* beard which [. . .] was *golden*'); 'los bigotes *grandes*, la boca *pequeña*' ('*large* moustache, *small* mouth'); 'la color viva, antes *blanca* que *morena*' ('fresh-faced, rather *fair* than *dark*'); 'algo *cargado* de espaldas, y no muy *ligero* de pies' ('somewhat stooping [literally: *heavily-laden* in the shoulders] and none too *light* on his feet'; all emphases added). Most significantly, though, the almost hypnotic rhythm of this prolonged toing and froing along with the perfect conceptual balance it seems to embody ('el cuerpo entre dos extremos' [his body between two extremes]) is amusingly punctured by the mention of the author's six rotting, badly-aligned, teeth, which, emphatically, '*no* tienen correspondencia los unos con los otros' (have *no* correspondence one with another'; emphasis added). What is the specific purpose of this exaggerated rhetorical patterning in what purports to be an image of Cervantes? With respect to 'Cervantes', one could say that the patterning and its subversion succeed in giving the reader an impression of someone with a certain lively, agile, witty, ironic cast of mind, and so, perhaps, after all ('le style c'est l'homme même'), in providing us with something like a true image – not of 'Cervantes's' *condición*, in the sense of his physical characteristics) but of his *ingenio*, his cast of mind. In the context of *novelas ejemplares* (exemplary stories), the terms used to generally describe the body – 'entre dos extremos' (between two extremes) – irresistibly, and appropriately, bring to mind Aristotle's famous definition of virtue ('virtus in medio') as always lying at a mid-point between opposite extreme vices.[19] With respect to that definition, this portrait presents us with what seems to be a, physically, very well

'invention', and, more specifically, the tendency of more pedantic writers to equate 'truth' with the accumulation of trivial detail is frequently parodied by Cervantes in *Don Quijote*. For example: 'Sucedió, pues, que en más de seis días no le [a Don Quijote] sucedió cosa digna de ponerse en escritura, al cabo de los cuales, yendo fuera de camino, le tomó la noche entre unas espesas encinas o alcornoques: que en esto no guarda la puntualidad Cide Hamete que en otras cosas suele' (II, 60) (And so it happened, then, after more than six days when nothing happened to him [Don Quijote] that was worthy of being written down, while he was travelling off the road, night overtook him amidst some densely-growing oaks, or cork-trees, for with regard to this matter Cide Hamete does not observe his customary exactitude). See Miguel de Cervantes, *Don Quijote*, ed. John Jay Allen, 2 vols (Madrid: Cátedra, 1992), I, p. 477.

19 Don Quijote appeals to it when, defending his 'rashness' in attacking the lions, he says: 'porque bien sé lo que es valentía, que es una virtud que está puesta entre dos estremos vicios, como son la cobardía y la temeridad' (II, 17, p. 154) (for I am well aware what courage is: a virtue set between the two extreme vices of cowardice and rashness).

balanced individual, but yet not perfectly so, as we have seen. Perhaps Cervantes is hinting that, by analogy, inner perfection, absolute virtue, is not to be found in him or in any individual, and, in a Christian context, fortunately so, since imperfection has its own point. Indeed, this portrait of their author may well be intended to serve also as an evocation and defence of the *Novelas ejemplares* – individually and as a 'body of work' – as deliberately and fruitfully lacking in formal 'perfection'.

Finally, there are at least two other ways in which the fiction of the missing engraving may be seen as having a particularly exemplary relevance to the *Novelas*. The reader is asked to imagine that, if Cervantes had had his wish, the first page of the published text would have featured an engraving of him with a complementary verbal description and biographical note set beneath it. The visual image is absent, but in a sense actually present. When Cervantes's 'friend' says: 'Éste que veis aquí [. . .]' (I, p. 51) ('This man you see here [. . .]' [I, p. 3]), we do see him at once. Thus, if we are open to it, we are offered a momentary glimpse of something normally taken completely for granted: the almost miraculous power of words and, by extension, the literary fictions woven out of them to engage the mind as if they were the reality they represent. The second point of comparison between the imaginary ekphrasis – at least the first part of it – and the *Novelas ejemplares* (only two of which come with an explicit moral attached) does not need to be laboured: if the engraving had (merely) accurately represented Cervantes's physical appearance, the reader would not need to be told what he should already be able to see in an engraving; if the engraving had also succeeded in communicating a sense of Cervantes's inner self, no mere catalogue of physical features could be an adequate substitute for that communication.

Turning now to look at the final element of this part of the text (the miniature biography): if this is examined as a piece of history writing, an interesting pattern emerges. The first two sentences consist of almost entirely objective statements of fact: 'Llámase comúnmente Miguel de Cervantes Saavedra. Fue soldado muchos años, y cinco y medio cautivo, donde aprendió a tener paciencia en las adversidades' (I, p. 51) ('He is commonly called Miguel de Cervantes Saavedra. He was many years a soldier, five and a half a prisoner, when he learned patience in adversity' [I, p. 3]). The tone of 'llamáse comúnmente [. . .]' ('He is commonly called [. . .]') implies an attitude of self-deprecatory modesty, an impression confirmed by the laconic reference to his period in captivity, 'donde aprendió a tener paciencia en las adversidades' ('when he learned patience in adversity'). It may very well be true that Cervantes did learn patience during those difficult years, but this is not an objectively verifiable statement of fact of the kind that 'fue soldado muchos años, y cinco y medio cautivo' ('He was many years a soldier, five and a half a prisoner') is. It represents, rather, an assessment, a judgement about attitude and disposition, and these types of judgement in historical writing are notoriously open to question, or at least to qualification. Having made this almost imperceptible incursion into the realm of the subjective, Cervantes immediately retreats into strict objectivity – 'Perdió en la batalla naval de Lepanto la mano izquierda de un arcabuzazo' (I, p. 51) ('He lost his left hand in the naval battle of Lepanto, from a blunderbuss wound' [I, p. 3]) – before returning, more decisively this time, to the subjective in the form of private opinion, at first acknowledged as such – 'herida que, aunque parezca fea, *él la tiene* por hermosa' (I, p. 51) ('a [. . .] wound, which, though it looks ugly, *he considers* beautiful' [I, p. 3]; emphases added), then passing on into understandable (even noble) patriotic sentiment, and finally accelerating pell-mell into a full-blown jingoistic tirade: 'por haberla cobrado en la más memorable ocasión que vieron los pasados siglos ni esperan ver los venideros, militando debajo de las vencedoras banderas del hijo del rayo de la Guerra, Carlo Quinto, de felice memoria'(I, p. 51) ('since he collected it in the greatest and most memorable event that past centuries have ever seen or those to come may hope to see, fighting beneath the victorious banners of the son of that glorious warrior, Charles V of happy memory' [I, p. 3]). Thus, in the very short space of two sentences a remarkable shift has been enacted: the quiet self-effacement of the opening phrases has been made to shade into a strident, boastful rant. But is the pride that is so overt at the climax of this passage not, perhaps, already lurking in the determined modesty of the first few phrases? If this is probably not a question that first-time readers ask themselves before passing on to encounter the *Novelas ejemplares*, it almost certainly is one that they will ask after prolonged, or not-so-prolonged, exposure to them. In conclusion, then, the last part of the description that could have accompanied the absent engraving tells us as little (or as much) about Cervantes as the first. It is hardly surprising, then, that he declares himself unhappy with the friend – 'de quien me quejo' (I, p. 51) ('of whom I complain' [I, p. 3]) – who supposedly produced it. He has fallen short of the truth's 'punto preciso' (I, p. 51) ('exact point' [I, p. 0]) through flattery. Ironically, 'Cervantes's' professed concern for the integrity of truth is itself shown to be hollow, since – because it is not flattering enough – he considers substituting for the description as it stands a text secretly dictated by him: 'yo me levantara a mí mismo dos docenas de testimonios y se los dijera en secreto con que extendiera mi nombre y acreditara mi ingenio' (I, p. 51) ('I would have put together a couple of dozen testimonials and passed them to him on the quiet so that he could extend my renown and bear witness to my inventiveness' [I, p. 3]). Despite this, however, the terms in which the statement about truth is couched are extremely interesting. This is especially so because of the clearly calculated use within the same sentence of the nominal and adverbial forms of the word 'punto': 'que dicen *puntualmente* la verdad' (which convey the truth *exactly*) and 'por no tener *punto preciso* ni determinado' (I, p. 51; emphases added) (because they have no *exact* or determined *point*). The purpose of the miniature biography with its remarkable shift from scrupulous objectivity to the most blatant subjectivity seems to be, fundamentally, to suggest how difficult it is for any human being (but here specifically the historian, and even more specifically, the writer) to know the truth, keep his mind fixed on it (the words 'punto' [exact] and 'puntualmente' [exactly], as we have seen, imply that it is something absolutely precise) and put it into words, even when it is the truth about himself. Of course, this clear enactment of how the human propensity to prejudice and vanity gets in the way of truth-telling only serves to increase Cervantes's credibility as an 'exemplary novelist', someone whose purpose is precisely to know and communicate the truth about human beings and their behaviour.

In conclusion, and as hardly needs pointing out, the centrality of Cervantes's presence in his 'Prólogo al lector' has nothing to do with self-advertisement. In fact, as it is hoped that this essay has helped to show, his enigmatic, uneven, contradictory, self-portrayal forms a multi-faceted, concentrically ordered *concepto* that provokes interesting, interconnected questions about the relationship of Cervantes (and, by implication, any human being) to himself, others, his past, his culture and his work, and about the relationship between language and truth, art and reality. Because of its richness of implication, the fiction of the missing engraving serves as an exemplary introduction to stories which, as a body, constitute a composite, self-consciously incomplete portrait of human nature and of the possibilities of fiction. Cervantes holds his own imperfect image before us, and offers the *Novelas ejemplares*, as an approximate 'imago hominis'.

Works cited

Aristotle, *On the Art of Poetry*, in *Aristotle, Horace, Longinus: Classical Literary Criticism*, tr. T. S. Dorsch (Harmondsworth: Penguin, 1965; repr. 1974).

Cervantes Saavedra, Miguel de, *Don Quijote*, ed. John Jay Allen, 2 vols (Madrid: Cátedra, 1992).

———, *Novelas ejemplares*, ed. Harry Sieber, 2 vols (Madrid: Cátedra, 1986).

———, *Exemplary Novels/Novelas ejemplares*, ed. B.W. Ife, 4 vols (Warminster: Aris & Phillips, 1992).

Civil, Pierre, '*Ut pictura poesis* en los preliminaries del libro español del siglo de oro: el poema al retrato grabado', in *Actas del IV Congreso Internacional de la Asociación Internacional Siglo de Oro (AISO)*, ed. María Cruz García de Enterría and Alicia Cordón Mesa, 2 vols (Alcalá: Universidad, 1998), pp. 419–32.

Covarrubias Orozco, Sebastián de, *Tesoro de la lengua castellana o española*, (Madrid, 1611; repr. Madrid: Turner, 1970).

Davies, Gareth Alban, ' "Pintura": Background and Sketch of a Spanish Seventeenth-Century Court Genre', *Journal of the Warburg and Cortauld Institutes*, 38 (1975), 288–313.

Forcione, Alban K., *Cervantes, Aristotle and the 'Persiles'* (Princeton, NJ: Princeton University Press, 1970).

Góngora, Luis de, *Soledades*, ed. and tr. Philip Polack (Bristol: Bristol Classical Press, 1997).

Horace, *Satires, Epistles, 'Ars Poetica'*, tr. H. Rushton Fairclough, Loeb Classical Library (London: Heinemann; New York: G. P. Putnam's Sons, 1929).

Lafuente Ferrari, Enrique, *La 'Novela ejemplar' de los retratos de Cervantes* (Madrid: Dossat, 1948).

Lee, Rensellaer W., *'Ut pictura poesis': The Humanistic Theory of Painting* (New York: W. W. Norton, 1967).

McSpadden, George E., *'Don Quijote' and the Spanish Prologues: Glimpses of the Genius of Cervantes at Work*, Vol. I (Potomac, MD: Porrúa Turanzas, 1979).

Padilla, Pedro de, *Jardín espiritual* (Madrid: Querino Gerardo, 1585).

Plato, *The Republic*, tr. Desmond Lee, 2nd edn rev. (Harmondsworth: Penguin, 1974).

Porqueras Mayo, Alberto, *El prólogo como género literario: Su estudio en el siglo de oro español* (Madrid: Consejo Superior de Investigaciones Científicas, 1957).

———, 'En torno a los prólogos de Cervantes', in *Cervantes: Su obra y su mundo: Actas del I congreso internacional sobre Cervantes*, ed. Manuel Criado del Val (Madrid: EDI-6, 1981), pp. 75–83.

Presberg, Charles, '"This is not a Prologue": Paradoxes of Historical and Poetic Discourse in the Prologue of *Don Quijote*, Part I', *MLN*, 110 (1995), 215–239.

Randel, Mary Gaylord, 'Cervantes' Portraits and Literary Theory in the Text of Fiction', *Cervantes* 6.1 (1986), 57–80.

Riley, E. C., *Cervantes's Theory of the Novel* (Oxford: Clarendon Press, 1962).

Rivers, Elias L., 'Cervantes' Art of the Prologue', in *Estudios literarios de hispanistas norteamericanos dedicados a Helmut Hatzfeld con motivo de su 80 aniversario*, ed. J. M. Sola-Solé and others (Barcelona: Hispam, 1975), pp. 167–71.

2

Enchantment and Irony: Reading *La gitanilla*

William Clamurro
Emporia State University, Emporia, Kansas

The second longest of the group (after the *Casamiento/Coloquio* [Marriage/Colloquy]) and the most deceptively complex of all the *Novelas ejemplares* is the text that Cervantes chose to open the entire collection.[1] *La gitanilla* (The Little Gypsy Girl) is also one of the most studied and popular. Re-read in the imagination, recomposed in memory, *La gitanilla* easily devolves into the genre of the formulaic, fortunate tale of loss and recovery: the beautiful baby daughter of a noble family is kidnapped at birth by gypsies; she is raised in a marginal world, but later she meets a handsome young aristocrat who has fallen in love with her and who is willing to undergo a period of testing disguised as a gypsy and living in their world. Strife and violence erupt, and this leads to the recovery and recognition of the long-lost girl by her rightful parents. At the end, all conflicts and problems are resolved, and a happy marriage of the two young lovers restores social unity and familial harmony.

Thus abbreviated, this *novela* is the simple, affirmative story of the triumph of love and inner virtue, and the fortunate restoration of order.[2] But a more full and attentive reading of the text reveals that this is a remarkably complex and suggestive work, strange in its structure and narrative order, full of seemingly

[1] See, for example, Juan Bautista Avalle-Arce's introductory comments in his edition of Cervantes's *Novelas ejemplares*, 3 vols (Madrid: Clásicos Castalia, 1982, 1987); especially his comment that '*La gitanilla*, como es evidente, forma el pórtico de esta colección de doce novelitas y es preciso indagar los motivos que pueden haber motivado a Cervantes para ponerla como primera muestra de un conjunto que le causaba la íntima satisfacción que he discutido en el primer apartado' (p. 19). (*La gitanilla*, obviously, forms the gateway to this collection of twelve little *novelas*, and one must ascertain the reasons that may have moved Cervantes to offer it as the first sample of a collection that gave him the deep satisfaction that I discussed in the first section).

[2] With regard to the largely affirmative implications of the *novela* and what we might call the un-ironic readings, see especially the studies by Joaquín Casalduero, *Sentido y forma de las 'Novelas ejemplares'* (Madrid: Gredos, 1974); Ruth El Saffar, *Novel to Romance: A Study of Cervantes's 'Novelas ejemplares'* (Baltimore, MD: Johns Hopkins University Press, 1974); and Balbino Marcos, 'Un exponente ideal de exaltación femenina: *La gitanilla*', *Letras de Deusto*, 15.3 (1985), 95–111.

gratuitous loose ends, and ultimately revealing of numerous troubling ironies that touch upon socio-cultural inequalities and tensions.[3] In the commentary that follows, I would like to explore a few of what strike me as the most fascinating and telling complexities of the work. What I hope to suggest, finally, is that the apparent excess of ironies, unresolved issues, and digressive actions all serve to make the *novela* more, rather than less, powerful and engaging and that, beyond this positive consequence of Cervantine complexity, the subtle dissonances of *La gitanilla* prepare us to be more astute and appropriately sceptical readers of the tales that will follow.[4]

The Gypsies and Their World

The implications of including the gypsies – a fascinating yet slightly threatening marginal ethnic group despised by the Spaniards of Cervantes's time – as a key part of the story's human dynamic have been much studied.[5] The opening paragraph of the *novela* sets forth a surprisingly flat and categorically dismissive judgement of the gypsies. After having finished all the *novelas* the reader will notice how this 'beginning' echoes a moment near the very end of the collection: Berganza's similar but somehow more cold and hostile view of gypsies.[6] Cervantes's narrator – and *who* exactly is this detached, but perhaps not fully 'reliable' narrator? – paints the gypsies of *La gitanilla* and their world

[3] Numerous more recent studies have focused upon the ironic and anti-ideal nature of much of this text. See especially the studies by Jonathan Burgoyne, '*La gitanilla*: A Model of Cervantes's Subversion of Romance', *RCEH,* 25.3 (2001), 373–95; E. Michael Gerli, 'Romance and Novel: Idealism and Irony in *La gitanilla.*' *Cervantes,* 6.1 (1986), 29–38; Lesley Lipson, '"La palabra hecha nada": Mendacious Discourse in *La gitanilla*', *Cervantes,* 9.1 (1989), 35–53; Tamara Márquez-Raffetto, 'Inverting the Paradigm: Preciosa's Problematic Exemplarity', *Mester*, 25.1 (1996), 49–78; Francisco Márquez-Villanueva, 'La buenaventura de Preciosa', *NRFH*, 34.2 (1985–86), 741–68; and Alison Weber, 'Pentimento: The Parodic Text of *La gitanilla*', *HR*, 62.1 (1994), 59–75.

[4] The following commentary is much indebted to the studies listed in the 'Works Cited' at the end, in particular, El Saffar, Casalduero, Alban K. Forcione, *Cervantes and the Humanist Vision: A Study of Four 'Exemplary Novels'* (Princeton, NJ: Princeton University Press, 1984), and Stanislav Zimic, *Las 'Novelas ejemplares' de Cervantes*, (Madrid: Siglo XXI, 1996). I would also like to acknowledge the incisive comments of my friend and colleague, Dr Henry Sayre, of Oregon State University, who read a preliminary draft of this essay.

[5] On the question of the gypsy community and attitudes toward them in this *novela*, see especially Isaías Lerner, 'Marginalidad en las *Novelas ejemplares, I. La gitanilla*', *Lexis*, 4.1 (1980), 47–59; Marie Laffranque, 'Encuentro y coexistencia de dos sociedades en el Siglo de Oro: *La gitanilla* de Miguel de Cervantes', in *Actas del Quinto Congreso Internacional de Hispanistas* (1974), ed. Maxime Chevalier and others (Bordeaux: Presse Universitaire de Bordeaux, 1977), pp. 549–61; Márquez-Raffetto; and Walter Starkie, 'Cervantes and the Gypsies', *The Huntington Library Quarterly*, 26 (1963), 337–49.

[6] As Berganza is made to express it, 'La [vida] que tuve con los gitanos fue considerar en aquel tiempo sus muchas malicias, sus embaimientos y embustes, los hurtos en que se ejercitan así gitanas como gitanos, desde el punto casi que salen de las mantillas y saben

in terms of simplistic, ethnically biased clichés: gypsies are by their very nature thieves:

> Parece que los gitanos y gitanas solamente nacieron en el mundo para ser ladrones, estudian para ladrones, y, finalmente, salen con ser ladrones corrientes y molientes a todo ruedo, y la gana del hurtar y el hurtar son en ellos como accidentes inseparables, que no se quitan sino con la muerte. (I, p. 61)
>
> (It seems that gypsies, both male and female, were born into this world to be thieves; they are born of thieving parents, they are brought up with thieves, they study to be thieves, and finally they become fully qualified thieves and the desire to steal and stealing itself are in them essential characteristics, which they lose only in death [I, p. 13])

This presentation of their world is thus made in rather crude and sweeping terms. Yet the passage serves to introduce the main character, Preciosa, and although she is described as having been schooled by her presumptive gypsy grandmother in all the 'gypsy arts' of stealing, Preciosa will never actually be seen stealing in the course of the narrative. Instead, she seems to make her living by singing and dancing, telling fortunes, and, in general, as an entertainer. She is more a kind of enchanting 'magnet for money', for coins willingly given by her audiences, than she is the conventional, and conventionally 'picaresque', thief or swindler. The notion that all the other gypsies routinely engage in stealing, meanwhile, is left only implicit in the story. The thievery and swindling essential to the nature of the gypsies are thus assumed, but are not really imputed to Preciosa as an individual, nor does theft become, even in the case of the other gypsies, a key part of the story.

Yet acts of stealing stand at the beginning and the end of the *novela*. These thefts are, however, of a very different sort. The first one exists in the 'pre-history' of the narrative and is alluded to in an indirect way. Speaking of Preciosa, the narrator notes that 'la crianza tosca en que se criaba no descubría en ella sino ser *nacida de mayores prendas* que de gitana' (I, p. 62) ('the coarse upbringing she had had only revealed that she had been *born of better stock* than that of the gypsies' [I, p. 13]; emphases added). This first and, as it were, extra-textual theft is, of course, the necessary kidnapping of the girl as an infant. By contrast, the second act of stealing is not technically a theft at all. It occurs near the end of the *novela* and is the alleged stealing of jewels fabricated by Juana Carducha, the spurned innkeeper's daughter, who plants the incriminating valuables in the baggage of the male hero of the tale, Andrés Caballero (in reality, the aristocrat, don Juan de Cárcamo). This false 'theft' provokes the crisis of the always latent

andar'. (see Miguel de Cervantes, *Novelas ejemplares*, ed. Harry Sieber, 2 vols (Madrid: Cátedra, 1980–81), II, p. 347 ('My life with the gypsies at that time made me ponder their malice, lies and deceits, the thefts which both man and women amongst them practise almost from the moment they leave their cradles and begin to walk' [Miguel de Cervantes, *Exemplary Novels / Novelas ejemplares*, ed. B. W. Ife, 4 vols (Warminster: Aris & Phillips, 1992), IV, p. 141]). Further quotations from the text are taken from these editions. Berganza's description continues at some length (II, pp. 347–49; IV, pp. 141, 143).

clash of hostile social strata, the conflict between a despised ethnic group and mainstream society. As an accused thief and presumed gypsy, Andrés Caballero is in danger of losing his life. But once he is revealed to be the aristocrat, don Juan de Cárcamo, he is above any such penalty and would have been exempt, no doubt, even if the crime of theft had been real. Even more important, he is also conveniently excused from punishment for his impulsive killing of a soldier who, thinking Andrés to be a gypsy, had insulted and struck him.

Theft, then, is a central but ironically treated motif in this story. Most tellingly, it is linked not so much to gain and loss of material wealth as it is to the question of the loss and recovery of identity. The first theft–kidnapping (of Preciosa) deprives the young woman of her authentic identity, or as we might say, temporarily displaces her from her original 'world'. The second and basically artificial theft, prompting the accusation against Andrés/don Juan, provokes the necessity of re-establishing and asserting the man's true identity. Ironically, given that Andrés is willing to maintain the fiction of his disguise and accept punishment, this revelation and restoration of his true identity is effected by the gypsy grandmother, evidently unwilling to let the youth be killed in what we might call a case of 'mistaken identity'. In fact, for the older gypsy woman the peril into which Andrés falls requires that she reveal both identities: that of the only recently gypsified Andrés (a willing identity shift on his part), and also that of Preciosa herself, whose identity has been so long fabricated for her that she is not aware of its inauthenticity.

What then is the meaning of 'theft' in this particularly complex, fictional world? It is clearly not the routine yet thematically necessary stealing or swindling so familiar to us from the picaresque narratives of Cervantes's time. Nor is theft the consequence of true material privation or desperation. As we see in the case of don Juan de Cárcamo, when he takes on his identity as Andrés Caballero the gypsy, he refuses to steal; but in order to satisfy and fit in with his new criminal companions, he feigns activity of this sort, using the money that he has brought with him to purchase items that he will later claim to have stolen. On another level, Preciosa herself is so adept at her song and dance routines, and she is also so beautiful, that people freely shower her with money, the gold coins that she thus has no need to steal. Given the assumed morality and customs of the gypsies, then, the absence of explicit stealing within the story is curiously jarring.

I would argue that in *La gitanilla* Cervantes develops a story whose logic of theme and narrative-structure has more to do with the juxtaposition and testing of identities, with volition and desire, and with the much more subtle contrasting of social levels and social order, than it has to do with either the material desperation of the picaresque world or with the situational tension and suspense that a story of authentic thieves would have generated.[7] The special and peculiarly

[7] Concerning the overtones of the picaresque, see Avalle-Arce (p. 23); see also my own treatment of this text in William H. Clamurro, *Beneath the Fiction: The Contrary Worlds of Cervantes's 'Novelas ejemplares'* (New York: Peter Lang, 1997), pp. 15–40.

restrained world of this *novela*'s gypsies serves instead as the backdrop for a more sly and subtle commentary on society's often hypocritical inconsistencies, as well as for the more idealizing implications of the testing and triumph of love and virtue, embodied in the two main characters.[8]

Temporary Inversions of Female versus Male Power

La gitanilla is not the only one of Cervantes's *novelas* in which one or more female characters is given an active role, a narrative centrality, or a symbolic value that overshadows that of any of the male characters; one thinks immediately of *La fuerza de la sangre* (The Power of Blood) and *Las dos doncellas* (The Two Damsels). But the dominance of Preciosa is not only greater. It is also of a markedly different nature. In the first place, one is surprised to notice that a good third of the text goes by with Preciosa and her mostly female gypsy companions engaged in a series of seemingly random incidents, before the principal male character, don Juan de Cárcamo, even enters the story. When the youth does appear and when he assumes the temporary persona of Andrés the gypsy, Preciosa nonetheless continues to dominate the action and the spirit of the tale. In a peculiar sense, and very much unlike some of the central and 'dominant' women in Cervantes's other *novelas*, Preciosa is not only the central object of desire and the focal point of beauty and enchantment, but also the informing force, the defining 'subject' who orders and illuminates much of the immediate world around her. This latter feature is manifest in many passages. For example, we see this dominance in Preciosa's bold sense of command and self-possession that is displayed in the early, more random episodes, before don Juan/Andrés comes in. We are reminded especially of this self-assured poise when Preciosa goes into the house where several idle noblemen are gambling (I, pp. 72–7) (I, pp. 25, 27, 29). This episode is followed a little later by Preciosa's visit to the home of doña Clara, wife of the government official (*teniente*). In this scene, when it is time for doña Clara, or someone of the household, to pay for the fortune-telling and it is discovered that no one there has any ready cash, Preciosa is given liberty (by Cervantes) to engage in some blunt satiric commentary on both the implicit hypocrisy of appearances and the irony of the fact that honesty in government service only leads to material privation for those who are virtuous.[9]

The other crucial moments in Preciosa's assumption of an authority that inverts the traditional roles of gender occur during her first encounter with don Juan de Cárcamo. In this scene, the young woman is neither overly impressed by the youth's slightly boastful presentation of his own aristocratic status nor tempted by the man's generous, if slightly crass and possibly suspect, offer of

[8] On the complexity of the social critique, see in particular the articles by Burgoyne and Márquez-Villanueva; even Forcione (pp. 208–15) acknowledges the contrary and critical elements in what he otherwise finds an affirmative, idealizing text.

[9] On the subtlety and complex satiric power of Preciosa's poem and comments in this episode, see especially Márquez-Villanueva.

gold (I, pp. 83–4) (I, pp. 37, 39). Nor does Preciosa yield to the judgement, both materialistically self-interested and foresightfully shrewd, of her gypsy grandmother. Rather the young woman claims and underlines her own autonomy, as the well-known passage puts it:

> Yo, señor caballero, aunque soy gitana pobre y humildemente nacida, tengo un cierto espiritillo fantástico acá dentro, que a grandes cosas me lleva. A mí ni me mueven promesas, ni me desmoronan dádivas, ni me inclinan sumisiones, ni me espantan finezas enamoradas; y aunque de quince años [. . .] soy ya vieja en los pensamientos y alcanzo más de aquello que mi edad promete, más por mi buen natural que por la experiencia. (I, p. 85)
>
> (I, my worthy gentleman, although I am but a poor and humbly-born gypsy girl, have within me a certain little impulse to fantasy, which inspires me to great things. Promises do not move me, presents do not break me down, humble submissions do not affect me, and fine declarations of love do not shake me; and although I am only fifteen [. . .] I am old in thoughts, and I grasp more than you might expect of my age, more from my natural intelligence than from experience. [I, p. 39])

So begins Preciosa's fairly long discourse, during which she not only claims a degree of female autonomy surprising for the culture of that epoch, but also eloquently asserts the importance of honour and virginity in the context of Christian marriage.[10] Most significantly, Preciosa concludes by turning the tables, as it were: the young man's declaration of love and offer of marriage become the pretext for her challenge to him to submit to a test of his sincerity and love. The conditions of this test (I, p. 86) (I, p. 41) – that don Juan de Cárcamo take on the identity of Andrés Caballero, a gypsy, and live with the gypsy band for two years – mean that don Juan will give up identity, wealth (along with the real protections of wealth), and the autonomy and relative power advantage that one would normally associate with his gender. This test imposed by Preciosa also sets in place the necessary conditions within which the final crisis of violence, mistaken identity, near death, and recognition can occur.

Preciosa's next crucial assertion of her rather surprising autonomy and gender-defying 'difference' happens during the curious scene of the ceremony in which don Juan, now called Andrés, is welcomed and initiated into the gypsy community (I, pp. 100–5) (I, pp. 57, 59, 61, 63). This moment is for many readers – or at least for *this* reader – striking for the troubling combination of certain quasi-utopian elements of the gypsies' generous and communal lifestyle and their apparent harmony with nature, on the one hand, with their immorality (incest) and cold brutality (dissolving marriages at a whim; murdering a wife who is unfaithful or suspected of being so), on the other.[11] The picture painted by the

[10] On this theme, see Forcione, especially pp. 136–84.

[11] Concerning the dimension of the grim, threatening, and (as he would have it) demonic within the world of the gypsies, see Forcione, in particular pp. 184–85.

discourse of the elder gypsy leader (I, pp. 100–3) (I, pp. 57, 59, 61) is, over-all, a most troubling one. It is emphatically not the world of don Juan de Cárcamo. But it is also, in a significant way, not really Preciosa's world either. The gypsy leader's grim and decidedly patriarchal if not male-chauvinist description of his community's rules and customs, again, as in the case of the presentation of theft in the text's first paragraph, serves as both a foil and a prelude to yet another of Preciosa's 'exceptions' and to her exercise of power. While the older gypsy, in effect, seems to have handed the young woman over to Andrés, Preciosa once more overturns and rejects the norm:

> Puesto que estos señores legisladores han hallado por sus leyes que soy tuya, y que por tuya te me han entregado, yo he hallado por la ley de mi voluntad, que es la más fuerte de todas, que no quiero serlo si no es con las condiciones que antes que aquí vinieses entre los dos concertamos. Dos años has de vivir en nuestra compañía que de la mía goces, por que tú no te arrepientas por ligero, ni yo quede engañada por presurosa. (I, p. 103)
>
> (Since these legislators have found by their laws that I am yours, I have found by the law of my will, which is the strongest law of all, that I do not want to be yours except under the conditions we agreed before you came here. You have to live in our company two years before you enjoy my company, so that you won't repent if you are fickle, and I won't be deceived into being too hasty. [I, p. 61])

This significant discrepancy – Preciosa's differentiation and distancing of herself from her apparent world – is necessary to the demands of both the quest and 'test of love' conventions and also to the underlying irony and paradox of the story's ideological implications: Preciosa both is and is not a gypsy. But of more interest is the fact that this initial period of her life, at least her life within the scope of the *novela*, provides a stage characterized by force of will, autonomy, and verbal precision on her part.[12] Preciosa can, in effect, lay down the law. She determines an environment in which don Juan's love and sincerity can be thoroughly tested, and also a situation in which she herself can articulate and embody a kind of witty, sometimes satirical, difference and curious distance from the norms of the gypsy way of life. Preciosa can both embody virtue and also test its authenticity in others.

This autonomy is most meaningful in its contrast with what will happen at the conclusion of the story. With Preciosa's restoration and recuperation of her 'true' aristocratic identity as the long-lost Costanza, her autonomy and self-possessed verbal power are replaced with obedience, restraint, and submission. This is a key question to which I shall return later; but for the moment, it is worth noting that this before-and-after contrast suggests that for Cervantes the world of the gypsies, as he constructs it here, and the obvious anomaly of the young woman's

[12] Concerning the question of Preciosa's temporary verbal autonomy, see Márquez-Raffetto, pp. 53–4.

freedom and force of will, all serve to provide the author and his story with a field of meta-realistic exploration and expression. Not unlike the case of another striking Cervantine anomaly – the mysterious and radically autonomous Marcela of *Don Quijote*, Part I – the woman in question and her temporary circumstances serve as a way of talking about a value carried to an extreme that is unlikely in the real world beyond the text, but all the more resonant for this same improbability.

The Role of Poetry in the 'Novela'

As many critics have noted, the number, variety, and complexity of the poems found in *La gitanilla* distinguish it from the other *novelas* of the collection.[13] These poems – both serious and comic, the idealized statements of beauty and the more frivolous and satiric – mirror in their contrary complexity the dual identity of Preciosa herself. In addition, the poetry serves to add resonance to several other key characters in the story, notably the mysterious page-poet Clemente and, toward the end, don Juan.

There are, in all, eight pieces of verse included in the *novela*, and the range of tone, theme, and purpose between them is striking. For one thing, not all of the poems belong to Preciosa: two (I, pp. 74–6, and p. 96) (I, pp. 27, 29, and p. 52) are given to her by the mysterious *paje-poeta* (page-poet) Clemente, and another (I, pp. 119–20) (I, pp. 81, 83) is in effect the improvised pastoral duet of Andrés and Clemente, in praise of Preciosa and her beauty. Nor are all the poems at the same level of seriousness. At least two – Preciosa's versified palm-reading or fortune-telling ('la buena ventura') at the home of doña Clara and the embarrassingly poor *teniente* (I, pp. 79–81) (I, pp. 33, 35), and her comic–curative *ensalmo* (incantation) (I, pp. 97–8) (I, p. 55), which is not what she really whispered into the ear of the half fainted-away don Juan, but rather what she later writes down – are somewhere between the satiric and the gratuitously silly. In the case of her fortune-telling verse, spoken out loud to doña Clara, it seems hard at first to find much beyond a witty and manipulative string of flatteries, combined with inconsistent and equivocating predictions – 'Has de heredar, y muy presto | hacienda en mucha abundancia' ('You'll come into money | and a lot of it quite soon'); or 'Si tu esposo no se muere | dentro de cuatro semanas, | verásle corregidor | de Burgos o Salamanca' ('If your husband does not die | within four weeks, | you'll see him as a magistrate | in Burgos or Salamanca') – and at least one rather questionable, or questionably off-colour, allusion: 'Guárdate de las caídas, | principalmente de espaldas | que suelen ser peligrosas | en las principales damas'

[13] With regard to the role and implications of the poems included in this *novela*, see the studies by Forcione; María Antonia Garcés, 'Poetic Language and the Dissolution of the Subject in *La gitanilla* and *El licenciado Vidriera*', *Calíope*, 2.2 (1996), 85–104; Georges Güntert, '*La gitanilla* y la poética de Cervantes', *BRAE*, 52 (1972), 107–34; and Joseph B. Spieker, 'Preciosa y poesía (Sobre el concepto cervantino de la Poesía y la estructura de *La gitanilla*)', *Explicación de Textos Literarios*, 4.2 (1975), 213–20.

('Take care about falls | [especially on your back] | they can be very dangerous | in ladies of position') (I, pp. 80) (I, pp. 33, 35). And yet, as Márquez-Villanueva has shown, even a seemingly frivolous satiric performance like this can, and does, contain a highly complex, penetrating and serious element of social critique.[14] The maintenance of a uniformly idealized tone and thematic pitch is, then, hardly a top priority for Cervantes – or for his temporarily free-spoken heroine.

The first two, longer poems, whose authorship is not made explicit, but which the reader is inclined to attribute to Preciosa, the two supposedly penned by the shadowy Clemente (I, pp. 74–6, and p. 96) (I, pp. 27, 29, and p. 52), and the last two (the first being the alternating song of Andrés and Clemente and the second Preciosa's reply [I, pp. 119–20, and p. 121] [I, pp. 81, 83, and pp. 83, 85]) appear to have more serious purposes. Among the several critics who have considered the deeper implications of the more serious pieces of verse in the *novela*, A. K. Forcione's study is perhaps the most thorough.[15] As he notes, 'the poems in the early part of the tale, which have been generally ignored by critics and occasionally omitted by editors and translators, can be understood as carefully integrated emblematic statements of its principal themes' (p. 136); and of the last two poems, he asserts that 'the most important poems in the work are those which Juan, Clemente, and Preciosa sing on the eve of the heroes' return to civilization' (p. 139). As different as these four poems are from each other, they nonetheless can be seen (as Forcione insists) as complementary, subtle, and allusive statements on idealized Christian marriage, transcendent beauty, and the value of chastity and virtue. With regard to the Cervantine concept of the nature and value of poetry itself, it is difficult, if not impossible, to miss the parallel, clearly implied, in the text between what Clemente says about poetry (I, pp. 90–1) (I, p. 45) – and in particular the familiar but elegant metaphoric treatment, 'la poesía es una bellísima doncella, casta, honesta, discreta, aguda, retirada, y que se contiene en los límites de la discreción más alta' (I, p. 91) ('poetry is a beautiful young girl, chaste, pure, sensible, acute, retiring, inclined to keep to herself within the bounds of the highest good sense' [I, p. 45]) – and what Preciosa herself has previously said, to don Juan, about herself and the value of chastity. As Preciosa puts it, 'una sola joya tengo, que la estimo en más que a la vida, que es la de mi entereza y virginidad, y no la tengo de vender a precio de promesas ni dádivas [. . .]' (I, p. 85) ('I have one jewel only, which I esteem more than life itself, which is the jewel of my virginity and integrity'

[14] As Márquez-Villanueva has stated, 'se halla de por medio el poder destructor de la imagen eufemística, origen de inesperadas pero no desconocidas polisemias que tocan ya en las mismas fronteras de la lengua como instrumento de comunicación' (in the way stands the destructive power of the euphemistic image, the origin of unexpected but not unfamiliar double meanings which reach to the very frontiers of language as an instrument of communication) (p. 751); see also p. 761.

[15] See in particular Forcione's sections 'The Matrimonial Ideal and the Poetry of *La gitanilla* (pp. 136–47) and also '*Preciosa* and the Theme of Poetry' (pp. 215–22).

[I, p. 39]). Thus, there is a strong inclination towards taking the female protagonist as, in part, an embodiment of poetry (in the ideal) and, by extension, her own poetry as a manifestation of herself as a unique individual woman.[16]

But the idealized commonplaces about beauty and purity in poetry, as expressed in Clemente's words, are not the whole story in this *novela*. As noted above, longer and shorter passages of verse can not only lend themselves to hymns of praise or encomia to beauty, but can also serve as vehicles for satire and sly mockery. The poems inserted by Cervantes into *La gitanilla* serve to intensify rather elevated and edifying themes, as with the two initial and two concluding poems, and also as examples of Preciosa's own earthy and anti-idealizing, satirical dimension. Preciosa and poetry, then, are not simply synonymous or interchangeable. Rather, the two entities occasionally come together in moments of coincidence and resemblance, and at other times, the poetry and its thematic focus seem to stand apart from the presumed ideal purity of the ostensible speaker, Preciosa. The *novela*'s poetry, the idea of poetry, belong to more than one character and to more than one abstract register of decorum.

The Mystery of the 'Paje-Poeta', and the Mission of Don Juan's Father at Court

The most peculiar and perplexing figure in the *novela* is surely the *paje-poeta* (page-poet), Clemente.[17] Various critics have referred to this character as a kind of 'doubling' figure to don Juan/Andrés, and in fact the device of paired characters, be they rivals or allies, is found in several of the *novelas* in this collection. One thinks of Rinconete and Cortadillo, the two women of *Las dos doncellas* (The Two Damsels), Ricardo and Mahamut in *El amante liberal* (The Generous Lover), the two Spanish students in *La señora Cornelia* (Lady Cornelia), the two boys in *La ilustre fregona* (The Illustrious Kitchen Maid), and certainly of Campuzano and Peralta in the *Casamiento* and the two dogs in the *Coloquio*, among others. But in sharp contrast to these other pairs, both the nature and the narrative function of Clemente are riddled with a studied and premeditated ambiguity. It begins with his social status: he is presented as a 'paje' (page) early on in the story; but later, when he returns to the narrative, in flight from the law, he styles himself more a 'companion', all but a social equal, to the nobleman whom he was ostensibly serving. With regard to his assumed identity as a poet, Clemente presents Preciosa with a couple of poems, promising more; but then he claims that he is not really a full-fledged poet. His poems, along with his apparently adoring attitude toward Preciosa, would suggest that he is in love with

16 On the issue of poetry in *La gitanilla*, in addition to the relevant sections of Forcione's study, see Garcés, Güntert, Monique Joly, 'En torno a las antologías poéticas de *La gitanilla* y *La ilustre fregona*', *Cervantes,* 13.2 (1993), 5–15; and Spieker.

17 Concerning the complex function of this character, see Forcione (pp. 149–51); for a very different view, one that sees Clemente as a serious love competitor to don Juan, see Zimic (pp. 9–11).

her, smitten by her beauty, and more than just a distant admirer. Yet, towards the end of the story, when he meets up with the gypsy band as he is trying to flee the country, and after he has fulfilled the more apparent than real narrative function of arousing jealousy in the heart of don Juan/Andrés, Clemente confesses that he does *not* love Preciosa and never did. Finally, in the chaos and confusion near the end of the *novela*, when Andrés has been arrested for killing the insolent soldier and the local authorities are trying to round up as many of the other gypsies as they can, Clemente (or don Sancho, or Alonso Hurtado, as he is variously called) simply disappears from the story, completely and without trace.

Who, then, and more significantly *what*, is this Clemente? His brief narrative functions – first as a presumed admirer of the beautiful gypsy girl, and later as a mysterious and intrusive cause of fear and jealousy in don Juan's heart – are quite clear. But beyond these convenient 'functions', his nature and identity strike me as being significant and revealing for other, subtler, and more interesting reasons.

Clemente is not quite a page and not fully a poet, but he is a little of both these things. More important, he is a creature of the courtly and aristocratic society of the city, Madrid. Likewise, as something of a hanger-on vis-à-vis his social superiors, he represents that ambiguously mobile group of persons who served and could come to feel identified with the interests of the authentic aristocracy.[18] His close friendship and perhaps too-close involvement with the affairs of his master – resulting in his direct participation in a sword fight that leaves two other men (noblemen, at that) dead – makes Clemente a representative of this extended aristocratic and socially complicated structure of greater and lesser nobility and their various sub-levels of dependents and companions. Clemente lives in and is part of this world. His master is evidently of sufficiently modest noble stature that his killing of the two other noblemen, despite the fact that it was in fair self-defence, could not be excused by recourse to the claim of some relatively higher and thus more protected social status.

The 'crime' that puts both Clemente and his master, or close companion, on the run from the authorities in Madrid is as important for its perpetrators and victims as it is for the act and fact of the homicide itself. In explaining to Andrés his reasons for fleeing Madrid, Clemente finally gives the most important, significantly 'identifying', information about himself (I, p. 114–15) (I, pp. 73, 75). In so doing, he also hints at the more complex social profile of his unnamed master: 'Yo estaba en Madrid en casa de un título, a quien servía no como a señor, sino como a pariente. Éste tenía un hijo único heredero suyo, el cual, así por el parentesco como por ser ambos de una edad y de una condición misma, me trataba con familiaridad y amistad grande' (I, p. 114) ('I was in Madrid, in the household of a titled nobleman, whom I served not as one does a master, but as a relation. This nobleman had an only son and heir, who, because we were related and of similar age and character, treated me as a great and intimate friend'

[18] Concerning the issue of the complex and changing relationships between the different levels, and margins, of the Spanish aristocracy, see José Antonio Maravall, *Poder, honor y élites en el siglo XVII* (Madrid: Siglo XXI, 1979).

[I, p. 73]). As we see, then, Clemente's status is to an extent intermediate: connected by an asserted 'familiar' relationship, and yet not fully in the family. At the same time, the young heir of the 'casa de un título' ('household of a titled nobleman') is presented as pursuing a social linkage not sanctioned by his parents, due to their own social ambitions: 'Sucedió que este caballero se enamoró de una doncella principal, a quien él escogiera de bonísima gana para su esposa, si no tuviera la voluntad sujeta como buen hijo a la de sus padres, que *aspiraban a casarle más altamente*' (I, p. 114) ('It happened that this young gentleman fell in love with a lady of rank whom he would gladly have married, except that his will was subject to that of his parents, and *they hoped to arrange a socially advantageous marriage for him*' [I, p. 73]; emphases added). It is, then, this hidden love and the young nobleman's desire and jealousy concerning the 'principal' ('high-ranking') but not sufficiently prominent woman, who gets the man and his companion-servant into trouble. Because the two men who are killed in the nocturnal sword fight turn out to be 'dos caballeros [. . .] y muy principales' (I, p. 115) ('two gentleman, for such they were, and of high rank too' [I, p. 75]), Clemente and the 'Conde mi pariente' (my relative, the Count) have to flee, in effect evading justice.

This incident is the cause of Clemente's presence at the end of the story and is also the clue to a larger question – of justice and social privilege – that will arise more dramatically at the climax of the *novela*. For when the putative gypsy 'Andrés' kills the insolent soldier (with the latter's own sword; the victim thus being in a sense defenceless), he is at first considered an irredeemably 'condemned man'. Yet when Andrés is revealed to be in fact the aristocrat, don Juan de Cárcamo, and it is further taken into account that the murdered soldier is of much lesser rank (little more than the nephew of the *alcalde* [mayor]), the guilty young man is essentially 'let off' with just a payment of money: 'Recibió el tío del muerto la promesa de dos mil ducados, que le hicieron por que bajase de la querella y perdonase a don Juan' (p. 133). ('The uncle of the dead man received the promise of two thousand crowns so that he would drop the criminal charge and pardon don Juan' [I, p. 99]). As I have noted in a previous study, in the worlds of Cervantes's *novelas*, and most especially in *La gitanilla*, the rendering of justice is extremely partial and inequitable, as much (or more) determined by the respective social rank and identity of perpetrators and victims as it is governed by any status-blind consideration of the nature and severity of the crimes themselves (see especially the Introduction, pp. 5–6).

All of these elements – Preciosa's gypsy 'identity', the *novela*'s use of poetry, its stark violence and unequal dispensing of justice – underscore the problems and complex limitations of social class. Clemente serves as a strange and, although a seemingly secondary thread of the narrative, potent clue and link to this larger issue of the grim force of society and its unforgiving demands. By his notably shadowy and ambiguous identity, actions, and motivations, Clemente reminds us of this phenomenon of intricate social-rank relationships. While the world of the gypsies, in juxtaposition to the presumed mainstream Spanish society and culture, also dramatizes the problem of arbitrary and inequitable justice as well as the differences of day-to-day customs, the curious behaviour and positioning of Clemente reminds us, in an indirect and more subtle manner, of certain social complexities in the lives and families of the other aristocratic, and thus supposedly 'respectable', participants in the story.

Finally, a most significant but little remarked passage occurs in the scene in which don Juan de Cárcamo first shows up and introduces himself to Preciosa. In the course of his attempt both to identify himself socially and to further his cause materially by documenting his personal and family wealth, don Juan mentions a detail that seems so unremarkable that little is made of it: the youth tells us that 'mi padre está aquí en la Corte pretendiendo un cargo, y ya está consultado, y tiene *casi ciertas esperanzas* de salir con él' (I, p. 84)) ('my father is here in the capital seeking a post, his application has been approved by the authorities and he has *every hope of being appointed*' [I, pp. 37, 39]; emphases added). What Cervantes's principal male character is in effect saying is that not only does the Cárcamo family live in Madrid, in the heart of 'la Corte' ('the capital') as it were, but also that his father is seeking some sort of government post, which, as the clear contextual thrust of this moment indicates, will increase the family's, and thus the young don Juan's, material wealth. The senior Cárcamo is thereby presented as a part of not only a social class (the aristocracy) but also of the subtle and complex dynamic of different levels or gradations within the nobility and the frequent need for some of its members to advance themselves by means of a basically dependent, if not parasitic, relationship with higher placed nobles or with the monarchy itself.[19] Thus, in this brief and seemingly innocuous phrase the text gives us a glimpse of the complexities of a social structure, one within which 'familias principales' ('high-ranking families') such as don Juan's may be relatively wealthy but are not broadly free or independent of the larger, quite rigid social structure.

Reading and the Unresolving Text

The central issues, or the main themes, of *La gitanilla* resolve neatly, perhaps all too neatly, at the conclusion of the *novela*. Preciosa is returned to her family and restored as the authentic Costanza; don Juan de Cárcamo endures his time of trial – including the unanticipated near-death 'trial' of being arrested for murder – and thus he both proves and earns the love that he at first claimed he felt. Finally, he achieves the union with Preciosa/Costanza that he had initially appeared to be trying to purchase. Virtue and fortitude triumph; social order is, after a fashion, restored; and even the gypsies are let off lightly: the gypsy grandmother becomes part of the new larger family (the combining through marriage of the Cárcamo and the de Azevedo y de Meneses families), while the other gypsies are spared punishment and are basically allowed to go free. But in the midst of all this,

[19] Once again, see Maravall, especially pp. 201–18.

several discords and ironic loose ends remain. The all-too-neat resolution of the problem of the murdered soldier has to be acknowledged. Likewise, the successful escape and complete disappearance of Clemente, not to mention the truth of his initial identity, suggest that there are broader problems having to do with the equitability of justice and with the questionable behaviour of members of the aristocracy, problems that not only disturb the modern reader but that probably also disturbed the sense of fairness of some of Cervantes's contemporary readers, however common such law-bending expedients may have been. Last, we have the irony of Preciosa, or shall we now say, Costanza, during her time as a gypsy. This was an identity in which she herself fully believed. It was not a 'role' (like that of don Juan when he played at being Andrés Caballero), but rather her original and authentic nature. Upon the disclosure that she is in fact the daughter of the de Azevedo y de Meneses family, she changes radically. From a wilful, articulate, and autonomous woman, Preciosa becomes a submissive and totally obedient, 'dependent' young girl. We are then prompted to wonder, if only on a secondary level, who this woman really is, or is meant by Cervantes to be and to represent.[20]

In effect, Cervantes has pulled off an admirable sleight-of-hand: the creation of a double, or even multiple, *novela*. *La gitanilla* is a work whose core story provides the familiar gratifications of a satisfying narrative form, retracing the almost folkloric pattern of loss and recovery. But, simultaneously, and in a way both integrated with and yet dissonantly distinct from the main plot, the author has taken us on a journey of subtle yet penetrating and disturbing glimpses into the often harsh inequalities and social tensions of the age. The totality of *La gitanilla*, however, is not simply a kind of picaresque narrative swindle – although (as Avalle-Arce and others have noted) it seems to begin that way and it does reiterate many picaresque elements throughout. Rather, it holds together, constantly in play, a multiplicity of thematic and social levels, as well as implications of ethical inconsistency and cultural conflict. In reading after reading, the text itself withstands reduction to a possible unity of tone or critical implications, triumphing over any and all attempts at simplification (e.g. that it is *merely* a sly but cynical tale of social inequality and corruption, or that it is just a fairly simple and straightforward celebration of love and virtue). The experience of reading this *novela*, not in spite of, but rather very much as a consequence of, these ironies and seeming 'loose ends' proves the text to be a continually renewing and fascinating construct of language and theme. Among its many other enchantments and ironies, *La gitanilla* is, I believe, also about the art and possibilities of the act of reading. It can, and in fact must, be seen as a story that is a constantly recreating experience, a challenge to our own acts

[20] On the irony of Preciosa's sudden silence when restored to her identity as Costanza (or Constanza, as the name is variously spelled in the text), see Márquez-Raffetto; see also my own treatment of the question, especially pp. 38–40.

of reading. *La gitanilla* ultimately educates us, making of us the readers required by this quintessentially Cervantine text and by the other *novelas ejemplares* to follow.

Works cited

Burgoyne, Jonathan, '*La gitanilla*: A Model of Cervantes's Subversion of Romance', *RCEH*, 25.3 (2001), 373–95.

Casalduero, Joaquín, *Sentido y forma de las 'Novelas ejemplares'* (Madrid: Gredos, 1974).

Cervantes Saavedra, Miguel de, *Novelas ejemplares*, ed. Harry Sieber, 2 vols (Madrid: Cátedra, 1984).

———, *Novelas ejemplares*, ed. Juan Bautista Avalle-Arce, 3 vols (Madrid: Castalia, 1987).

———, *Exemplary Novels / Novelas ejemplares*, ed. B. W. Ife, 4 vols (Warminster: Aris & Phillips, 1992).

Clamurro, William H., *Beneath the Fiction: The Contrary Worlds of Cervantes's 'Novelas ejemplares'* (New York: Peter Lang, 1997).

El Saffar, Ruth, *Novel to Romance: A Study of Cervantes's 'Novelas ejemplares'* (Baltimore, MD: Johns Hopkins University Press, 1974).

Forcione, Alban K., *Cervantes and the Humanist Vision: A Study of Four 'Exemplary Novels'* (Princeton, NJ: Princeton University Press, 1984).

Garcés, María Antonia, 'Poetic Language and the Dissolution of the Subject in *La gitanilla* and *El licenciado Vidriera*', *Calíope*, 2.2 (1996), 85–104.

Gerli, E. Michael, 'Romance and Novel: Idealism and Irony in *La gitanilla*', *Cervantes*, 6.1 (1986), 29–38.

Güntert, Georges, '*La gitanilla* y la poética de Cervantes', *BRAE*, 52 (1972), 107–34.

Hart, Thomas, *Cervantes' Exemplary Fictions: A Study of the 'Novelas ejemplares'* (Lexington: University Press of Kentucky, 1994).

Joly, Monique, 'En torno a las antologías poéticas de *La gitanilla* y *La ilustre fregona*', *Cervantes*, 13.2 (1993), 5–15.

Laffranque, Marie, 'Encuentro y coexistencia de dos sociedades en el Siglo de Oro: *La gitanilla* de Miguel de Cervantes', in *Actas del Quinto Congreso Internacional de Hispanistas* (1974), ed. Maxime Chevalier and others (Bordeaux: Presse Universitaire de Bordeaux, 1977), 549–61.

Lerner, Isaías, 'Marginalidad en las *Novelas ejemplares, I. La gitanilla*', *Lexis*, 4.1 (1980), 47–59.

Lipson, Lesley, '"La palabra hecha nada": Mendacious Discourse in *La gitanilla*', *Cervantes*, 9.1 (1989), 35–53.

Maravall, José Antonio, *Poder, honor y élites en el siglo XVII* (Madrid: Siglo XXI, 1979).

Marcos, Balbino, 'Un exponente ideal de exaltación femenina: *La gitanilla*', *Letras de Deusto*, 15.3 (1985), 95–111.

Márquez-Raffetto, Tamara, 'Inverting the Paradigm: Preciosa's Problematic Exemplarity', *Mester*, 25.1 (1996), 49–78.

Márquez-Villanueva, Francisco, 'La buenaventura de Preciosa', *NRFH*, 34.2 (1985–86), 741–68.

Spieker, Joseph B., 'Preciosa y poesía (Sobre el concepto cervantino de la Poesía y la estructura de *La gitanilla*)', *Explicación de Textos Literarios*, 4.2 (1975), 213–20.

Starkie, Walter, 'Cervantes and the Gypsies', *The Huntington Library Quarterly*, 26 (1963), 337–49.

Weber, Alison, 'Pentimento: The Parodic Text of *La gitanilla*', *HR*, 62.1 (1994), 59–75.

Zimic, Stanislav, *Las 'Novelas ejemplares' de Cervantes*, (Madrid: Siglo XXI, 1996).

3

The Play of Desire: *El amante liberal* and *El casamiento engañoso y El coloquio de los perros*

Peter N. Dunn
Wesleyan University

> En esta vida los deseos son infinitos, y unos se encadenan a otros, y se eslabonan y van formando una cadena que tal vez llega al cielo, y tal se sume en el infierno. (Miguel de Cervantes Saavedra)[1]

> Readers do not only work on texts, but texts work on readers, and this involves a complex double dialectic of two bodies inscribed in language. (Elizabeth Wright)[2]

My argument about the play of desire in these *novelas* is twofold: I shall consider, first, how desire plays, how it plays out in a narrative; how the plot plays with desire, and the role of desire in driving the actions of characters. Second, I hope to show how we readers, in our negotiation with the text, are enticed to endure the vicissitudes of the characters and to pursue our own quest for the satisfying ending. There is, however, another sense for the '*play* of desire', and that is the playfulness of the author in the representation of the desires of the characters in, for example, the characters' misconstruals of their own desire and of the desire of others. There is, in addition, the 'readerly' desire formed in us by our previous readings, and by our being members of a reading community. To quote Peter Brooks, 'the tale as read is inhabited by the reader's desire and [. . .] further analysis should be directed to that desire, not his individual desire and its origins in his own personality, but his transindividual and intertextually determined desire as a reader including his expectations for, and of, narrative meanings'.[3]

El celoso extremeño (The Jealous Old Man from Extremadura) would be an obvious choice for this approach, but I have chosen not to use it because of its

[1] 'In this life desires are infinite, and they follow on from each other, linking together to form a chain that sometimes reaches up to heaven, and other times plunges down into hell'. Miguel de Cervantes Saavedra, *Los trabajos de Persiles y Sigismunda*, ed. Juan Bautista Avalle-Arce (Madrid: Castalia, 1969), VI, 10, pp. 458–59.

[2] Elizabeth Wright, *Psychoanalytic Criticism*, 2nd edn (New York: Routledge, 1998), p. 16.

[3] Peter Brooks, *Reading for the Plot. Design and Intention in Narrative* (Cambridge, MA: Harvard University Press, 1992), pp. 111–12.

very obviousness. In that story, Carrizales's obsessive desire to possess, to enclose, and, Pygmalion-like, to shape his human material, arouses counter-desires. These are the givens of the plot; they stand out in plain view and they forewarn us of the inevitability of a destructive ending. The subtleties and the political implications of the story lie elsewhere. I have just referred to the inevitability of *an* ending, not of *the* ending, because all readers of *El celoso* have found something disconcerting in the resolution, as if the powerful engines of desire and counter-desire had failed to achieve their promised climax, or their appointed catastrophe. But then, if we can say this, it is because we have not taken into account how the narrative engages, shapes, directs, and plays with the desire of the reader for a specific outcome. We read for the ending that we expect and wish for, though this may not be the necessary end; in the words of Peter Brooks again, 'the improper end lurks throughout narrative' (p. 104). The *novela* plays with our anticipations of a final coherence. All of this stands out with such obviousness in *El celoso extremeño*, as the narrative displays on the surface of the text its patterns of desire, sex, and power, with an explicitness that is not to be found in any of the others except *La fuerza de la sangre* (The Power of Blood). (Here we may possibly have a clue to the reason why these two together occupy the mid point of the set of *Novelas ejemplares*.)

Rather than discuss *El celoso extremeño* or *La fuerza de la sangre*, I will focus on *El amante liberal* (The Generous Lover) and *El casamiento engañoso y El coloquio de los perros* (The Deceitful Marriage and The Dialogue of the Dogs), in both of which the play of desire is manifested in ways that are less overt, but that are muted or absorbed by conventions of genre. However, I am going to leave aside generic expectations in favour of readerly ones, so I will first focus on the reading experience and state my conviction that Cervantes was quite aware of the role of readers in creating a meaning, *their* meaning, for his stories. In order to approach this question, we should pause and think back over the scholarship of the last century, so as to recall where its focus has been directed. Two related questions concerning the *Novelas* have claimed scholarly attention. The first and most prominent one concerns what Cervantes meant by calling them 'exemplary'. Does the epithet carry a moralizing or admonitory weight, telling us what examples to follow and what to avoid, what pays and what bankrupts? Or is their exemplarity located rather in the skilful variety, so that we should admire the collection as a showcase of the art of writing stories? The second question is: what did Cervantes mean by that tantalizing declaration that if he had time (a crafty Cervantine evasion, if ever there was one), 'si no fuera por no alargar este sujeto, *quizá* te mostrara el sabroso y honesto fruto que se podría sacar, así de todas juntas, como de cada una de por sí' ('if it were not for the fact that it would make this over-long, *perhaps* I would show you the delicious and wholesome fruit which could be pulled both from the collection as a whole and from each one alone'; emphases added)?[4] What meaning should we

[4] Miguel de Cervantes, *Novelas ejemplares*, ed. Harry Sieber, 2 vols (Madrid: Cátedra, 1986), I, p. 52. The English translation is from Miguel de Cervantes, *Novelas ejemplares /*

take from 'todas juntas' ('as a whole')? Does Cervantes challenge us here to discover some totalizing meta-narrative? Many scholars, provoked by the absence of any literary frame of the kind that was common practice among the Italian *novellieri* and the Spanish *novelistas* of the period from about 1620, have asked what holds the collection together. Does the very togetherness of the collection suggest a subtle, implicit frame?[5] Does the order of the stories in their sequence offer a clue to their cumulative meaning? Is there perhaps an internal frame, a vertebral column that the critic's X-ray eyes ought to be able to detect by careful scrutiny? For Joaquín Casalduero, 'la colección es un organismo' ('the collection is an organism') and the unity is thematic, the modalities of love being the sequencing element.[6]

At about the same time, Walter Pabst suggested that the final story, the *Casamiento y coloquio* functions as a retroactive frame, by ironizing all the preceding ones.

> En él se refleja una vez más todo el mundo abigarrado y vario de las precedentes novelas. Bañados de ironía, los personajes desfilan una vez más ante nuestros ojos. Es como en una comedia, en la que al final aparecen todos una última vez en el escenario, para inclinarse ante las carcajadas del público.
>
> (In it, the various, many-hued world of the preceding *novelas* is reflected once again. The characters, steeped in irony, parade in front of us once more. Just as at the end of a play, when all the characters appear on stage one last time and bow to acknowledge the loud laughter of the audience.)[7]

In other words, the *Coloquio* becomes, for Pabst, a kaleidoscopic vision of the types of humanity that populate the preceding *novelas*, but seen now through the lens of *desengaño* (disillusionment). In the preceding pages of his study of the *Novelas,* Pabst imagines the reader shaking his head over the strange behaviour of the characters,

> sorprendido por el curioso comportamiento de los personajes, por la inverosímil y falsa psicología, por la generosa falta de memoria, la contradicción entre el ser y el obrar que imperan [. . .] en este mundo ora cómico, ora diabólico, ya poético, ya puesto cabeza abajo. (p. 215)
>
> (surprised by the curious behaviour of the characters, by the unrealistic, false psychology, by the plethora of memory lapses, the contradiction between

Exemplary Novels, ed. B. W. Ife, 4 vols (Warminster: Aris & Phillips, 1992), I, pp. 3, 5. Further references are to these editions.

5 For a more extensive discussion of narrative framing and its implications, see Peter N. Dunn, 'Framing the Story, Framing the Reader: Two Spanish Masters', *MLR*, 91 (1996), 94–106.

6 Joaquín Casalduero, *Sentido y forma de las 'Novelas ejemplares'* (Madrid: Gredos, 1962), p. 20.

7 Walter Pabst, *La novela corta en la teoría y en la creación literaria* (Madrid: Gredos, 1972), p. 221.

> being and doing that prevail [. . .] in this sometimes comic, sometimes diabolic, now poetic, now topsy-turvy world.)

This view of the *Coloquio*, I suggest, is not so much a retroactive frame as a solvent that deconstructs the previous stories. It seems to be a rather desperate stratagem, devised by an intelligent reader formed by twentieth-century realism, in order to save the text and the reputation of Cervantes.

I am not convinced that we have gained much insight into these stories by doing what scholarly criticism has mostly done in the twentieth century: seeking thematic unity, be it ideological or ethical; or by locating a tension of opposites (*concordia oppositorum*), whether emphasizing modes (the critical game of idealism versus realism), or genre (romance versus novel) or structure (closed versus open-ended), though Cervantes is a masterful exploiter of open-endedness. In short, I believe Cervantes is here manipulating our readerly desire for directions and signposts. He is sending us on one of his false quests, in search of that mysterious *quid* that would give us an additional helping of 'sabroso y honesto fruto' ('delicious and wholesome fruit'), a quest that is surely as fruit-less as looking for the six plays that Lope de Vega said he composed in accordance with the classical precepts.[8]

It has been said that there are three classes of problem: those problems that either have been or can be solved; those that can never be solved; and those that, with the passage of time, cease to be problems. I would like to think that we have reached a moment when we can perceive this 'problem' as belonging to the third category, so that rather than speak of the problem of Cervantes's intention, we can focus on how the *Novelas* play upon readerly desire. Thomas R. Hart has pointed to an undogmatic assumption current in Italian Renaissance writing, with which Cervantes was familiar, namely that each reader should take whatever lesson she or he needs (or, I would add, no lesson at all), thereby recognizing the role of the reader's desire in constructing meaning.[9] Evidently, it was a part of the humanist project to locate exemplarity at the level of reading.[10] Garci Rodríguez de Montalvo in his prologue to *Amadís de Gaula* had already declared his desire 'porque assí los cavalleros jóvenes como los más ancianos hallen [. . .] *lo que a cada uno conviene*' ('so that both young and older gentlemen may find [. . .] *what is appropriate to each one of them*'; emphasis added).[11] We might also propose, in passing, the uncontroversial reflection that Cervantes's *novelas* offer what modern novels have repeatedly offered – the

[8] See Lope de Vega, *Arte nuevo de hacer comedias en este tiempo,* ed. Juana de José Prades (Madrid: Consejo Superior de Investigaciones Científicas, 1971), 370–71.

[9] Thomas R. Hart, *Cervantes and Ariosto. Renewing Fiction* (Princeton, NJ: Princeton University Press, 1989), pp. 116–17.

[10] Timothy Hampton, *Writing From History. The Rhetoric of Exemplarity in Renaissance Literature* (Ithaca, NY: Cornell University Press, 1990), p. 5.

[11] Garci Rodríguez de Montalvo, *Amadís de Gaula,* ed. Juan Manuel Cacho Blecua, 2 vols (Madrid: Cátedra, 1991), I, p. 225.

possibility of entering into other worlds and alternative lives that are both like and unlike our own. Already we are beginning to see how Cervantes's refusal to demonstrate the 'sabroso y honesto fruto' ('delicious and wholesome fruit') to be gained from all the stories taken together enables the creation of spaces where readerly desire can become operative.

I will shortly consider how these stories interpellate (in Louis Althusser's sense of the word) a modern reader, but for now I want to examine two things: first, the terms relating to pleasure that are used to describe the kind of reader reception Cervantes envisaged, and second, how the concept of play, broadly conceived, is an apt one both for the author's mode of writing and for the reader's mode of engagement with this writing. Bruce Wardropper approached the first question in a paper on *eutrapelia* delivered to the International Association of Hispanists in 1980.[12] In it he drew attention to the *aprobación* (censor's report) of the volume of *Novelas* written by Fray Juan Bautista Capataz. This censor, who was a friend of Cervantes, praises the stories for embodying the virtue of *eutrapelia*, or wholesome pleasure, with these words:

> supuesto que es sentencia llana del angélico doctor Santo Tomás, que la eutropelia [sic] es virtud, la que consiste en un entretenimiento honesto, juzgo que la verdadera eutropelia está en estas Novelas, porque entretienen con su novedad, enseñan con sus ejemplos a huir vicios y seguir virtudes. (I, p. 45)
>
> (since it is the clear opinion of the Angelic Doctor, St Thomas, that eutropelia [sic] is a virtue that consists in wholesome entertainment, my judgement is that true eutropelia lies in these Novelas, for they provide entertainment by their originality, and through their examples teach one to flee vice and pursue virtue.

The idea that pleasure and entertainment are good things to be sought for themselves has a long history, which goes back to before the time of the Angelic Doctor. Critics of a moralizing bent, as we know, cited Horace's line in the so-called *Ars poetica*: 'Aut prodesse volunt aut delectare poetae' (Poets wish either to instruct or to entertain), forcing a disjunction between profit and pleasure in order to hierarchize them, with *prodesse* in the superior position. Less frequently cited was the phrase, eleven lines later, which awards the prize to the poet who 'miscuit utile dulci, lectorem delectando pariterque monendo', who 'blended profit and pleasure, equally delighting and instructing the reader'. Christian writers of the Middle Ages had no difficulty endorsing the 'profit motive' (if I may call it that), but pleasure required some determined advocacy. Wardropper cites the dire warning against merriment in Luke's gospel: 'Woe to you who are laughing, for you will mourn and weep' (Luke 5: 26), as well as other similar admonitions

[12] Bruce W. Wardropper, 'La *eutrapelia* en las *Novelas ejemplares* de Cervantes', in *Actas del Séptimo Congreso de la Asociación Internacional de Hispanistas* (1980) (Rome: Bulzoni, 1982), pp. 153–68.

by early Fathers of the Church. Nevertheless, from Isidore of Seville on, we can find writers who not only defended, but positively asserted the value of pleasure. Petrarch wrote to his brother to protest that the external beauty of poetry should be appreciated for its own sake, and not simply as the shell to be broken in order to reveal a kernel of meaning.[13] Also, we cannot forget that the more racy works of Ovid were some of the most widely read works of the medieval centuries, especially the *Ars amatoria* and its many vernacular spin-offs.

There were, in addition, authoritative medical arguments for pleasurable activity. Medical treatises explained that physical exercise and all activities that conduce to cheerfulness help to preserve health, and they can do this because the emotions, the *accidentia animae*, affect the body. One of the three divisions of theoretical medicine was that of the *res non naturales*, that is to say, those things that are not part of the body but which affect its health, such as air, food, drink, exercise. Also, anything that could provoke strong feelings could affect the body and its health. Extreme joy or sorrow were said to be dangerous, and could even result in death by suddenly upsetting the balance of the humours. Arnold of Villanova states that cheerfulness is a necessary part of a regimen of health because it strengthens bodily energy. Story-telling was understood to fall into this category of beneficial activities. Boccaccio's ten well-to-do young people tell stories in delightful surroundings not only in order to escape from the plague, but in order to counter its baneful effects on their minds and perhaps even on their bodies. It was an 'act of self-remedy against the plague' (Olson, p. 57). While it is not difficult to find 'bad' examples in the *Decameron*, stories of immoral acts, the company receives them with wholesome laughter, and Boccaccio makes a strong point in his afterword about the reader's responsibility for the reception of them. The subtitle (*Galeotto*) that he gave to his *Decameron* can be read both as a commendation and as a warning, signalling the importance of reading maturely and critically. At the least, Boccaccio's work suggests the power of fiction to alleviate psychological distress (Olson, p. 206). Time and mortality are beguiled in pleasurable delay. Many medieval writers accepted delight as being a valid goal of literature without always demanding moral benefit. In the twelfth century, Walter Map's *De nugis curialium* has a preface that anticipates Cervantes's defence of literature as recreation ('Prologue' to the 'Third Distinction'). The medical theory on which the therapeutic effect of story-telling was based was common property among Christian, Islamic, and Hebrew physicians, so it is no surprise to find stories from the *Arabian Nights* and on into the seventeenth century in which depression, distress, or love-sickness in a leading character is cured by an aptly chosen and skilfully told story.

In his *Prólogo al Lector* (Prologue to the Reader) Cervantes justifies his stories on the same basis, namely, pleasurable recreation: 'Horas hay de recreación, donde el afligido espíritu descanse' (I, p. 52) ('There is time for recreation, when

[13] Glending Olson, *Literature as Recreation in the Later Middle Ages* (Ithaca, NY: Cornell University Press, 1982), pp. 31–2.

the tormented spirit can rest' [I, p. 5]). This is a value for which each reader must assume responsibility. Consider the analogies that Cervantes provides: 'Para este efeto se plantan las alamedas, se buscan las fuentes, se allanan las cuestas y se cultivan, con curiosidad, los jardines' (I, p. 52) ('That is why poplar groves are planted, springs are made into fountains, slopes are levelled and gardens created in wonderful designs' [I, p. 5]). All of these – planting, designing, levelling, laying out – are *activities*. The 'afligido espíritu' must not remain passive, because those things will not come to him; he must seek them out with a desire that matches the desire for order and proportion that shaped them. Recreation has to be a self-rewarding activity, which is to say some form of play. *A propos* of Cervantes's analogy of the 'mesa de trucos' (billiard table) that he has set up for public recreation, Alban Forcione has commented on 'the game as community-building activity':

> In the writings of humanists such as Castiglione, Erasmus, and Rabelais, we discover that the game emblematically represents man's capacities to organize the potentially chaotic and destructive interaction of individual impulses and desires into a social framework in which self-fulfillment and group harmony are part of a single process. In short, the game is the image of society in its essential and ideal condition.[14]

If there is a frame for the *Novelas*, perhaps it is a compact, or invitation, to engage in the game of *serio ludere* by means of which an integrated community of desires may be forged between author and readers.

* * * * *

We are now in a position to discuss *El amante liberal*. The fact that it is the *novela* which most faithfully replicates the form of the Greek romance in miniature has been sufficient to devalue it for many twentieth-century readers, myself included, readers conditioned either by classic realism, or by the modernist project of privileging aesthetic autonomy, self-reflexivity, and the immanence of the author in the text.[15] A text only becomes a story in the act of reading, when we

[14] Alban K. Forcione, 'Afterword: Exemplarity, Modernity, and the Discriminating Games of Reading', in *Cervantes' Exemplary Novels and the Adventure of Writing*, ed. Michael Nerlich and Nicholas Spadaccini (Minneapolis: Prisma, 1989), pp. 331–52 (pp. 346–47).

[15] In a previous study I dismissed it as 'la menos atractiva' (the least attractive). See 'Las *Novelas ejemplares*', in *Suma cervantina*, ed. J. B. Avalle-Arce and E. C. Riley (London: Támesis, 1973), pp. 81–118 (p. 93). In one of Italo Calvino's novels a character says: 'I, too, feel the need to reread the books I have already read [. . .] but at every rereading I seem to be reading a new book. Is it I who keep changing and seeing new things of which I was unaware? Or is reading a construction that assumes form, assembling a great number of variables, and therefore something that cannot be repeated twice according to the same pattern?' See *If on a Winter's Night a Traveller*, tr. William Weaver (New York: Harcourt Brace, 1981), p. 255.

compose a virtual text in our heads in response to the actual text on the page.[16] We re-read stories in endlessly changing ways, according to our experiences, to the cultural processes of which we are a part, and to the cultural products we have absorbed – what Roland Barthes called the *déjà-lu*.[17] Whether or not Cervantes was a 'perspectivist', readers surely are.[18] In the classic realism that enabled the approach of a Walter Pabst, the reader (I cite Catherine Belsey) is 'invited to perceive and judge the "truth" of the text, the coherent, non-contradictory interpretation of the world as it is perceived by an author whose autonomy is the source and evidence of the truth of the interpretation'.[19] Given such a set of assumptions, by which a unified intrinsic meaning in the text is guaranteed by the author, and is valid for all times and all readers, it is not difficult to understand Pabst's desperate attempt to project the satiric mode of the *Coloquio* retroactively over the whole collection of the *Novelas.*

My approach to *El amante liberal* is different. This *novela*, unlike the others, begins with a disembodied, unnamed voice, which is not that of a narrator. It speaks out from the page: '¡Oh lamentables ruinas de la desdichada Nicosia, apenas enjutas de la sangre de vuestros valerosos y mal afortunados defensores [. . .]!' (I, p. 137) ('"Oh pitiful ruins of unhappy Nicosia hardly dry of the blood of your brave but ill-fated defenders"' [I, p. 111]), and so forth. The beginning of a story always presents an enigma. There is a prehistory to be explained, and a voice that has to be located. When we read, for example, in Jane Austen's words, that it is 'a truth universally acknowledged that [. . .]', we are challenged (interpellated in Althusser's language) to ask what kind of narrator would assert such a truth-claim?[20] There can be no story of someone about whom nothing is known. In *El amante liberal* information about who is speaking here is withheld and we are kept in suspense. We perceive that the lamenter's sorrows are in some way bound up with those of the city of Nicosia. We wonder why it is Nicosia and how he has lost his liberty, but we must wait to find out, and delay is of the essence in story-telling, mobilizing our desire to press on, to learn more. (We will find that this desire and this delay are thematized in the dialogue of Cipión and Berganza.) A narrative bears generic markers, which may not be immediately revealed, but when they are detected they will serve to direct or, perhaps deliberately, to misdirect the reader. Cervantes, a master of all narrative kinds,

16 See Jerome Bruner, *Actual Minds, Possible Worlds* (Cambridge, MA: Harvard University Press, 1986) and Wolfgang Iser, *The Act of Reading* (Baltimore, MD: Johns Hopkins University Press, 1978).

17 Roland Barthes, *S/Z* (Paris: Seuil, 1970), XII.

18 The debate provoked by Leo Spitzer's 1948 essay, 'Linguistic Perspectivism in *Don Quijote*', in *Linguistics and Literary History: Essays in Stylistics* (Princeton, NJ: Princeton University Press, 1948), pp. 68–73 is ably summed up by Thomas R. Hart in '¿Cervantes perspectivista?', *NRFH*, 40 (1992), 293–303.

19 Catherine Belsey, *Critical Practice* (London: Methuen, 1980), pp. 68–9. Later reprints by Routledge.

20 See Louis Althusser, 'Ideology and Ideological State Apparatuses', in *Lenin and Philosophy*, tr. Ben Brewster, 2nd edn (London: NLB, 1977), pp. 123–175 (pp. 160–70).

naturally presupposes a correlative competence in his audience, readers who are experienced in recognizing and decoding the markers of every narrative genre and mode. In this case, the markers are there from the outset: a voice of desolation, abandonment, hopeless captivity, densely rhetorical in its enunciation. (Hart, *Cervantes*, pp. 46–52). Here the *lector amantísimo* (dearest reader) can be counted on to respond to the model of romance, specifically that model epitomized in the *Ethiopian Story* of Heliodorus.[21]

In Italo Calvino's *If on a Winter's Night a Traveller*, one of the characters asks: 'Do you believe that every story must have a beginning and an end? In ancient times a story could end only in two ways: having passed all the tests, the hero and the heroine married, or else they died' (p. 259). It was either romance or tragedy. The spirit that presides over *El amante liberal* is that of romance, not that of tragedy. We become aware of the generic pull of romance as soon as the unnamed speaker, who is soon to be revealed as Ricardo, refers to the miseries of captivity and loss. The end is already foreshadowed, even as Cervantes defers the introduction of the other essential component of the romance plot: the ineffably beautiful woman with whom the hero is in love. If the beginning provokes our desire to know what follows, the end has to satisfy our need to decipher the beginning. It is our desire for the anticipated end, for final coherence, that enables us to navigate the middle, reading its clues, mastering its codes. This middle, with its false promises and wrong turnings, is what Roland Barthes called the 'dilatory space', the space of errors, delay, and postponement (Brooks, p. 287).

In *El amante liberal*, Cervantes creates that dilatory space immediately. The cause of Ricardo's expressions of grief is not given until after Mahamut has explained to him how the Turks effect the transfer of power from one provincial governor to his successor. The passage from exclamatory grief to explanatory narration – a narrative composed typically of kidnap, shipwreck, and near rape – is interrupted by Mahamut's explanation; but the transfer ceremony itself is postponed until after Ricardo has told his story. Thus, we have delay interlaced with delay, desire for narrative resolution along with desire for the dramatic representation of the real-world exotic ceremony of the transfer of authority.[22] Then, Ricardo's narrative finally brings us back to the point of entry into the text, to the moment of narration, but it does so in a false resolution because Leonisa is presumed to be

[21] Stanislav Zimic gives preference to *Leucippe and Clitophon* by Achilles Tatius in his *Las 'Novelas ejemplares' de Cervantes* (Madrid: Siglo XXI: 1996), pp. 47–8, n.2.

[22] In reality, only the costumes and the setting are exotic. The ceremony closely resembles the pattern of the Spanish *residencia* (visit of inspection), as others have noted. Carroll Johnson, in *Cervantes and the Material World* (Urbana, IL: University of Illinois Press, 2000), cites it as 'a positive example to be profitably imitated by imperial Spain' by suggesting that the narrative voice describes 'a system in which no one, not even the viceroy, is above the law, a system clearly superior to the Spanish double justice system for *hidalgos* (nobles) and *pecheros* (ordinary taxpayers) [. . .]' (p. 125). In reality, the 'double justice system' could not obtain in the practice of the *residencia*, since viceroys were necessarily *hidalgos*. I suggest that the scene may be simply the novelist's way of explaining the exotic in terms of what is familiar.

dead – and this is the cause of Ricardo's grief. In fact, of course, she will shortly reappear as a captive for sale, covered with silks and jewels. Already, we can define the roles according to the functions described by Vladimir Propp in his *Morphology of the Folktale*: Hero, Prize, Rival, Helper, Villain.[23] The Hero is Ricardo, Leonisa is both the Prize and the object of desire of Ricardo and the Rival Cornelio; Mahamut is the Helper; the Turks collectively are the Villain. Cornelio is also what Propp called a Blocking Figure, but with a characteristically Cervantine variation, since the real impediment to Ricardo's union with Leonisa is within Ricardo himself: namely, his rashness, his anger, his arrogant assumption that only he is worthy of her. Cornelio, we later discover, is an obstacle only to the extent that her parents seem to favour him. He himself is unmanly, shrinking from the fight, effeminate, a *lindo* (pretty boy), with curly locks. He is not only generically the wrong match (meaning that he does not fit the requirements of the genre) but he is a genetically impossible suitor.[24] Having in mind the sexual stereotype of the Turk for Cervantes's audience, we could characterize Cornelio as 'the Turk within', differentiated from real Turks only by his blond hair. He is the foreign body that will be expelled at the end of the story, the only character who is not paired off with a partner.

For the Turks, Leonisa, the Prize, is both the object of immediate, uncontrollable desire, and also a valuable commodity.[25] For Ricardo, in contrast, Leonisa is priceless, and he offers all his wealth for her ransom. All the finery that the Turks put on her does not enhance her beauty – rather her beauty adds lustre to the jewels. For the Turks she is the supreme erotic object; but for Ricardo she is the agent of self-knowledge and therefore of self-transformation. Thus, at the end of their odyssey he 'nobly' renounces her, she refuses to be renounced, her parents accept him, and they are married on the spot by a bishop who is conveniently there. It is quite literally a question of 'end of story'. All the characters, in short, are roles rather than 'characters' in a modern sense. They fit perfectly into A. J. Greimas's system of classifying literary figures, not ontologically according to who they are, but functionally, according to what they do, as *actants* in his terminology.[26] Likewise, the Ottoman milieu, which Carroll Johnson (*Cervantes and the Material World*) has filled in and glossed extensively from contemporary evidence and historical scholarship, has but little function in the narrative, other than to broadly differentiate 'them' from 'us'.

I have so far not mentioned the middle section of the *novela* where most of the action takes place. Ricardo's earlier narration prepares us for the ensuing romance of shipwrecks, pirates, lecherous and avaricious Turks with their absurd

23 Vladimir Propp, *The Morphology of the Folktale*, tr. Laurence Scott, 2nd edn rev. (Austin, TX: University of Texas Press, 1971).

24 Adrienne Martin, 'Rereading *El amante liberal* in the Age of Contrapuntal Sexualities', in *Cervantes and His Postmodern Constituencies*, ed. Anne J. Cruz and Carroll B. Johnson (New York: Garland, 1999), pp. 151–69 (p. 154 and pp. 160–62).

25 Johnson has noted the relation between desire and commodification (pp. 144–50).

26 Algirdas Julien Greimas, *Sémantique structurale: recherche de méthode* (Paris: PUF, 1986), Ch. X.

plots, all playing with the expectations aroused by the codes characteristic of the genre. All of this, I suggest, is marked as parody.

The urge to parody in Cervantes is not confined to *Don Quijote*. In fact, almost all his work can fit Linda Hutcheon's ample definitions of parody as 'authorized transgression', or 'repetition with critical difference', or 'repetition with ironic distance'.[27] We may recall *El celoso extremeño* once again, where Cervantes gives an age-old comic story-line a turn toward tragedy. There he confronts the challenge of retelling an ancient chestnut, the farce of the old man in love with a young girl, but in a radically different mode, no longer as farce, acknowledging its tragic potential, and humanizing it against the grain of the bawdy *fabliau* tradition from which he lifted it. Thus, we might also define the dynamic of parody as transcoding from one generic matrix to another.

In *El amante liberal,* parody is signalled very early by a sudden change of register, an abrupt rhetorical downshift. After the high declamatory opening expressing Ricardo's woes, Mahamut picks up Ricardo's passionate reference to 'ruinas' (ruins) with a naïve comment: 'Por las de Nicosia dirás,' ('You mean the ruins of Nicosia') to which Ricardo retorts: 'Well, what others are there?' ('Pues ¿por cuáles quieres que lo diga [. . .] si no hay otras [. . .]' [I, p. 138]). Parody becomes more pronounced shortly after when Ricardo asks Mahamut if he knows a lady who is the most beautiful ever seen,

> la de más perfecta hermosura que tuvo la edad pasada, tiene la presente, y espera tener la que está por venir, una por quien los poetas cantaban que tenía los cabellos de oro, y que eran sus ojos dos resplandecientes soles, y sus mejillas purpúreas rosas, sus dientes perlas, sus labios rubíes, su garganta alabastro [. . .], esparciendo naturaleza sobre todo una suavidad de colores tan natural y perfecta que jamás pudo la envidia hallar cosa en que ponerle tacha. (I, p. 142)
>
> (hers was the most perfect beauty that the past had known, the present knows or the future can hope to know; one of whom the poets sang that she had hair of gold, that her eyes were two shining suns, her cheeks purple roses, her teeth pearls, her lips rubies, her throat alabaster [. . .], over all of which Nature sprinkled such a perfect natural softness of colours that never would envy discover anything with which to find fault. [I, p. 115])

and so on. Mahamut replies that, of course, that must be Leonisa. Here the Petrarchan conventions have been turned on their heads – made absurd by being made to do what they cannot possibly do – serve as the identification marks of an individual. The whole text now oscillates between high drama and low comedy. Our contemporary experience of pulp fiction, of the movies of James Bond and Indiana Jones, and of *Pulp Fiction* itself, which often parody serious genres – our *déjà-lu* – makes us receptive to Cervantes's play with diverse genres. At a crucial moment in the story, all three Turks, two pashas and a cadi, fall violently

27 Linda Hutcheon, *A Theory of Parody. The Teachings of Twentieth-Century Art Forms* (London: Methuen, 1984), pp. 6, 26, and 31–4.

in love with Leonisa and begin to plot against one another. These high dignitaries rapidly descend into being scheming lovers and lecherous clowns. The cadi plots to sail to Constantinople, ostensibly taking Leonisa as a gift to the Grand Turk, but he will throw his wife overboard, declare that it was Leonisa who died, and so keep her for himself. In the meantime, his wife Halima has fallen in love with Ricardo, who is now a slave with a false name, and she has Leonisa, who also has a false name, convey her declaration of love to Ricardo. At the same time, the cadi has Ricardo convey his proposition to Leonisa. Thus Ricardo and Leonisa are made to press upon each other the amorous claims of the hateful Turks. En route to Constantinople the cadi's ship is attacked simultaneously by the warships of his amorous rivals, the two pashas, and the melée in which the Turks all set about killing one another is a wild scene of guignol, presented in anti-heroic discourse: at one moment the cadi is saved from an enemy's sword by his 'cien varas de toca' (I, p. 180) (hundred yards of turban).[28] Our heroes watch the carnage, peeking out from the hatch, 'por ver en qué paraba aquella grande herrería que sonaba' (I, p. 181) (to see what the upshot of this din of iron-mongery would be). When that din subsides and they see that only four badly wounded Turks are left lying there, they now come bravely forth, courageously seize some weapons, and finish them off. This subversion of discursive conventions (romance typically demands the backs-to-the-wall heroic defeat of the many by the few) extends also to gender stereotyping. Woman, the narrator tells us, is 'fácil, 'móvil' (I, p. 168) (impressionable, changeable) but both Leonisa and Halima are better planners and more resourceful and cool under pressure than the men who rescue them.

What this summary discloses, I think, is that by abbreviating and condensing the given form, by reducing multiple plots to a single one, and including contemporary reference, Cervantes has produced a playful and ironic critique of the generic conventions of Greek romance. The critique encompasses, of course, the commonplace tropes: the labyrinth of fortune, and virtue tested like gold in a crucible. The form is thus ironized, and its anti- (not merely non-) realism is exposed. After *Don Quixote*, with its demonstration of the impossibility of exemplarity,[29] how could Cervantes seriously present a sequence of events in a heroic mode without leaving them open to the play of irony, given the banality of his readers' world?

[28] Other examples of stylistic parody: Ricardo recalls to the precise hour the time elapsed since his captivity ('éste de hoy hace un año, tres días y cinco horas' [I, p. 143] ('which today is one year three days and five hours ago' [I, p. 117]); the tears of Ricardo are self-consciously literary, 'las lágrimas que *como suele decirse*, hilo a hilo le corrían por el rostro en tanta abundancia que llegaron a humedecer el suelo' (I, p. 154; emphasis added) (the tears which, *as they usually say*, streamed down his face so abundantly that they even moistened the ground); the sighs of the enamoured Moor served only to drive the ship away faster (I, p. 176) (I, p. 157).

[29] 'Instead of exhorting his readers to virtuous action, Cervantes narrates the impossibility of exemplarity'. See Hampton, p. 293.

Cervantes has achieved two results by condensing the romance form and stripping it of multiple plots: first, he has produced the playful parody I have indicated; and second, he has revealed the seriousness of the folktale message that inheres in this type of narrative fiction. In their study of classic fairy tales, Iona and Peter Opie have shown that the story of Cinderella 'is not one of rags to riches, but of reality made evident'.[30] Cinderella is not transformed into nobility; she is restored to her original noble condition. Whatever magic there is in these tales 'lies in people and creatures being shown to be what they really are' (Opie, p. 14). This revelation of a destiny that is deserved is also the dynamic of romance. The story of Ricardo in *El amante liberal* can end only when he has faced his fear of rejection by Leonisa, and the knowledge that life can be unfair.

* * * * *

We shall now turn our attention to the last story in Cervantes's collection, *El casamiento engañoso y El coloquio de los perros*, which problematizes both beginnings and endings. It engages our desire to know the origins of stories but, more radically, it engages with our blindness to the origin of desire itself. Sigmund Freud was preoccupied for a long time with the case of the person known as the Wolf Man, and in his later years he came to suspect that his patient might not have seen what he believed he saw as an infant, that is, that the 'primal scene' may really have been a primal fantasy (Brooks, p. 276). This illustrates the point that in the stories we tell about ourselves, we can never reach back beyond the fantasy that generates them, and we seldom recognize that they are generated by fantasy. This is the reality that both the *alférez* (Ensign) Campuzano and the dog Berganza must confront.

In this combined story, Cervantes abandons most decisively the providential master plot guided by an authorial hidden hand, resulting in poetic justice, rewards or punishments. Here there is no narrative voice to provoke scepticism and to alert us to our responsibility as readers. The mystery of desire (rather than of 'lawlessness', *pace* Alban Forcione) articulates both of these combined stories. In the story of infatuation caused by the glimpse of Estefanía's little white hand, the *alférez* Campuzano persists in spite of the warning signs given by his friend the captain and by Estefanía's servant. Campuzano's story is clearly not a love story. Sexual desire, though, is not enough to explain his infatuation, nor is his evident machismo, nor his plan to deceive her as she deceived him. Sexual desire is desire in its most conspicuous manifestation and the one most familiar to us in fiction. Desire is a drive, which has to be distinguished from instinct and from need, as Freud explained. Instinct is directed towards a specific object; desire '[. . .] cannot be reduced to need since, by definition, it is not a relation to

30 Iona and Peter Opie, *The Classic Fairy Tales* (Oxford: Oxford University Press, 1974), p. 13.

a real object independent of the subject, but a relation to phantasy [. . .]'.[31] Fantasy is, indeed, the *mise-en-scène* of desire.[32] Desire must also be distinguished from love; for both Freud and Lacan, desire is not love but lack. Campuzano's fetishistic pursuit of the little white hand betrays the existence of a psychic need, and his narcissistic self-regard fits Lacan's account of the 'scopic drive', 'making oneself seen'[33] where the eye is an organ of incorporation (Burgin, p. 94; Lacan, pp. 67–104). Moreover, his story of his *casamiento engañoso* is a *texto engañoso* (deceitful text). It has been shaped into a self-conscious narrative, with internal symmetries and stylistic felicities quite unlike a soldier's spontaneous, unrehearsed talk. In the attempt to represent a transparent personal self-revelation, it becomes snared in its self-revelatory and self-justifying rhetoric and in the trappings of written fiction. So much is this the case that his literate companion Peralta does not hesitate to cap it with Petrarch's epigrammatic couplet: 'Che chi prende diletto di far frode; | Non si de' lamentar s'altri l'inganna' (II, p. 291) ('He who takes pleasure in deceiving others should not complain when he himself is deceived' [IV, p. 79]).

Immediately after this follows the *Coloquio*, which I take to be Campuzano's dreamwork, a dog's eye view of a world riddled with deceit and brutality. The web of desires that is figured in the conversation of the dogs – the dogs' own desires which range all the way from the basic ones for food and shelter to justice in a wicked world; those of the people Berganza encounters during his life, people driven by lust, greed, ambition, pride, and self-conceit; there are also the desires produced in the reader by the encounter with the text – forming a web that is too complex to be explored here. Cipión wants his friend to produce a narrative that is orderly, like that of Campuzano, to turn his life, if not into art, at least into a shapely construction: 'Sigue tu historia y no te desvíes del camino carretero con impertinentes digresiones' (II, p. 321) ('Continue your story and do not go off the beaten track with irrelevant digressions' [IV, p. 109]). As we know, it is precisely in the apparently irrelevant digression that desire may betray itself. Cipión also embodies the double desire of a listener or a reader for the story both to continue and also to conclude, the tense play of the opposing pleasures of delay, and discovery of the appropriate end. His motive, however, like that of most readers, is not entirely pure: he is eager for Berganza to finish so that he can begin his own story the following day.

31 Jean Laplanche and J-B. Pontalis, *The Language of Psycho-Analysis*, tr. Donald Nicholson-Smith (New York: Norton, 1974), p. 483.

32 Victor Burgin, 'Diderot, Barthes, *Vertigo*', in *Formations of Fantasy*, ed. Victor Burgin, James Donald, and Cora Kaplan (London: Methuen, 1986), pp. 85–108 (p. 98).

33 Jacques Lacan, *The Four Fundamental Concepts of Psycho-Analysis*, ed. Jacques Alain-Miller, tr. Alan Sheridan (New York: Norton, 1978), pp. 194–95. 'Estaba yo entonces bizarrísimo [. . .] y tan gallardo a los ojos de mi locura que me daba a entender que las podía matar en el aire' (II, pp. 283–84) ('At that time, I myself was rather flash [. . .] and so splendid was I in the eyes of my own delusion, that I believed that I could have any woman I wanted' [IV, p. 69]).

The dialectical relation between Berganza and Cipión has often been commented on, but I want to stress one particular aspect of it. Even before they came to possess the power of speech, the two dogs have been driven by the desire to talk, to narrate the story of themselves: 'desde que tuve fuerzas para roer un hueso tuve deseo de hablar' (II, p. 301), says Berganza ('I too, ever since I was strong enough to gnaw at a bone, had the desire to speak' [IV, p. 87]). The story of oneself is, ultimately, the only story that we ever do tell, though it is impossible to tell, having no beginning that we can reach back to, and no end that we can foresee, which would confer a final meaning on this middle in which we are forever immersed. The told is shadowed by the not-told. (That is what I take to be the pathos of the narratives of Samuel Beckett.) And just as we are driven by the desire to tell, we are also deflected by the desire to put our story in a certain order, with emphases and omissions, to make it convincing, negotiating as it were a second, virtual self to install between our always veiled, occluded selves and the listener. This is what Campuzano has done in the account of his marriage, and it is also what Berganza does in response to Cipión's interruptions and to his mere presence as a desiring listener. Thus, between them Berganza and Cipión play out opposing desires, which they hold in a creative tension: to frame, contain, and stabilize the text on one side, and to let it flow freely on the other.

In their desire for meaning, the dogs puzzle over the mystery of their speech, which they see as miraculous. Cipión suggests that their command of speech is what humans call a portent. If this is so, then whatever they say has to be subsumed in a greater teleological discourse that is speaking them, in which case they are not agents but signs constituting a message, but they can then have no access either to that message, if one really exists, or to its origin. It can be neither confirmed nor denied unless, of course, its purpose is embodied in the very discourse in which they reveal the world's evil – but evil scarcely requires a miracle to make itself known.

If Campuzano's story begins with a desire incited by the fluttering white hand, which he imagines will lead him into a new life, Berganza looks to another hand, a 'mano poderosa' (powerful hand) for deliverance from his canine condition. According to the witch Cañizares, he was born a human child but was changed into a puppy at birth, a revelation he has hinted at but held back more than once in the course of his narrative. He is destined to remain in his doggy condition until the apocalyptic moment when

> Volverán a su forma verdadera
> cuando vieren con presta diligencia
> derribar los soberbios levantados
> y alzar a los humildes abatidos,
> por mano poderosa para hacello. (II, p. 346)

> (They will return to their true form
> when they see how quickly and surely
> the haughty are brought down
> and the meek exalted
> by the hand with the power to do it. [IV, p. 139])

This hand has only a textual existence, but it is powerful enough to beguile him throughout his narrative, and there is no more insidious desire than the desire to be beguiled. His restoration to human form is to be deferred until the moment when he can take his place in a state of universal justice, a reversal of the present condition of the world. Had he recalled the lessons he attended at the Jesuit school, he would have learned that the bogus prophecy is a mishmash of words taken from Isaiah, the Magnificat, and Virgil. But, as we see every day, formal education is no match for the enchantments of desire or bewitching fantasies.

I have written elsewhere of the problems of framing, of authority, and of the positioning of the reader in this *novela* (Dunn, 'Framing'). To conclude here, I want to mention briefly the reader's role in unravelling the temporal sequences that Cervantes has knotted together. We are made to begin each part of the composite story at a different point in time, and each new beginning leaves something unexplained, some desire unrecognized, some origin unacknowledged. We are not told how the two friends, Campuzano and Peralta, became friends, nor how they separated. Indeed, as we finish reading this strange and marvellous work we become aware that *not* to strive after hidden beginnings or the fantasy of lost origins is an important message for the exemplary reader. The homology of Berganza's and Campuzano's desires demonstrates that desire is forever displaced and forever eludes us. Cipión debunks the witch's prophetic verses that Berganza has fostered in his memory (II, pp. 346–47) (IV, pp. 139, 141). At the end of his recital of the examples of human perversity and folly he has encountered, Berganza tells of his meeting with Cipión.

> Digo, pues, que viéndote una noche llevar la linterna con el buen cristiano Mahudes, te consideré contento y justa y santamente ocupado; y lleno de buena envidia quise seguir tus pasos, y con esta loable intención me puse delante de Mahudes, que luego me eligió para tu compañero y me trujo a este hospital. (II, p. 355)
>
> (What I mean is that, seeing you one night carrying the torch with the good brother Mahudes, it seemed that you were happy and occupied in a just and holy task and, full of a healthy envy, I decide to follow your steps, and with this laudable intention I stood in front of Mahudes who straightaway chose me for your companion and brought me to this hospital. [IV, p. 151])

In Cipión he has found a role model and a companion. He accepts the fact that he is a dog and also that he still has a function in the world of people. The two of them are guard dogs at the charity hospital in Valladolid, not far from where Cervantes resided, the place where humans confront the consequences of their desires: pain, disease, loneliness, remorse, even madness. Berganza's solitude is ended, and the friendship of the two dogs is affirmed; likewise, as Peralta finishes reading and Campuzano awakes, these two friends cease their little dispute and abandon their fruitless desire for a literal truth in stories. The *alférez* and the *licenciado* (Licenciate), traditional antagonists as personifications of arms and letters, go out to the riverside promenade to look at the world. 'Vámonos al

Espolón a recrear los ojos del cuerpo, pues ya he recreado los del entendimiento' says Peralta (II, p. 359) ('Let's repair to the Espolón to entertain our eyes for we have already entertained our minds' [IV, p. 157]). Here is exemplified the *eutrapelia* that closes the collection of *Novelas ejemplares.*

There arises the question, now, of what are we left with at the end of this *novela.* There is Peralta, about whom we know nothing except his friendship with Campuzano. There is Campuzano, a derelict soldier who is far from representing the noble career of arms, whose sword serves only as a cane to steady his trembling frame. All we know of him is his story of desire that has brought him to poverty, shame, and remorse. He is haunted still by his memory of Estefanía as well as by his shame. That story is so skilfully told that his friend Peralta has given it the epigrammatic coda taken from Petrarch, stamping it as a work of literary art. There is the story of a dog, whose desiring fantasy of a human origin is debunked by his companion Cipión. The *Casamiento* and the *Coloquio* interact and interrogate each other. Do we, as desiring readers, read the *Casamiento* as a specific case of the world's deceit as Berganza experienced it and described it, or do we read the *Coloquio* as the context within which to generalize Campuzano's story? Can we do either when truth-claims are denied on each level of the fiction? Finally, the two friends who frame the story walk out of it into the 'real world' to resume a friendship about which we know nothing, with Campuzano bearing the unresolved story of his shameful marriage.

In this last story of the collection of *Novelas ejemplares*, Cervantes, I would assert, plays his last trick on the desiring reader, frustrating every desire for explicit origins and for narrative closure.

Works cited

Althusser, Louis, 'Ideology and Ideological State Apparatuses', in *Lenin and Philosophy*, tr. Ben Brewster, 2nd edn (London: NLB, 1977).

Avalle-Arce, J. B., and E. C. Riley (ed.), *Suma cervantina*, (London: Támesis, 1973).

Barthes, Roland, *S/Z* (Paris: Seuil, 1970).

Belsey, Catherine, *Critical Practice* (London: Methuen, 1980). Later reprints by Routledge.

Brooks, Peter, *Reading for the Plot. Design and Intention in Narrative*, (Cambridge, MA: Harvard University Press, 1992).

Bruner, Jerome, *Actual Minds, Possible Worlds* (Cambridge, MA: Harvard University Press, 1986).

Burgin, Victor, 'Diderot, Barthes, *Vertigo*', in *Formations of Fantasy*, ed. Victor Burgin, James Donald, and Cora Kaplan (London: Methuen, 1986), pp. 85–108.

Calvino, Italo, *If on a Winter's Night a Traveller*, tr. William Weaver (New York: Harcourt Brace, 1981).

Casalduero, Joaquín, *Sentido y forma de las 'Novelas ejemplares'* (Madrid: Gredos, 1962).

Cervantes Saavedra, Miguel de, *Los trabajos de Persiles y Sigismunda*, ed. Juan Bautista Avalle-Arce (Madrid: Castalia, 1969).

Cervantes Saavedra, Miguel de, *Novelas ejemplares*, ed. Harry Sieber, 2 vols (Madrid: Cátedra, 1986).

———, *Exemplary Novels / Novelas ejemplares*, ed. B. W. Ife, 4 vols (Warminster: Aris & Phillips, 1992).

Dunn, Peter N., 'Las *Novelas ejemplares*', in *Suma cervantina*, ed. J. B. Avalle-Arce and E. C. Riley (London: Támesis, 1973), pp. 81–118.

———, 'Framing the Story, Framing the Reader: Two Spanish Masters', *MLR*, 91 (1996), 94–106.

———, 'Afterword: Exemplarity, Modernity, and the Discriminating Games of Reading', in *Cervantes' Exemplary Novels and the Adventure of Writing*, ed. Michael Nerlich and Nicholas Spadaccini (Minneapolis: Prisma, 1989), pp. 331–52.

Greimas, Algirdas Julien, *Sémantique structurale: recherche de méthode* (Paris: PUF, 1986).

Hampton, Timothy, *Writing From History. The Rhetoric of Exemplarity in Renaissance Literature* (Ithaca, NY: Cornell University Press, 1990).

Hart, Thomas R., *Cervantes and Ariosto. Renewing Fiction* (Princeton NJ: Princeton University Press, 1989).

———, '¿Cervantes perspectivista?', *NRFH*, 40 (1992), 293–303.

Hutcheon, Linda, *A Theory of Parody. The Teachings of Twentieth-Century Art Forms* (London: Methuen, 1984).

Iser, Wolfgang, *The Act of Reading*, (Baltimore, MD: Johns Hopkins University Press, 1978).

Johnson, Carroll, *Cervantes and the Material World*, (Urbana, IL: University of Illinois Press, 2000).

Lacan, Jacques, *The Four Fundamental Concepts of Psycho-Analysis*, ed. Jacques Alain-Miller, tr. Alan Sheridan (New York: Norton, 1978).

Laplanche, Jean, and J.-B. Pontalis, *The Language of Psycho-Analysis*, tr. Donald Nicholson-Smith (New York: Norton, 1974).

Martin, Adrienne, 'Rereading *El amante liberal* in the Age of Contrapuntal Sexualities', in *Cervantes and His Postmodern Constituencies*, ed. Anne J. Cruz and Carroll B. Johnson (New York: Garland, 1999), pp. 151–69.

Olson, Glending, *Literature as Recreation in the Later Middle Ages*, (Ithaca, NY: Cornell University Press, 1982).

Opie, Iona, and Peter, *The Classic Fairy Tales* (Oxford: Oxford University Press, 1974).

Pabst, Walter, *La novela corta en la teoría y en la creación literaria* (Madrid: Gredos, 1972).

Propp, Vladimir, *The Morphology of the Folktale*, tr. Laurence Scott, 2nd edn rev. (Austin, TX: University of Texas Press, 1971).

Rodríguez de Montalvo, Garci, *Amadís de Gaula*, ed. Juan Manuel Cacho Blecua, 2 vols (Madrid: Cátedra, 1991).

Spitzer, Leo, 'Linguistic Perspectivism in *Don Quijote*', in *Linguistics and Literary History: Essays in Stylistics* (Princeton, NJ: Princeton University Press, 1948), pp. 68–73.

Vega, Lope de, *Arte nuevo de hacer comedias en este tiempo,* ed. Juana de José Prades (Madrid: Consejo Superior de Investigaciones Científicas, 1971).

Wardropper, Bruce W., 'La *eutrapelia* en las *Novelas ejemplares* de Cervantes', in *Actas del Séptimo Congreso de la Asociación Internacional de Hispanistas* (1980) (Rome: Bulzoni, 1982), pp. 153–68.

Wright, Elizabeth, *Psychoanalytic Criticism*, 2nd edn (New York: Routledge, 1998).

Zimic, Stanislav, *Las 'Novelas ejemplares' de Cervantes* (Madrid: Siglo XXI, 1996).

4

Language as Object of Representation in *Rinconete y Cortadillo*

Alan K. G. Paterson
St Salvator's College, University of St Andrews

Cervantes's *Rinconete y Cortadillo* (Rinconete and Cortadillo) is an object-lesson in how the reader's heavy investment in understanding the text has not generally been paid back in critical kind. I mean by this that few critical readings work at the linguistic density that characterizes the text. Aden W. Hayes proves one of the exceptions when he identifies the linguistic behaviour of characters with the meaning of the story.[1] Language is an artefact wrought by the character with the intention of constituting a distinctive persona. This focus safeguards my experience as the reader of a text that has a high level of linguistic complexity by acknowledging that the complexity is essential to the critical gloss. In the course of his reading, Hayes singles out Monipodio for detailed attention, in particular justifying the factual errors he commits by placing them in the context of the leader's need to reinforce his authority; the truthfulness of words to experience is secondary to Monipodio's assertion of his will through the manipulation of language. In the formulation of this argument, Hayes avoids attributing errors to the author, in contrast to a positivistic critique which habitually laid textual contradictions at Cervantes's door. Instead, textual contradictions are to be attributed to what Hayes calls the character's 'delusory and self-serving use of language' (p. 14). What would happen, however, if we were to include the narrator among the manipulators of language in the *novela*? The question has a certain resonance with those studies which have raised an awareness of the fact that the narrator is a presence in the tale, a not entirely transparent mediator between us and the events that are told. This study in part resumes the enquiry into the narrator, but within the frame of reference set by language. By reason of the latter qualification, there are times when I will find it more natural to refer to the narrator as the writer, though not of course meaning Cervantes.

The narrator in *Rinconete y Cortadillo* exercises great care over certain aspects of his practice in the narrative. He makes a clear effort to get the names of things –

[1] A. W. Hayes, 'Narrative "errors" in *Rinconete y Cortadillo*', *BHS*, 58.1 (1981), 13–20 .

notably places and objects – precisely right. I know this from the number of times I still have to reach for the dictionary, consult the atlas or pause over a footnote. Support is proffered generously from within the narrative, for the narrator is well disposed to help me keep up with his exacting discipline in words. The first location is defined by the inn being named, then the region ('los famosos campos de Alcudia' ['the famous plain of Alcudia']), and finally its relevance to a traveller's map of Spain ('como vamos de Castilla a la Andalucía' ['on the road from Castile to Andalusia']),[2] all done with a care and precision that leave little margin for further enquiry into the significance of this particular geography for the start of the tale. Consonant with this studied air of precision, there is a striving that borders on pedantry to get the right word. The opening paragraph sets the standard. Autocorrection is evident when the 'zapatos' (shoes) of one boy are correctly redefined as 'alpargatas' (II, p. 559) ('rope sandals' [I, p. 175]), articles of clothing, worn or imaginary, are identified with a punctiliousness worthy of a tailor, and the 'zapatos' of the other boy are redefined by being compared to 'cormas' ('más le servían de cormas que de zapatos' [II, p. 559]) ('more like walking-stocks than walking shoes' [I, p. 175]), which the editorial footnotes all tell us are shackles fitted to slaves or small boys to stop them from running away. There are always cases where it is the literary text we read which supplied the lexicographer in the first place with both the lexis and the meaning, but not so in the case of 'cormas', for our own John Minsheu by 1599 corroborates the meaning generally accepted for our story: 'a little pair of stockes. Also a clog of wood or such like for horses, or to put on boyes feete that runne from their masters'.[3] This definition of 'cormas' does not strike me as referring to everyday footwear but to a specialized article, and the word would thus belong to a relatively more recondite lexis than the footnotes let on. If that is so, the narrator's comparison is carefully fetched into the narrative, without being too far-fetched. These shoes may be in need of the cobbler's craft, but at least they have received close attention from the word-smith. In a brief space the word-smith has exercised his ingenuity yet further, for these alpargatas 'tan traíd[a]s como llevad[a]s' (I, p. 559) ('more worn out than worn' [I, p. 175]) invite a second thought, a conscious gloss to the effect that the phrase 'traído y llevado' (*Diccionario de la Real Academia Española*: '1fr. 'Trasladado con frecuencia de un lugar a otro; frecuentemente usado, manoseado' [Frequently moved about from one place to another; frequently used, handled]) – 'well-worn' – has been significantly modified so as to highlight the reason for the footwear being well-worn in that it had been much worn. In this instance and many others the narrator exercises unqualified authority over

2 Miguel de Cervantes Saavedra, *Obra completa*, ed. Florencio Sevilla Arroyo and Antonio Rey Hazas, 3 vols (Alcalá de Henares: Centro de Estudios Cervantinos, 1993–95), II, pp. 559–603 (p. 559). The translation is from Miguel de Cervantes, *Exemplary Novels / Novelas ejemplares*, ed. B. W. Ife, 4 vols (Warminster: Aris & Phillips, 1992) I, p. 175. Unless otherwise specified, all quotations are from these editions.

3 John Minsheu, *A Dictionarie in Spanish and English* (London: E. Bollifant, 1599), p. 78.

his text; he is well ahead of his reader and confident in a writing stratagem which renders language into not-so-everyday speech, investing it with a special, even recherché quality. The problems I experience reading the narrator's text are, to a large extent, due to my own linguistic awareness being stretched to deal with the not-so-familiar features that the narrator has put into lexis and idiom. And as I say, when the going gets hard, his habit is to interpolate a linguistic gloss: 'el uno tenía una media espada, y el otro un cuchillo de cachas amarillas, que los suelen llamar vaqueros' (II, p. 560) (one had half a sword; the other a yellow-handled knife, one of the ones they call *vaqueros*) and 'un tiesto, que en Sevilla llaman maceta, de albahaca' (II, p. 575) ('a flowerpot, known in Seville as a *maceta*' [I, p. 193]) instance two of his many interventions throughout, the second illustrating equally well a keen ear for regional usage.[4] So a persistent, irrepressible concern over language is the marked and perhaps unique trait of this narrator. As he makes clear his linguistic interests he lays down a reading of *Rinconete y Cortadillo* to which this study is directed.

It would simplify matters if we were to attribute this persistent concern over words and phrases to Cervantes,[5] but by doing so we erase that beguiling presence who is ever active at the centre of the tale, who indefatigably names persons and things, records linguistic manners and sociolects, glosses the process of writing. Indeed, without this tireless attention to language on the part of this someone there would scarcely be any tale to tell. Yet the narrator's authority and control over matters of language are partial. It is not that he is unreliable, untrustworthy or ill informed, for his good intentions and commitment to getting things right are not called seriously to account.[6] His authority and control

[4] This manner of intervention is the most obvious marker of the narrator's active presence in the narrative.

[5] This is the position taken up by Ronald G. Keightley; he elides the narrator with Cervantes the author, as the following observation makes clear: 'it is the omniscient author-narrator Miguel de Cervantes who chooses to end his story of *Rinconete y Cortadillo* in this way [by cutting it short]).' See his 'The Structure of *Rinconete y Cortadillo*', in *Essays on Narrative Fiction in Honour of Frank Pierce*, ed. R. B. Tate, (Oxford: Dolphin, 1982), pp. 39–54 (p. 50). Keightley's drastic dispatch of the narrator is not unusual. Few studies have cared to notice him. Ruth El Saffar occupies an ambiguous position, recognizing the narrator as the initiator of the narrative, but seeing him then as one who 'retires to the background, allowing Rincón to represent him in inviting Cortado to emerge from his solitude' (*Novel to Romance: A Study of Cervantes' 'Novelas ejemplares'* [Baltimore: Johns Hopkins University Press, 1974], p. 39). The strongest affirmation of the narrator to date is by Bernard P. E. Bentley in 'El narrador de *Rinconete y Cortadillo* y su perspectiva movediza', in *Studia aurea, Actas del III Congreso de la AISO* (Toulouse, 1993), ed. I. Arellano and others, 3 vols (Toulouse-Pamplona: GRISO-LEMSO, 1996), III (Prosa), pp. 55–65. Bentley's narrator exerts a significant presence in the narrative, precisely by shifting his perspective, and it is suggested that he could even be identified with Rincón – a surprising sequela to El Saffar's retiring narrator. My own reading radically foregrounds the narrator, for as the organizer, commentator and provider of the heteroglossic text he more than any other can be said to occupy its centre.

[6] Striving to get things right is not the same as getting them right, hence I take it that the uncertainty over the boys' ages is due to the narrator's scrupulousness rather than a sign of his

are limited because he is not the only source of what we read; the content and movement of the story are determined by characters' words and encounters. Once we are aware that the narrator's particular competency lies in language, we are also made aware that in this respect he enjoys no monopoly. He has to share his expertise in the linguistic domain with other adepts. The conversation between Rincón and Cortado in the porch of the inn is paradigmatic. For the first and by no means last time the narrator's voice is replaced by one that is shared between the couple of boys. They engage in a special and novel form of discourse, characterized by a register and by social semiotics, with origins in *Lazarillo de Tormes*, which capture the phenomenon of social deception practised through a linguistic tactic of pretence. The scene is paradigmatic also because there is a bemused eavesdropper, the landlady of the inn, caught up in the contradiction between what she sees (two ragamuffins) and what she hears (a conversation between two well-brought up children). On the one hand, we have those who deliberately assume a linguistic register for their own, private purpose and on the other we have someone who tries to make sense of her language being turned unfamiliar. This configuration is repeated across the story. Indeed, Rinconete and Cortadillo will take on the role of the bemused and foxed listener on several occasions. The student will provide another vivid case of how a shared language turns into a linguistic subterfuge, a trap so well laid for the listener that he fails to understand the true meaning of the communication.

But my focus remains on the narrator, who is not explicitly novelized into the plot yet is linked by association with those who listen and register their responses to the matter and manner of discourse inside the story he tells. He, more than any other character, occupies what I have signalled above as the *novela*'s paradigmatic situation. The narrator is not the controlling agent of language so much as the recipient; he records the dialogic process that is performed by others who exercise linguistic competencies that lie beyond his own specialized competency as the writer of the story. He goes about his job of capturing this process with a degree of fidelity made evident by the predominance of direct and indirect free speech, both markers of a bold dialogic style. It is his commitment to putting on record these varieties of speech that qualifies his own monopoly over words; his voice becomes only one in a medley of voices. For parts of his narration his interventions are limited to comments on what he has received, true to the central paradigm that Cervantes develops of speakers and their listeners. Indeed, he closes his narration on himself as the reflective narrator summarizing highlights of the dialogic experience in the thieves' den. In novelized terms, the agent of this recall is Rinconete, whose consciousness the narrator taps. The summarizing impulse and the concluding promise of a sequel mark this conclusion out as metatextual; it deals with writing itself. In other words, the narrator who taps into Rinconete's recollections of the howlers he has heard in Monipodio's den is reassembling the

unreliability. Not knowing their years for sure, he delivers a second thought (seventeen years) on the first thought (fourteen to fifteen years). It is an instance of the metatextuality that will be fundamental to this reading i.e. the detail tells us about writing.

phenomenon of discourse as a move preliminary to putting it into a narration. The closing paragraph stands in a propaedeutic relationship not to another story – a sequel, which he may or may not tell – but to the one we have read.

A metatext that leads us in circular fashion from endings back to beginnings is a strategy familiar to us from the modern novel, one which we may think of as serving to focus on the act of writing itself. Metatext may invite us to consider the processes that enter into *poiesis*, suggesting for example the complex nature of the narrator, who only once he has traversed the experiences of which we have read is fitted to set them out in fiction. Such a function is not so distant from the metatextual ending of *Rinconete y Cortadillo* provided we keep in our sights what constitutes the narrator's writerly identity; he is the one who writes, who is marked out by his dedicated interest in language, evident not only in his compulsion for finding the right word that will exactly link up with experience but also in his taking cognizance of the distinctive voices in the Babel of others. The turning moment at the end, the metatext, is when he catches himself mulling over the phenomena of language that he has somehow experienced, in preparation for writing the story we have read. A reading of the *novela* which observes this emphasis on the writer who writes his compulsive engagement with language is distinguished from its 'costumbrista' ('period-detail') readings. There is nothing wrong with applying the term 'costumbrista' to the *novela*, except that it locks the work into an inadequate taxonomy. It restricts what the story tells us to a unitary content (customs) which is linguistically undifferentiated, whereas the phenomenon which the narrator captures is the multivalent factor of style. Of course, like the dedicated linguist he is, the narrator contextualizes distinctive forms of discourse by putting them into concrete settings, a notable example being the jargon (*germanía*) of *la hampa* (criminal underworld). As he does so, he introduces a sense of how language divides those whom it seems on the face of it to unite. What is impressed upon listeners to the hybrid versions of their own language is how alien the common possession can become. Needless to say, the reader is an interested party in the sociolinguistic phenomenon that motivates the writer, for it is our language too that is exposed to this treatment.

The episode of the student is a good case in point, if only because of the particular brilliance with which it attaches a sociolect to a concrete situation and actions. The stylistic variant at work is *bernardinas*, an equivalent to 'patter' or 'jaw' in English. It is a linguistic device fashioned out of irrelevancies and downright nonsense by the petty thief in order to distract his intended victim, in this case the student. The victim himself, incidentally, straddles a semiotic frontier, since like many of his peers at University then and now he moonlights, as a sacrist. His dual working-role (he is referred to as a 'medio estudiante' [semi-student]) has a linguistic consequence. Cortado calculates his *bernardinas* on the assumption that the student is a cleric, and he steers the opening patter, composed of proverbs and sayings, towards ecclesiastical nonsense – 'Cuanto más, que cartas de descomunión hay, paulinas [. . .]' (II, p. 569) ('What is more, there are such things as letters of ex-communication, the edicts of Pope Paul III [. . .]' [I, p. 187]) and so forth – ending out of his depth with the howler that since his victim is in holy orders then the thief 'había cometido algún grande incesto, o sacrilegio' (II, p. 570) ('had [. . .] done something quite incestuous or sacrilegious' [I, p. 187]). The tactic meets with success, for the student, ignoring the malapropism, picks up the cue, corrects the matter of his job, but preposterously concurs with the cheap-jack that indeed it is 'dinero sagrado y bendito' (II, p. 570) ('money that is holy and sanctified' [I, p. 187]). At that point Rincón enters the sting, fires off more proverbs and sayings, and returns to the ecclesiastical plane, making an enquiry about the chaplaincy's annual income that tries the student's self-control beyond its limits. His sober piety flips into a full-blooded student oath: '¡Renta la puta que me parió!' (II, p. 570) (Income! What damned income?) providing an object-lesson in the psychological mechanisms and semantics of profanity. The phenomenon of *bernardinas* is irresistible, for Cervantes re-runs it to include the theft of the student's lace handkerchief. True to form, the narrator makes a statement about the linguistic device in play ('al modo de lo que llaman bernardinas' (II, p. 571) (in the manner of 'patter' [my translation]) as well as elaborating on the psychological state induced in the victim by the said *bernardinas* ('el pobre sacristán estaba embelesado escuchándole' and 'Este tan grande embelesamiento [. . .]' [II, p. 571]) ('the poor benighted sexton was quite bemused, listening to him'; 'he was so transfixed [. . .]' [I, p. 187]). In due time the boys receive their come-uppance, when they are in turn accosted by the Babel of *la hampa*. This is when they are obliged by El Ganchuelo to concede their own verbal inadequacy, though not before suffering humiliation. They guess incorrectly and wildly at what the boy had said in what they assume to be their own language badly spoken: 'No somos de Teba ni de Murcia' (II, p. 571) ('Murcia, we're not from Murcia, nor from Thebes for that matter' [I, p. 189]). As El Ganchuelo concludes, these linguistic babes need to be spoon-fed.

This is good instructive stuff, repaying close study. But these performances in various linguistic styles and their relationship to social and psychological behaviours are not an isolated case. The phenomenon of styles is persistent throughout the *novela*. Direct speech enables characters to add their share of linguistic identity directly to the whole pool. Early in the narrative Rinconete and Cortadillo bring the distinctive voice of the con man cum parvenu into their first dialogue, and also allow us into the obscure but vividly metaphorized area that is the lingua franca of the card-sharper. Rinconete's later listing of the card-tricks he knows, beginning 'Yo sé un poquito de floreo de Vilhán' (II, p. 579) ('I have a modicum of skill at Vilhan's feint' [I, p. 197]) is just a taster, as Monipodio, the past master, makes clear and not without true verbal wit on his part: '–Principios son, –dijo Monipodio, –pero todas esas son flores de cantueso viejas y tan usadas' (II, p. 580) (' "They're good for a start," said Monipodio, "but all those tricks are old hat, and [. . .] commonplace" ' [I, p. 199]). Gender determines voices. Repolido's physical abuse of La Cariharta provokes the discriminated styles of male defence by threat and female retaliation through insult. Old age carries a distinctive voice. La Pipota recreates la madre Celestina, bowing out to attend to her devotions with the bawd's counsel to make hay while the sun shines: 'Holgaos, hijos, ahora que tenéis tiempo; que vendrá la vejez y lloraréis en ella los ratos que perdistes en la mocedad como yo los lloro' (II, p. 586) ('"Have fun, my children," she said to them, "now, whilst you've got the time: for come old age and you'll regret the times that you wasted in your youth"' [I, p. 207]). I am now doing as reader what the text enjoins me to do – to acknowledge the rich multiplicity of voices as well as identify each one's uniqueness inside the narrative.

In this array of voices, I must include above all the narrator, not only for being the word-smith who creates his own style as the writer/narrator, but also for exercising his sense of occasion. His appetite for language is prompted by a range of stimuli. He responds, for example, to place-names that have inscribed in them diachronic traces of another language and culture ('a la entrada de la ciudad, que fue a la oración, y por la puerta de la Aduana, a causa del registro y almorifazgo [. . .]'(II, p. 566) ('when they entered the city, which happened to be at the time of public prayer, and had stopped at the Custom-house Gate for inspection and for payment of import duty [. . .]' [I, p. 181]) – here he captures, on cue, the Arabic element retained in Sevilla's commerce, appropriately as his characters cross the city boundary). Personal names, too, gain his attention; in particular the use of nicknames and the process of their invention. He is master of ecphrasis, or description, abandoning the narrative, on cue, to engage with an object, person or event with a lexical precision and procedural order that leave an impression of an underlying repertoire of exercises dutifully fulfilled. Monipodio's portrait, for example, is exemplary as a framed and vividly differentiated digression. Indeed, in the portrait there is a momentary intersecting of the plane of representational art and the object of representation when the narrator concludes his *tour de force* with 'En efecto, él [Monipodio] representaba el más rústico y disforme bárbaro del mundo' (II, p. 577) ('In other words, he was the spitting image of the world's most uncouth and ugliest barbarian' [I, p. 195]), implying that it was this farouche individual who had modelled himself on the prototype of the barbarian, not the narrator who had modelled him. The narrator did no more than accurately describe Monipodio; the art had been laid down beforehand by his subject. Of course the effect of language being marked out as something special is enhanced by this process, so we savour its status as belonging to the special craft of those who invent characters like Monipodio, feasts like the abundant supper provided from the washing hamper, panics like the one that attends the approach of the police – to add two other notable examples in *Rinconete y Cortadillo* of ecphrasis, in the sense of digressionary description.

Who the narrator is we are not told; he plays no role as character in the story he tells, but he is, nonetheless, an active agent in it. It is he who has collected other people's utterances, he who shows a care bordering on pedantry over his own and their language. It is he who demonstrates (without advertisement) how to write about things. On this last point, we can sense him writing by the book, as instanced in that glorious moment when Monipodio breaks out in anger over the student's filched purse, 'de manera que parecía que fuego vivo lanzaba por los ojos' (II, p. 582) (until it seemed as though fire blazed forth from his eyes [my translation]), the simile complying neatly and with hindsight so predictably with the writer's manual par excellence, Ravisius Textor's *Epitheta*. It is as if we catch him in the very act of turning its pages.[7] But in a paradoxical way, he is just one voice among the many that he registers; he makes up part of the rich, dialogic texture of the whole tale. Yet his language is clearly marked out as a different 'voice zone' from the others, just as theirs is well differentiated from his. My acknowledgement of terms that come from Mikhail Bakhtin is overdue, now that my commentary is leading towards Cervantes's text being taken as an ideal exemplar of Bakhtin's heteroglossic or multi-voiced text. The heteroglossic text constitutes Bakhtin's notion of what the genre of novel is as style. For him, it is the mix and opposition of voices that make up the 'dialogized system' that every novel is. In one of the essays in *The Dialogic Imagination*, Bakhtin raises the interesting question of where the author is to be found in a multi-voiced, novelistic system.[8] It goes without saying that Cervantes is not the voice, or style of speech present in any one of the stylistic zones that are drawn out over the text of the *novela*. The *bernardinas* sample the language of the cheap-jacks who con gullible victims; La Pipota speaks as her prototype in *Celestina*; Monipodio, a character as linguistically motleyed as his appearance, draws his language eclectically from *la hampa*, from the *refranero* (proverbs), from the law, from guildry, from courtliness, according to the kinds of challenge that others make to his authority. And suffice to say it raises tricky problems if we assume that Cervantes's voice coincides with that of the narrator/writer. If we were to make such an assumption, it would then lead us on to ask if the narrator's outlook on writing is fused with Cervantes's outlook, and possibly to conclude that he, Cervantes, like the narrator, believes that readers will draw moral advice from the tale that he – the narrator – has told; or that, for unspecified biographical

[7] I cite Ravisius's *Epitheta* since along with his *Officina* it was a widely known and used commonplace book. We remember that these compilations were directed towards those learning to write, and the *Epitheta* in particular to teaching them to 'weave a richer, more attractive – which is to say more commonplace! – texture', in the words of Walter J. Ong ('Commonplace Rhapsody: Ravisius Textor, Zwinger and Shakespeare', in *Classical Influences on European Culture A.D. 1500–1700*, ed. R. R. Bolgar [London: Cambridge University Press, 1976], pp. 91–126 [p. 101]). 'Ira' is prefaced by a definition of the passion which includes among the symptoms 'blazing eyes' ('ut ardescant oculi') and among the epithets are cited 'fervens' (fiery) with its Ovidian quotation 'saepe suum fervens oculis dabat ira ruborem' (often burning anger would redden his eyes), and 'fulminea' (related to lightning). (I quote from *Epitheta* [Basle, 1599], pp. 430–32.) Here are the ingredients for the vivid yet commonplace description of Monipodio's outburst of anger: 'de manera que parecía que fuego vivo lanzaba por los ojos' (II, p. 582) (until it seemed as though fire blazed forth from his eyes). This analysis is not concerned to show that Cervantes relied on commonplace collections; it points out that the language of the narrator/writer, when it enters the narrator's direct language zone, shows tell-tale signs of the exercise book. To use a Bakhtinian expression, the language 'images' the style of literary story-telling, thus reflecting to us its own process of composition and its context.

[8] The essay in question is 'From the Prehistory of Novelistic Discourse', in *The Dialogic Imagination. Four Essays by M. M. Bakhtin*, ed. Michael Holquist, tr. Caryl Emerson and Michael Holquist (Austin: University of Texas Press, 1981), pp. 41–83.

reasons, Cervantes had to postpone telling the whole story of the boys' life in the underworld of crime.[9] This *reductio ad absurdum* serves as a reminder of the need to separate the writer/narrator from the real author, a separation which is particularly relevant when the narrator acquires such a distinctive style of being narrator.

Yet where Cervantes is is crucial to understanding the story. Let me try out the hypothesis that he is present in a level of critical awareness towards language that is higher than the narrator's. After all, our narrator draws his story to a close on a lame and trivial note, listing the malapropisms committed in the thieves' den – a pedant to the end. True, he also records the laughter caused by their solecisms, but the laughter is Rinconete's. Perhaps it is the narrator's lack of humour we sense by the end, for he seems impervious to the enormous joke that from the outset envelops his narrative. For his Babel is wracked by humour, being a place of constant parody, where the norms of trusted discourse are subverted by those who take the shell of proper discourse to conceal their own alternative and subversive behaviours within. Cervantes is the manager of this comic yet serious Babel. Comic it undoubtedly is. Take the memorable improvised band that celebrates the bonds of friendship – its instruments consisting of a slipper, a broom, two pieces of a broken plate rapidly clicked between the huge fingers of Monipodio's hand. The band is as cacophonous with regard to music as the mangled references to 'Negrofeo, que sacó a la Arauz del infierno' (II, p. 594) ('Black Orpheus who led What's-her-name from the underworld' [I, p. 217]) and 'Marión, que subió sobre el delfín y salió del mar como si viniera caballero sobre una mula de alquiler' (II, p. 594) ('Marion who rode on the dolphin's back and escaped from the sea as if he were some gent on a hired mule' [I, p. 217]) are to the mythology of harmony. But this is the sound of the underworld, an untuned and tuneless travesty of music, deprived of its worldly harmonies, not to speak of its divine origins. Or take again the farouche portrait of Monipodio, hugely comic in the detail (the deep-set eyes, the hirsute chest) and for the grotesque disproportions of his clothes, ending with his broad, buniony feet ('los pies eran descomunales, de anchos y juanetudos', (II, p. 577) ('his feet were outsized knobbly monstrosities' [I, p. 195]). But this is no gentle, eccentric giant, for his physique denotes his choleric humour, and we are vouchsafed one awful rage before which his underlings quail. This is the terrible Lord of Misrule, a law unto himself, laughable yet fearsome. And finally, there is the comedy of language; the inventions, the howlers, the exuberant shows of style. But these represent

[9] We remember that both positions are stated at the conclusion of the *novela* and belong to the narrator's direct plane, or voice: 'y así se deja para otra ocasión contar su vida y milagros, con los de su maestro Monipodio, y otros sucesos de aquéllos de la infame academia, que todos serán de grande consideración y que podrán servir de ejemplo y aviso a los que las leyeren' (II, p. 603) ('thus we will leave for another occasion an account of his life and wondrous doings together with those of his master, Monipodio, and of what happened to those other members of the academy of vice. All such stories will be of great moment and will provide an example and warning to all who'll read them' [I, p. 229]).

a deep travesty done to the purpose of language; contextualized, the violence done to language is part of the violence done to others. The narrator participates in this drama in a way that makes him, too, subject to its comedy. Bent on collecting the myriad voices of Babel which employ the gift of speech to subject, trick, betray, and harass, he is unaware of his own paradoxical situation, for he patiently perfects his own voice as the lone defender of language that stands for clarity, exactitude, duty, and decent social purpose. He does not seem even to enjoy the laugh. Indeed, in the pure archaism he employs when finally explaining that the full tale would require 'más luenga escritura' (II, p. 603) ('deserve to be written about at greater length' [I, p. 229]), where the voice lingers on the archaic phoneme, do we not catch his tedium over the endless task of putting words and things into order?

This reading recovers the writer. In effect, the *novela* turns around his[10] effort at writing it. His position at the centre highlights the paradox that marks all narrators. This is the paradox inherent to authorial omnipresence, sensed when we ask how could he know all that is said and done at any juncture without being himself a palpable presence at the actual exchanges of speech and in the course of events? His high visibility to us readers as the one who engages with language makes strange his utter invisibility to those whose words and acts he observes first hand and records. Cervantes's engagement with this paradox is familiar from elsewhere in his fiction. It is enshrined in the paradigmatical Cide Hamete in *Don Quijote*, the omnipresent but invisible writer whom Quijote believes is or should be committing his acts of chivalry to paper. But this paradox of omnipresence is only one of the various products of the fiction commenting on its own composition, that is, operating as metatext. *Rinconete y Cortadillo* tells us about its writer and the incessant engagement with language which marks the writer's special relationship with reality. In this respect, the multiple zones of style that make up the dialogized system of the whole, including the style cultivated by the writer of a literary *novela*, bring us to reflect on Bakhtin's dictum on the novel: 'Language in the novel not only represents, but itself serves as the object of representation' (Bahktin, p. 49). *Rinconete y Cortadillo* renders this transaction with language with a density that is natural to the genre of short story. As the tale draws the reader into language as the object of its representation, linguistic awareness is the meaning we carry away from it.

[10] I make no defence of the gender specificity adopted here and elsewhere, other than that of avoiding the stylistically clumsy compromise 'his/her' that English would otherwise enforce. The narrator, as far as I can see, could be either male or female at discretion; or could be voiced according to the sexual identity of the reader. This gender neutrality is part of his/her disembodied nature.

Works cited

Bakhtin, M. M., 'From the Prehistory of Novelistic Discourse', in *The Dialogic Imagination. Four Essays by M. M. Bakhtin*, ed. Michael Holquist, tr. Caryl Emerson and Michael Holquist (Austin: University of Texas Press, 1981), pp. 41–83.

Bentley, Bernard P. E., 'El narrador de *Rinconete y Cortadillo* y su perspectiva movediza', in *Studia aurea, Actas del III Congreso de la AISO* (Toulouse, 1993), ed. I. Arellano and others, 3 vols (Toulouse-Pamplona: GRISO-LEMSO, 1996), III (Prosa), pp. 55–65.

Cervantes Saavedra, Miguel de, *Exemplary Novels / Novelas ejemplares*, ed. B. W. Ife, 4 vols (Warminster: Aris & Phillips, 1992).

———, *Rinconete y Cortadillo*, in *Obra completa,* ed. Florencio Sevilla Arroyo and Antonio Rey Hazas, 3 vols (Alcalá de Henares: Centro de Estudios Cervantinos, 1993–95), II, pp. 559–603.

El Saffar, Ruth, *Novel to Romance: A Study of Cervantes' 'Novelas ejemplares'* (Baltimore, MD: Johns Hopkins University Press, 1974).

Hayes, A. W., 'Narrative "errors" in *Rinconete y Cortadillo*', *BHS*, 58.1 (1981), 13–20.

Keightley, Ronald G., 'The Structure of *Rinconete y Cortadillo*', in *Essays on Narrative Fiction in Honour of Frank Pierce*, ed. R. B. Tate (Oxford: Dolphin, 1982), pp. 39–54.

Minsheu, John, *A Dictionarie in Spanish and English* (London: E. Bollifant, 1599).

Ong, Walter J., 'Commonplace Rhapsody: Ravisius Textor, Zwinger and Shakespeare', in *Classical Influences on European Culture A.D. 1500–1700*, ed. R. R. Bolgar (London: Cambridge University Press, 1976), pp. 91–126.

Ravisius, Iohannes, *Epitheta* (Basle, 1599).

5

Now You See it, Now You . . . See it Again? The Dynamics of Doubling in *La española inglesa*

Isabel Torres
Queen's University of Belfast

La española inglesa (The English Spanish Girl) is, on the surface, an engaging tale of loss and recuperation, separation and reconciliation, and ultimately the triumph of the human spirit over adversity. The surface text, however, is but a beguiling pretext carefully constructed by Cervantes to draw his readers into an often ambiguous and paradoxical interpretative space. Cervantes's more receptive contemporary readers, caught up in the complexities of an ever-changing plot, see their reality distorted and filtered through a utopian imaginary which challenges their relationship with their world and the value systems which inform it. We shall see, in this glimpse into the structural workings of the tale, how *La española inglesa* is skilfully crafted in terms of binary systems and oppositional rhythms, so that its readers are offered a double vision of events within the fictional world, which has uneasy ramifications for the one-dimensional perspectives which (perhaps ironically) constitute early Baroque reality. What might seem to be a confirmation of conservative systems of belief is converted, through an awareness of contrapuntal argument and multiperspectivism, into a challenging of a collectively complacent and persistently static world-view. Despite the familiar trappings of the romance genre, engagement with *La española inglesa* is no easy ride. The reader is pushed and pulled towards a false dénouement, an anticlimactic moment, which makes the final resolution uncomfortably satisfying and takes the overtly utopian sting out of the traditional romance ending. Cervantes toys with his readers (contemporary and modern), frustrates at every turn their preconceived notions of the complicated intrigue of romance (and, therein, the liminal potentialities offered by the inevitable twists and turns of fate), until the closure which, when it comes, is at once satisfying and disturbing.

Before looking more closely at the text itself, we should broach a question, framed in broader terms, which has had significant implications for critical reception of *La española inglesa* in the twentieth century. In stark terms the question is the following: if the author of *La española inglesa* had not also written *Don Quijote* (Don Quixote), would we consider the tale worthy of critical attention in its own right? Américo Castro's suggestion that we would not, that we would probably talk about it a lot less, has impacted very negatively upon subsequent readings of the tale.[1] We could argue the reverse of course, on the basis that Cervantists have tended to devote relatively little critical attention to *La española inglesa*. Whatever the truth, there is no denying that until Ruth El Saffar's more comprehensive elucidation of the tales,[2] *novela* criticism was dominated by a selective approach which prioritized those tales deemed more compatible with the novelistic art of the *Quijote*. Alban K. Forcione identifies the roots of this exclusive approach in the modern reader's problematic attitude to the generic, structural and thematic complexity of Cervantes's tales, which frustrates all expectations of the short story genre.[3] The result has been a tendency among critics to invoke a dualistic typology which classifies the tales according to contrived literary genres, for instance, 'romantic and realistic [. . .] idealistic and sceptical, Italianate and Spanish, imitative and original, literary and representational' (Forcione, p. 25). This might be considered a generically focused reflection of the critic's fondness for the biographical dichotomy of the 'two-Cervantes theory', summarized by Forcione in a later study as: 'reactionary-progressive, imitator-innovator, classical-romantic, conformist (or hypocrite)-authentic, and so on'.[4] By imposing this dichotomy on the stories themselves, literary criticism has generated a damaging dual perspective which foregrounds for serious discussion more progressive and creatively original stories (in other words those thought to resemble the *Quijote*), and relegates to the background those stories, such as *La española inglesa*, which display more romantic and (as twenty-first-century value judgement would have it) more naïvely idealistic tendencies.

Cervantes's apparently contradictory evocation of the poetics of exemplarity has also yielded problematic reception. The uncompromising criticism of exemplarity in the *Quijote* has made the *Exemplary Novels* difficult to account for. Once again the 'two Cervantes's' theory has provided a tempting refuge in this context. Recently, however, this issue has been resolved through an appeal to reception aesthetics, more specifically to an application of reader-response theory that owes a substantial debt to Iser.[5] By placing the responsibility for the

1 See Américo Castro, *Hacia Cervantes* (Madrid: Taurus, 1967), pp. 466–67. In the same context Castro also implicitly denigrates the significance of the following texts: *Las dos doncellas* (The Two Damsels), *El amante liberal* (The Generous Lover), *La señora Cornelia* (Lady Cornelia) and the *Persiles*.

2 See Ruth El Saffar, *From Novel to Romance. A Study of Cervantes's 'Novelas ejemplares'* (Baltimore, MD: Johns Hopkins University Press, 1974).

3 See Alban K. Forcione, *Cervantes and the Humanist Vision: A Study of Four 'Exemplary Novels'* (Princeton, NJ: Princeton University Press, 1982), pp. 24–6. Forcione emphasizes the disorienting effect which Cervantes's claim to be the first to *novelar* in Spanish has had on his readers, both contemporary and modern.

4 Alban K. Forcione, 'Afterword: Exemplarity, Modernity, and the Discriminating Games of Reading', in *Cervantes's 'Exemplary Novels' and the Adventure of Writing*, ed. Michael Nerlich and Nicholas Spadaccini, Hispanic Issues 6 (Minneapolis: Prisma Institute, 1990), pp. 331–51.

5 See, for instance, Marsha S. Collins, 'Transgression and Transfiguration in Cervantes's *La española inglesa*', *Cervantes*, 16.1 (1996), 54–73. This study operates within the

creation of exemplary meaning with the reader, rather than with the author, we can finally dispense with the facile categorizing that has effectively closed down the interpretative possibilities of a work like *La española inglesa*. This is the approach advocated by Nicholas Spadaccini and Jenaro Talens, whose evocation of exemplarity displaces it from 'the conventional realm of the ethical (where an author assumes the responsibility for conveying a conventional moral lesson)' to one in which the imagination of the reader is activated, and the act of reading itself becomes a productive project 'connected to an exploration of the self in the world'.[6] In *La española inglesa*, the readers' successful collaboration in this project is dependent upon their awareness of the game of perspectives operating throughout the text, and their willingness to explore with Cervantes the complexities of truth. This dialogical exploration will involve a challenging engagement with their world and, even more provocatively, a level of interrogation of the self/world relationship in which the boundaries between reality/fiction, real history/romance, familiar/other are obscured, confused and subverted.

La española inglesa's membership of the 'romance' group of the *Exemplary Novels* has been qualified to some extent by the disputed significance of the socio-historical data which pervades the text. The hard facts of history, the concrete minutiae of names, places and events, have always been an integral touchstone with reality for the readers of Cervantes's fiction, adding a verisimilar dimension to the artistic illusion. However, in *La española inglesa,* in addition to the presence of purely historical content, such as the opening reference to the sack of Cadiz, the reader has to contend with the benevolent portrayal of the English and their Queen during a period of mutual hostility and intolerance, not to mention the tension between such specific historical referentiality and the idyllic patterns of romance within which it is cast.[7] Obviously for the modern reader, distanced

theoretical framework of Wolfgang Iser's *The Fictive and the Imaginary: Charting Literary Anthropology* (Baltimore, MD: Johns Hopkins University Press, 1993).

6 See Nicholas Spadaccini and Jenaro Talens, *Through the Shattering Glass: Cervantes and the Self-Made World* (Minneapolis: University of Minnesota Press, 1993), pp. 117 and 120 respectively.

7 Mostly critics have evoked and assessed the integration of history in the *novela* as evidence for an early or late dating of the text. See El Saffar, pp. 150–51, notes 10 and 11, in which she reviews the lines of enquiry which have produced a range of dates from 1596 to 1611. Those who support an early dating suggest that the story follows the sack of Cadiz by the English in 1587, e.g. Mack Singleton, 'The date of *La española inglesa*', *Hispania*, 30 (1947), 329–35. Geoffrey Stagg argues for an even earlier date, with subsequent revisions around 1584 and 1604; see 'The Composition and Revision of *La española inglesa*', in *Studies in Honor of Bruce W. Wardropper*, ed. Dian Fox and others, *Homenajes* No. 6 (Newark, Delaware: Juan de la Cuesta, 1989). Those who argue for a date of composition after 1605 establish a connection between the positive depiction of the English monarch and the peace treaty signed between England and Spain in Valladolid that year, e.g. Thomas Hanrahan, 'History in the *española inglesa*', *MLN*, 83 (1968), 267–71 and Carroll B. Johnson, '*La española inglesa* and the Practice of Literary Production', *Viator*, 19 (1988), 377–416. The more generally accepted late date of 1611 is based on an analysis of the development of Cervantes's thought and writing, e.g. Rafael Lapesa, 'En torno a *La española inglesa* y *El*

from the work both culturally and temporally, the task of identifying, let alone reconciling, the pervasive textual presence of historical referents and romance conventions will be much more difficult. While some critics have seen the integration of historical data in the story as something of a red herring, a distraction from the main thematic axis (El Saffar, pp. 152–53), for others the significance of the text is seriously diminished without some appreciation of the socio-historical backdrop, 'which offers a privileged terrain on which to consider the purely literary questions of mediation and the transmutation of particular historical experience into a fictional text of greater or lesser transcendence' (Johnson, p. 379). We could opt out of this debate on the basis that 'history only endures as an articulation of interpretations that one may accept or argue about and not as a past reality' (Spadaccini, p. 85), though, perhaps, not without some qualification. In *La española inglesa* Cervantes certainly rewrites history according to his own vision, but in so doing he also evokes events that occurred and places and people whose existence is 'a past reality'.[8] From the perspective of the present study, the most interesting aspect of this implicitly conflicting narrative strategy is the very active role which it imposes on the receiver. If, as Forcione has pointed out, romances are like games in that both 'presuppose the acceptance of clear-cut rules' (Forcione, 'Afterword', p. 350), then the integration of socio-political data in a *mundo al revés* (topsy-turvy) environment which undermines the readers' expectations will ensure their dynamic participation. In other words, while we might expect to find in a typical romance 'an unambiguous value system, a moral vocabulary of good and evil [. . .] (a) [. . .] decisive and reassuring conclusion' (Forcione, 'Afterword', p. 350), Cervantes does not adhere to these conventions unproblematically in the tale under discussion.[9]

It would be wrong, however, to assume that active participation on the part of the reader implies complete interpretative freedom. Throughout the text structural signposts guide the receptive reader towards identifying counterbalancing elements and mirrored events. Beyond the point of identification (the balanced

Persiles', in *Homenaje a Cervantes*, ed. Francisco Sánchez-Castañer, 2 vols (Valencia: Mediterráneo, 1950), II, pp. 367–88; and El Saffar.

8 Joseph V. Ricapito's analysis of the tale insists upon the significance of political and historical resonances for a complete understanding of Cervantes's critical engagement with his own historical moment and extends beyond Johnson's economic reading to incorporate a religious, historical focus. For Ricapito, Cervantes's text works on two levels which are readily accessible to the seventeenth-century reader: 'The initial text addresses the quandary of English Catholics, but there is a subtext that in fact deals with the dilemma of the Jews and *conversos*'. See *Cervantes's 'Novelas ejemplares'. Between History and Creativity* (West Lafayette, Indiana: Purdue University Press, 1996), chapter two, '*Católicos secretos, Conversos*, and the Myth of the Maritime Life in *La española inglesa*', p. 53.

9 As Forcione also points out, Cervantes tends to exploit the value system of his society in the construction of his fiction: 'If the reader looks closely at Cervantes's Gypsies, he discovers that their perverse social order, with its institutionalization of thievery, its patriarchal representation of woman, and its authoritarian morality, resembles the real world of Gypsies [. . .] a lot less than it does the socio-political establishment of Spain' ('Afterword', p. 350).

structure of the tale has not gone unnoticed),[10] the perceptive reader is challenged to see the rationale behind such structural precision. Jennifer Lowe was perhaps the first critic to approximate an analytical stance, and her view of the story as a game of two halves has become the accepted norm.[11] The structural pattern proposed by Lowe is based on an identification of the obstacles to be overcome by the young protagonists, Ricaredo and Isabela. They emerge as equal in all respects and, therefore, ultimately worthy of each other. The problem with Lowe's schematic reading, however, is that while she does attempt to recognize the complementary relationship between structure and content, her analysis takes no account of the nature of the resolution of the obstacles which she has identified. David Cluff does confront the question of how obstacles are resolved at specific moments in the text, but stops short of joining the dots and addressing the question of their wider implications.[12] His recognition, however, of a double plot (he stresses the role of Isabel's parents and links the loss of their daughter to loss of their fortune), which operates on the creation of rising expectations and their interruption on the point of fulfilment, at least implicates the reader in the process of exemplarity (Cluff, p. 264).

In a more recent study, which functions within an intellectual framework explicitly informed by reader-response theory, Collins puts the symmetrical and doubling patterns of the tale in generic context:

> Gemination, a common feature of romance, emerges as one of the primary structural components in *La española inglesa*. The story divides symmetrically in two sections, with the poisoning of Isabela as the peripetal point signalling the narrative's ascending movement towards greater spirituality and powerful, emotional evocation. The locus of dramatic activity shifts from Protestant England, the court of Elizabeth I, and the home of Ricaredo's parents in part one, to Catholic Spain, the convent of Santa Paula, and the home of Isabela's parents in part two. (p. 60)[13]

[10] See for instance J. Casalduero, *Sentido y forma de las 'Novelas ejemplares'* (Madrid: Gredos, 1962), p. 121, who identifies four main sections in the story (set in London, at sea, in London again, and finally in Spain), in which a binary movement in the narrative connects and contrasts events, and also a tertiary movement that highlights the essential elements of both action and plot (encapsulated in Isabel/beautiful; Isabel/ugly; Isabel beautiful). More recently, María Catarina Ruta has developed Casalduero's argument by adding a focus on the development of Ricaredo into a true hero, whose journey mirrors Isabela's in reverse. See M. C. Ruta, '*La española inglesa*: El desdoblamiento del héroe', *AC*, 25–26 (1987–88), 371–82.

[11] See Jennifer Lowe, 'The Structure of Cervantes' *La española inglesa*', *Romance Notes*, 9 (1967–68), 287–90. See also E. T. Aylward, 'Patterns of Symmetrical Design in *La fuerza de la sangre* and *La española inglesa*', *Crítica Hispánica*, 16.2 (1994), 189–203, who demonstrates that the tale consists of two virtually identical halves both in terms of narrative and chronological order.

[12] See David Cluff, 'The Structure and Theme of *La española inglesa*: A Reconsideration', *Revista de estudios hispánicos*, 10 (1976), 261–81. Cluff identifies three main turning points in the narrative around which the events of the story are organized: the intervention of the Queen; the poisoning of Isabela by Arnesto's mother; news of Ricaredo's death (see pp. 265–67).

[13] This view is completely at variance with that of Aylward: 'he (Cervantes) arranges his narrative in a symmetrical pattern, but [. . .] without any key episode or turning point on

While assenting entirely to Collins's assessment of the division of the tale into two parts, I would argue the point from a slightly different perspective, stressing how the contemporary readers' awareness of the conventions of romance could influence the way in which they negotiate and receive this key episode. A completed and, therefore, retrospective interpretation of the tale will inevitably place Isabela's poisoning and subsequent disfigurement at the centre of the narrative. However, a recuperation of the reading process in chronological terms demonstrates how the competent reader of romance could receive this reversal of fortune from a dual perspective: both as the frustrated ending of a romance gone wrong and as the catalyst for a new one in which the climactic scene will confirm a conventionally authentic anagnorisis. Interestingly, an English version of Cervantes's story, the anonymous *The Captive Lady*, does end at the Spanish tale's centre, that is, when the female protagonist's father is brought to England among a group of captives and consents to his long-lost daughter's marriage to his captor.[14] The recreated English tale clearly yields to the narrative expectations of the reader and constructs its dénouement from the raw material of romance found in the first half of Cervantes's story. *The Captive Lady*, in its reduction of *La española inglesa* 'to its pure romantic essence' (Johnson, p. 378), 'calls attention to the massive presence of real history and real society in *La española inglesa*' (p. 379), as well as to the relationship which Cervantes forges between parts one and two of his story. Although it is beyond the scope of this study to read the entire text in detail, a sustained analysis of textual multi-layering in part one and a brief identification of doubling in part two should be sufficient to demonstrate how any attempt to follow a linear reading route through the story is deliberately frustrated. The doubling, circular dynamics of Cervantes's text force the reader to assimilate the textual ambiguities of the first half, to interpret the second half back against the frustrations of the first, and, ultimately, to participate in the construction of the story's exemplarity by reading ending 'two' back against the instability of ending 'one'.

The very title of the work foregrounds the oppositional forces and the multiperspectivism that will operate on readers' perceptions throughout. However, at the beginning of the story the anticipated cultural clashes, Catholic–Spain/Protestant–England, are evoked only as background scenery against which other more complex conflicts and unexpected alliances are enacted. The female protagonist, Isabel, is seven when the story opens and exists objectified for the reader as one more prize to be carried off from Cadiz by the English gentleman Clotaldo, who seizes her as a beautiful gift for his wife. Clotaldo's perspective is perversely, albeit subtly, reinforced on a metaphorical level by Isabel's parents, whose simultaneous evocation of the loss of their luminous daughter and the loss of their fortune anticipates the network of materialistic imagery which will

which to balance the structure; the two halves are simply intended to be identical in their execution' (p. 199).

14 See Anon., *The Captive Lady*, ed. A. R. Braunmuller (Oxford: Oxford University Press, 1982) as cited by Johnson, p. 378, n.5.

underline Cervantes's representation of Isabel as victim/possession throughout part one. Moreover, the polarized reactions to the abduction of Isabel set Clotaldo against his commanding officer, the Earl of Leicester, and force an alliance between the English invader Leicester and Isabel's parents. When the action moves to England, Clotaldo's subsequent characterization as a loving, god-fearing husband and father is contaminated by his sinister subterfuge in Spain, and by the disconsolate grief of Isabel's parents, which lurks in the shadows of the readers' memory: 'Tenía Clotaldo un hijo llamado Ricaredo, de edad de doce años, enseñado de sus padres a amar y temer a Dios, y a estar muy entero en las verdades de la fe católica' ('Clotaldo had a son called Ricaredo, of twelve years of age, who had been brought up by his parents to love and fear God, and to be a firm believer in the truths of the Catholic faith').[15]

Clotaldo's aristocratic household functions in microcosmic opposition to the social structures that support it. The secret practice of Catholicism within a Protestant state renders the family's performance on the social stage artificial and illusory, while their familial existence is a fragile and neurotically-charged reality. Isabel is thrust into this double life, handed over as a 'ríquisimo despojo' (p. 218) ('a rich piece of booty' [II, p. 5]), and taught to play the role of daughter imposed on her. Her new identity as Isabela is easily constructed. Despite a residual longing for her lost parents, she learns to move easily between the shifting signifiers of her dual identity. On the surface she is treated 'as if' she were their daughter, and she responds to their role playing, their lessons (linguistic and social), and their material generosity, as only a child of such excellent natural disposition could, by treating them 'as if' they were her parents. However, the contrived family circle is threatened by the natural inclinations of the young Ricaredo. His initial acquiescence to the 'as if' world created by his parents, one in which he loves Isabela as his sister, is overthrown by 'ardentísimos deseos de gozarla y de poseerla' (p. 219) ('most ardent desire to possess and enjoy her' [II, p. 6]). There is an uncomfortable mirroring of father and son in this development. Just as we were reassured at the beginning of the story that Clotaldo's intentions were wholly honourable, although his choice of Isabela was motivated in great part by her incomparable beauty, we are now informed that Ricaredo's ultimate objective is marriage. The mutually reinforcing scenarios cast a sinister shadow over Clotaldo in retrospect and undermine any attempt by the narrative to disassociate the son from the sins of the father. Isabela, first taken by the father as a possession for his wife, is now sought after again in possessive terms by the son, despite the legitimizing framework of marriage within which his desire is located.

Cervantes never really desensualizes Ricaredo's passion for Isabela, although the text plays some lip-service to a more elevated neo-Platonic dimension. In his

[15] All references to *La española inglesa* will be taken from Miguel de Cervantes, *Novelas Ejemplares*, ed. Jorge García López (Barcelona: Crítica, 2001); here p. 218. Translations will be taken from Miguel de Cervantes, *Exemplary novels / Novelas ejemplares*, ed. B. W. Ife, 4 vols (Warmister: Aris & Phillips, 1992); here II, p. 5.

complete submission to *amor hereos* (love sickness), Ricaredo becomes tainted with the narcissistic neurosis of the courtly lover. His retreat into self-serving, self-destructive cowardice has all the linguistic hallmarks of the egocentric poetic voice of fifteenth-century lyric poetry. Indeed the inherent ambiguities of the language of courtly love render his need for a 'remedio' (cure) particularly problematic. His illness has the effect, whether intentional or not, of distressing his parents to the point that they might even be prepared to give their consent to a marriage to Isabela, despite having already promised him to a Scots lady, who is in every respects his equal – rich, aristocratic and a secret Catholic.[16] Ricaredo's initial reluctance to broach the topic is coloured by his own still negative perception of Isabela's status within the household: 'y estaba claro, según él decía, que no habían de querer dar a una esclava – si este nombre se podía dar a Isabela – lo que ya tenían concertado de dar a una señora' (p. 220) ('and it was obvious, he said to himself, that they would not want to give to a slave – if you could call Isabella a slave – what they had decided to give to a lady' [II, p. 7]). When he finally does declare himself to Isabela, it is in private and with the intention of keeping their betrothal a secret from his parents. Ricaredo's understanding of what it means to be 'a true and catholic Christian' (II, p. 7) is as flawed as Clotaldo's. Isabela, however, although receptive to his proposal, is reluctant to be hidden away for a second time. When Ricaredo's mother finally consents to the marriage, and persuades Clotaldo to do the same, the reader cannot be certain whether she is motivated by a desire to pull her son back from the brink of death, or persuaded by his elaborate eulogy of Isabela's virtues. Cervantes's text leaves both interpretative doors open:

> [. . .] que si no le casaban con Isabela, que el negársela y darle la muerte era toda una misma cosa. Con tales razones, con tales encarecimientos subió al cielo las virtudes de Isabela Ricaredo, que le pareció a su madre que Isabela era la engañada en llevar a su hijo por esposo. (p. 221)
>
> (If they did not marry him to Isabela, then refusing him would be the same thing as killing him. With so many reasons and praises did he laud her virtue that his mother thought that Isabella indeed would be the one who came off worse if she married her son. [II, p. 9])

The reader is not told what excuses are invented to stop the wedding to the Scots lady, but the ease with which the fabrications are executed is somewhat disconcerting. Moreover, textual assertions regarding the joy with which Clotaldo and Catalina preside over the wedding preparations are undermined by subtle evocations of Isabela's questionable social status. The arrival of the Queen's messenger

16 Ricapito draws attention to the textual evidence which suggests Cervantes's awareness of the historical reality of 'secret Catholics' in England and the circumstances surrounding the penalizing attitude of the English government. The character of the Scottish Clisterna is a further signifier of the Catholic/Protestant conflict, evoking Mary Stuart's quest for the throne and subsequent execution (p. 50).

just four days before the wedding, requesting that Clotaldo bring to the court 'su prisionera, la española de Cádiz' (p. 222) '(their prisoner, a Spanish girl from Cadiz' [II, p. 9]), is a sharp reminder that Isabela's 'otherness' might not be so easily assimilated beyond the confines of Clotaldo's alternative England, where the state religion does not even pertain. The monarch's intervention threatens to pull down the fragile structure of the family's world. Fears that Isabela will betray their secret Catholicism throw the family into chaos, despite her assurances to the contrary. This would, of course, be the worst-case scenario. Clotaldo recognizes that they are also guilty of lesser offences, such as arranging the marriage without the Queen's permission.

Until this point in the story, the strategies of self-preservation which inform the continued survival of the English family's world have mostly existed for the reader at the level of narrative inferences. The fact that Clotaldo's family are as 'other' as Isabela is now ironically apparent. The inauthenticity of their existence is underlined by the elaborate theatricality which surrounds their journey to the court of Elizabeth I. Every aspect of the procession is carefully stage-managed by Clotaldo to ensure that the experiential effects on the audience at court confirm an elaborate deception; Isabela had been chosen by them as a worthy bride for their son from the outset and should be so received by the Queen. This important passage is worth quoting in full:

> [. . .] acordaron que Isabela no fuese vestida humildemente como prisionera, sino como esposa, pues ya lo era de tan principal esposo como su hijo [. . .] otro día vistieron a Isabela a la española, con una saya entera de raso verde acuchillada y forrada en rica tela de oro, tomadas las cuchilladas con unas eses de perlas, y toda ella bordada de riquísimas perlas; collar y cintura de diamantes, y con abanico a modo de las señoras damas españolas; sus mismos cabellos, que eran muchos, rubios y largos, entretejidos y sembrados de diamantes y perlas, le servían de tocado. Con este adorno riquísimo y con su gallarda disposición y milagrosa belleza, se mostró aquel día a Londres sobre una hermosa carroza, [. . .] Iban con ella Clotaldo y su mujer, y Ricaredo, en la carroza, y a caballo, muchos ilustres parientes suyos. Toda esta honra quiso hacer Clotaldo a su prisionera, por obligar a la reina la tratase como a esposa de su hijo. (pp. 223–24)
>
> ([. . .] they agreed that Isabella should not go to see the Queen dressed humbly, but as a bride, since she was the bride of a nobleman, their son [. . .] on the following day they dressed Isabella in the Spanish style, with a long dress of slashed green satin, lined with cloth of gold, the slashes pinned by 'esses' of pearls, and the whole edged with rich pearls, a necklace and waistband of diamonds, and with a fan in the style of Spanish ladies; her own long thick fair hair woven and sewn with diamonds and pearls served as a headdress. With her rich dress, her noble bearing and miraculous beauty, she drove through London that day in a fine coach; [. . .] Clotaldo, his wife and Ricaredo went with her in the coach, and they were escorted by many noble relations on horseback. Such was the honour that Clotaldo did to his prisoner, so that the Queen should treat her as the wife of his son. [II, p. 11])

Nothing in this mini drama is quite what it seems. The pomp and ceremony of Isabela's arrival at court only serves to bring more sharply into focus the cultural chasm which separates her from the others as well as the unjustifiable origins of her presence among them. She may not be dressed as a prisoner, but the material extravagance of her Spanish costume functions as a symbolic concretization of the treasure so often plundered from the enemy ships. Her prominence in the procession is a sham, a hollow inversion of the social reality, exposed by the pearl letters embroidered on her dress.[17] In this passage Cervantes manipulates a delicate dialectic of apparent power and authority on the one hand and the realities of imprisonment on the other. The procession scene on the whole works as a perfect visual corollary to the binary tensions which have pervaded the story so far, while the description of Isabela accentuates the double vision the author expects of his readers.

Isabela's reception by the English Queen is everything that Clotaldo could have wished for, though Cervantes's contemporary readers might be shocked to find a benevolent 'fairy godmother', rather than a powerful adversary (Collins, p. 64). At the most obvious level of sharing the same name, the Queen has been usually perceived as Isabela's double in the story, and no doubt Cervantes intends an elevation of his protagonist through what might be seen as a perverse connection. They are certainly not equals. In fact, in terms of the power dynamics which influence their relationship, we could argue that the Queen doubles for and displaces Catalina as the latest illegitimate maternal figure in the young girl's life: 'que ya la estimo como si fuese mi hija' (p. 225) ('for I esteem her as if she were my own daughter' [II, p. 13]). Much has been made of the fact that the Queen takes Isabela under her wing despite the girl's steadfast devotion to her own religion. The text makes clear, however, that the handing over of Isabela to the Queen is viewed by the monarch in terms of the recuperation of treasure (booty) which was rightfully hers to begin with. Isabela will have no more agency at court than she did in the home of Clotaldo. Renamed ('the Spanish Isabella' [II, p. 13]) and then handed over yet again, this time to the chief lady-in-waiting, she is to be further reconstructed and re-educated in the ways of the English royal court. The Queen will consent to the marriage, but first Ricaredo must step out from the shadow of his father's service to the crown and earn his right to win the 'greatest prize' (Isabela) by leading an attack on Catholic and/or Turkish shipping. The Queen's promise to guard Isabela in his absence, while recognizing that her virtue is guard enough, is yet another subtle indication of Isabela's lack of self-determination and perhaps also a hint for the reader of

[17] See Monique Joly, 'Dos notas al margen de *El amante liberal* y *La española inglesa*', in *Hommage à Robert Jammes*, ed. Francis Cerdan, 3 vols (Toulouse: Presses Universitaires du Mirail, 1994), II, pp. 591–94. Joly points out that it was customary to mark slaves on the cheek with the letter 's' as a sign of their slavery, quoting Covarrubias's commentary on the word 'esclavo' and alluding to jokes from the period. Joly, however, interprets this visual reminder of Isabela's servitude in idealistic terms, stressing that she will become the servant of the Queen.

the danger which lies ahead. The sense of fear and abandonment which Isabela experiences when Ricaredo leaves, works against any utopian interpretation of her position at court: 'Quedó Isabela como huérfana que acaba de enterrar sus padres, y con temor que la nueva señora quisiese que mudase las costumbres en que la primera la había criado.' (p. 227) ('Isabella stayed behind like an orphan who has just buried her parents, fearing that her new mistress would want her to change the ways in which her former mistress had brought her up' [II, p. 15]).

Ricaredo's seafaring mission is as significant for what does not happen, as it is for what does happen. Good fortune (a standard supporting player in all romance plots) has a part to play in this. Ricaredo does not have to draw his sword against Catholics nor is he revealed (at least openly) as a Catholic or a coward. The ill wind which carries their ships to Spain, on this occasion, seems to augur well for everyone. There is no possibility that Ricaredo can reproduce his father's act of insubordination at sea. His commanding officer dies suddenly and the way is conveniently clear for Ricaredo to exercise free will in a way that will rewrite and set right Clotaldo's earlier crime in the same location. He opts not to slay the Spanish prisoners – captives of the two Turkish vessels the English defeat at sea – nor the few Turks who are still alive at the end of the battle. Instead he liberates the captives and gives them enough money and provisions to get them back to their respective homelands. Moreover, among the captives are the parents of Isabela who, having lost everything in the raid on Cadiz, were en route to America. Ricaredo agrees to take them to England without telling them the truth about their daughter.

The narrative would seem to be moving towards the conventional dénouement, characterized by anagnorisis and closed out by marriage. The problem is that the text continues to operate on at least two levels, simultaneously denying what it suggests. Ricaredo's heroism and magnanimity are as ambiguous as his speech, and as easily stripped away by the sceptical reader as the Spanish flags that falsely camouflage the English ships he sails in. When he says to his men: 'Soy de parecer que ningún cristiano católico muera; no porque los quiero bien, sino porque me quiero a mí muy bien' (p. 231) ('I think that no Catholic Christian should be killed, not because I esteem them at all, but because of my own self-esteem' [II, p. 19]), both his men and the readers are confronted with the problematic partiality of truth. Indeed, throughout the episode the mixed reaction of the English sailors to all that Ricaredo does and says is highlighted by Cervantes: 'Nadie osó contradecir lo que Ricaredo había propuesto, y algunos le tuvieron por valiente y magnánimo, y de buen entendimiento; otros le juzgaron en sus corazones por más católico que debía' (pp. 231–32) ('No one dared to question Ricaredo's proposal, and some indeed thought him brave, magnanimous and clever. Others thought privately that he was more pro-Catholic than he ought to be' [II, p. 21]). These silent witnesses play almost a metadramatic role in mirroring, directing, expanding and limiting the potential reactions of the reader (spectator). Above all, Cervantes's insistence on multiperspectivism forces the reader to confront in the real world the fact that truth can be relative and manipulated, that its articulation can be deceptive, and the interpretation of words and actions often informed by subjectivity.

The account of Ricaredo's triumphant return to England continues to underline that things and people can often be perceived in more ways than one. The ships' opposing standards of victory and mourning confound the crowd watching from the shore, while Ricaredo's extravagant entrance at court, in full Milanese armour, sends out equally conflicting signals:

> Con este adorno, y con el paso brioso que llevaba, algunos hubo que le compararon a Marte, dios de las batallas, y otros, llevados de la hermosura de su rostro, dicen que le compararon a Venus, que para hacer alguna burla a Marte de aquel modo se había disfrazado. (p. 236)
>
> (So dressed and with his spirited gait, some people compared him to Mars, god of battles, and others, moved by the beauty of his face, compared him to Venus, who might have disguised herself like this to play a trick on Mars. [II, p. 25])

While on one level, the apparently irreconcilable forces of love and war are brought powerfully together in this depiction of Ricaredo as idealized chivalric knight, on another level, the deliberate confusion of mythical markers evokes a sexual indeterminacy which undermines any positive heroic representation.[18] Moreover, the detailed description of Ricaredo's clothing which precedes this passage recalls Isabela's elaborate introduction to the court and gives greater ironic depth to the concept of Ricaredo as a 'disguised Venus'. The image of Ricaredo as warrior is just that, a falsely forged identity, just bright enough to blind a materialistic sovereign who exchanges the prize 'joya', Isabela, for the rich booty brought back from sea. Isabela is handed over again ('Isabela es vuestra [. . .] podéis tomar su entera posesión' [p. 237]) ('Isabela is yours [. . .] you can take her into your possession' [II, p. 25]), for what should be the last time. But the male protagonist who receives her is not elevated in the narrative, but debased by the frivolous interventions and mocking comments of the ladies of the court. When a child uses Ricaredo's sword as a mirror, and when Lady Tansi compares him to the sun 'descended to earth' (II, p. 27), the laughter of the crowd activates the reader to recognise the narcissistic core of Ricaredo's self-fashioning and the illegitimacy of his claims to authority in this setting. At a superficial level the comparison of Ricaredo with the sun might well suggest an equality with Isabela, whose beauty had earlier been described in the conventional terms of Petrarchist hyperbole; on the other hand, the deflation of Apollo which is implicit in Lady Tansi's 'outrageous simile', as well as insinuating a burlesque effeminacy, quite literally brings the male protagonist down to earth with a bump and suggests that his union to the ethereal beauty Isabela may indeed be some light years away.

[18] For an analysis of this story as a corrective rewriting of the *Amadís de Gaula* in which Ricaredo displays all the characteristics of a knight of chivalry, see Stanislav Zimic, 'El *Amadís* cervantino: apuntes sobre *La española inglesa*', *AC*, 25–6 (1987–88), 469–83. For a more problematic reading of Ricaredo as a *Venus armata* figure and as a projection of a crisis of male identity, see Mar Martínez Góngora, 'Un unicornio en la corte de una reina virgen: "Gineocracia" y ansiedades masculinas en *La española inglesa*', *Cervantes*, 20.1 (2000), 27–46, especially p. 36.

At every turn Cervantes ingeniously undercuts his story to move the reader towards a finale that clearly cannot be final. The stage is set for the reunion at court of Isabela and her parents, but envy of Ricaredo's newly acquired status shrouds the scene like dry ice and the main characters seem to be wearing the wrong costumes. Isabela, having been schooled in the ways of the English court, is now wearing again the elaborate Spanish outfit which defines her difference. Meanwhile, her parents, recently arrived with the Spanish cargo, are 'vestidos de nuevo a la inglesa' (p. 238) ('dressed for the first time in the English style' [II, p. 27]), their inability to communicate in the language of their hosts making glaringly apparent the artificiality of their appearance. In fact, although the entire event has been stage-managed by Ricaredo, he is pushed into the audience of a recognition scene which inevitably acquires a dynamic of its own. The Queen still commands a certain agency, but this is somewhat displaced now by her sudden inability to understand Spanish. Isabela's roles as recuperated daughter, prized beloved, and now interpreter, cast her as object and mediator of the action taking place around her. Such ventriloquizing serves only to underline her reactive and inauthentic identity. When the Queen announces that she will 'hand Isabela over four days from then' (II, p. 31), the reader recalls the last time Ricaredo and Isabela were exactly this close to matrimony, and no doubt expects 'la contraria suerte' ('contrary fortune'), which signals the frustration of resolution. Moreover, the Garcilasian echo in 'sin sobresalto de perderla' (p. 242) ('with no fear of losing her again' [II, p. 31]) is sufficiently ambiguous to prepare us to participate all over again in a corrective search for significance.[19]

The rewriting of part one focuses especially on the transformation of Isabela and Ricaredo. Isabela must move beyond the circumstances of her constructed identity, and overcome the limitations of her objectivized existence to find an authentic position in the narrative. Ricaredo, on the other hand, must cast off the duplicity of his background, conquer the pretentious egocentricity of his character and develop the spiritual purity that will make him a suitable husband for Isabela. The introduction of Arnesto as Ricaredo's aristocratic nemesis is the first stage in the manipulation of the reader towards a more positive reception of the hero. Arnesto's passion for Isabela follows the same neurotic pattern as Ricaredo's. However, while the prognosis might be the same, the symptoms and their projection into violent aggression are vastly different. The threatened duel is prevented by the arrival of the Captain of the Queen's guard, but Arnesto's threat to seek out Ricaredo converts the latter into the innocent victim of a

[19] While most editors have identified Garcilaso, *Eclogue* I, 407 as the source of this line, one critic has gone further and identified Garcilaso de la Vega as the primary model for the depiction of Ricaredo as lover and soldier. See Mercedes Alcázar Ortega, 'Palabra, memoria y aspiración literaria', *Cervantes*, 15.1 (1995), 33–45. There is no doubt that Cervantes adhered to the Renaissance tradition of *imitatio* and to the concept of immortalizing art (as evidenced by the stress on literary creation at the end of this *novela*), but Alcázar's unquestioning acceptance of an autobiographical dimension to the poetic voice of Garcilaso's sonnets is problematic in the light of more recent criticism and to some extent works against her own argument by prioritizing autobiography over art.

demented rival and anticipates a stereotypical victory of good over evil later in the story.

Both Ricaredo and Arnesto manipulate the maternal instincts of their mothers to ensure their salvation. Catalina's influence over Clotaldo, however, fades into innocent insignificance in the light of the lady-in-waiting's thwarted efforts to manipulate the Queen and the attempted murder of Isabela which ensues. The poisoning and disfigurement of Isabela marks the third 'illness' of the story and, read against the metaphorical lyricism of the others, acquires a substantiality that renders it more powerfully evocative. The transformation of Isabela from miraculous beauty into a 'monstruo de fealdad' (p. 247) ('a grotesque monster' [II, p. 39]) is ironically the consequence of a successful remedy.[20] It is also, despite the fact that she is handed over once again by the Queen into the dubious care of Clotaldo's family, the beginning of a move towards greater agency and freedom. The stripping away of Isabela's external appearance is also in direct contrast to the elaborate cloaking and emphasis on disguise and deceptive appearances that characterize part one. Ricaredo now experiences a forced epiphany when he recognizes the spiritual depth of his attachment to her. His secret strategy for the survival of their love in the face of his parents' renewed plans for a marriage to the Scottish Clisterna, might suggest that he has not yet lost a propensity towards subterfuge and deception, but he has at least put a foot on the neo-Platonic ladder and the reader is becoming more confident of his spiritual ascent.

We are not, however, permitted to feel any reassurance with regard to the motivations or actions of Clotaldo and Catalina. Their rejection of Isabela as a suitable bride for their son confirms the more sinister axis of potential interpretations opened up by the first half of the story. In their willingness to accept the same level of superficiality in their son as in themselves, they demonstrate the gulf that separates them from him and prepare us for the definitive separation to come. Moreover, both Ricaredo and the Queen assume the worst when they request that Clotaldo not take from Isabela the riches that she and her family have acquired in England. In the first half of the story Isabela stood as a concretization of Spanish booty, plundered from its rightful home and misappropriated. In the hands of Clotaldo and Catalina, this wealth continues to function in place of integrity, a generous balm on a damaged conscience. On the whole, however, what seemed to be a symbolic emphasis on wealth and finance in the first half of the story is revealed in retrospect as an integral structuring device at the level of the plot, acquiring a positive, utilitarian function.[21] The accumulation of

[20] On the association of women with magic and the ambiguous symbolism of the unicorn (both betokening purity, and phallic), see Martínez Góngora, pp. 33–4.

[21] Johnson suggests that the families of Isabela and Ricaredo represent two opposing economic orders. Isabela's father is a member of a sophisticated economic system based on credit in which wealth is generated through investment of capital and processes of exchange. On the other hand, Clotaldo participates in a primitive, unproductive economic order based on antagonism, rapine and deceit. In this context, Catholicism is redefined in economic terms (pp. 401–2).

diamonds, pearls, and the hefty fine levied against the lady-in-waiting, will constitute the rightful restoration of Isabela's father's fortune which, with his daughter, was taken in the raid on Cadiz. Indeed, only back in Spain can authentic resolution be effected.

Spain displaces England now as the dominant space within which the action evolves, free from cultural ambivalence and religious suppression. The house which Isabela's parents rent, opposite the convent of Santa Paula, replaces Clotaldo's household as the reader's window on the world the family inhabit. But Isabela's house exists as a microcosmic projection, not rejection, of its world. Whereas the English family lived in the shadow of a court dominated by material extravagance and political machinations (in fact a power centre where they were impostors), Isabela's house looks out on the devout cloisters of a convent in which a family member is a nun. All is just as it should be; no tension, no opposition, just fluid reintegration into a natural and spiritual home. In this mutually supportive environment Isabela finds the strength to forgive Clotaldo and Catalina, to withstand the advances of numerous suitors, and finally to confront the news of Ricaredo's death. Worldly goods are not denigrated in this world, but riches are not valued as adornments. Instead the emphasis is on income, investment and social regeneration in the hands of a hardworking and honest merchant class.[22] Moreover, the textual healing process stretches beyond the restoration of the family fortune. Isabela recovers completely from the disfiguring illness from which she showed only the slightest sign of recuperation in England.

Ironically, perhaps, the news of Ricaredo's death is the catalyst that liberates Isabela from the baggage of her constructed, ventriloquizing past. Her decision to enter the convent is, perversely, her first act of self-determinacy. In opting to hand herself over to God, she takes a first step towards a more proactive future. The scene that takes place on the day of Isabela's profession deliberately fuses and inverts two episodes associated with the English court. First the procession that accompanies Isabela to the door of the convent deliberately recalls for the reader the dramatically organized procession that led her to the Queen. But what is mirrored in detail is shattered in significance:

> Y como es costumbre de las doncellas que van a tomar el hábito ir lo posible galanas y bien compuestas, como quien en aquel punto echa el resto de la bizarría, y se descarta della, quiso Isabela ponerse la más bizarra que le fue posible; y así se vistió con aquel vestido mismo que llevó cuando fue a ver a la reina de Inglaterra, que ya se ha dicho cuán rico y cuán vistoso era. Salieron a luz las perlas y el famoso diamante [. . .] (p. 256)

[22] Johnson proposes a convincing anti-aristocratic reading of the story: 'one way to consider the paradoxical joining of the idealistic love story and the detailed descriptions of financial operations would be to consider how *La española inglesa* is a reflection of the dialectic of history. The idealised love story is or had been traditionally the province of the aristocracy, but Cervantes eliminates aristocratic protagonists in favour of the bourgeoisie. When Cervantes belabors the financial infrastructure of the bourgeois lifestyle he is insisting on the emergence of the bourgeoisie onto center stage in both history and fiction' (p. 408).

(And since it is the custom of girls who are taking the veil to present themselves as handsomely as possible, as people who are abandoning and ridding themselves of all their worldly splendour at that point in their lives, Isabella decided to dress with as much splendour as possible; and so she put on the dress she wore when she went to be presented to the Queen of England, the richness and magnificence of which has already been described. She brought out the pearls and the famous diamond. [II, p. 49])

In every sense Isabela has ownership of her destiny now. She is no longer Clotaldo's puppet, dressed up to perform and scripted in advance. Her retinue is comprised of her family, her friends and the hierarchy of the Catholic Church, a faith that at least in Spain can dare to say its name. Isabela, of course, will not enter the convent, the conventional refuge of the widowed (and violated), for Ricaredo is not actually dead. He turns up now as the only obstacle of any merit in the story, to ensure that the conventional happy-ever-after resolution can take place. He is, however, barely recognizable. Gone is the shiny armour, and with it the false posturing that characterized his pretentious return to court from battle. The emblem of the Holy Trinity that marks his chest emulates the pearl letters of Isabela's gown and resonates with their symbolic significance. In Ricaredo's case, however, capture and rescue are necessary stages in his journey towards spiritual purification and union with Isabela.[23] When he kneels before her and pleads for recognition, his words and their world are finally in tune, and his declarations no longer reach us through the contrived rhetoric of courtly love. Indeed it is Isabela who now usurps the traditional male voice of amorous lyric: 'sois sin duda la mitad de mi alma [. . .] estampado os tengo en mi memoria y guardado en mi alma' (p. 257) ('you are the half of my soul [. . .] you are imprinted upon my memory and engraved upon my soul' [II, p. 51]).[24] The love which Ricaredo and Isabela share is a perfect reconciliation of body and soul. It is in this context that Isabela can finally articulate her own destiny in marriage: 'Venid, señor, a la casa de mis padres, que es vuestra, y allí os entregaré mi posesión por los términos que pide nuestra santa fe católica'(p. 257) ('Come, sir, to my parents' house, which is yours as well, and there I shall hand myself over in marriage, in the manner required by our Holy Catholic faith'[II, p. 51]).

23 See Thomas A. Pabón, 'The Symbolic Significance of Marriage in Cervantes' *La española inglesa*', *Hispanófila*, 63 (1978), 59–66, in which he argues that the story has a labyrinthine structure within which both lovers purge themselves symbolically in order to be worthy of the sacrament of marriage.

24 These words echo an earlier comment made by Ricaredo to Isabela: 'con intención que la mucha belleza desta doncella borre de mi alma la tuya, que en ella estampada tengo' (p. 248) ('with the idea that her great beauty will erase your beauty from my soul, even though it is engraved there' [II, p. 39]). Alcázar Ortega (p. 44) identifies Garcilaso's Sonnet V, 1 as the inspiration for Ricaredo's declaration of eternal devotion. Isabela's expansion of this verse is a clear development of the Garcilasian preoccupation with the power of the poetic word over time. Isabela hints at the role of memory in literary creation and anticipates the role she will be accorded at the end when she must carry her own story forward in writing.

This final anagnorisis is confirmed by one of the onlookers, who recognizes Ricaredo as the English corsair who had liberated him and three hundred others from the Turks. This single voice, raised in support, offers an unquestionably positive perspective on Ricaredo's earlier seafaring mission and has the effect of closing down those ambiguous avenues of interpretation which had been opened up by the text's earlier insistence on multiperspectivism.[25] Ricaredo is drawn further and further from the character-contaminating associations of his life in England. Even his parents are conspicuous by their absence.[26] The doubling dynamic which has underpinned the narrative structure throughout the text now compels the reader to participate in a more explicitly challenging and revisionist reading process. We now receive the first half of the tale again, in theory from the 'tongue and wisdom of Isabela' (p. 51), although her reclaimed linguistic subjectivity is in fact mediated in summary form by the narrator. This doubling back on the story is entirely transformative in its complete suppression of subversive resonance. Paradoxically, however, this absence of alternative and conflicting perspective serves to underline the implications of its earlier evocation. Indeed, when Isabela temporarily allows Ricaredo to fill in the gaps in the recreated narrative, the contrast which emerges between the depiction of the ambiguous hero of part one and the exemplary protagonist of this one-dimensional romance in miniature, is deliberately exaggerated. The man who speaks now is not the demi-god who recalled his triumphs for the court. That counterfeit English hero, defined and distanced from the contemporary reader in terms of chivalric knights and mythical abstractions, has indeed been killed off. In his place stands the spiritually cleansed, true Catholic hero of his time, whose fantastical trials and tribulations are in fact informed by the biographical realism of Cervantes's own life experiences.[27]

The dénouement of Cervantes's story is, it would seem, 'decisive and reassuring'. The good are rewarded and the not so good achieve a measure of poetic justice.[28] But despite the apparent purity of the romance ending, the reader is not allowed to disengage so comfortably from Cervantes's tale. Marriage is not evoked as the conventional terminus of an author-manipulated fictional journey, nor does it offer an aperture into an undisclosed, but happy-ever-after imaginary. Instead it represents a spiritual and societal contract which not only binds the couple to one another, but also commits them to financial investment in the real world of the contemporary reader. The evocation of the marital home as contemporary real estate, coupled with a pseudo-familiar name-dropping strategy

[25] When the Turks take Ricaredo captive, he is also recognized by one of their number who had been aboard the ships attacked by the English. His identity remains undisclosed, however, in gratitude for the great magnanimity he displayed in battle (see p. 262 [II, p. 55]).

[26] Note that Isabela's father speaks for the first time in the narrative now, finally assuming his legitimate role as *paterfamilias*.

[27] In 1580 the Fathers of the Holy Trinity also ransomed Cervantes, held captive like Ricaredo in Algiers.

[28] Ruta stresses how the restoration of order in a Spanish context implies a 'justa punición' (just punishment) for Clotaldo (p. 375).

(Hernando de Cifuentes), pulls the fictional world into the historic present and lends greater relevancy to the shared focus of the *exemplum*:

> Esta novela nos podría enseñar cuánto puede la virtud y cuánto la hermosura, pues son bastantes juntas y cada una de por sí a enamorar aun hasta los mismos enemigos, y de cómo sabe el cielo sacar de las mayores adversidades nuestras, nuestros mayores provechos. (p. 263)
>
> (This novel can teach us the power of virtue and of beauty, since separately and together they are sufficient to make even enemies love each other, and also how heaven can draw out of our greatest adversities the greatest blessings for us. [II, p. 57])

In the second half of *La española inglesa* Cervantes's readers encounter an idealized Spain where the combined force of beauty and virtue promotes racial harmony, tolerance and financial prosperity. Such a comprehensive and comforting Erasmian vision is provocative in the sense that it runs counter to the obsessive questions which usually characterize the artistic imagination of Baroque Spain.[29] The intellectual uncertainties of the age, so often explored in terms of the complex relationships between appearance and reality, truth and illusion, fact and fiction, are evoked at an ironic, critical distance. England becomes the Spain that Spaniards should leave behind, an extravagant illusion of unity and prosperity that disguises difference and promotes performance. The text plays radically with notions of perspective and interpretation in order to unsettle the contemporary reader's assumptions and to challenge received ideas and ideals. Part two is a utopian rewriting of part one, and the creation of significance depends on the readers' active engagement with the mirrored fictional worlds reflected there and, beyond that, with their own uncertain and changing reality. The doubly dialogic nature of *La española inglesa* would suggest that this very unconventional romance has a lot more in common with the *Quijote* than we have been prepared to acknowledge.

Works cited

Alcázar Ortega, Mercedes, 'Palabra, memoria y aspiración literaria en *La española inglesa*', *Cervantes*, 15.1 (1995), 33–45.

Anon., *The Captive Lady*, ed. A. R. Braunmuller (Oxford: Oxford University Press, 1982).

Aylward, E. T., 'Patterns of Symmetrical Design in *La fuerza de la sangre* and *La española inglesa*', *Crítica Hispánica*, 16 (1994), 189–203.

[29] Some commentators have commented on the problematic reception which a positive vision of secret Catholics might provoke in a contemporary reader who could draw parallels with the situation of the Spanish converts to Catholicism who continued to practise Judaism in secret. See for instance: Manuel da Costa Fontes, 'Love as an Equalizer in *La española inglesa*', *Romance Notes*, 16 (1975), 742–48 (especially p. 744) and Ricapito's insistence on Cervantes's portrayal of secret Catholics as 'a pretext for self-criticism of Spain with the objective of promoting a religious norm that worked towards tolerance of faiths' (p. 55).

Casalduero, J., *Sentido y forma de las 'Novelas ejemplares'* (Madrid: Gredos, 1962).
Castro, Américo, *Hacia Cervantes* (Madrid: Taurus, 1967).
Cervantes Saavedra, Miguel de, *Exemplary Novels / Novelas ejemplares*, ed. B. W. Ife, 4 vols (Warminster: Aris & Phillips, 1992).
———, *Novelas Ejemplares*, ed. Jorge García López (Barcelona: Crítica, 2001).
Cluff, David, 'The Structure and Theme of *La española inglesa*: A Reconsideration', *Revista de estudios hispánicos*, 10 (1976), 261–81.
Collins, Marsha, S., 'Transgression and Transfiguration in Cervantes's *La española inglesa*', *Cervantes*, 16.1 (1996), 54–73.
El Saffar, Ruth, *From Novel to Romance. A Study of Cervantes's 'Novelas ejemplares'* (Baltimore, MD: Johns Hopkins University Press, 1974).
Fontes, Manuel, 'Love as an Equalizer in *La española inglesa*', *Romance Notes*, 16 (1975), 742–48.
Forcione, Alban, K., *Cervantes and the Humanist Vision: A Study of Four 'Exemplary Novels'* (Princeton, NJ: Princeton University Press, 1982).
———, 'Afterword: Exemplarity, Modernity, and the Discriminating Games of Reading', in *Cervantes's 'Exemplary Novels' and the Adventure of Writing*, ed. Michael Nerlich and Nicholas Spadaccini, Hispanic Issues 6 (Minneapolis: Prisma Institute, 1990), pp. 331–51.
Hanrahan, Thomas, 'History in the *española inglesa*', *MLN*, 83 (1968), 267–71.
Iser, Wolfgang, *The Fictive and the Imaginary: Charting Literary Anthropology* (Baltimore, MD: Johns Hopkins University Press, 1993).
Johnson, Carroll, B., '*La española inglesa* and the Practice of Literary Production', *Viator*, 19 (1988), 377–416.
Joly, Monique, 'Dos notas al margen de *El amante liberal* y *La española inglesa*', in *Hommage à Robert Jammes*, ed. Francis Cerdan, 3 vols (Toulouse: Presses Universitaires du Mirail, 1994), II, pp. 591–94.
Lapesa, Rafael, 'En torno a *La española inglesa* y *El Persiles*', in *Homenaje a Cervantes*, ed. Francisco Sánchez-Castañer, 2 vols (Valencia: Mediterráneo, 1950), II, pp. 367–88.
Lowe, Jennifer, 'The Structure of Cervantes' *La española inglesa*', *Romance Notes*, 9 (1967–68), 287–90.
Martínez Góngora, Mar, 'Un unicornio en la corte de una reina virgen: "Gineocracia" y ansiedades masculinas en *La española inglesa*', *Cervantes*, 20.1 (2000), 27–46.
Pabón, Thomas, A., 'The Symbolic Significance of Marriage in Cervantes' *La española inglesa*', *Hispanófila*, 63 (1978), 59–66.
Ricapito, Joseph, V., *Cervantes's 'Novelas ejemplares'. Between History and Creativity* (West Lafayette, Indiana: Purdue University Press, 1996).
Ruta, María Catarina, '*La española inglesa*: El desdoblamiento del héroe', *AC*, 25–6 (1987–88), 371–82.
Singleton, Mack, 'The date of *La española inglesa*', *Hispania*, 30 (1947), 329–35.
Spadaccini, Nicholas, and Jenaro Talens, *Through the Shattering Glass: Cervantes and the Self-Made World* (Minneapolis: University of Minnesota Press, 1993).
Stagg, Geoffrey, 'The Composition and Revision of *La española inglesa*', in *Studies in Honor of Bruce W. Wardropper*, ed. Dian Fox and others, *Homenajes* No. 6 (Newark, Delaware: Juan de la Cuesta, 1989).
Zimic, Stanislav, 'El *Amadís* cervantino: apuntes sobre *La española inglesa*', *AC*, 25–6 (1987–88), 469–83.

6

Soldiers and Satire in *El licenciado Vidriera*

Stephen Rupp
University of Toronto

The narrative of *El licenciado Vidriera* (The Glass Graduate) traces the progress of its titular character from his apprenticeship of study and travel through an episode of madness to his final efforts to establish a court career in Valladolid and a life of military service in Flanders. To record this fictional life Cervantes engages a series of literary genres. The particular affliction that the text describes – the delusion that one's body is made of glass – has explicit associations with the transparency and keenness of satirical discourse, and during his madness the licentiate speaks with the traditional voice of the urban satirist, offering harsh commentary on the weaknesses of the tradesmen and officials who throng the streets around him. A number of other generic patterns inform the narrative frame that encloses the central episode of the madman's railing. The conventions of picaresque fiction shape the initial description of the young Tomás Rodaja; the patterns of Renaissance travel literature and of the rhetorical praise of cities influence the schematic account of his journey through Italy and the Lowlands; the trajectory of romance is present in his rise from modest origins to a valiant death in the army of Flanders.[1] The juxtaposition of different generic models is particularly marked in the text's laconic ending. The licentiate takes leave of the court with a traditional complaint against its inconstancy and sets forth for the wars:

> Esto dijo y se fue a Flandes, donde la vida que había comenzado a eternizar por las letras la acabó de eternizar por las armas, en compañía de su buen amigo el capitán Valdivia, dejando fama en su muerte de prudente y valentísimo soldado.

[1] Michael E. Gerli discusses the evocation and rewriting of picaresque models in this *novela* in *Refiguring Authority: Reading, Writing, and Rewriting in Cervantes* (Lexington, KY: University Press of Kentucky, 1995), pp. 10–23. Alban K. Forcione's extended analysis in *Cervantes and the Humanist Vision: A Study of Four 'Exemplary Novels'* (Princeton, NJ: Princeton University Press, 1982) includes commentary on Tomás Rodaja's journey in relation to Renaissance travel literature (see especially pp. 225–40). The standard discussion of rhetorical topics for eulogies of cities and countries is E. R. Curtius, *European Literature and the Latin Middle Ages*, tr. Willard R. Trask (Princeton, NJ: Princeton University Press, 1953), pp. 157–58. The parallel between Tomás Rodaja's aspirations – a projected ascent from humble

(This said, he went off to Flanders, where, accompanied by his good friend Captain Valdivia, he added eternal fame by deeds of arms to that which he had begun to acquire by learning, leaving behind him after his death a reputation as a prudent and most valiant soldier.)[2]

The Renaissance debate over the claims of arms and letters shapes the protagonist's choice of careers, and this closing statement reaffirms the structuring force of these terms. At the same time, this conventional theme is cast in a commemorative language that recalls the Roman practice of inscribing military curricula on gravestones and a parallel tradition of literary epitaphs recording the virtues and deeds of soldiers.[3] The text's lapidary conclusion also grants priority to the licentiate's late commitment to the life of arms. The completion in Flanders of his long quest for fame suggests that death on active service has given order and meaning to the complex and varied life that preceded it. Critical discussion of the licentiate's previous roles as student and satirist should take into account his final decision to embark on military service, in relation to the representation of soldiers in the various literary genres that the *novela* engages.

Such consideration of the literary image of the soldier can begin with his ambivalent place in satire. Since the satirist often catalogues the pretensions and failings of humankind through a survey of social types, the soldier offers an easy target of his discourse, both for the vanity of military ambition on any scale and for the conventional propensity of soldiers to impress comrades and civilians alike by bragging and bullying. Juvenal's *Satires* present soldiers and the life of arms in this unflattering light.[4] In Satire 3 Umbricius condemns the affronts and discomforts that have driven him from Rome, including in his parade of parasites and louts a soldier who has struck him in the street with his hob-nailed boot (243–48). Satire 10 derides the spoils of war (133–41), discredits the high ambitions of famous generals (142–87), and adds marauding soldiers to the

origins to a position of honour and wealth in society – and Mediterranean folktales is noted in Stanislav Zimic, *Las 'Novelas ejemplares' de Cervantes* (Madrid: Siglo Veintiuno, 1996), p. 165.

2 Miguel de Cervantes, *Novelas ejemplares*, ed. Harry Sieber, 2 vols (Madrid: Cátedra, 1986), II, p. 74. English version from *Exemplary Stories*, tr. C. A. Jones (Harmondsworth: Penguin, 1972), p. 146. Further translations from *El licenciado Vidriera* follow Jones's version; other translations of Spanish texts are my own.

3 Sonnet 16 of Garcilaso de la Vega illustrates the continuity of this tradition in Golden-Age verse. In the initial note on this poem in his annotations on Garcilaso's poetry, Fernando de Herrera comments that 'Este epitafio, o título sobre sepultura hizo G. L. a su hermano don Fernando de Guzmán' (Garcilaso composed this epitaph, or funerary inscription, for his brother Fernando de Guzmán). See *Garcilaso de la Vega y sus comentaristas*, ed. Antonio Gallego Morell, 2nd edn (Madrid: Gredos, 1972), p. 354. Although Guzmán died of the plague, the sonnet clearly evokes his heroic service in war.

4 Line references and quotations from Juvenal's *Satires* are to the Oxford Classical Text of Persius and Juvenal: *A. Persi Flacci et D. Iuni Iuuenalis Saturae*, ed. W. V. Clausen (Oxford: Oxford University Press, 1959); translations are from *The Satires*, tr. Niall Rudd (Oxford: Oxford University Press, 1992).

many risks that threaten wealth accumulated through avarice (12–18). The incomplete Satire 16 offers ironic praise of soldiers' privileges before the civil courts and their casual right to abuse civilians. In such texts the violent habits and martial allegiances that define soldiers as a distinct social group are the object of the satirist's anger and moral outrage.

The arguments of satire are often reversible, and from the satirist's perspective the discipline of military service can also stand as a positive alternative to the licence and disorder endemic among civilians. This opposition can be articulated by setting a heroic past against a decadent present or by offering enlistment as a form of escape from civilian vices. Juvenal's Satire 14 includes affairs of war in a list of honest occupations:

> Gratum est quod patriae ciuem populoque dedisti,
> si facis ut patriae sit idoneus, utilis agris,
> utilis et bellorum et pacis rebus agendis. (70–72)
>
> (It is an excellent thing to provide a son for the state and nation,
> if you see to it that he's an asset to his country, a capable farmer,
> capable, too, of discharging the business of peace and war. [p. 122])

Here satire displays its preference for the traditional values and activities of a social elite. To work one's land, and to attend to the state's affairs in war and peace, are the only occupations that Juvenal's speaker will allow the true citizen. His satire, however, suggests that few will practise such offices, since avarice now leads the young to follow careers that promise prompt and easy gain. The contrast between the heroic ethos of a lost republican past and the vices of imperial society is clearly marked. Renaissance satire presents similar arguments. In his verse epistle to the Count of Olivares, Quevedo recalls the honour and valour of Spain's martial past (46–54) and urges Olivares to confront present dangers by restoring military discipline (190–98).[5] Ben Jonson's 'Epistle to a Friend, to Persuade Him to the Wars' presents military service as a form of ethical flight from the evils of urban life. The speaker rails against the conventional types who have reduced civil society to chaos – 'flatterers, spies, | Informers, masters both of arts and lies' (163–64) – and exhorts his friend to seek the rewards of an honourable career at arms: 'These take, and now go seek thy peace in war: | Who falls for love of God, shall rise a star' (195–96).[6] This variant of satire praises the soldier's trade as a repository of traditional virtues and a school of enduring fame.

As Alban Forcione and E. C. Riley in particular have noted, *El licenciado Vidriera* investigates the limitations of satirical discourse.[7] As part of this

[5] Francisco de Quevedo, *Poemas escogidos*, ed. José Manuel Blecua (Madrid: Castalia, 1972), pp. 116–24.

[6] Ben Jonson, *The Complete Poems*, ed. George Parfitt (Harmondsworth: Penguin, 1975), pp. 150–55.

[7] Forcione discusses in detail Cervantes's critique of the attitudes and techniques of satire (see especially pp. 281–96). The engagement with the ancient tradition of cynicism in

scrutiny, Cervantes plays on the varying judgements that satire offers on the life of arms and on the other professions to which that life can be opposed. The licentiate's decisive act of abandoning the court for the army, and the fame that he acquires in Flanders, clearly evoke the positive view of military service as an ethical alternative to the folly and hypocrisy of civil society. Yet the *novela* does not present this view without qualification. The account of the licentiate's career as a satirist, and the motives for his progress from one career to another, call into question the conventional oppositions of satirical discourse and the value traditionally attached to fame. The play of generic frames within the text leads to a complex reassessment of the soldier's life as a subject of rhetorical debate and literary representation.

Cervantes's general remarks on the qualities and purposes of satire reveal an awareness of its range and diversity.[8] *El licenciado Vidriera* engages several variants of Golden-Age satire. Recent criticism of this *novela* has emphasized its debt to the formal patterns and satirical attitudes of picaresque fiction. Michael Gerli argues that the central character's initial circumstances recall the geography and the social relations of the picaresque – particularly the search for a position in service to a master – and that the narrative in general recalls the 'peripatetic stride' characteristic of such fiction, as it traces the protagonist's formative travels through the cities of Italy and his trajectory as a keen observer and social critic in Valladolid (pp. 12, 14). For Gerli, Cervantes emphasizes the ethical force that informs picaresque narrative, presenting a 'critical, cutting view of a social reality', in which an astute and morally aware protagonist 'confronts the community in which he lives, mercilessly exposing hypocrisy, dishonesty, and deceit wherever he perceives it' (p. 15). This reading finds support in a general line of interpretation that stresses the protagonist's role as a teller of bitter truths. Stanislav Zimic proposes that the licentiate speaks with true judgement and moral sense, and that his delusion suggests both the clarity and the precariousness of truth in society (pp. 185–88). Such interpretation aligns *El licenciado Vidriera* with a reading of the picaresque as social satire directed against the failings and hypocrisy of early modern Spain.

Other satirical traditions also assert their presence in this *novela*. In Valladolid the licentiate surveys the offices and professions of urban life, and both before his descent into madness and after his recovery he attempts to find a profession to practise. Such concern with the trades and professions of urban society, and with the careers open to talent, is a common feature of ancient verse satire.

Cervantes's *novelas* is the subject of E. C. Riley, 'Cervantes and the Cynics: *El licenciado Vidriera* and *El coloquio de los perros*', *BHS*, 53 (1976), 189–99.

8 In his remarks on poetry to don Diego de Miranda, Don Quijote distinguishes between satire based on personal attack and Horatian satire directed against the general vices of humanity (*Don Quijote,* ed. Martin de Riquer, 2 vols [Barcelona: Juventud, 1955], II, 16, pp. 650–51). Clear and informed commentary on Cervantes's attitudes toward satire is offered in Anthony Close, *Cervantes and the Comic Mind of his Age* (Oxford: Oxford University Press, 2000), pp. 17–59.

As Juvenal's Satire 14 indicates, the number of acceptable professions is predictably limited and reflects the conservative bias of the genre. Often the satirist details the false professions of a corrupt society and the humiliations that afflict those who are driven by need or ambition to practise them. In Satire 7 Juvenal's speaker complains of the inadequacies of official literary patronage and describes the numerous futile occupations on which the young can misspend their talents. The profession of poetry may yield few tangible rewards, but conditions are even less auspicious for the historian, the advocate, the rhetorician, and the schoolmaster. The search for an honourable vocation in *El licenciado Vidriera* recalls the sad parade of trades and professions in a long tradition of satirical verse.

The licentiate's pursuit of a career traces the contours of the debate on arms and letters. As in the discourse on this theme in *Don Quijote* (I, 37–38, pp. 388–94), Cervantes articulates the traditional opposition in terms appropriate to his own time, setting the discomforts and benefits of university study against the dangers and rewards of service in an early modern army. In both texts the goal of the career of *letras* is to become a *letrado*, a term which referred in sixteenth-century usage to someone who had secured a university degree and so qualified himself for office in the royal bureaucracy.[9] Tomás Rodaja studies *letras* because he aspires to join what Richard Kagan has called 'the letrado hierarchy', a widely graded ladder of government service that led to the prestige of high state office (*Students*, pp. 82–87). This path to honour was well worn. Kagan has shown that legal studies dominated the curricula of Castilian universities, and that university students fixed their attention on the rewards of bureaucratic or ecclesiastical service (pp. 77, 214–15). In Cervantes's time the University of Salamanca had engraved above its façade the motto 'Kings for Universities, Universities for Kings' (p. 212), and his protagonist's path begins in this imperial institution and leads to the circle of court power in Valladolid.

The account of Tomás Rodaja's initial progress in the study of *letras* shows little tendency to irony. The young Tomás expresses his faith in education as a high road to honour: 'Con mis estudios –respondió el muchacho –siendo famoso por ellos; porque yo he oído decir que de los hombres se hacen los obispos' (II, p. 43) ('By the fame I win through my studies –replied the boy– because I have heard that even bishops start off as men' [p. 121]). His early success in Salamanca suggests that his confidence is well founded. Supported by two young patrons Tomás displays extraordinary gifts of intellect and character that quickly attract the esteem and affection of all who make his acquaintance. This favourable view of the protagonist's aspirations contrasts sharply with the standard literary treatment of the *letrado* class. In a *letrilla* that catalogues the failings of various social types, Góngora comments astutely

[9] Richard L. Kagan, *Students and Society in Early Modern Spain* (Baltimore, MD: Johns Hopkins University Press, 1974), p. 70.

that a degree from Salamanca guarantees neither the signs nor the substance of material gain:

> Que sea el otro letrado
> por Salamanca aprobado,
> *bien puede ser*;
>
> mas que traiga buenos guantes
> sin que acudan pleiteantes,
> *no puede ser*. (ll. 55–60)
>
> (That the other *letrado* should hold a degree from Salamanca may well be; but that he should wear good gloves if litigants do not turn up cannot be) [10]

Góngora stands with other Golden-Age authors in a long tradition of satire directed against lawyers, judges, and other servants of the law. In Satire 7 Juvenal remarks bitterly on the connection between legal success and fine clothing – 'purpura uendit | causidicium uendunt amethystina' (135–36) (the expensive clothes of purple and violet sell the barrister) – and the law is prominent among the corrupt professions that plague the society of his satires. In its treatment of the *letrado* Spanish satire trades in conventional tropes and attitudes, and *El licenciado Vidriera* is striking in its initial refusal of this tradition.

This *novela* also departs from the conventions that define the social situation and the perspective of the protagonist in picaresque fiction. The relationship of master and servant is central to the genre; although the *pícaro* comments sharply on the failings of others, he is aware of his own limitations of birth and talent and so strives to accommodate himself to his masters, so that he may 'become part of the social order with its security, comfort, and privileges'.[11] In Tomás Rodaja, however, the need for such accommodation is attenuated. Despite his early interest in the life of *letras* and the friendship of his patrons in Salamanca, his chance acquaintance with Captain Valdivia prompts him to abandon Salamanca for the attractions of foreign travel and the Spanish garrisons in Italy. Throughout this period of studies and travels his engaging personal qualities persuade others to solicit his company while making few demands in return. His early life offers a multitude of experiences but requires commitment to none.

The protagonist maintains his attitude of detachment during his madness. As he wanders through the streets of Salamanca and Valladolid, passers-by solicit his opinions and he replies in each case with a pointed saying. Standing apart from the society around him, he uses his intellectual acuity to categorize and judge others. The narrative modulates here into the pattern of formal satire inspired by Juvenal, in which 'the satirist stands before some scene, usually a bustling city street, and

[10] *Góngora y el 'Polifemo'*, ed. Dámaso Alonso, 5th edn, 3 vols (Madrid: Gredos, 1967), II, p. 69.

[11] Ronald Paulson, *The Fictions of Satire* (Baltimore, MD: Johns Hopkins University Press, 1967), p. 61.

comments, to the world at large or to a specific *adversarius*, on the foolishness and depravity of those who pass before him or those whom he remembers'.[12] Many features of the episode confirm this generic affiliation. The licentiate's madness can be traced to a well-attested connection between the satirist's obsession with human weakness and a disposition to melancholy, and his paratactic, discontinuous discourse maintains the disordered and non-linear character of all satirical forms.[13] During his madness the licentiate assumes the role of a traditional ambulatory satirist, railing with bitterness and ingenuity against the crowds who surround and pursue him.

Cervantes's detailed account of the licentiate's sayings reflects his interest in the techniques and the limitations of satire. It is of course conventional in satire to renounce technical artistry, but in most cases this claim cannot support close scrutiny. To reinforce his protestations of honesty and directness, the traditional satirist asserts that he speaks without art, and the structural shapelessness of his tirade lends substance to this claim. Yet in the smaller units of his discourse – the verbal sallies that he levels against specific social types – the satirist shows himself to be 'an extremely clever poetic strategist', employing 'an incredibly copious and colorful vocabulary and an almost limitless arsenal of rhetorical devices' (Kernan, *Cankered Muse*, p. 4). Cervantes's mad licentiate confirms these general principles. His tirade is structured only in the sense that if offers a broad survey of the offices and trades of society in which certain related groups are treated together: carters, sailors and mule-drivers (II, p. 61; p. 135); tailors and shoemakers (II, p. 65; pp. 138–39); notaries, bailiffs, attorneys and solicitors (II, pp. 69–70; pp. 142–43). In critiquing specific trades, however, he employs an impressive range of rhetorical and affective strategies: word-play, amplification, comparison, anecdotes and vignettes, reframing of conventional attitudes and social prejudices, play on the contrast between his past experience of society and his present perspective as a man of glass. His sayings exert a dual appeal, displaying both intellectual virtuosity and aesthetic excellence. The licentiate captures the attention and regard of others through the cultivation of wit, that is, by means of a consciously difficult literary style. He speaks with *agudeza de ingenio* (sharpness of wit) and his remarks reduce the objects of his satire to hopeless folly and elicit from his interlocutors a reaction of *admiración* (wonder), the standard response in baroque aesthetics to an effective display of wit.[14]

[12] Alvin B. Kernan, *The Plot of Satire* (New Haven, CT: Yale University Press, 1965), p. 97.

[13] The connection between the satirist's harsh discourse and the state of melancholia is noted in Alvin B. Kernan, *The Cankered Muse: Satire of the English Renaissance* (New Haven, CT: Yale University Press, 1959), p. 113. See also his *plot of satire*, p. 100.

[14] The discourse of Cervantes's mad licentiate parallels a frequently cited definition of the *concepto* (conceit) as 'una armónica correlación entre dos o tres cognoscibles extremos, expresada por un acto del entendimiento' (a harmonious correlation between two or three extreme terms, expressed through an act of understanding), from a standard seventeeth-century treatise on baroque aesthetics, Baltasar Gracián's *Agudeza y arte de ingenio* (Sharpness and the Art of Wit), ed. Evaristo Correa Calderón, 2 vols (Madrid: Castalia, 1969), I, p. 55.

The licentiate's remarks on a passing judge illustrate his strategies of rhetoric and judgement:

> Yo apostaré que lleva aquel juez víboras en el seno, pistoletes en la cinta y rayos en las manos, para destruir todo lo que alcanzare en su comisión. Yo me acuerdo haber tenido un amigo que en una ocasión criminal que tuvo dio una sentencia tan exorbitante, que excedía en muchos quilates a la culpa de los delincuentes. Preguntéle que por qué había dado aquella tan cruel sentencia y hecho tan manifiesta injusticia. Respondióme que pensaba otorgar la apelación, y que con esto dejaba campo abierto a los señores del Consejo para mostrar su misericordia moderando y poniendo aquella su rigurosa sentencia en su punto y debida proporción. Yo le respondí que major fuera haberla dado de manera que les quitara de aquel trabajo, pues con esto le tuvieran a él por juez recto y acertado. (II, p. 64)
>
> (I'll bet that judge has enough vipers in his bosom, pistols in his belt and lightning in his hands to destroy everything within his jurisdiction. I remember that I had a friend who was working on a criminal charge and who gave a sentence which was far in excess of the crime. I asked him why he had given such a cruel sentence and committed such a manifest injustice. He replied that he intended to grant the appeal, and by this means he was leaving the field open to the members of the Council to show their mercy by moderating and reducing to its proper proportions the harsh sentence he had passed. I replied that it would have been better to have given a sentence which would save them this trouble, for in this way they would consider him to be an upright and just judge. [p. 138])

Tactics of rhetorical magnification and moral critique work together in this passage. The licentiate first expands the judge's physical image to a grotesque and monstrous size, anatomizing his body as an instrument filled with venomous animals, material tools of destruction, and the emblematic lightning bolts of divine rage and vengeance. He then turns to his memory, relating an anecdote – presumably from his student days – concerning an unnamed friend who meted out a patently unjust sentence in a criminal case. The point of the anecdote is that justice has been sacrificed to social hypocrisy: the friend has sentenced with severity only so that his superior judges may make a show of mercy when the case is heard on appeal. In this context, justice and mercy can be counted upon only when they advance social ambition. Finally, the licentiate paints himself in memory as an innocent observer and honest counsellor, advising his friend of the ethically appropriate course that he should have followed. This summary pronouncement on the judge is an impressive piece of rhetorical manipulation, through which the licentiate manages to present himself simultaneously as a practised wit and as an ingenuous spokesman for traditional values.

The calibre of the licentiate's wit guarantees him an audience, but it also represents one of the crucial limitations of satirical discourse. His remarks respond to a double intent: to offer a moral critique of Spanish society and to assert the speaker's extraordinary acuity of intellect. As one pronouncement crowds upon another, the technical mechanisms of wit take precedence over moral judgement.

Forcione has isolated a troubling paradox in the text's treatment of satire: its discourse places a complex rhetorical technique – the 'striking combination of disparate elements' into an abstract conceit which displays and demands intellectual sophistication – at the service of a simple moral vision, grounded in a dark view of human weakness and an insistence on conflict at all levels of social intercourse (p. 269). In his eagerness to pass judgement on others, the licentiate discounts individual variation and human particularity, reducing his fellow citizens to types and playing on received opinion and traditional prejudice. His ambulatory critique illustrates the general principle that 'in no art form is the complexity of human existence so obviously scanted as in satire' (Kernan, *Cankered Muse*, p. 23). Despite his declared intention to survey the trades and professions of his society, the licentiate consistently sacrifices social complexity and diversity to the virtuosity of wit.

In its rhetorical attack on judges the text also turns to traditional satire against the law. Although the licentiate refuses to indulge in conventional criticism of notaries, rejecting such complaints as the rudiments of backbiting and defending notarial work as a public service essential to the administration of the law (II, pp. 69–70) (pp. 142–43), he does not hesitate to offer a reductive portrayal of a vengeful magistrate. The object of his rhetoric extends beyond the single figure that occupies his immediate attention. As satirists know well, to attack the highest servants of the law is to suggest that the entire system of justice is partial. In Quevedo's satirical vision *El alguacil endemoniado* (*The Bailiff Bedevilled*) a demonic voice describes the pleasure that devils take in the damnation of judges, since each judge yields a rich harvest of corrupt lawyers, officers and litigants:

> Los jueces son nuestros faisanes, nuestros platos regalados, y la simiente que más provecho y fruto nos da a los diablos; porque de cada juez que sembramos, cogemos seis procuradores, dos relatores, cuatro escribanos, cinco letrados y cinco mil negociantes, y esto cada día. De cada escribano cogemos veinte oficiales; de cada oficial, treinta alguaciles; de cada alguacil, diez corchetes.
>
> (Judges are our pheasants, our delicate dishes, and the seed that brings most profit and gain to us devils; because from every judge that we sow, we harvest six attorneys, two prosecutors, four scribes, five *letrados* and five thousand litigants, and this happens every day. From every scribe we harvest twenty clerks; from every clerk, thirty bailiffs; from every bailiff, ten constables).[15]

Satire's harsh view of the law finds confirmation in the licentiate's own attempt to practise his profession as a *letrado* following the end of his madness. The text records the stages of his short, frustrated career: his public confession that divine mercy has restored his sanity, his declaration concerning his legal training in Salamanca, his appeal for fair treatment as a member of a professional class and his failure on successive occasions to discourage the curious who

[15] Francisco de Quevedo, *Sueños y discursos*, ed. Felipe C. R. Maldonado (Madrid: Castalia, 1972), p. 99.

continue to pursue him. Unable to secure material survival by exercising his intelligence, he abandons the court in Valladolid for the sieges of Flanders.

The final transition to a career of arms appears to grant priority to the variant of satire that presents military service as an ethical alternative to the failings and vanities of civil society. The urban crowd that the licentiate has anatomized through his ambulatory satire denies him the conditions for practising his profession and forces him to turn his ambitions to warfare. The *novela*'s conclusion suggests that in Flanders the licentiate has found a place of honour and a set of values conspicuously absent in his critical survey of urban life: male friendship, prudence and courage. This pattern inverts the conventional features of the picaresque search for a place in the social order. The standard *pícaro* finds a social accommodation within the limited options imposed by his abilities and genealogy; Cervantes's licentiate is unable to enter the civil profession to which he aspires, despite the extraordinary talents at his command. Picaresque narrative can also end its trajectory in the life of arms, but not on heroic terms. As Anne Cruz has shown, late exemplars of the *pícaro* find a place among the riot and mock-heroics of common soldiers.[16] For the restored licentiate, however, military service appears to retain a conservative function as a repository of virtues and a school of fame.

The ending of *El licenciado Vidriera* is striking in its brevity. Cervantes's typical practice in describing the final disposition of his characters runs to length and detail; some of the other *Novelas ejemplares* end with lapidary statements, but these tend to cap and summarize more extended accounts of the characters' motives and reactions. In contrast, the single closing sentence of *El licenciado Vidriera* records the protagonist's journey to Flanders, his final change of career, his reunion with Captain Valdivia, and the fame that he obtains through a valiant death. Although the text anticipates the life of arms in its earlier account of travels in Italy and the Lowlands, the protagonist does not commit himself to military service until the conclusion. Given the compression of the narrative at this point, any interpretation must make assumptions concerning questions of motive and continuity. The reading that stresses the positive value of arms appeals to three such assumptions: that the licentiate suffers innocently the persecution of the crowd, that the pursuit of honour is the primary motive for his enlistment, and that the fame he wins in arms is continuous with the fame he has sought through letters. The final sentence can sustain all of these assumptions, but prior sections of the *novela* qualify each one and so invite us to question the value attributed to the licentiate's final career as a soldier.

The text evokes the image of the licentiate driven from Valladolid by the hostile curiosity of the crowd, but it also suggests that he is in some measure responsible for the popular reaction against him. In his career as a satirist he has criticized the trades and offices of society in terms that are both harsh and partial, and the public is reluctant to accept at face value his restored commitment to the *letrado*'s profession. Since claims of expertise in legal practice are not

[16] Anne J. Cruz, *Discourses of Poverty: Social Reform and the Picaresque Novel in Early Modern Spain* (Toronto, ON: University of Toronto Press, 1999), pp. 191–206.

easily reconciled with an ingenious and exaggerated critique of judges and other ministers of the law, the licentiate's satirical discourse compromises his capacity to convince others that his abilities are genuine. In addition, a strikingly consistent feature of the protagonist's conduct is his refusal to accept the compromises and accommodations demanded by the normal mechanisms of social exchange, and this relentless attitude seems singularly at odds with the civil profession that he hopes to enter. Legal proceedings depend on negotiation and compromise, and in the courts of early modern Spain a confusing array of competing legal codes, and a corresponding set of overlapping jurisdictions, generated a strong need for such practices.[17] By turning to the army the licentiate opts for a demanding code of honour and discipline, and this choice is governed in part by his self-imposed exclusion from the social accommodations that influence conduct in civilian life.

The desire for a strong code of values may lead the licentiate to abandon the court for the army, but the text of the *novela* shows a broad range of motives for enlistment. When the protagonist first meets Captain Valdivia, the ensign of his company is on recruitment close to Salamanca, and Valdivia enumerates to the young student the immediate rewards of military existence:

> Alabó la vida de la soldadesca; pintóle muy al vivo la belleza de la ciudad de Nápoles, las holguras de Palermo, la abundancia de Milán, los festines de Lombardía, las espléndidas comidas de las hosterías; dibujóle dulce y puntualmente el *aconcha, patrón*; *pasá acá, manigoldo*; *venga la macarela, li polastri, e li macaroni*. Puso las alabanzas en el cielo de la vida libre del soldado y de la libertad de Italia; pero no le dijo nada del frío de las centinelas, del peligro de los asaltos, del espanto de las batallas, de la hambre de los cercos, de la ruina de las minas, con otras cosas deste jaez, que algunos las toman y tienen por añadiduras del peso de la soldadesca, y son la carga principal della. (II, p. 45)
>
> (He praised the soldier's life, and gave him a vivid picture of the beauty of Naples, the delights of Palermo, the prosperity of Milan, the banquets in Lombardy, and the splendid food in the inns. He gave a delightful and exact account of the way they shouted, 'Here, landlord', 'This way, you rogue', 'Let's have the *maccatella*, the *polastri* and the macaroni'. He praised to the skies the soldier's free life and the easy ways of Italy; but he said nothing to him about the cold of sentry duty, the danger of attacks, the horror of battles, the hunger of sieges, the destruction of mines, and other things of this kind, which some consider to be the extra burdens of a soldier's life, when in fact they are the main part of it. [p. 122])

Like many accounts of life in Flanders by contemporary observers, this report of Valdivia's words is marked by understated irony. The narrator balances the

[17] Richard L. Kagan remarks that 'Castilian justice in the sixteenth and seventeenth centuries was a hodgepodge of confused laws and competing jurisdictions that crafty litigants exploited to their own advantage'. See *Lawsuits and Litigants in Castile 1500–1700* (Chapel Hill, NC: University of North Carolina Press, 1981), p. 31.

dangers of siege warfare in the Lowlands against the pleasant conditions of service in the citadels of Italy, and plays on the distinction between the principal duty of military service and its supplementary burdens. The passage nonetheless describes the immediate pleasures that could lead young men to enlist: release from the petty ordinances and restrictions of civil society, access to food and drink at the expense of a foreign population, easy comradeship in the taverns and barracks of Italian cities. Cervantes alludes here to the tradition of satire that stresses the riot of common soldiers, reminding us that the licentiate's school of honour could also be an arena of disorder.

The protagonist's long search for honour ends in Flanders, and the text suggests that the trajectory of his fame follows a unifying line, beginning with his studies in letters and ending in a soldier's death. This gesture toward continuity neatly frames the tale, but it is surprising in a text so clearly marked by formal shifts and breaks. As Felipe Ruan has shown, the *novela*'s narrative movement traces a series of faults and disjunctions that deny stability or closure.[18] Fame itself shifts in meaning over the course of the narrative. Gwynne Edwards has isolated four variants of fame attributed to the protagonist: the distinction that he earns through eight years of diligence and dedication at the University of Salamanca, the notoriety that he acquires in the space of six days through his sharp satirical remarks, the reputation that he hopes to obtain as a *letrado*, and the reports of prudence and valour that survive his death in Flanders.[19] The differences among these variants call into question any single, unitary concept of fame. Edwards argues that 'the true and lasting fame of *Armas* and *Letras* sets in its true perspective the debased values of the Court' (p. 565), but the clear affiliation of *letras* and *letrados* qualifies such an equation of the two careers, since the successful pursuit of bureaucratic office is unlikely to cultivate military virtues or to confer enduring fame. According to the discourse on arms and letters in *Don Quijote* the *letrado*'s career offers pleasant rewards – wealth, influence, the privilege of governing the world from a comfortable chair – but not a soldier's hard-won honour. The licentiate's fame would surely be of a different kind had he followed without deviation his initial career of *letras*.

In *El licenciado Vidriera* Cervantes explores the techniques and limitations of literary satire. The protagonist mimics the satirist's frustrated search for an honourable profession, rails against the trades and offices of society during his madness, and finally turns to military service in Spain's imperial armies. This closing gesture follows a traditional satirical pattern in opposing the conservative virtues of warfare to the vanity that plagues the professions of civilian life. At the same time, however, Cervantes engages satire's tendency to dramatize the licence and disorder that attracted common soldiers to the life of arms and disturbed the good

[18] Felipe Ruan, 'Carta de guía, carto-grafía: fallas y fisuras en *El licenciado Vidriera*', *Cervantes*, 20 (2000), 151–62.

[19] Gwynne Edwards, 'Cervantes's *El licenciado Vidriera*: Meaning and Structure', *MLR*, 68 (1973), 559–68 (p. 565).

order of civilian life. Even as it presents service in Flanders as an ethical alternative for the licentiate, the text recognises the range of contingencies and motives that induced men to enlist and the complex, shifting character of fame. Like many of Cervantes's *novelas*, this work is exemplary in its sense of play and exploration; by displacing generic and discursive boundaries, it questions conventional patterns of thought and rhetoric.

Works cited

Alonso, Dámaso (ed.), *Góngora y el 'Polifemo'*, 5th edn, 3 vols (Madrid: Gredos, 1967).

Cervantes Saavedra, Miguel de, *Don Quijote de la Mancha*, ed. Martin de Riquer, 2 vols (Barcelona: Juventud, 1955).

———, *Exemplary Stories*, tr. C. A. Jones (Harmondsworth: Penguin, 1972).

———, *Novelas ejemplares*, ed. Harry Sieber, 2 vols (Madrid: Cátedra, 1986).

Clausen, W. V. (ed.), *A. Persi Flacci et D. Iuni Iuuenalis Saturae* (Oxford: Oxford University Press, 1967).

Close, Anthony, *Cervantes and the Comic Mind of his Age* (Oxford: Oxford University Press, 2000).

Cruz, Anne J., *Discourses of Poverty: Social Reform and the Picaresque Novel in Early Modern Spain* (Toronto, ON: University of Toronto Press, 1999).

Curtius, E. R., *European Literature and the Latin Middle Ages*, tr. Willard R. Trask (Princeton, NJ: Princeton University Press, 1953).

Edwards, Gwynne, 'Cervantes's *El licenciado Vidriera*: Meaning and Structure', *MLR*, 68 (1973), 559–68.

Forcione, Alban K., *Cervantes and the Humanist Vision: A Study of Four 'Exemplary Novels'* (Princeton, NJ: Princeton University Press, 1982).

Gallego Morell, Antonio (ed.), *Garcilaso de la Vega y sus comentaristas*, 2nd edn (Madrid: Gredos, 1972).

Gerli, Michael E., *Refiguring Authority: Reading, Writing, and Rewriting in Cervantes* (Lexington, KY: University Press of Kentucky, 1995).

Gracián, Baltasar, *Agudeza y arte de ingenio*, ed. Evaristo Correa Calderón, 2 vols (Madrid: Castalia, 1969).

Jonson, Ben, *The Complete Poems*, ed. George Parfitt (Harmondsworth: Penguin, 1975).

Juvenal, *The Satires*, tr. Niall Rudd (Oxford: Oxford University Press, 1992).

Kagan, Richard L., *Students and Society in Early Modern Spain* (Baltimore, MD: Johns Hopkins University Press, 1974).

———, *Lawsuits and Litigants in Castile 1500–1700* (Chapel Hill, NC: University of North Carolina Press, 1981).

Kernan, Alvin B., *The Cankered Muse: Satire of the English Renaissance* (New Haven, CT: Yale University Press, 1959).

———, *The Plot of Satire* (New Haven, CT: Yale University Press, 1965).

Paulson, Ronald, *The Fictions of Satire* (Baltimore, MD: Johns Hopkins University Press, 1967).

Quevedo, Francisco de, *Poemas escogidos*, ed. José Manuel Blecua (Madrid: Castalia, 1972).

Quevedo, Francisco de, *Sueños y discursos*, ed. Felipe C. R. Maldonado (Madrid: Castalia, 1972).

Riley, E. C., 'Cervantes and the Cynics: *El licenciado Vidriera* and *El coloquio de los perros*', *BHS*, 53 (1976), 189–99.

Ruan, Felipe, 'Carta de guía, carto-grafía: fallas y fisuras en *El licenciado Vidriera*', *Cervantes*, 20 (2000), 151–62.

Zimic, Stanislav, *Las 'Novelas ejemplares' de Cervantes* (Madrid: Siglo Veintiuno, 1996).

7

Exemplary Rape: The Central Problem of *La fuerza de la sangre*

Anthony Lappin
University of Manchester

La fuerza de la sangre is a tale difficult to stomach or understand, and even the title of this article will be deemed unacceptable by some readers – but then, the article's title but mirrors the dilemma provoked by the story itself. Can one talk of exemplarity and unpunished rape in the same breath? At the end of the essay, I shall consider the concept of exemplarity as Cervantes expresses it in his prologue to the collection, but my primary focus will be the exemplary tale itself. *La fuerza de la sangre* is usually translated as 'The Power of Blood', although, as will become evident from my discussion, 'Overpowering Blood' is perhaps nearer the mark.[1] The story is the following.

A young girl, Leocadia, living in Toledo, is walking home one night from the river to the city with her elderly parents and younger brother. The family is noble but rather poor. A gang of young good-for-nothings, led by a spoilt noble brat, surprise the family, and stare impudently at the women's faces. Rodolfo, the high-born leader of the group, is overcome with desire to have sex with the girl, who is sixteen years of age and extremely beautiful. He communicates this to his companions and, while they retrace their steps, Rodolfo carries her off. She faints. Rodolfo carries her back to his bachelor pad, where, while she is still senseless, he rapes her. She comes to, and asks him to kill her to put an end to her dishonour. Confused by what she has said, and by the spirit of the girl when he attempts to rape her again, he leaves her to go and ask his friends what he should do. Leocadia is now able to explore the room in which she is held prisoner and conceal a silver crucifix about her person as evidence of what happened to her and who did it. When Rodolfo returns, she asks him to leave her by the main church of Toledo so that she can find her way home, and that he not say to anyone what has happened to her so that she may not be publicly defamed for being raped. He agrees, and leaves her where she

[1] Citations of both text and translation are taken from Miguel de Cervantes, *Exemplary Novels / Novelas ejemplares*, ed. B. W. Ife, 4 vols (Warminster: Aris & Phillips, 1992), II, pp. 102–27. Translations of other texts are by the author.

requested. He goes off to live as a soldier in Italy, and thinks no more of his adventure.

The story is not over, however, since Leocadia has conceived a child as a result of the rape. She gives birth in secret, and hands her son over to a wet-nurse for four years, after which he is brought back to Toledo. The son is called Luis after his maternal grandfather, but he is, of course, not publicly recognized as her son, being passed off as a cousin who is living with them. Time passes. One day, Luis is knocked over by a horse, and receives a serious wound to the head. Whilst the bystanders are wondering what to do with him, Rodolfo's father, moved by the similarity between Luis and his own son, brings him to his own house, where he is placed in Rodolfo's room, in the very bed in which he was conceived. Luisico's family are summoned. Leocadia recognizes the room, and eventually explains what has happened to Rodolfo's mother, who has her son recalled from Italy with the promise of marriage. Leocadia and Luis remain as guests of the family until he returns.

Rather than confronting her son with his deeds, Rodolfo's mother plays a trick on him. She hands him a fake portrait of a woman in whom the delights of virtue clearly outweigh those of the flesh, and declares that it will be she who will be his wife. Rodolfo complains that he likes beautiful girls, so that he could not possibly enjoy being married to someone deprived of a pretty face. The matter is left suspended, and they go to dinner. Whilst sitting at table, Rodolfo's mother pretends to suddenly remember Leocadia – whom she presents as a guest – and summons her to table. Leocadia enters the room in a highly staged entrance designed to show her innumerable charms to their most attractive degree. Rodolfo is bowled over. As dinner progresses, Leocadia is overcome by emotion and faints. Rodolfo, getting up to give her assistance, also faints. It is thought that they have both died, and there is a general clamour: Leocadia's parents, who, together with the parish priest, were hiding behind a curtain, come out to join in the grief; so do the musicians, who were similarly hidden; Rodolfo's mother is about to faint, but Rodolfo regains his senses. He is told Leocadia is to be his wife. He kisses her. Leocadia then comes to, and makes a sententious remark about how he had robbed her honour and was now returning it. They are married on the spot. They live happily ever after in Toledo and have many children.

Most twentieth-century critics of this story have considered it as somehow unreal, as somehow miraculous or allegorical.[2] I shall argue that the structure of the tale and its events are ordered methodically to provide a precise legal, theological and psychological picture whose bedrock is that *it rings true*. Yet in asserting

[2] A theological allegory in which Leocadia and Rodolfo are Adam and Eve, the rape is the Fall (a sin of the flesh), and they are redeemed by the salvific action of Christ (the crucifix) through their marriage is proposed by Joaquín Casalduero, *Sentido y forma de las 'Novelas ejemplares'*, *Revista de Filología Hispánica* Anejo 1 (Buenos Aires: Facultad de Filosofía y Letras de la Universidad de Buenos Aires, Instituto de Filología, 1943), pp. 123–26; miracle tale: Alban K. Forcione, *Cervantes and the Humanist Vision: A Study of Four 'Exemplary Novels'* (Princeton, NJ: Princeton University Press, 1982), pp. 354–78.

Cervantine realism, I wish to stress that the author is doing more than producing an accurate picture of the customs and *mores* of by-gone Toledo; he is also using that realism to produce some very baroque effects indeed, effects that depend upon a knowledge of the theological and legal presuppositions that structure the tale.

Casalduero (pp. 123–24) takes it as axiomatic that Leocadia's fainting fit (which allows her to be raped) is fictional, in the sense that it responds to a literary commonplace and is there for the stylistic symmetries that it allows Cervantes to produce. However, for many noble women fainting fits would have been a natural consequence of experiencing strong emotion, due to their wearing corsets or stiff bodices, and the likelihood of a swoon could only be increased by Leocadia's tender innocence. One modern account of rape, given by an eleven-year old Australian girl (she was attacked by her eighteen-year-old cousin when in a playhouse), noted that 'I must have fainted or passed out because when I woke up he was gone and there was blood everywhere'.[3] Leocadia's total innocence is later confirmed by her assertion – to Rodolfo after he had raped her – that the only men she had ever spoken to were her father and her confessor. We are given a picture of innocence as complete as it is possible to have, and we are consequently meant to consider the rape as an outrage. Leocadia cannot in any sense be judged as having precipitated her own downfall, having participated in the rape, or having secretly desired it – an important point to which we shall return.[4]

The fainting fit allows the rape to occur, just as Leocadia's two later fainting fits mark turning points in the narrative: giving time to Rodolfo's mother to believe the story she has just heard; precipitating Rodolfo into marriage. Leocadia was more than able to defend herself from the attack, since she does so when Rodolfo attempts to rape her again. We are thus left in no doubt about Leocadia's determination to protect her honour. But we are also left in no doubt about Rodolfo's normal sexual responses. He is cooled, as the normal male response would be, by determined opposition on the part of his

3 Paul R. Wilson, *The Other Side of Rape* (St Lucia, Queensland: University of Queensland Press, 1978), p. 40.

4 For the concept of victim precipitation, see Menachim Amir, *Patterns of Forcible Rape* (Chicago: University of Chicago Press, 1971), pp. 260–61 and p. 266. On that of 'victim participation', particularly in relation to child-abuse, see Sedelle Katz and Mary Ann Mazur, *Understanding the Rape Victim: A Synthesis of Research Findings* (New York: John Wiley and Sons, 1979), p. 138, and John M. Macdonald, *Rape: Offenders and their Victims* (Springfield, IL: Thomas, 1971), pp. 112–13; such behaviour was not lost on earlier writers: Marcus Torre and Jacobus Balsarini, *De poena stupri cum puella immatura. Disertatio Marci Torre, patritii Veronensis et Jacobi Balsarini, patritii Methonensis. Accedit elucubratio anatomica desumpta ex operibus D. Cajetani Petrioli Romani, S. R. M. Regis Sardiniae &c. &c. &c. chirugiae professoris, una cum tabula aere incisa, et ad calcem impressa* (Rome: Generosus Salamoni, 1754), pp. 10–11. Sigmund Freud's view of women's masochistic subconscious desire for rape is discussed sympathetically by John Forrester, 'Rape, Seduction and Psychoanalysis', in *Rape: An Historical and Social Enquiry*, ed. Sylvana Tomaselli and Roy Porter (Oxford: Basil Blackwell, 1986), pp. 57–83 – see below, n. 22. Leocadia's family's reaction of fear to the initial insult may have prompted Rodolfo's course of action since 'a terrified victim is ripe for rape' (Katz and Mazur, p. 153).

victim.[5] Rodolfo is no pervert. But he is part of a class (young, disengaged, with few trammels upon his actions) that was likely to commit the crime he did:

> Young men may be dampened down (e.g. as apprentices) or syphoned off (e.g. deflected elsewhere as soldiers); but where such safety valves are not available, adolescents often turn to rape. Rapists are thus the waste of patriarchy, but they are its wayward sons not its shock troops, not its life-blood but a diseased excrescence.[6]

This description fits happily with Cervantes's introduction of Rodolfo into the story:

> Hasta veintidós tendría un caballero de aquella ciudad a quien la riqueza, la sangre ilustre, la inclinación torcida, la libertad demasiada y las compañías libres, le hacían hacer cosas y tener atrevimientos que desdecían de su calidad y le daban renombre de atrevido. (II, p. 102)
>
> (About twenty-two years indeed would be the age of a gentleman of that city, in whom riches, noble blood, perverted inclinations, too much liberty, and evil companions, were the causes of his perpetrating excesses of arrogance quite out of keeping with his social position, acts which had earned him the reputation of hot-headedness. [II, p. 103])

Similarly, if we compare the events of the rape with what is known about the patterns of modern rape, then here too we may say that the narration Cervantes constructs rings true, and that it would have been understood as anecdotally accurate by his contemporary readers. According to studies carried out in the 1970s, female adolescents between 13 and 17 were most at risk of rape, and offender and victim were usually of the same age group; the place of meeting was not usually the place of the rape – some form of abduction therefore had to take place – and the rapist's home (usually close by) was the most likely place for the crime to be committed, whereas the street was the most likely place for the first contact; rapes were more likely in summer, and during the evening or night; and half of the number of rape victims were, like Leocadia, held captive for more than half an hour. Captivity sometimes ended with the offender driving the abducted victim back to her home or near the vicinity where he found her. Leocadia's initial request when she regains consciousness to be killed (II, p. 104; II, p. 105) is unusual in the modern setting, where the fear of death is actually greater in adult rape victims (although much less common in adolescents), yet there is a strong link between female attempted suicide and a past history of rape – cultural

[5] Howard E. Barbaree and Ralph C. Serin, 'Role of Male Sexual Arousal during Rape in Various Rapist Subtypes', in *Sexual Aggression: Issues in Etiology, Assessment and Treatment*, ed. Gordon C. Nagayama Hall and others (Washington, DC: Vermont & Taylor, 1993), pp. 99–114, (p. 103).

[6] Roy Porter, 'Rape – Does it have a Historical Meaning?' in *Rape: An Historical and Social Enquiry*, ed. Sylvana Tomaselli and Roy Porter (Oxford: Basil Blackwell, 1986), pp. 216–36, (p. 235).

conditioning may accentuate the desire for death either during or after a rape.[7] In 1940s Spain, a mother could say to her daughter, who had fallen pregnant after being raped by her boyfriend, 'que si a ella le hubiese sucedido cosa semejante se hubiese tirado al tren para morir antes que vivir deshonrada' (that if something similar had happened to her, she would have thrown herself under a train to be killed rather than live with dishonour).[8] Leocadia's pregnancy, too, is not to be wondered at, since 'the probability of pregnancies resulting from rape appear to be almost as high as the probability associated with voluntary copulations'.[9] Her initial feelings of shame and gradual recovery are mirrored in the experiences of modern women.[10] Gibbens and Prince, in their 1963 study, noted that: 'Although pregnancy from rape can be very traumatic, some girls made a good recovery from the disaster.'[11] The subsequent marriage of rapist and victim is not unheard of in the modern world, either (Macdonald, pp. 44, 95–97).

From a legal perspective, Cervantes's structure shows a precision which suggests that he was well aware of the canonical requirements for both rape and marriage. In canon law, 'Rape must involve the use of violence, it must involve abduction, it must involve coitus, and it must be accomplished without the free consent of one partner.'[12] In *La fuerza de la sangre*, we clearly have abduction, coitus and lack of consent. Violence is also present, since 'satis erit quouis modo adsit

7 Katz and Mazur, pp. 34, 102, 126, 130–33, 166, 172–73, 222; see also Macdonald, pp. 28–32, 36, 54, 98.

8 León del Amo, *Sentencias, casos y cuestiones en la rota española* (Pamplona: Universidad de Navarra, 1977), p. 819.

9 Lee Ellis, 'Rape as biosocial phenomenon', in *Sexual Agression: Issues in Etiology, Assessment and Treatment*, ed. Gordon C. Nagayama Hall and others (Washington, DC: Vermont & Taylor, 1993), pp. 17–41, at p. 21; see also M. N. Islam and M. N. Islam, 'Retrospective study of alleged rape victims', *Legal Medicine*, 5 (2003), S351–53.

10 Macdonald, pp. 98–101; Katz and Mazur, p. 229: 'Within a year most victims seemed to have recovered from the rape. Only those with pre-existing psychiatric or emotional difficulties still required more extensive psychiatric treatment.'

11 T. C. N. Gibbens and Joyce Prince, *Child Victims of Sex Offences* (London: ISTD, 1963), p. 16.

12 James A. Brundage, 'Rape and Seduction in the Medieval Canon Law', in *Sexual Practices in the Medieval Church*, ed. Vern L. Bullough and James Brundage (Buffalo, NY: Prometheus, 1982), pp. 141–60 (p. 143). In the twelfth century, the term *raptus* (and therefore the seriousness of the offence) could be applied not only to the physical abduction but also to the 'carrying off' of the girl's virginity: Rufinus, *Summa Decretorum*, C. 36 q. 1, in *Die Summa Decretorum des Magister Rufinus*, ed. Heinrich Singer (Paderborn: Ferdinand Schöningh, 1902), p. 534. This idea was repeated down the centuries (Torre and Balsarini, p. 35), but was not considered relevant by the great canonistic authority and contemporary of Cervantes, Tomás Sánchez, SJ (d. 1610), in his *Disputationum de sancto matrimonii sacramento libri decem in tres tomos distribuiti* (Venice: Ioannes Antonii and Iacopo de Francisci, 1606–7), VII.12, §3, vol. II, p. 38B. The popularity and influence of Sánchez's work can be glimpsed in the number of printings it received – Genua: Pavone 1602; Madrid: Sánchez 1602–5; Antwerp: Nutius 1607, 1617, 1620 and 1624; Venice: Guerilius 1619; Lyons: Societas Typographorum 1621 and 1637; Madrid: 1623; Venice: Iuntas 1625; Antwerp: Aertssius 1626 and 1652; Lyons: Borde 1654 and 1681, Anisson 1669 and 1690; Avignon: Duperier 1689; Nuremberg: Lochner 1706; Venice: Polidorus 1712, and Pezzana

violentiae; ut si puella inspiciat homines armis munitos, ad eam renitentem cogendam' (Sánchez, VII 12, §5, vol. II, p. 38B; it is enough that violence be present in whatever way, such as if a girl should see armed men intent on seizing her against her will), exactly the sight presented to Leocadia before she fainted in Rodolfo's constraining arms. Leocadia is noble, an important consideration when weighing the significance of the rape.[13] We later see Rodolfo expatiating upon one of the 'secondary goods' of marriage (which was for him his own enjoyment of sex, but these secondary goods were considered quite differently by the canonists – that is, as the avoidance of fornication or the fulfilment of desire, the latter being at times sinful).[14] At the end of the tale, Cervantes is careful to specify how the marriage took place at a time when it could still be solemnized by vows of present consent, before the parish priest and families as witnesses, and as such the process differed from the Tridentine legislation in effect at the time he was writing. Cervantes notes that, on the instructions of doña Estefanía the priest carries out the *desposorio* 'que por haber sucedido este caso en tiempo cuando con sola la voluntad de los contrayentes, sin las diligencias y prevenciones justas y santas que ahora se usan, quedaba hecho el matrimonio, no hubo dificultad que impidiese el desposorio' (II, p. 124) (for, since this tale occurred during the time when marriage was complete with only the agreement

1712 and 1754; Lyons: 1739. An abbreviation of Sánchez's work, entitled *Compendium tractatus de S. Matrimonii*, was carried out by Emanuel Laurentius Soares (Seville: de Lyra, 1623; Venice: Fontana, 1625).

13 For example, see Torre and Balsarini: 'paupercula mulier praesumitur facili in corpus suum peccare' (p. 11) (it is to be presumed that the poor woman will easily sin with her body). Sánchez, VII.12, §3, vol II, p. 38B, stipulated that for *raptus* to occur the victim must be 'honestae vitae' (of honourable behaviour).

14 Raymund of Penyafort, *Summa*, IV.2: De matrimonio, §§7–8, ed. Honoratus Vincentius (Verona: Augustus Carattonius, 1744), p. 478:

> Bona matrimonii principaliter sunt tria, fides, proles et sacramentum. In fide attenditur, ne post uinculum coniugale cum alio, uel alia coeatur. In prole, ut amanter suscipiatur, et religiose educetur. In sacramento, ut coniugium non separetur [. . .] Valent haec bona ad excusationem peccati, si seruat fide thori, causa prolis conueniant coniuges. Unde nota, quod aliquando commiscentur coniuges caussa [*sic*] suscipiendae prolis, aliquando causa reddendi debitum, aliquando causa incontinentiae, siue uitande fornicationis, aliquando cause exsaturandae libidinis. In primo et secundo casu nullum est peccatum: in tertio ueniale: in quarto mortale.
>
> (The principal goods of marriage are three: faith, offspring and sacrament. In faith one must pay attention that after the bond of marriage one does not have sex with anyone else; in offspring, that they may be lovingly raised and devoutly brought up; in the sacrament, that the spouses should not separate [. . .]. These goods are strong enough to excuse sins, if in order to maintain fidelity, the spouses come together for the reason of [generating] children. Whence it is to be noted that sometimes spouses have sex for the conception of children, sometimes to render the other spouse their rights to have sex, sometimes due to incontinence or the avoidance of fornication, sometimes for the satisfaction of lust. In the first and second case, there is no sin; in the third, a venial sin; in the fourth, a mortal sin.)

of those contracting the marriage – without the just and holy precautions which are now in use – there was no difficulty which should prevent the marriage).[15] The priest was not necessary for the validity of the marriage; he does serve, however, to increase the drama and comedy of Leocadia's faint, rushing to absolve her of her sins but being confronted with the swooning Rodolfo's face between her breasts:

> Llegó el cura presto, por ver si por algunas señales daba indicios de arrepentirse de sus pecados para absolverla de ellos; y donde pensó de hallar un desmayo halló dos, porque ya estaba Rodolfo puesto el rostro sobre el pecho de Leocadia. (II, p. 124)
>
> (The priest hastened to see if by some sign she was indicating repentance for her sins, in order to absolve her; but where he expected to find one person unconscious, he found two, because Rodolfo had fainted, with his head on Leocadia's breast. [II, p. 125])

It is easy to forget how radical the change was that Trent made in marriage practices, a change which led many authors to look back with a nostalgic eye to the narrative possibilities provided by the freer arrangements that held sway in ecclesiastical jurisdiction for the best part of five hundred years. Cervantes has taken care over his plot and characterization, and we should recognize this and respond to it.

From the points of view of theology and philosophy, *La fuerza de la sangre* is at its most baroque. For any reader with a theological education, it was certain that Leocadia, despite her rape and subsequent childbirth, had remained a virgin. This, perhaps the most interesting aspect of the story, is in itself a narrative

The sinfulness of the third category (which Rodolfo thinks of as a good, which only serves to underline the sensual nature of his character) was much debated, and even the fourth at times was classified by some authorities, although mortally sinful, as being punished only as if it were a venial sin.

15 My translation; Rees Price mistranslates: '[. . .] when marriages could be performed at the will alone of both the persons concerned', annotating (*Exemplary Novels*, II, p. 136, n. 18) that 'before the Council of Trent established preliminaries to a wedding, it was possible for a priest to carry out the ceremony, before witnesses, whenever convenient', a misapprehension that explains his slip. Rather, Trent enforced the church ceremony as an essential part of marriage (Prospero Fagnani, *Commentaria in quinque libros decretalium*, 8 vols [Rome: Iacobi Fei And. F., 1661], 4: *De Sponsalibus et Matrimonio*, cap. Is qui fidem, §8, at VI, 13). The medieval dispensation allowed marriage by an agreement between parties: either a present agreement (where both say, 'I accept you as my wife/husband'), which constituted the marriage *by itself*; or a future agreement (where both say, 'I will accept you as my wife/husband'), termed *sponsalia* (engagement), and which was turned into marriage by subsequent sexual intercourse or the fulfilment of stipulated clauses: see Raymond of Penyafort, *Summa*, IV.1: *De Sponsalibus*, §1, pp. 459A–460A; IV.2: *De Matrimonio*, §2, pp. 470A–471A. The Castilian word, *desposorio*, is defined in the *Diccionario de autoridades* (Madrid, 1732), II, 223A, as 'La promessa que el hombre y muger se hacen mutuamente de contraher Matrimonio. Oy regularmente se entiende por esta voz el casamiento por palabras de presente' (The mutual promise which the man and woman make to contract marriage. Today this word is usually understood as meaning marriage by words of present consent).

triumph, and calls for some explanation. I refer to Article 1 of *Quaestio* 152 of the Secunda Secundae of the Angelic Doctor's *Summa Theologiae*, in which he answers the question, 'Does virginity consist in the integrity of the flesh?' Aquinas distinguishes three levels in the loss of virginity: the breaking of the hymen, the experience of sexual pleasure, and the decision of the soul to seek such sexual pleasure. It is the third which is the important one: virginity is essentially a sign of *pudicitia*, purity, the refusal to aim for sexual pleasure in one's actions. Pleasure is here defined as orgasm (*seminis resolutio*) which may come about without the consent of the mind:

> vel in dormiendo, vel per violentiam illatam, cui mens non consentit, quamvis caro delectationem experiatur, vel etiam ex infirmitate naturae, ut patet in his qui fluxum seminis patiuntur: et sic non perditur virginitas; quia talis pollutio non accidit per impudicitiam, quam virginitas excludit.[16]
>
> (either in sleeping, or through violence, to which the mind does not consent, although the flesh might experience pleasure, or even from the infirmity [or imperfection] of nature, as is evident in those who undergo an orgasm; and thus virginity is not lost, since such pollution does not come about through impurity, which excludes virginity.)

Leocadia most definitely does not consent in her defloration, or to any pleasure that might be involved. So Leocadia remained a virgin, despite her ravishment. This classification of the girl has various ramifications, but there is another victim of rape whose ghostly figure haunts this story, and to whom we should turn.

That figure is Lucretia, whose legendary rape was held to have led to the expulsion of Tarquinius Superbus, last king of Rome, and the founding of the Republic. Lucretia was a troubling figure for Humanists. Held up as a paradigm of womanly virtue by pagan authors, her virtue was brilliantly held up to question by Augustine.

> In Renaissance terms, Lucretia is a *topos*, interesting because it brings pagan and Christian frameworks into play simultaneously, and the issue is whether or

[16] Thomas Aquinas, *Summa theologiae*, 2a 2ae, CLII.1, resp. ad 4 (*Divi Thomae Aquinatis Ordinis Praedicatorum, Doctoris Angelici a Leone XIII P. M. gloriose regnante Catholicarum scholarum patroni Coelestis renunciati Summa theologica editio altera romana ad emendatiores editiones impressa et noviter accuratissime recognita*, 4 vols [Rome: Forzani et Sodales, 1922], III, p. 980). Aquinas's fleeting reference to the 'infirmity of nature' looks ahead to modern feminists' explanations of the fact that some women do experience orgasm during rapes ('Like a child who wets his pants when excited, a victim may have had a sexual orgasm as a result of the excitement caused by fear. [. . .] The result is that a woman may have a physical reaction [orgasm] while she is mentally horrified and revolted': Katz and Mazur, p. 179; cp. p. 147, where one rapist assumed that his victim would both desire and have an orgasm). For medieval legal interest in (male) orgasm during rape, see John Marshall Carter, *Rape in Medieval England: An Historical and Sociological Study* (Lanham, MD: University Press of America, 1985), p. 37.

not she is to be admired, or whether a Christian or a pagan view should be taken of her case.[17]

By her chastity Lucretia inflamed the lust of the son of Tarquinius Superbus, Sextus Tarquinius; he broke into her room and threatened that, should she not consent to intercourse with him, he would kill her and her slave, and claim that he had found them having sexual relations. Lucretia, determined to preserve her honour (and therefore the honour of her family), acceded to Sextus Tarquinius's demands, and the following morning confessed what had happened to her husband and male relatives, then committed suicide as a proof of her purity and guiltlessness in the matter. Augustine turned the praise on its head: 'Si adulterata, cur laudata; si pudica, cur occisa?' ('If she was an adulteress, why is she praised? If she was pure, why was she slain?').[18] Perhaps, speculated Augustine, she killed herself because of a 'latens consensio' (secret consent) (*De civitate dei*, I.19, l. 56, vol. I, p. 21) to the rape, and was therefore at some level guilty. Leocadia explicitly rejects the option taken by Lucretia after her rape: 'No quiero desesperarme' (II, p. 106) ('I will not fall into despair' [II, p. 107]; as Rees Price noted in his translation, '*Desesperarse* means "to commit suicide" but it does not seem appropriate here', but only because suicide as a response to rape is not considered.[19]

Leocadia is prepared to die rather than be raped again: 'que si ahora, despierta, sin resistencia concediese a tan abominable gusto, podrías imaginar que mi desmayo fue fingido cuando te atreviste a destruirme' (II, pp. 106–8) ('because, if I, now conscious, were to accede to your abominable desires without resistance, you might imagine that my fainting was feigned when you dared to destroy me' [II, pp. 107, 109]).[20] It was not only Rodolfo who might have thought that. Augustine pushed his charges against Lucretia further:

> Quod ergo seipsam, quoniam adulterum protulit, etiam non adultera occidit, non est pudicitiae caritas, sed pudoris infirmitas. Puduit enim eam turpitudinis alienae in se commissae, etiamsi non secum, et Romana mulier, laudis auida nimium, uerita est ne putaretur, quod uiolenter est passa cum uiueret, libenter

17 Norman Bryson, 'Two Narratives of Rape in the Visual Arts: Lucretia and the Sabine Women', in *Rape: An Historical and Social Enquiry*, ed. Sylvana Tomaselli and Roy Porter (Oxford: Basil Blackwell, 1986), pp. 152–73, at p. 171. A feminist analysis of the importance of Lucretia for Florentine Humanism has been carried out by Stephanie H. Jed, *Chaste Thinking: The Rape of Lucretia and the Birth of Humanism*, Theories of Representation and Difference (Bloomington-Indianapolis: Indiana University Press, 1989).

18 Aurelius Augustinus, *De civitate dei*, II.19, l. 62, ed. Bernardus Dombart and Alphonsus Kalb, 2 vols, Corpus Christianorum Series Latina 47–8 (Turnhout: Brepols, 1955), I, p. 21; *Augustine: The City of God against the Pagans*, trans. R. W. Dyson, Cambridge Texts in the History of Political Thought (Cambridge: Cambridge University Press, 1998), p. 31.

19 *Exemplary Novels*, II, p. 136, n.5.

20 Thirteenth-century canonists insisted that a woman should offer resistance with all her force, in a discussion which centred upon the example of Lucretia: Wolfgang P. Müller, 'Lucretia and the Medieval Canonists', *Bulletin of Medieval Canon Law*, 19 (1989), 13–32.

> passa si uiueret. Vnde ad oculos hominum testem mentis suae illam poenam adhibendam putauit, quibus conscientiam demonstrare non potuit. Sociam quippe facti se credi erubuit, si, quod alius in ea fecerat turpiter, ferret ipsa patienter. (I.19, ll. 69–78, vol. I, p. 21)
>
> (In that case, therefore, when she slew herself because she had endured the act of adultery even though she was not an adulteress herself, she did this not from love of purity, but because of a weakness arising from shame. She was made ashamed by the infamy of another, even though committed against her without her consent. Being a Roman lady excessively eager for praise, she feared that, if she remained alive, she would be thought to have enjoyed suffering the violence that she had suffered when she lived. Hence, she judged that she must use self-punishment to exhibit the state of her mind to the eyes of men to whom she could not show her conscience. She blushed, indeed, to think that, if she were to bear patiently the infamy that already had been inflicted upon her, she would be believed to have been an accomplice to it. [Dyson, p. 31])

Here we have just the nexus suffered by Leocadia: she is guiltless, but who will believe that she is? And at this point, Leocadia's pregnancy is a key element in the scales. It was held by canonists and physicians alike that without mutual orgasms pregnancy could not be achieved.[21] Leocadia could not have conceived her bastard child without an orgasm, without experiencing sexual pleasure. This is why it is crucial that Leocadia's swoon should not be false. Otherwise, the charges that were laid against Lucretia could be laid against Leocadia – that she had in some way been a willing participant in the rape – a view which would have been eloquently proved by her falling pregnant. Essentially, what Cervantes has done has been to create a Christian retelling of the Lucretia story, in which the heroine is completely innocent, blameless and without need for shame. However, as Leocadia's father observes of public opinion: 'advierte, hija, que más lastima una onza de deshonra pública que una arroba de infamia secreta' (II, p. 110) ('And bear in mind, dear girl, that an ounce of public dishonour hurts more than a hundredweight of secret shame' [II, p. 111]) – not that, he adds, Leocadia has any

[21] Although the belief that male sperm was itself sufficient to produce pregnancy arose in the late thirteenth century amongst certain canonists (see Francisco Javier Hervada Xiberta, *La impotencia del varón en el derecho matrimonial canónico*, Publicaciones del Estudio General de Navarra 20, Colección Canónica del Estudio General de Navarra 1 (Pamplona: Estudio General de Navarra, 1959), pp. 66–71), it remained the minority opinion. Sánchez (II.21, §§10–11, vol. I, p. 158AB) opted for the mutual orgasm theory, not least because the Blessed Virgin must have emitted seed in the conception of Christ – an argument which has some bearing on our story as well. See also James A. Brundage, *Law, Sex, and Christian Society in Medieval Europe* (Chicago: University of Chicago Press, 1987), p. 450. The belief in the mutual orgasm theory only began to decline during the seventeenth century: Mark Breitenberg, *Anxious Masculinity in Early Modern England*, Cambridge Studies in Renaissance Literature and Culture, 10 (Cambridge: Cambridge University Press, 1996), p. 26. Medieval English secular courts would consider that a woman was lying about rape if she became pregnant as a result, because it was 'believed that conception could not occur if a woman were forced to have intercourse against her will' (Carter, p. 170).

infamy. Leocadia, unlike Lucretia, is innocent, without any stain of suspicion. Yet she must hide what has happened to her, since the general opinion is less informed by the truth than by a topos drawn from Ovid that Augustine had used (and implicitly criticized) in the passage cited above:

> uim licet appelles: grata est uis ista puellis;
> quod iuuat, inuitae saepe dedisse uolunt.
> quaecumque est Veneris subita uiolata rapina,
> gaudet, et inprobitas muneris instar habet.
> at quae, cum posset cogi, non tacta recessit,
> ut simulet uultu gaudia, tristis erit.
>
> (You may use force; women like you to use it; they often wish to give unwillingly what they like to give. She whom a sudden assault has taken by storm is pleased, and counts the audacity as a compliment. But she who, when she might have been compelled, departs untouched, though her looks feign joy, will yet be sad.)[22]

Seven years pass after the rape, and another misfortune, this time in the street, sets the wheels in motion that will lead to Leocadia's marriage and Luisico's retrospective legitimacy. The scene of the accident is meant to be a parallel to that of the abduction and rape. Just as Leocadia was carried off by Rodolfo (who had lost control of himself through the passions), so Luisico is knocked over by a horse which had run out of control – and the horse was a symbol of ungovernable passions at least from the time of Plato. Luis is carried by Rodolfo's father, acting on an impulse; Leocadia was carried away by Rodolfo, again acting on impulse; both ended up in Rodolfo's bed. But Luisico is carried to the bed to be cured; Leocadia was carried to the bed to be injured. Yet Luisico's cure will also bring about his mother's return to the health of honour that is no longer built upon pretence.

Leocadia had conceived a plan as well as a child after her rape. Taking (*not* stealing, specifies Cervantes with unwonted casuistry) a silver crucifix from the room of her captivity, she intended to trap her rapist into identifying himself when he went to claim it from the priest who would have advertised that it had been found. Her father disabused her of her simplicity, and recommended that she commend herself to the crucifix so that she might one day have a judge to rectify her misfortune. When she reveals all to Rodolfo's mother, doña

22 Publius Ovidius Naso, *Ars amatoria*, ed. A. S. Hollis (Oxford: Clarendon, 1977), p. 26; tr. J. H. Mozley and G. P. Goold, *The Art of Love and Other Poems*, Loeb Classical Library 232, 2nd edn (Cambridge, MA: Harvard University Press, 1979), pp. 13–175 (p. 59). This *topos* was given another twist by Sigmund Freud, who speculated that women may subconsciously desire rape, and therefore not struggle with all their force to avoid it. In relation to this, Freud used Cervantes, but the *Quijote*, not *La fuerza de la sangre*, describing Sancho Panza's famous judgement on the alleged rape as psychologically unjust (Forrester, p. 61; see also Macdonald, pp. 91–92).

Estefanía, it is the latter's turn to draw up a plan, and from this point the control of the situation passes out of male hands into female ones. Rodolfo's and his father's impulsive actions had provided two turning points in the story, one to the bad, the other to the good. Now the control of events is with doña Estefanía, and it is characterized by deceit and cunning. Rodolfo is summoned back from Naples, where he is having a grand old time, with the promise of marriage. Yet when he arrives, he is handed a fake portrait of his bride-to-be by his mother. She promises that the woman is virtuous, but Rodolfo is not to be taken in (he has no idea of the depths of his mother's cunning): 'Si los pintores, que ordinariamente suelen ser pródigos de la hermosura con los rostros que retratan, lo han sido con éste, sin duda creo que el original debe ser la misma fealdad' (II, p. 120) ('If the painters, who are usually very prodigal in adding beauty to the faces they paint, have done so with this one, I believe that the original must undoubtedly be ugliness itself' [II, p. 121]). Rodolfo smells a rat, but he is mistaken about which way the wind is blowing. He thus finds himself in an uncomfortable position. He has returned from the good life to be faced with an appalling prospect: an ugly wife, for a man who prizes beauty above all things. He is left weak and impressionable, desiring a way out of his wholly imaginary troubles, and ready to seize it. And doña Estefanía is not above playing ironic games with her son. She says, as she presents him with the portrait, 'Yo quiero, Rodolfo hijo, darte una gustosa cena con mostrarte a tu esposa' (II, p. 120) ('I would like, my son, to give you a pleasant supper by showing you your future wife' [II, p. 121]) – of course, her plan *is* to show Rodolfo his true *esposa* at the real dinner, and she is well aware that the metaphorical *cena*, the portrait, will thoroughly revolt him.

At the dinner itself, Estefanía lies again. Everyone sits down, and she says, 'al descuido, "¡Pecadora de mí, y qué bien trato a mi huéspeda!"' (II, p. 122) ('as if forgetful, "Goodness me! I am not treating my guest very well!"' [II, p. 123]). She then orders for her to be summoned. Leocadia's entrance is finely staged, theatrical in the extreme. She enters dressed fashionably and fascinatingly, covered in gold, pearls and diamonds, holding her son by the hand and with two acolytes carrying candles going on before. 'Levantáronse todos a hacerle reverencia, como si fuera alguna cosa del cielo que allí milagrosamente se había aparecido' (II, p. 122) ('Everyone rose to do her honour, as if she were something divine which had miraculously come among them' [II, p. 123]). Several critics have noticed the similarity between this description of Leocadia and representations of the Blessed Virgin Mary.[23] This is quite justified: both Leocadia and the Theotokos had been privileged to have had virgin births. Both conceived without any sin in the conception

[23] Jeremy Robbins, *The Challenges of Uncertainty: An Introduction to Seventeenth-Century Spanish Literature*, New Readings: Introductions to European Literature and Culture 2 (London: Duckworth, 1998), p. 91. Her dress also recalls the portrait of a pregnant woman (*c.* 1595) attributed to Marcus Gheeraerts II (d. 1636), now in the Tate Gallery, London (a reproduction of the painting can be viewed at www.tate.org.uk).

(on Leocadia's part at least, if not Rodolfo's). That Leocadia, a rape victim, is to be compared to the Virgin Mary, should not surprise us. Several of Ovid's ravished nymphs and maidens in his *Metamorphoses* were allegorically understood within the medieval Christian tradition as figures of the Blessed Virgin.[24] Yet Leocadia's appearance, and the wholly intended and ravishing effects it has on Rodolfo, is not 'miraculous', or even particularly religious. It is a contrivance of artifice and virtue. Leocadia's marriage to Rodolfo is not a miracle in the sense that critics generally explain it. It is based upon a series of rational, virtuous and cunning choices on the part of Rodolfo's mother to manoeuvre her son into the psychological frame of mind that he would willingly accept marriage to Leocadia to avoid marriage to 'la misma fealdad' (ugliness itself). As he says to himself during the meal, 'Si la mitad de esta hermosura tuviera la que mi madre me tiene escogida por esposa, tuviérame yo por el más dichoso hombre del mundo' (II, p. 122) ('If the lady my mother has chosen for me to marry had even half of this beauty, I should think myself the happiest man on earth' [II, p. 123]).[25] The Blessed Virgin's marriage to Saint Joseph was brought about by the mediation of an angel; here, Rodolfo's appreciation of Leocadia is that she is 'algún ángel humano' (II, p. 122) ('some human angel' [II, p. 123]) – but he desires to do with Leocadia what one may not do with angels. As Robbins notes (p. 94), the appearance of Leocadia in a manner that recalls Marian iconography is, in part, a parody of contemporary aesthetic theory: Rodolfo is led towards greater sensual arousal rather than, as the theory posited, awareness of the spiritual dimension of things.

The resolution of the scene is provided by Leocadia's fainting. It had all become too much for her, both the memories of the past and the dazzling possibilities of the present. She swoons and Rodolfo rushes to her aid, faints himself, comes to, and doña Estefanía feigns that she has changed her mind about making him marry the woman whose portrait she had shown him, and will allow him to marry Leocadia, whom he accepts as his wife. With its evocation of the wedding night and its reference to the numerous offspring with which the two were blessed the narrative ends with its focus firmly upon the sexual and familial satisfactions of Rodolfo and Leocadia.

Leocadia ceases to be anomalous, a virgin who has given birth; is returned to normality, to normal sexual intercourse; and is given an honourable marriage. Luisico is retrospectively legitimized and Rodolfo makes amends for his crime by making an honest woman of Leocadia. He also avoids (or rather his mother engineers that he avoids) a charge of violent rape, for which there was no limit

24 Mark Amsler, 'Rape and Silence: Ovid's Mythography and Medieval Readers', in *Representing Rape in Medieval and Early Modern Literature*, ed. Elizabeth Robertson and Christine M. Rose, The New Middle Ages (Palgrave: New York, 2001), pp. 61–96, (pp. 72–3 [Proserpina], p. 80 [Daphne]).

25 Perhaps a glance at the common recommendation in contemporary guides to marriage that the proposed bride should be of 'mediana formosura' (middling beauty). See Maria de Lurdes Correia Fernandes, *Espelhos, Cartas e Guias: Casamento e Espiritualidade na Península Ibérica 1450–1700* (Oporto: Instituto de Cultura Portuguesa, 1995), p. 95.

on the life of the action in an ecclesiastical court.[26] Marriage to the victim essentially voided the charge of rape, as Leocadia admits, when recalling her own rape as a *felix culpa* now that she is to marry Rodolfo: 'Yo lo doy por bien empleado' (II, p. 126) ('I consider it well done' [II, p. 127]).[27] Critics seem united in considering Leocadia to have been rewarded for her virtue, but given her situation, there was little else that she could have done, other than throwing herself down a well. Forcione (pp. 374–77) sees her being in love with Rodolfo as miraculous, but it is not: she had been promised him by his mother, and had been treated as a daughter of the family during the three weeks that Rodolfo took to return from Italy. Her marriage would bring her honour, would legitimize her son and would allow her own family to escape their genteel poverty and keep up a position which conformed to their own nobility; their poverty, Leocadia was fully aware, had given occasion to the rape, since, on the evil night, had her family been rich she would have returned home ensconced in a carriage, not on foot. It would take a heart of stone not to love someone who could offer such advantages, although Cervantes does point to contrary feelings, the emotional turmoil of which brings on her fainting fit. Yet she still chooses freely to marry Rodolfo, even though she is again constrained by his arms as she awakes from her swoon in what is a carefully contrived symbolic replay of the initial rape. She is again in the power of her rapist, although her consent is freely given, a contrast made more acute for contemporary readers since the Council of Trent had insisted that no marriage could take place between rapist and victim unless the latter was removed from

[26] Henricus Cardinalis Hostiensis, *Summa aurea. Interiectae recèns fuêre eruditae ex Summa F. Martini Abbatis, I.V.D. celeberrimum, Azonis et Accursius (ut ferunt) coaetanei adnotationes, et hae cum antiquis Nicol. Superantij in finem cuiuslibet §. reiectae* (Lyons, 1568), V: *De adulteriis, stupro et aliis criminibus ad incontinentiam pertinentibus et de nocturna pollutione*, §10, fol. 364rB, 'Et certè intra quinquennium admittitur accusatio; quando vi commissum est stuprum si autem per vim sit oppressus masculus vel foemina sine praefinitione' (And the accusation [of rape] is to be heard certainly within five years; when the rape is committed with force, if either a male or female is oppressed by force, there is no limit).

[27] Roman law prohibited the marriage between *rapta* and *raptor* (Brundage, 'Rape and Seduction', p. 146). Twelfth-century canonists sometimes distinguished between elopements (in which the girl connived in her abduction and subsequent defloration), after which they would allow subsequent marriage; and sexual ravishment, after which there was no possibility of subsequent marriage; this distinction was swept away by Innocent III: Jean Dauvillier, *Le Mariage dans le droit classique de l'Église depuis de Décret de Gratien (1140) jusqu'à la mort de Clément V (1314)* (Paris: Recueil Sirey, 1933), pp. 160–61. The civil punishment for *raptus* varied between execution, servitude or consignment to the galleys, imprisonment, fines, whipping, and infamy (Nicasius de Voerda Macliniensis, *Ennarationes in quatuor libros Institutionum imperialium, iam recens fidelius ac exactius, quam vsquam antea castigatae* [Venice: Pietro Dehucini, 1584], fol. 455r; Thomas Traugott, *Problema iuris matrimonialis an iuramentum reo de stupro delatum acceptatum et adiudicatum a consistorio suppletorium mutari possit si actix ante eius praestationem stuprum semiplene probet?* [Leipzig: Langenhemiana, 1746], p. 20; Torre and Balsarini, p. 38]. The *Partidas* (III.20, §7) prescribed the death penalty and the transfer of the offender's property to the victim (Sánchez, VII.12, §20, vol. II, p. 41B). Before Trent, canon law stipulated that no punishment should be enacted if a marriage took place (Sánchez, VII.12, §16, vol. II, p. 40B).

her assailant's power. However, canonists such as Sánchez (VII.12, §42; VII.13, §§1–6, vol. II, pp. 46A–49A) dismissed that stipulation, arguing that the woman's free consent was what alone mattered.[28] Cervantes, in the very ending of the *novela*, focuses upon a hotly debated topic within marriage legislation.

The belief that *La fuerza* is essentially a miracle tale has led at least one critic to claim we should simply ignore Rodolfo.[29] He is, it must be said, deeply unpleasant. He undergoes no repentance, he is not even reproved sternly for what he has done, his priority in a wife is her looks. His only thought, once married, is to get Leocadia into bed. He shows no sign of grief for his crime, and Leocadia even removes the need for him to apologize. Yet Rodolfo's character is consistent. He marries Leocadia because, essentially, he is seduced. His own hypersensual nature and his worries about his impending marriage to a woman who is no oil painting push him towards the beautiful Leocadia, just as his mother intends. His consent seems free, but it is as constrained as Leocadia's. The rape that began the story involved physical violence; it was naked sexual intercourse, deprived of anything else to clothe it, certainly deprived of love and affection, but deprived even of opposition to the intercourse, even of the sight of the two bodies involved (the room is completely dark), and of everything but the barest narration.

The seduction of Rodolfo, in contrast, is carried out through images and appearances: the false portrait, Leocadia's theatrical entrance. But these merely echo the role-playing and pretending that go on throughout the story. The name Rodolfo (not his real name), his mask, his speaking to Leocadia in a mixture of Spanish and Portuguese when he dumps her after the rape; the fiction that Leocadia's family creates to explain Luisico's existence.[30] Even the good have need of simulation.[31] Indeed, in *La fuerza*, the faints are almost the only thing not feigned. But seduction, in the canonical sense of the corruption of the will

28 Cervantes's interest in internal constraint and free will has been pointed out in relation to the *Persiles* by Theresa Ann Sears, 'Sacrificial Lambs and Domestic Goddesses, or, Did Cervantes Write Chick Lit? (Being a Meditation on Women and Free Will)', *Cervantes*, 20:1 (2000), 47–68; seventeenth-century canon law recognized only 'metus reverentiae' (the fear born of reverence) towards an excessively bad-tempered and grudging parent or tutor as a reason for annulling a marriage on the grounds of what would now be considered internal constraint (Sánchez, IV.6, §8, vol. I, p. 374B), although modern canon law has developed this area in great detail: see Angelo D'Auria, *Il difetto di libertà interna nel consenso matrimoniale come motivo di incapacità per mancanza di discrezione di giudizio*, Pontificia Universitas Lateranensis, Theses ad Doctoratum in Utrioque Iure (Rome: Pontificia Università Lateranense, 1995).

29 R. M. Price, 'The Force of Blood: Introduction', in *Exemplary Novels*, II, pp. 99–101 (p. 100).

30 Cervantes explores the difference between appearance and reality in the deception over the child's origins – 'El niño abrazaba a su madre por su prima y a su abuela por su bienhechora'(II, p. 118) ('The child embraced his mother, as his cousin, and his grandmother because she had been good to him' [II, p. 119]) – just at the moment when it is revealed who Luisico actually is.

31 A process in the *Novelas* recognized by don Álvaro Antonio Enríquez de Almansa y Borja, seventh Marqués de Alcañices (d. 1643), in his sonnet in praise of the book: 'con el arte quiso | vuestro ingenio sacar de la mentira | la verdad' (Miguel de Cervantes, *Novelas*

through promises (rather than threats), was linked to rape. Medieval illustrations of Gratian usually chose to illustrate scenes of seduction rather than the rape described at Causa 36, to draw attention to the similarity between them.[32] Leocadia's rape, then, is mirrored at the end. Rodolfo is again overcome with passion, but the conniving of the women turns it towards a socially respectable end: immediate marriage. The first half of the story features the actions and decisions of men (Rodolfo's rape of Leocadia, her father's decision that she cannot pursue her plan to track down the rapist, Rodolfo's father's decision to take Luis home). The second half of the story involves the decisions of women. Social form is preserved or (re-) established by women who manipulate appearances, who create fictions which manipulate, which seduce, and, with Leocadia, who is also seduced.[33] *La fuerza de la sangre*, then, is a *tour de force*; yet it is anything but a miracle story. It uses the concept of Providence, certainly, as its basic causational structure. Nevertheless, as in life, the action of grace must be guessed at behind the scenes; it is not made visible. In any case, the basic structure of a miracle tale is violated at the very outset: 'In hagiography, no rape is ever completed. [. . .] The wicked seducers are always thwarted and punished, the faithful protected and rewarded.'[34] Cervantes's story works by different rules. And at bottom, it is about the power and triumph of fiction.

Yet what of its moral message? Leocadia's father at first expects justice, a judge, to right the wrong his daughter has suffered, and instructs her to commend herself to the crucifix to gain this justification. The silver of the crucifix points towards the fifty silver coins a rapist is instructed to pay to his victim's father in

ejemplares, ed. Harry Sieber, 2 vols, Letras Hispánicas 105–6 (Madrid: Cátedra, 1992–94), (I, pp. 54–55) (your wit has managed to take truth out of lies through art).

32 See Diane Wolfthal, *Images of Rape: The 'Heroic' Tradition and its Alternatives* (Cambridge: Cambridge University Press, 1999), pp. 108–10, although she confuses seduction with 'consensual lovemaking', thus misunderstanding the purpose of the illustrations which were intended to impress upon clerics the severity of the crime of seduction, later considered to be worse than rape since in seduction both body and mind were corrupted, in rape only the body (Torre and Balsarini, p. 34). Sánchez recorded the opinion of some canonists who equated strong and importunate persuasion with force, but counselled caution in the application of the heavy penalties for *raptus* in such cases (VII.12, §10, vol. II, p. 39B).

33 Jean Baudrillard, *De La Séduction*, Bibliothèque Médiations (Paris: Éditions Galilée, 1979), p. 36: 'La loi de la séduction est d'abord celle d'un échange rituel ininterrompu, d'une surenchère où les jeux ne sont jamais faits, de qui séduit et de qui est séduit, pour la raison que la ligne de partage qui définirait la victoire de l'un, la défaite de l'autre, est illisible – et qu'il n'y a pas de limite à ce défi à l'autre d'être plus séduit encore, ou d'aimer plus que je l'aime, sinon la mort' (The law of seduction is, in the first place, that of an uninterrupted ritual exchange, of a process of raising the stakes in which the bidding is never closed, between the one who seduces and the one seduced, because of the fact that the dividing line that would define the victory of one, and the defeat of the other, is always indecipherable – and because there is no limit to this challenge to the other to be even more seduced, or to love more than I love, except that of death [editor's translation]).The seduction is carried on into the sexually-productive marriage, whose basic component is the refusal to allow a withdrawal from this 'jeu' (game).

34 Kathryn Gravdal, *Ravishing Maidens: Writing Rape in Medieval French Literature and Law,* New Cultural Studies 4 (Philadelphia: University of Pennsylvania Press, 1991), p. 24.

Deuteronomy 22: 28–29 – the number commented upon by Ambrose as signifying 'vice being turned into grace', and it is *gracia* (mercy, forgiveness) which the Alfonsine *Partidas* use to explain the motivation of a woman who chooses to marry her rapist.[35] Yet the crucifix is also a reminder of the saving death of Christ, who died for sinners, not for the just. Indeed, justice for Leocadia is only achievable through the lack of justice meted out to Rodolfo. Contemporary legal commentarists had begun to consider the law that allowed a rapist to escape punishment by marrying his victim as unjust and as being itself an incitement to sin (Sánchez, VII.12, §16, vol II, p. 40B). Yet Rodolfo's punishment would serve nothing, and would be highly detrimental to Leocadia. The wheat and the tares must grow together (Matthew 13: 24–30). The moral, then, is a Christian one: do not judge (Matthew 7: 1; cf. I Corinthians 4: 5). The mother who has a child out of wedlock (and therefore must be dishonoured and dishonourable) may well be guiltless and thus a type of the Blessed Virgin. Yet the means by which justice is achieved for her may not be recognisably 'holy'. Justice may involve a (perhaps allowable) deception, but it may also require that the guilty get off scot-free, without even saying sorry: the marriage between rapist and victim did not require any repentance or penance for it to be valid (Sánchez, VII.12, §42, vol. II, p. 38B). Human law and human expectations of justice are both transgressed and transcended by forgiveness.[36] The power of the blood which Luisico's grandfather saw spilt on the ground ('la fuerza de la sangre que vio derramada en el suelo el [. . .] abuelo de Luisico' [II, p. 126]) ('the power of the blood which the [. . .] grandfather of Luis saw spilled on the ground' [II, p. 127]) does not cry out for

[35] Ambrosius Mediolanensis, *Apologia David*, §42, in *Ambroise de Milan: Apologie de David. Introduction, texte latin, notes et index*, ed. Pierre Hadot, tr. Marius Cordier, Sources Chrétiennes 239 (Paris: Le Cerf, 1977), p. 126, l. 21 'hoc ergo numero etiam uitia uertuntur in gratiam *Gracia: Siete Partidas*, III.20, §7, cited by Sánchez, VII.12, §27, vol. II, p. 43B. The stipulation of Deuteronomy is the following:

> Si invenerit vir puellam virginem, quae non habet sponsum, et apprehendens concubuerit cum illa, et res ad iudicium venerit: dabit qui dormivit cum ea, patri puellae quinquaginta siclos argenti, et habebit eam uxorem, quia humiliavit illam: non poeterit dimittere eam cunctis diebus vitae suae. (*Biblia sacra iuxta Vulgatam Clementinam nova editio*, ed. Albertus Colunga, OP, and Laurentius Turrado, Biblioteca de Autores Cristianos, 14 [Madrid: BAC, 1994], p. 160B)
>
> (If a man meets a virgin who is not engaged and, seizing her, lies with her, and the matter should come to court, he who slept with her shall give fifty silver shekels to the girl's father, and he shall have her as his wife, because he humiliated her, he shall not be able to divorce her all the days of his life.)

[36] See Sánchez, VII.12, §27, vol. II, p. 44B, where he notes that 'supponi esse delictum stante valore legis humane. Atque ita ait: *Mulier humanam legem trangrediens [raptorum nuptias eligens]*. Ea tamen iure canonico correcta, cessat delictum' (it is to be supposed that the crime [of *raptus*] stands as far as human law is operative, and so it is said, 'A woman transgressing human law in marrying her rapist'. However, the crime ceases when human law is corrected by canon law).

vengeance, as Abel's did after Cain murdered him (Genesis 4: 10). Instead, it moved a man both 'ilustre y cristiano' (II, p. 126) ('noble and Christian' [II, p. 127]) to an act of mercy, a virtuous response which would also undo his fault in allowing his son too much liberty in the first place. The rape (*fuerza*) and Rodolfo's noble blood (*sangre*) are united in the Christ-like child, Luisico, who will be the engine of redemption.

Cervantes, in his introduction to the *Novelas ejemplares*, was outright in his admission of the moral worthiness of his labours. The censor, an affable Thomist, considered that the *novelas* 'enseñan con sus ejemplos a huir vicios y seguir virtudes' (Sieber [ed.], I, p. 45) ('teach us by their example to flee vice and follow virtue'), an ethics of reading which is amply attested in the medieval Christian interpretation of Ovid's *Metamorphoses* (Amsler, p. 65), which provided a system of interpretation that did not consider the representation of sin as being necessarily an incitement to sin. It is in the light of this tradition, which demanded that readers be both sophisticated and subtle, that Cervantes's claims of morality should be seen. It is nevertheless depressing how often critics take Cervantes, master of irony and paradoxical statement, at his (seeming) word in discussing the key passage that assures us of the benign intention behind these stories. For Forcione, for example, the prologue is a 'closed, conventional discourse', made up of 'emphatically doctrinaire pronouncements' (Forcione, p. 4). The topic, however, was anything but conventional. In the middle of his prologue to the reader, Cervantes lets fly with a straightforward attack, echoing the most prevalent criticism of hypersensitive and easily offended moralists concerned to limit in the extreme the types of behaviour represented in fiction and stage: 'Sí, que no siempre se está en los templos; no siempre se ocupan los oratorios; no siempre se asiste a los negocios, por calificados que sean. Horas hay de recreación, donde el afligido espíritu descanse' (I, p. 4) ('After all, we cannot always be in church; the oratories are not always occupied; we cannot always be doing business, no matter how important it is. There is time for recreation, when the tormented spirit can rest' [I, p. 5]). Yet Cervantes goes even further, with a deliberate parody of the purity of intention and of subject-matter that such moralists were starting to insist upon ever more ferociously, considering the depiction of sin to be in itself sinful and offering sinful encouragement to those who read or watched it.[37]

> Una cosa me atreveré a decirte, que si por algún modo alcanzara que la lección destas novelas pudiera inducir a quien leyera a algún mal deseo o pensamiento, antes me cortara la mano, que sacarlas en público. Mi edad no está ya para burlarse con la otra vida, que al cincuenta y cinco de los años gano por nueve más y por la mano. (I, p. 4)
>
> (One thing will I dare to say to you, that if by any way it should fall out that the reading of these *novelle* might lead whoever should read them to some

[37] See the material assembled by Thomas Austin O'Connor, *Love in the 'Corral': Conjugal Spirituality and Anti-Theatrical Polemic in Early Modern Spain*, Ibérica 31 (New York: Peter Lang, 2000), especially pp. 60, 70 and 194.

> ill desire or thought, I would rather cut off my hand than bring them out in public. My age will no longer allow me to bite my thumb at the other life, for I will get ahead of myself if I even reach sixty-four, nine years hence.)[38]

For Ife,

> Cervantes was offering his readership a new, more respectable and worthwhile form of narrative which, contrary to their expectations, would not shock or offend them. And he backed up this assertion by saying that he would rather cut off the hand with which he wrote than have anyone come to harm from reading them; no idle promise, in view of what he has just told us about having lost his other hand in battle.[39]

This passage should perhaps be read in the light of Cervantes's own judgement on the *Novelas ejemplares*, given in the *Viaje del Parnaso*, that they showed how to 'mostrar con propiedad un desatino' (set forth an absurdity with due concern to form).[40] Were Cervantes really to decide to cut his hand off – considering he had lost the other in battle for the Faith against the Turk – how would he do it? Holding the knife between his teeth, or with spectacularly prehensile toes? Indeed, he says he does not intend to take chances with his salvation, but that is what he would be doing: self-mutilation in canon law was akin to murder, a gross and serious mortal sin, which performed by a cleric on himself would cause his demotion; which Hostiensis (perhaps the greatest of the thirteenth-century decretalists) described as an example of tyranny; and which Sánchez defined as simply unnatural, 'quae nullo modo manum ad eum usum concessit' (because in no way is the hand given for such a use).[41] Second, Cervantes mixes two evangelical precepts:

> Et quisquis scandalizaverit unum ex his pusillis credentibus in me: bonum est ei magis si circumdaretur mola asinaria collo eius, et in mare mitteretur. Et si

38 An alternative translation of the last sentence would be: 'My age is not one which can afford to make fun of the next life, for to my fifty-five years I have to add the equivalent of another nine, and some more for my hand.'

39 B. W. Ife, 'General Introduction', *Exemplary Novels / Novelas ejemplares*, ed. B. W. Ife, 4 vols (Warminster: Aris & Phillips, 1992), II, pp. vii–xvi (p. xi). Other straightforward readings: Aubrey F. G. Bell, *Cervantes* (New York: Collier, 1961), p. 155; Ruth El Saffar, *Cervantes: 'El casamiento engañoso' and 'El coloquio de los perros'*, Critical Guides to Spanish Texts 17 (London: Grant & Cutler-Tamesis, 1976), p. 10. Juan Bautista de Avalle-Arce, in his introduction to the edition of the *Novelas ejemplares*, Clásicos Castalia 120–23, 3 vols (Madrid: Castalia, 1982), I, pp. 120–22, at least realized that it was supposed to be funny: 'Y no hay que desatender la regocijada ironía encerrada en la risueña amenaza "antes me cortara la mano". ¡Bien hubiese quedado la historia de la literatura española!' (p. 16) (And there is no reason to avoid paying attention to the merry irony enclosed by the playful threat, 'I'd rather cut off my hand' – that would have worked out well for the history of Spanish literature!).

40 Miguel de Cervantes Saavedra, *Viaje al Parnaso*, ed. Vicente Gaos, Clásicos Castalia 57 (Madrid: Castalia, 1973), IV, 27 (p. 103).

41 Raymund of Penyafort, *Summa*, II.1: *De homicidio*, §7, p. 46A; Hostiensis, *Summa aurea*, I: *De corpore vitiatis ordinandis, uel non*, §4, fol. 56rB; Sánchez, VII.13, §5, vol. II, p. 52B.

> scandalizaverit te manus tua, abscide illam: bonum est tibi debilem introire in vitam, quam duas manus habentem ire in gehennam, in ignem inextinguibilem.[42]
>
> (If any of you put a stumbling block before one of these little ones who believe in me, it would be better for you if a great millstone were hung around your neck and you were thrown into the sea. If your hand causes you to stumble, cut it off; it is better for you to enter life maimed than to have two hands and go to hell, to the unquenchable fire.)[43]

Here Jesus does not say that self-mutilation was what one should do if one led *others* into sin.

The form of Cervantes's declaration makes it look as though he was sincere in adopting an impossible puritanism; the content, however, shows that he was parodying it, drawing the reader who was prepared to pay attention back into an earlier, more robust and more wholesome tradition. The 'virtuous' ending of *La fuerza de la sangre* shows precisely the limits of any world-view which insisted upon total purity of intention and response, a world-view at once inhuman and profoundly unchristian. Rodolfo remains unchanged. That is his character. But since that *is* his character, he must be manipulated through his own sensual and ungodly reactions into a socially acceptable expression of sexual desire. His reaction to Leocadia's appearance as the Blessed Virgin Mary is not to be struck with wonder and repentance, but to be overwhelmed with concupiscence. He is shallow, as Robbins notes (p. 95). But then, many human beings are. A view of salvation or even simple political economy must take them into account as well. Pious and prudish readers' desires to witness the reward for patient virtue and to see the fulfilment of the biblical injunction that a woman should marry her rapist demand that they accept the near-blasphemy of a virgin birth and that the iconography of the Blessed Virgin Mary be evoked in a scene of highly-charged eroticism, because these lead to the 'right' ending. The happiness and prolific fecundity of the marriage is in part an endorsement of Rodolfo's seeking marriage for sensual pleasure rather than virtue – quite contrary to what serious moralists were advising (Correia Fernandes, p. 262 and pp. 273–76). If God can draw good out of evil, so an author can imagine it. But beautiful, irreproachable, innocent goodness, like Leocadia heading homewards from the river, can give rise to evil, and heaven may permit that evil to occur.[44] No aesthetic theory can guard against malice and nature combined; and, as Robbins shows, aesthetic theory in Leocadia's and doña Estefanía's case can be turned inside out, and a representation which (in another context) should inflame the soul inflames the passions

42 Mark 9: 41–3 (cf. Matthew 5: 29–30 and 18: 6–9; Luke 17: 1–2); *Biblia sacra*, ed. Colunga and Turrado, p. 1001B.

43 *The Holy Bible. New Revised Standard Version: Catholic Edition* (London: Geoffrey Chapman, 1989), p. 45B.

44 Paul Lewis-Smith, 'Fictionalizing God: Providence, Nature, and the Significance of Rape in *La Fuerza de la sangre*', *MLR*, 91 (1996), 886–97 (p. 887).

instead. To continue the allusion to the biblical passage where Cervantes left off: 'Quod si oculus tuus scandalizat te, eiice eum' ('and if your eye causes you to stumble, pluck it out'). Readers, like writers, have a responsibility to themselves.[45]

Works cited

Ambrosius Mediolanensis, *Apologia David*, in *Ambroise de Milan: Apologie de David. Introduction, texte latin, notes et index*, ed. Pierre Hadot, tr. Marius Cordier, Sources Chrétiennes 239 (Paris: Le Cerf, 1977).

Amir, Menachim, *Patterns of Forcible Rape* (Chicago: University of Chicago Press, 1971).

del Amo, León, *Sentencias, casos y cuestiones en la rota española* (Pamplona: Universidad de Navarra, 1977).

Amsler, Mark, 'Rape and Silence: Ovid's Mythography and Medieval Readers', in *Representing Rape in Medieval and Early Modern Literature*, ed. Elizabeth Robertson and Christine M. Rose, The New Middle Ages (Palgrave: New York, 2001), pp. 61–96.

Aurelius Augustinus, *De civitate dei*, ed. Bernardus Dombart and Alphonsus Kalb, 2 vols, Corpus Christianorum Series Latina 47–8 (Turnhout: Brepols, 1955).

———, *The City of God against the Pagans*, tr. R. W. Dyson, Cambridge Texts in the History of Political Thought (Cambridge: Cambridge University Press, 1998).

Barbaree, Howard E., and Ralph C. Serin, 'Role of Male Sexual Arousal during Rape in Various Rapist Subtypes', in *Sexual Aggression: Issues in Etiology, Assessment and Treatment*, ed. Gordon C. Nagayama Hall and others (Washington, DC: Vermont & Taylor, 1993), pp. 99–114.

Baudrillard, Jean, *De La Séduction*, Bibliothèque Médiations (Paris: Éditions Galilée, 1979).

Bell, Aubrey F. G., *Cervantes* (New York: Collier, 1961).

Biblia sacra iuxta Vulgatam Clementinam nova editio, ed. Albertus Colunga, OP, and Laurentius Turrado, Biblioteca de Autores Cristianos 14 (Madrid: BAC, 1994).

Breitenberg, Mark, *Anxious Masculinity in Early Modern England*, Cambridge Studies in Renaissance Literature and Culture 10 (Cambridge: Cambridge University Press, 1996).

Brundage, James A., *Law, Sex, and Christian Society in Medieval Europe* (Chicago: University of Chicago Press, 1987).

———, 'Rape and Seduction in the Medieval Canon Law', in *Sexual Practices in the Medieval Church*, ed. Vern L. Bullough and James Brundage (Buffalo, NY: Prometheus, 1982), pp. 141–60.

Bryson, Norman, 'Two Narratives of Rape in the Visual Arts: Lucretia and the Sabine Women', in *Rape: An Historical and Social Enquiry*, ed. Sylvana Tomaselli and Roy Porter (Oxford: Basil Blackwell, 1986), pp. 152–73.

[45] My thanks are due to all those who have sought that I should avoid scandal, or at least stumbling, through their comments on this piece: Jon Beasley-Murray, Esther Gómez Sierra, Alistair Malcolm, Joseph Munitiz SJ, Rebeca Sanmartín Bastida, Patience Schell, Alistair Watson. I dedicate the article to Rees Price.

Carter, John Marshall, *Rape in Medieval England: An Historical and Sociological Study* (Lanham, MD: University Press of America, 1985).

Casalduero, Joaquín, *Sentido y forma de las 'Novelas ejemplares', Revista de Filología Hispánica* Anejo 1 (Buenos Aires: Facultad de Filosofía y Letras de la Universidad de Buenos Aires, Instituto de Filología, 1943).

Cervantes Saavedra, Miguel de, *Viaje del Parnaso*, ed. Vicente Gaos, Clásicos Castalia 57 (Madrid: Castalia, 1973).

———, *Novelas ejemplares*, ed. Juan Bautista de Avalle-Arce, Clásicos Castalia 120–123, 3 vols (Madrid: Castalia, 1982).

———, *Novelas ejemplares*, ed. Harry Sieber, 2 vols, Letras Hispánicas 105–6 (Madrid: Cátedra, 1992–94).

———, *Exemplary Novels / Novelas ejemplares*, ed. B. W. Ife, 4 vols (Warminster: Aris & Phillips, 1992).

Correia Fernandes, Maria de Lurdes, *Espelhos, Cartas e Guias: Casamento e Espiritualidade na Península Ibérica 1450–1700* (Oporto: Instituto de Cultura Portuguesa, 1995).

D'Auria, Angelo, *Il difetto di libertà interna nel consenso matrimoniale come motivo di incapacità per mancanza di discrezione di giudizio*, Pontificia Universitas Lateranensis, Theses ad Doctoratum in Utrioque Iure (Rome: Pontificia Università Lateranense, 1995).

Dauvillier, Jean, *Le Mariage dans le droit classique de l'Église depuis le Décret de Gratien (1140) jusqu'à la mort de Clément V (1314)* (Paris: Recueil Sirey, 1933).

Diccionario de autoridades (Madrid, 1732).

El Saffar, Ruth, *Cervantes: 'El casamiento engañoso' and 'El coloquio de los perros'*, Critical Guides to Spanish Texts 17 (London: Grant & Cutler-Támesis, 1976).

Ellis, Lee, 'Rape as biosocial phenomenon', in *Sexual Agression: Issues in Etiology, Assessment and Treatment*, ed. Gordon C. Nagayama Hall and others (Washington DC: Vermont & Taylor, 1993), pp. 17–41.

Fagnani, Prospero, *Commentaria in quinque libros decretalium*, 8 vols (Rome: Iacobi Fei And. F., 1661).

Forcione, Alban K., *Cervantes and the Humanist Vision: A Study of Four 'Exemplary Novels'* (Princeton, NJ: Princeton University Press, 1982).

Forrester, John, 'Rape, Seduction and Psychoanalysis', in *Rape: An Historical and Social Enquiry*, ed. Sylvana Tomaselli and Roy Porter (Oxford: Basil Blackwell, 1986), pp. 57–83.

Gibbens, T. C. N., and Joyce Prince, *Child Victims of Sex Offences* (London: ISTD, 1963).

Gravdal, Kathryn, *Ravishing Maidens: Writing Rape in Medieval French Literature and Law,* New Cultural Studies 4 (Philadelphia: University of Pennsylvania Press, 1991).

Henricus Cardinalis Hostiensis, *Summa aurea. Interiectae recèns fuêre eruditae ex Summa F. Martini Abbatis, I.V.D. celeberrimum, Azonis et Accursius (ut ferunt) coaetanei adnotationes, et hae cum antiquis Nicol. Superantij in finem cuiuslibet §. reiectae* (Lyons, 1568).

Hervada Xiberta, Francisco Javier, *La impotencia del varón en el derecho matrimonial canónico*, Publicaciones del Estudio General de Navarra 20, Colección Canónica del Estudio General de Navarra 1 (Pamplona: Estudio General de Navarra, 1959).

The Holy Bible. New Revised Standard Version: Catholic Edition (London: Geoffrey Chapman, 1989).

Ife, B. W., 'General Introduction', in Miguel de Cervantes Saavedra, *Exemplary Novels / Novelas ejemplares*, ed. B. W. Ife, 4 vols (Warminster: Aris & Phillips, 1992), I, pp. v–xiv.

Islam, M. N., and M. N. Islam, 'Retrospective study of alleged rape victims', *Legal Medicine*, 5 (2003): S351–53.

Jed, Stephanie H., *Chaste Thinking: the Rape of Lucretia and the Birth of Humanism*, Theories of Representation and Difference (Bloomington-Indianapolis: Indiana University Press, 1989).

Katz, Sedelle, and Mary Ann Mazur, *Understanding the Rape Victim: A Synthesis of Research Findings* (New York: John Wiley and Sons, 1979).

Krueger, M. M., 'Pregnancy as a Result of Rape', *Journal of Sex Education and Therapy*, 14 (1988), 23–7.

Lewis-Smith, Paul, 'Fictionalizing God: Providence, Nature, and the Significance of Rape in *La fuerza de la sangre*', *MLR*, 91 (1996), 886–97.

Macdonald, John M., *Rape: Offenders and their Victims* (Springfield, IL: Thomas, 1971).

Müller, Wolfgang P., 'Lucretia and the Medieval Canonists', *Bulletin of Medieval Canon Law*, 19 (1989), 13–32.

O'Connor, Thomas Austin, *Love in the 'Corral': Conjugal Spirituality and Anti-Theatrical Polemic in Early Modern Spain*, Ibérica 31 (New York: Peter Lang, 2000).

Porter, Roy, 'Rape – Does it have a Historical Meaning?', in *Rape: An Historical and Social Enquiry*, ed Sylvana Tomaselli and Roy Porter (Oxford: Basil Blackwell, 1986), pp. 216–36.

Price, R. M., 'The Force of Blood: Introduction', in Miguel de Cervantes Saavedra, *Exemplary Novels / Novelas ejemplares*, ed. B. W. Ife, 4 vols (Warminster: Aris and Phillips, 1992), II, pp. 99–101.

Publius Ovidius Naso, *Ars amatoria*, ed. A. S. Hollis (Oxford: Clarendon, 1977).

———, *The Art of Love and Other Poems*, tr. J. H. Mozley and G. P. Goold, Loeb Classical Library 232, 2nd edn (Cambridge, MA: Harvard University Press, 1979), pp. 13–175.

Raymund of Penyafort, *Summa*, ed. Honoratus Vincentius (Verona: Augustus Carattonius, 1744).

Robbins, Jeremy, *The Challenges of Uncertainty: An Introduction to Seventeenth-Century Spanish Literature*, New Readings: Introductions to European Literature and Culture 2 (London: Duckworth, 1998).

Rufinus, *Summa Decretorum*, in *Die Summa Decretorum des Magister Rufinus*, ed. Heinrich Singer (Paderborn: Ferdinand Schöningh, 1902).

Sánchez, Tomás, SJ, *Disputationum de sancto matrimonii sacramento libri decem in tres tomos distributi*, 3 vols (Venice: Ioannes Antonii and Iacopo de Francisci, 1607).

Sears, Theresa Ann, 'Sacrificial Lambs and Domestic Goddesses, or, Did Cervantes Write Chick Lit? (Being a Meditation on Women and Free Will)', *Cervantes*, 20:1 (2000), 47–68.

Soares, Emanuel Laurentius, *Compendium tractatus de S. Matrimonii* (Seville: de Lyra, 1623; Venice: Fontana, 1625).

Thomas Aquinas, *Summa theologiae: Divi Thomae Aquinatis Ordinis Praedicatorum, Doctoris Angelici a Leone XIII P. M. gloriose regnante Catholicarum scholarum patroni Coelestis renunciati Summa theologica editio altera romana ad emendatiores editiones impressa et noviter accuratissime recognita*, 4 vols (Rome: Forzani et Sodales, 1922).

Torre, Marcus, and Jacobus Balsarini, *De poena stupri cum puella immatura. Disertatio Marci Torre, patritii Veronensis et Jacobi Balsarini, patritii Methonensis. Accedit elucubratio anatomica desumpta ex operibus D. Cajetani Petrioli Romani, S. R. M. Regis Sardiniae &c. &c. &c. chirugiae professoris, una cum tabula aere incisa, et ad calcem impressa* (Rome: Generosus Salamoni, 1754).

Traugott, Thomas, *Problema iuris matrimonialis an iuramentum reo de stupro delatum acceptatum et adiudicatum a consistorio suppletorium mutari possit si actix ante eius praestationem stuprum semiplene probet?* (Leipzig: Langenhemiana, 1746).

de Voerda Macliniensis, Nicasius, *Ennarationes in quatuor libros Institutionum imperialium, iam recens fidelius ac exactius, quam vsquam antea castigatae* (Venice: Pietro Dehucini, 1584).

Wilson, Paul R., *The Other Side of Rape* (St Lucia, Queensland: University of Queensland Press, 1978).

Wolfthal, Diane, *Images of Rape: the 'Heroic' Tradition and its Alternatives* (Cambridge: Cambridge University Press, 1999).

8

Remorse, Retribution and Redemption in *La fuerza de la sangre*: Spanish and English Perspectives

B. W. Ife and Trudi L. Darby
King's College London

In the Prologue to the *Novelas ejemplares*, Cervantes famously offered an astonishing guarantee of the high moral tone of the collection: he would rather cut off the one remaining hand with which he wrote them than publish stories which could drive a reader to evil thoughts or desires.[1] Despite these protestations, Cervantes makes frequent use of plots which have their origin in acts of rape or abduction, and the *Novelas ejemplares* are notable for the amount of sexual violence they contain. Even so, *La fuerza de la sangre* (The Power of Blood) is exceptional in several ways: the opening rape scene is startlingly graphic; the rapist is shockingly brutal, callous and lacking in remorse; and the extraordinary *dénouement* poses some of the greatest interpretative challenges of any story in the collection.[2]

[1] '[. . .] que si por algún modo alcanzara que la lección destas novelas pudiera inducir a quien las leyera a algún mal deseo o pensamiento, antes me cortara la mano con que las escribí que sacarlas en público' ('[. . .] if by any chance it should happen that the reading of these novels might lead my readers into evil thoughts or desires, I would rather cut off the hand with which I wrote them than have them published'. Quotations from the text are from Miguel de Cervantes, *Exemplary Novels / Novelas ejemplares*, ed. B. W. Ife, 4 vols (Warminster: Aris & Phillips, 1992), I, pp. 4, 5.

[2] The earlier critical history of *La fuerza de la sangre* is conveniently summarized in Ruth S. El Saffar, *Novel to Romance: A Study of Cervantes's 'Novelas ejemplares'* (Baltimore: Johns Hopkins University Press, 1974), p. 128. R. P. Calcraft builds on El Saffar's approach, which sees the *novela* as an 'abstract combination of forces whose initial oppositions finally dissolve within a greater unity', in 'Structure, Symbol and Meaning in Cervantes's *La fuerza de la sangre*', *BHS,* 58 (1981), 197–204. Alban K. Forcione, in *Cervantes and the Humanist Vision* (Princeton NJ: Princeton University Press, 1982) develops an approach first used by J. J. Allen, '*El Cristo de la Vega* and *La fuerza de la sangre*', *MLN,* 83 (1968), 271–75, which emphasizes the parallels with the miracle narrative in general, and the life of St Leocadia, patron saint of Toledo, in particular. Both critics, however, lay stress on the way in which Cervantes, while using the forms and structures of the miracle narrative, 'secularizes' the miracle of *La fuerza de la sangre* by underlining the important role played by Leocadia's prudence and discretion. Paul Lewis-Smith, in 'Fictionalizing God: Providence, Nature, and the Significance of Rape in *La fuerza de la sangre*', *MLR*, 91 (1996), 886–97, builds further

In fact, there is nothing inherently contradictory in writing a story about a sex crime and using it to deliver a moral message. The conventional 'exemplarity' of the *novelas* is hardly ever manifested in the use of positive models to be imitated, and is more often found in negative examples to be avoided. But Cervantes's brand of exemplarity goes well beyond the conventional, and is most often realized through the way he presents examples, or 'working models', of human behaviour which raise issues that are rarely cut and dried and require the reader's active engagement to make sense of them. Rather than using fiction to teach, still less to preach, Cervantes's aim is to provoke. Readers of *La fuerza de la sangre* will find much to admire in its subtle artifice and invention, but their reading will not be complete unless they also find themselves mystified and outraged by what is going on in the story.

Cervantes

The clue to what makes Cervantes's fiction mysterious and provocative can be found in the gaps between what is conventional in his work and what is not. Some features of his work are so characteristic that they appear to be non-negotiable: that a suppressed truth must inevitably come to light, for example, or that a state of order, once disturbed, must be restored. But the pursuit of the 'happy ending' can be misleading if we are not responsive to the ways in which the plot architecture can be contradicted by narrative details which jag and jar. A conventional reading of *La gitanilla* (The Little Gipsy Girl), for example, will foreground the apparent inevitability in the chain of events at the end of the story:

> Juana Carducha's revenge against Andrés for spurning her offer of marriage leads to his arrest; in response to an insult he reverts to his social type, kills the insolent soldier and is brought before the *Corregidor* (chief magistrate); the *Corregidor*'s wife recognizes Preciosa as her long-lost stolen daughter, and Preciosa's gipsy *abuela* (grandmother) confirms the fact; Preciosa is revealed to be Constanza de Azevedo y de Meneses and is now free to marry Andrés, otherwise known as don Juan de Cárcamo.

But there is an alternative reading that is much more problematic:

> Andrés kills the insolent soldier and is brought before the *Corregidor*; the *Corregidor*'s wife fails to recognize Preciosa as her long-lost stolen daughter until the *abuela* puts two lots of evidence before her; the *Corregidor* leaves Andrés rotting in a dungeon long after he knows the true identity of the lovers,

on this work by showing how the *novela* illustrates the working out of divine providence through nature rather than through miracles. Adriana Slaniceanu, 'The Calculating Woman in Cervantes'*s La fuerza de la sangre*', *BHS*, 64 (1987), 101–10 and Marcia L. Welles, 'Violence Disguised: Representation of Rape in Cervantes' *La fuerza de la sangre*', *Journal of Hispanic Philology*, 13 (1989), 240–52 change the balance of emphasis away from the figural to the literal, focusing on the role of Leocadia and giving more direct attention to the implications of the violence done to her. The present essay continues this trend.

> tortures him by pretending that he is going to hang him once the two of them are married, and sends for a priest who refuses to marry them because the banns have not been read and there is no licence. Only then does the *Corregidor* let on that he knows who Preciosa and Andrés really are, and the marriage does not take place until several weeks later.

The fact that don Juan has absconded from home, and killed a soldier, is swept aside, as are the false witness of Juana Carducha and the old gipsy's thieving that started it all. Both readings are 'correct', that is, they are both consistent with the text. One foregrounds the plot structure; the other pays more attention to the detailed texture of the narrative. One results in a conventional happy ending; the other gets there eventually, but feels more like a chapter of accidents.[3]

Like *La gitanilla* and like many other *novelas* in the collection, *La fuerza de la sangre* also describes, at its simplest, a perfect arc:

> Leocadia, daughter of a poor *hidalgo* (noble) family from Toledo, is abducted by Rodolfo, son of an aristocrat. He rapes her and dumps her in the street. She gives birth to a son, Luisico, who is brought up as her cousin. Luisico is knocked down in the street by a horse, and taken into a nearby house for treatment. Leocadia recognizes the room as the one in which she was raped. Rodolfo's parents summon him back from Italy, he falls in love with Leocadia when he sees her again, and marries her.

In many ways this is the quintessence of the Cervantine plot, beginning with the violent disruption of a stable harmony, and speeding like an arrow towards the restoration of that harmony. The incidentals of the plot simply postpone the inevitable as much as they help to bring it about. The fact that *La fuerza de la sangre* is written with great economy of means, and has no sub-plot which might intrude on the inevitability of this process, merely serves to speed the arrow on its way and sharpen its impact when it hits the target.

There are also some very nice narrative devices which strengthen the symmetrical structure: the crucifix which Leocadia removes from the scene of the crime, and which symbolizes the redemptive power of Christ's blood as well as bearing witness to the veracity of her story; the return to the scene of the crime brought about by Luisico's accident in which, again, blood is a significant narrative detail as well as a potent symbol of redemption; the family resemblance between Luisico and his father, which catches the attention of Rodolfo's father and ushers in the *dénouement*; and the fainting fits to which Leocadia is victim during her rape and again when she is confronted by Rodolfo for the second time.

We need to be on guard, though, against too reductive a reading of the story driven by its admittedly strong underlying structural symmetry. For this happy ending is not reached without a degree of anguish which is almost without equal

[3] See B. W. Ife, 'Miguel and the Detectives: Crimes and their Detection in the *Novelas ejemplares*', *Journal of Hispanic Research*, 2 (1993–94), 355–68.

in the *Novelas ejemplares*. The violence of Leocadia's rape, and the apparent lack of remorse on the part of the rapist, are startling by any standards. Even Diego Carriazo senior's cynical violation of Costanza's mother in *La ilustre fregona* (The Illustrious Kitchen Maid) offers no comparison with the opening pages of *La fuerza de la sangre*. Cervantes sets the scene with compelling details: a family group is returning home after a nice day out by the river; five young louts, rich and idle, 'todos alegres y todos insolentes' (II, p. 102) ('uncaring and [. . .] insolent' [II, p. 103]), come marauding down the street;[4] they ogle disrespectfully at the three women in the family group; Leocadia's elderly father upbraids them for their insolence only for them to turn round and connive at Rodolfo's sudden urge to abduct her. And later, when Leocadia regains consciousness to find that she has been raped, Rodolfo responds to her entreaties by trying to rape her again. Few readers could remain unmoved by an episode which is all too credible: decent people's happiness and peace of mind is trampled by mindless arrogance; a young woman is brutally raped and dumped in the street, the flower of her youth and beauty destroyed, her family distraught, all decency put to shame. The episode is, and is clearly meant to be, sickening.

The reader's outrage will be compounded by the ending of the story. Rodolfo clears off to Italy and leaves Leocadia and her family to pick up the pieces of their lives. The truth comes to light through Luisico's accident, and Rodolfo is summoned back by his family not, as we might have expected, to get the rough edge of his father's tongue and to be made to face up to his responsibilities and make amends. No, he returns home to take part in one of the most bizarre charades it would be possible to imagine. First, his mother plays a childish trick on him by showing him a portrait of a plain Jane they have arranged for him to marry; and then when he objects, she produces Leocadia from behind an arras at dinner, so that she can blind him, for the second time in his life, with her beauty. He is not required to show any remorse for the crime he committed against Leocadia, nor does he volunteer any. When he marries her, he does so from choice, almost as if he were being rewarded rather than punished; indeed, no punishment is expected or extracted. An indignant reader might argue that he not only gets away with the crime – he gets a beautiful wife into the bargain.

On the question of Rodolfo's apparent lack of remorse, Paul Lewis-Smith has written that

> For some critics, Rodolfo remains a distasteful figure to the end. These are critics who fail to see that the mature Rodolfo loves Leocadia or who overlook the

[4] Elizabeth Teresa Howe, 'The Power of Blood in Cervantes' *La fuerza de la sangre*', *FMLS*, 30 (1994), 64–76, points out in passing that Rodolfo and his friends are riding horses (p. 67). While this is not explicit in the text, it is strongly implied by the use of the word 'caballero' in its sense of rider rather than 'gentleman': it becomes clearer later in the story that Rodolfo's social rank is higher than that of a mere gentleman. A mounted Rodolfo makes the swift abduction more plausible, and also sets up a parallel between Leocadia's abduction, perpetrated by a rider against a pedestrian, and Luisico's accident, in which he is run down by a horse as he is crossing the street to get a better view of the race.

> distinction that Cervantes draws between erotic love and lust [. . .] or who find it hard to forgive Rodolfo for failing to show remorse. To expect Rodolfo to show remorse when he is blissfully happy is to expect more than God expects and is morally unrealistic. We do not morally condemn Leocadia for failing to reprehend her husband and it behoves us not to condemn Rodolfo for failing to wear sackcloth and ashes. (p. 893, n. 8)

Nevertheless, if read at a purely literal level, *La fuerza de la sangre* provokes such strong feelings of injustice that only by suppressing wholly or in part the literal sense in favour of some form of metaphorical or symbolic reading can the opposing forces be reconciled. Even a reading as persuasive as Forcione's entails some 'explaining away': 'That Leocadia could love such an archetypal villain is quite implausible; it is in fact miraculous' (p. 363). Many readers may find that figural or symbolic interpretations, or recourse to miracles, whether secularized or not, do not allow them to keep faith with the outrage they experience when they read the story, or to see where their outrage leads them as critics or interpreters of the text. For the sense of outrage is real, and is caused by something that Cervantes put there in the text, and put there for a purpose. To recognize this is not to deny that God might use evil to achieve good;[5] it is simply to admit that that knowledge might not give a reader any consolation, or might not stop them from wanting revenge, from wanting Rodolfo to suffer as he made Leocadia suffer, from wanting him to shed bitter tears of remorse, or at least to say he is sorry.

Middleton and Rowley

A fascinating contemporary perspective on Rodolfo's lack of remorse comes from an English source, Thomas Middleton and William Rowley's play *The Spanish Gipsy*. Middleton and Rowley were two of a group of five Jacobean playwrights whom we can identify as having an interest in Spanish literature. The others are John Fletcher, Francis Beaumont and Philip Massinger.[6] Their interest may originally have been scholarly – certainly they were all well educated and interested in language – but it was enhanced by the events going on in London at the time they were writing. Their careers happened to coincide with a *rapprochement* between England and Spain, which began with the Treaty of London in 1604 and which James I hoped to consolidate in the early 1620s by marrying his son and heir, Charles, to the Spanish Infanta. Since England was a Protestant country, this was a controversial policy which was much discussed and commented on, and was one of the main topics for debate in the Parliaments of 1621 to 1624. *The Spanish Gipsy* was performed at

[5] 'Cervantes places special emphasis on the marvellous and paradoxical truth that Providence works through evil.' Lewis-Smith, p. 886.

[6] Trudi Laura Darby, 'Cervantes in England: the Influence of Golden-Age Prose Fiction on Jacobean Drama', *BHS,* 84 (1997), 425–41.

court in Charles's presence on 5 November 1623, one month to the day after his return from an unsuccessful attempt to marry into the Spanish royal house.

The Spanish Gipsy weaves together the plots of two of the *Novelas ejemplares*, *La gitanilla*, from which it gets its title, and *La fuerza de la sangre*.[7] Middleton and Rowley faced two types of problem in adapting Cervantes's prose fiction to verse drama for the Jacobean stage, and the changes they made were both logistical and ideological. As regards the plot of *La fuerza de la sangre*, there were three principal changes. First, they cut two characters, Estefanía (Rodolfo's mother) and Luisico (Leocadia's son). The loss of Estefanía was almost certainly governed by practical considerations: heroes and heroines are often motherless in Jacobean plays, because all the parts were played by men. Women were played by boy apprentices, but few companies would have enough boys to allow a playwright completely free rein in the gender-mix when putting together his cast. *The Spanish Gipsy* already has six female roles, which would stretch the company's resources to its limits. So Estefanía has to go, but Rodolfo (now called Roderigo) acquires in exchange a powerful father, Fernando, the *Corregidor* of Madrid, who will turn out to be a key player in the shift of emphasis within the English play.

The loss of Luisico is more interesting. Again, there will have been logistical reasons. Drama, unlike prose fiction, is not good at handling long time-spans and the playwrights would have wanted to avoid having to cover the gap between the rape, the pregnancy and birth, and Luisico's accident at the age of seven. But losing the small boy also, of course, cut down on the number of roles requiring boy actors: the play has to be more compact than the *novela*, covering a shorter time span and with fewer characters. But no boy means no blood, no recognition device and, potentially, no *dénouement*. Middleton and Rowley handle the need for a recognition device simply by having Leocadia (now called Clara) rather than Luisico knocked down by a horse, and having her recover in the very room in which she was raped.

But the child's blood, which is central to the symbolism of Cervantes's original text is completely missing from the English version, and this omission is clearly ideological. To the extent that there is a blood motif in *The Spanish Gipsy*, the emphasis is very different. Clara, the wronged woman, tells Fernando, the rapist's father, that 'Sinners are heard farthest, when they cry in blood' (3.3.65),[8] but the image here is not one of Christ's redemptive blood streaming in the firmament, as it did forty years earlier for Marlowe's Dr Faustus, but of the medieval proverb that 'murder will out', particularly when a murderer stands near the body of his victim and the body bleeds. The moral system underlying the statement is not one of redemption, but of retribution.

7 A list of characters and a summary of the plot are given in the Appendix (pp. 187–89).

8 Quotations are taken from Thomas Middleton and William Rowley, *The Spanish Gipsie and All's Lost by Lust*, ed. Edgar C. Morris (Boston, USA: D. C. Heath, 1908).

The second main change concerns the episode with the portrait of the ugly woman, which Middleton and Rowley handle as a play-within-a-play, written by Fernando, with Roderigo playing the lead role. The pseudo-play helps the playwrights to negotiate an episode which they clearly felt was rather awkward in Cervantes's original, allows the episode to be played for comic effect, but also taps into the tradition in which the play-within-a-play is used as a device to prick a conscience. *Hamlet* is an obvious example.

And conscience provides a link with the playwrights' third main change, which bears heavily on the central issue of remorse. For Roderigo is, from the outset, a very different character from his Spanish counterpart, begging forgiveness of his victim as soon as she remonstrates with him:

> [. . .] and since I find
> Such goodness in an unknown frame of virtue,
> Forgive my foul attempt, which I shall grieve for
> So hartily, that could you be your self
> Eye-witness to my constant vow'd repentance,
> Trust me, you'd pitty me. (1.3.75–80)

Roderigo's strong sense of guilt is reinforced by his father's reaction when he hears later what his son has done. Fernando, who has a double role as father and judge, throws himself on his knees before Clara, sheds 'tears of rage' and disowns his son:

> I do not plead for pitty to a villain;
> Oh, let him dye as he hath liv'd, dishonourably,
> Basely and cursedly! I plead for pitty
> To my till now untainted blood and honour;
> Teach me how I may now be just and cruell,
> For henceforth I am childlesse. (3.3.84–9)

Fernando's gesture of chilling self-abnegation is, significantly, not matched anywhere in *La fuerza de la sangre*. Here we begin to appreciate the shortened time-frame created by the omission of Luisico. Fernando is reacting to an act of violence committed within the past few days and with no redeeming feature; Estefanía is responding to an event which by the time she hears of it must have happened some eight years before, and which is mitigated, in part, by the fact that she now has a beautiful grandson. Nevertheless, the difference in intensity between Estefanía's reaction and Fernando's is striking.

Fernando's anger and Roderigo's guilty conscience intersect in the play-within-a-play. Fernando tells his son that the play was not entirely make-believe: he has lost his fortune and Roderigo must marry the rich but ugly woman whose portrait he was shown in the drama. Roderigo protests that he would rather marry a beautiful woman whom he saw watching the play, a woman he does not recognize as Clara, his victim. Fernando agrees, if Roderigo can persuade her. After the marriage, Fernando has one more surprise for Roderigo, when he tells him 'Thy wife's a wanton' and accuses him of having committed some terrible sin to deserve this. Under the onslaught of Fernando's cross-examination, Roderigo breaks down and confesses:

> [. . .] Turn from me then,
> And as my guilt sighes out this monster, rape,
> Oh, do not lend an ear! (5.1.23–5)

Like a skilful psychotherapist, Fernando has got the subject to confront his guilt, and further, brings him to acknowledge what remedy he should have made: 'Oh! had I married her, | I had been then the happiest man alive!' he exclaims; at which point, '*Enter Clara, Maria and Pedro, from behind the arras*' (5.1.37), as the stage direction puts it, and Clara's identity as his victim is discovered by production of the crucifix. That Roderigo's cure is complete is testified to by his reply: 'How can I turn mine eyes and not behold | On every side my shame?' (5.1.49–50) Cervantes, by contrast leaves us with no indication that Rodolfo ever acknowledges anything wrong with his actions.[9]

Middleton and Rowley have substantially rewritten Cervantes's text to make it say many of the things we might want it to say, but which it pointedly does not say. At the same time, they have stripped the *novela* of much of its core symbolism. This is hardly surprising, since they were writing for a particular audience within a Protestant context. Prince Charles was a follower of William Laud and the new 'High Church', Arminian theology; in this theology, images and ceremony were acceptable to enhance the dignity of the communion service. The crucifix which Clara takes from Roderigo's bedroom would not have been problematic. But a preference for decoration in churches should not be mistaken for a rejection of Protestant doctrine: the Church of England was still a Church which attached paramount importance to the Word rather than to images, and which put responsibility for its salvation on the individual soul rather than on any intercessory. An important text was St Paul's *Epistle to the Romans*, which is particularly strong on repentance and says in the second chapter:

> But after thy hardness and impenitent heart [thou] treasurest up unto thyself wrath against the day of wrath and revelation of the righteous judgement of God;
> Who will render to every man according to his deeds:
> To them who by patient continuance in well doing seek for glory and honour and immortality, eternal life:
> But unto them that are contentious, and do not obey the truth, but obey unrighteousness, indignation and wrath,
> Tribulation and anguish, upon every soul of man that doeth evil. (5–9)

[9] It should be noted, however, that after the rape Rodolfo goes to seek advice from his companions about what he should do next, perhaps indicating that he at least realizes he is in some trouble.

This, surely, was a strong encouragement to penitence, and one with which any English Protestant would have been familiar. The cultural framework in which Middleton and Rowley were writing required self-knowledge as a way to repentance and was keen on retribution and punishment: this was a society in which the sermon, the homily and biblical exposition were woven into the fabric of life, and collections of sermons were best-sellers. As Patrick Collinson notes

> [. . .] since for Protestants religion was not one compartment of a segmented life but all-enveloping, this must also mean that the Bible only is the *culture* of Protestants. [. . .] The Bible was not a straitjacket but a rich and infinitely varied source of imaginative and formal inspiration.[10]

In this society, Roderigo *has* to take responsibility for his actions: it is part of the confessional culture in which he is created. Cervantes, however, is writing for a different culture, one in which intercession is still possible and blood representing Christ's sacrifice can in itself be redemptive. For Cervantes, then, it is sufficient to rely on the pattern of events to bring about a satisfactory ending to his story, which one might view as a hagiography of Leocadia rather than a study of Rodolfo's conscience, of justice achieved through the patterning of events rather than the development of character. It is notable that, in bringing about the remorse and confession in Roderigo which we *think* we want from Cervantes, Middleton and Rowley move the focus of the play from the wronged woman to the man who wronged her. For the English playwrights the man is at the centre of our vision and it is a story of a troubled conscience. For Cervantes, however, it is the woman who is in focus and the story is of her courage and virtue.[11]

Spanish and English Versions

A comparison between Cervantes's *La fuerza de la sangre* and Middleton and Rowley's *The Spanish Gipsy* shows two things: first, that it is not at all anachronistic for a modern reader to respond indignantly to Rodolfo's behaviour and attitudes, because some of Cervantes's contemporaries clearly did the same to the extent that they felt the need to 'correct' the lack of remorse shown by Rodolfo by creating their own character, Roderigo, who does demonstrate that remorse; and second, Cervantes's provocative lack of interest in the question of Rodolfo's conscience shows that, for him, Leocadia is at the centre of his

[10] Patrick Collinson, *The Birthpangs of Protestant England. Religion and Cultural Change in the Sixteenth and Seventeenth Centuries* (Basingstoke: Macmillan, 1988), p. 95.

[11] The French dramatist Alexandre Hardy also wrote a version in 1626 which depicted Rodolfo passing though stages of remorse and repentance. See Esther J. Crooks, *The Influence of Cervantes in France in the Seventeenth Century* (Baltimore, 1931), p. 140, cited in Forcione, p. 361.

interest, not Rodolfo. What is challenging about *La fuerza de la sangre* is that it presents its readers with a series of deafening silences and asks them to interpret those silences in terms of what else is said. The absences from the story throw into relief what is there but which could easily be overlooked.

It is intriguing to note, for example, how Cervantes frames the story of *La fuerza de la sangre* with multiple references to the family. The story opens with Leocadia's family returning to Toledo from the riverside on a warm summer night. There are five of them in the group: 'un anciano hidalgo con su mujer, un niño pequeño, una hija de edad de diez y seis años y una criada' (II, p. 102) ('an old gentleman, with his wife, a small boy, a daughter of sixteen and a maid-servant' [II, p. 103]). If we leave aside the maid, this appears to be a family of four. The sixteen-year-old girl is Leocadia, but who is the little boy? Is he her brother? And why does Cervantes emphasize the father's age? This is a family which is particularized with great care: the father is quite old, the eldest child appears to be the girl, and there appears to be a son who is quite a bit younger, and who never appears in the story again. Why is he there, and why that age gap? Were there other children who did not survive? Is he an afterthought?

It is tempting to see the little boy as a harbinger of the nephew Luis who is yet to be born, and who will spend the first seven years of his life cast in the role of nephew/cousin rather than son. Cervantes appears to underline the link by using the diminutive ending '-ico' for Leocadia's brother and son.[12] But if we assume, as it seems we must, that he is Leocadia's brother, his presence on the first page of the novel, and his absence from the rest, might be much more significant. For, as Adriana Slaniceanu reminds us (p. 107), revenge in matters of honour is traditionally the role of the brother.[13] Leocadia has a brother, but he is conspicuously absent, by virtue of his age if nothing else, from the stage on which this drama will be acted out. This is clearly a story, Cervantes seems to be saying, in which the wronged woman will have to fend for herself.

If Leocadia is to bring about her own retribution, she makes a very promising start. What several critics have noted about the rape scene is Leocadia's extreme rationality once she has regained consciousness, and her exceptional presence of mind in observing the details of the room, and her foresight in removing the silver crucifix 'no por devoción ni por hurto, sino llevada de un discreto designio suyo' (II, p. 108) ('not for devotion, or as a theft, but inspired by a clever plan she had' [II, p. 109]). Both the reasoned arguments with which she meets and fends off Rodolfo's attempts to repeat his assault, and the 'discreet design' with which she removes the crucifix, point in one direction: honour and vengeance. At the very moment in which she is raped she appears to understand that the only way she is going to be able to right the wrong done to her is to take deep cover within

12 After Leocadia is abducted Cervantes writes 'lloró su hermanico' (II, p. 102) ('her little brother wept' [II, p. 105]) and her son is referred to as 'Luisico' throughout.

13 It is surprising that neither she nor Welles, who repeats the point (p. 247), noticed the disappearing brother, because it would have strengthened both their arguments.

the patriarchal social system, and bide her time. Don't get mad, she seems to say to herself; get even.[14]

This also appears to be the message she receives from her father when she is reunited with her family. Critics have often commented on the enlightened reception she is given. Far from disowning her, or throwing her out, which might have been the expected responses, her loving father teaches her two lessons, one soft and one hard. On the one hand he tells her quite rightly that she has committed no sin 'ni en dicho, ni en pensamiento, ni en hecho' (II, p. 110) ('neither in thought, word or deed' [II, p. 111]) and so has lost no private honour. But on the other hand he counsels against using the theft of the crucifix to trap her assailant, on the grounds that it can only work against her: 'más lastima una onza de deshonra pública que una arroba de infamia secreta' (II, p. 110) ('an ounce of public dishonour hurts more than a hundredweight of secret shame' [II, p. 111]). It is difficult to know whether this is wisdom, complacency or a world-weary acceptance that people of their social rank could not expect justice in these circumstances,[15] but either way, it is a salutary lesson in the way of the world. Leocadia now knows what Preciosa knew that fateful day she met don Juan de Cárcamo on the road into Madrid, that virginity has a cash value, is a tradable commodity in the sexual economy of the age: 'una sola joya tengo [. . .] que es la de mi entereza y virginidad y no la tengo de vender a precio de promesas ni dádivas, porque en fin será vendida' (I, p. 38) ('I have one jewel only [. . .] and I am not selling it for gifts and promises, because that would be, at the last, merely selling it' [I, p. 39]).

We have constantly to remind ourselves that words like 'honra' (honour) which are apparently so glibly bandied about in the literature of the time are merely euphemistic shorthand for this socio-economic fact of life. This was a society which was obsessed by the transmission of property through legitimate patrilineal descent, a society defined by *mayorazgo* (primogeniture). And the high value placed on legitimacy placed an equally high value on the virginity of an unmarried woman. In *La fuerza de la sangre*, Cervantes graphically reveals the sordid reality of honour and its loss. Robbed of her virginity, Leocadia is literally worthless within the patriarchal system. And her attendant loss of identity is intensified when she gives birth, and her son is sent away to be fostered until he can be passed off as a nephew. Leocadia cannot be identified as a mother, nor Luis as her son. It is easy for the reader, who is present at both the conception and the birth, to overlook this fact.

In some ways, then, there were two crimes committed by Rodolfo when he raped Leocadia: he not only took away her personal, physical integrity but also her sense of self in a social context. She ceased to be the person she once was. In

[14] Both Howe and Welles show how this *novela* is a very atypical example of the honour/vengeance theme in Spanish literature, and one in which the women break the cycle of violence endemic to honour/vengeance plots.

[15] Slaniceanu, p. 103: 'He seeks no aid from the forces of law and order, for *hidalgos pobres* (poor gentlemen) have no recourse to official justice.'

this respect, Leocadia is like a number of Cervantine women who are the victims of a crime which takes away their identity.[16] Three obvious examples come to mind from within the *Novelas ejemplares*: *La gitanilla*, *La española inglesa*, and *La ilustre fregona*. These are all reworkings of a very common narrative structure in Cervantes, the narrative of captivity and redemption, in which a character is abducted, stolen or otherwise misplaced geographically, culturally or socially, lives as another person, and is eventually 'redeemed' or repatriated to their proper place. Examples can be found throughout Cervantes's work: in *Persiles y Sigismunda* (the three 'mediterranean' narratives in Book I), and in *Don Quijote*, where the Captive's tale (I, 39–41) is the most obvious but by no means the only example.

The importance of the captivity narrative in early modern culture has been underlined by the English historian Linda Colley.[17] Colley has examined over one hundred English narratives of this type, both printed and manuscript, from 1600 to the middle of the nineteenth century, and although she does not mention captivity narratives in other languages, she does point out that she wrote the book to show that such narratives, which have usually been studied in the American context, are not unique to that context. The prevalence of this narrative type is undoubtedly a function of the high probability that early modern Europeans would find themselves captive at some time in their lives. Colley estimates that some 20,000 British and Irish captives were held in North Africa between the beginning of the seventeenth century and the mid eighteenth century (p. 56), and that at least 15,000 Spanish men and women had to be redeemed from North African captivity in the seventeenth century alone (p. 45). Cervantes's experience as a prisoner in Algiers (1575–80) was by no means exceptional.

What is striking about this phenomenon is not the number of people taken captive, but the number who wrote about the experience, which was clearly a formative one for many of them. Colley defines the captivity narrative as a mode of writing rather than a genre:

> [. . .] captivity narratives commonly describe how a single individual or a group was seized, how the victim/s coped (or not) with the challenges and sufferings that ensued, and how they contrived in the end to escape or were ransomed or released [. . .] (p. 13)

The examples were not always heroic: many individuals who underwent the experience

> [. . .] remained bitterly resentful throughout at being forced to cross into trauma and difference. Some captives, however, chose or were compelled

[16] Forcione, p. 357: 'The first half of the tale is marked by the loneliness of the heroine and her alienation from a society that deprives her of her very being'.

[17] Linda Colley, *Captives* (London: Jonathan Cape, 2002).

> to adjust to their new settings, while others learnt from their experiences to question the very validity of divides between peoples, and the meaning of what they had once regarded as home. Virtually all British captives though were compelled by the nature of their predicament to re-examine – and often question for the first time – conventional wisdoms about nationality, race, religion, allegiance, appropriate modes of behaviour, and the location of power. (p. 16)

Two things are helpful from this account: first, the importance given to the process of redemption itself – how the captives came to be restored to their rightful place in the scheme of things, which is why the form would appeal to writers of fiction[18] – and second, the lessons to be learned from contrasting two modes of being. If we put these observations into the context of the *Novelas ejemplares* we find a striking pattern emerges which may help to resolve some of the problems surrounding *La fuerza de la sangre* in particular.

Figure 1 summarizes the main structural features of four of the *novelas*, including *La fuerza de la sangre.* They can all be analysed into a number of basic elements: an initial crime results in some form of displacement, captivity or exile; an agent appears who brings about the redemption of the heroine, that is her restitution to her 'real' self and her proper place in society.

Figure 1: Captivity and redemption structures in four *Novelas ejemplares*

	La gitanilla	***La española inglesa***	***La ilustre fregona***	***La fuerza de la sangre***
Heroine	Preciosa	Isabel	Costanza	Leocadia
Crime	Theft	Theft	Rape	Rape
Criminal	*abuela*	Clotaldo	Diego Carriazo snr	Rodolfo
Displacement	Social/ethnic (gipsies)	Geographical/ religious (Spain and England)	Social	Social
Agent	Don Juan/Andrés	Ricaredo, son of Clotaldo	Tomás de Avendaño, friend of Diego Carriazo jnr	Rodolfo[19]

[18] A good contemporary example from England is that of Robert Greene's short novel *Pandosto: The Triumph of Time*, first published in 1588 and best known today as the source of Shakespeare's play *The Winter's Tale*. See Lori Humphrey Newcomb, *Reading Popular Romance in Early Modern England* (New York: Columbia University Press, 2002).

[19] It might be argued that Luisico could be the agent, but the paradigm favours Rodolfo because in each case it is the heroine's own qualities of integrity and fortitude, represented by her physical beauty, which attract the attention of the man who will rescue her. Moreover, Luisico does not have the power to reinstate her to her rightful place in society; only Rodolfo can do that.

In every case, the agent of redemption is a man who is attracted by the displaced girl, her physical beauty, and her character, integrity, and resistance to her alien environment. In every case, the first cause of the narrative is a crime which causes the suppression of a truth, and the narrative is concerned with the ways in which that truth will out, for out it must.[20]

Although less obvious than in the other examples, this pattern is also present in *La fuerza de la sangre*: the initial crime (Rodolfo's rape) leads to social displacement (Leocadia is robbed of her honour and her place in the marriage market and is forced to deny her role as mother); the agent is, and in this case can only be, the man who committed the original crime; and the outcome is that Leocadia regains her place in society, underlined by the further children she and Rodolfo give birth to.

In *La fuerza de la sangre*, the suppressed truth is Leocadia's role as mother and Luis's role as son, and the moment of revelation comes with the accident, and the intersection of these two family narratives in the bloodstained body of a beautiful little boy. After seven years of internal exile, Leocadia senses that the moment has come, and takes what is really a very brave step in revealing the truth to Rodolfo's family: 'this boy is your grandson' (II, p. 116; II, p. 117). It hardly bears thinking about how badly that moment could have gone: would they deny it and have her thrown out; would they try and pay her off to protect themselves and their son against social blackmail?[21] But Leocadia plays it to perfection, bringing the biological and the social realms into phase and creating a perfect alignment of three generations of patrilineal descent. All they need to do is supply the missing third term, and it is significant that from now on Leocadia and her parents-in-law will act in concert to ensure that Rodolfo plays his part.

Once the truth has been revealed and Leocadia's story has been verified, Cervantes moves quickly to get Rodolfo back from Italy and all other matters resolved. But there remains the oddity of the episode with the portrait. Several critics follow Ray Calcraft in arguing that Rodolfo's response to the picture of the plain lady is evidence of maturity gained from his years in Italy. It is true that his reply to his mother's suggestion that he should marry the plain but virtuous wife they have selected for him is extremely polite. But many readers will prefer to read Rodolfo's response as a spoiled brat's plea not to make him marry an ugly woman.[22] If he ever does become a changed man, the moment is not yet.

[20] The sole exception to this rule appears to be the episode in *Persiles y Sigismunda* (II, 7) where Auristela decides not to reveal the contents of the offensive note she has received from Clodio.

[21] This thought is voiced, quietly, at several points in the text. The exceptional wealth of Rodolfo's family is clear from the furnishings in his bedroom, and his mother is careful to verify Leocadia's story, just in case she is a gold-digger.

[22] He describes himself, somewhat disingenuously, with the words 'mozo soy' (II, p. 120) ('I am a young man' [II, p. 121]) (he is twenty-nine by this stage), and his mother entices him back from Italy with 'la golosina de gozar tan hermosa mujer' (II, p.118) ('the appetite to enjoy such a beautiful woman' [II, p. 119]); she clearly knows what kind of child she is dealing with.

It is difficult to fathom why Cervantes has Estefanía play this trick on him, and it may be necessary to conclude that it is simply a manoeuvre, another kind of 'discreet design'; its function is to prepare the ground for the replay of the first encounter between Leocadia and Rodolfo, a return match from which she intends this time to get a result that suits her. Like some stallion who has to be made ready to cover a prize mare, Rodolfo has to be softened up for the great revelation at dinner, the moment when Leocadia and her son will be revealed in all their miraculous glory and the male gaze will finally come into focus.

It is clear from the final pages of the story, however, that Rodolfo and the state of his conscience are not as significant for Cervantes's purpose as Leocadia is. For Cervantes, and for Leocadia, Rodolfo is simply a means to an end, a cipher, an agent. He has performed a biological function and he is now required to perform a matching social function, to marry her and give her back what he stole from her. This story is entirely about Leocadia, about how she is the victim of a vicious crime, about how she is robbed of meaning and value within the society in which she lives; about how she bides her time and when the chance presents itself, how she engineers her own release and that of her son from social exile into the social mainstream, as measured by 'la ilustre descendencia que en Toledo dejaron [. . .] que muchos y felices años gozaron de sí mismos, de sus hijos y de sus nietos' (II, p. 126) ('the noble descendants [. . .], which [they] left in Toledo; and they enjoyed many happy years together, with their children and grandchildren' [II, p. 127]).

Our response to Rodolfo and how he behaves is, then, simply a by-product of Cervantes's concern to show the brutal reality behind the word 'deshonra' (dishonour) and the mere functionality of his male character; it has no real bearing on the story itself. Rodolfo's role is simply to redeem both Leocadia and her son, to rescue them from the social exclusion to which his action has banished them. This might have been brought about by his father getting the shotgun out, but as the comparison with other *novelas* shows, that is not what seems to interest Cervantes. What he seems interested in is how all of these women – Preciosa, Isabel, Costanza and Leocadia – bring about their own redemption, how their qualities, their integrity and fortitude, symbolized by their physical beauty, motivate and inspire the men who will rescue them. Those qualities are rewarded by their ultimate redemption from captivity or repatriation from exile. Like Ricaredo, Avendaño and don Juan de Cárcamo, Rodolfo is inspired by a well-managed, hieratic *coup de foudre*, rescues Leocadia from social exclusion and restores her to marriage, domesticity and fecundity. Unlike them, he was also the cause of her initial captivity. In this respect, perhaps *La fuerza de la sangre* represents the most perfect expression of Cervantes's narrative structure of captivity and redemption.

At the end of *La gitanilla*, Cervantes introduces a note of irony at the moment when Preciosa is restored to her proper place in the social order. As a gipsy she is bright and self-motivated; as the Corregidor's daughter she is dutiful and submissive. There is a similar irony in this story, perhaps an inescapable one; for all of Cervantes's female leads illustrate the virtual impossibility of defining a role for themselves in other than patriarchal terms. However much they shine in their various struggles, they are all ultimately ingested into the status quo. Fulfilment entails submission, loss of individuality, absorption, invisibility. Perhaps Leocadia stands out in this context, because, although she too takes her place in the reproductive cycle, she does not simply slot into her place, she sets out to achieve marriage as a form of revenge. And since her family is clearly poorer and socially inferior to Rodolfo's she achieves more than restoration, she manages to achieve betterment. And in a world where we do well to come out even, we can only admire a woman who comes out ahead.

Appendix

Thomas Middleton and William Rowley, *The Spanish Gipsy* (1623)

List of characters

Don Fernando, *corregidor* of Madrid
Don Pedro de Cortes
Don Francisco de Carcomo
Roderigo, son to don Fernando
Lewys, son to de Castro, slain by Alvarez
Diego, friend to don Lewys
Don John, son to Francisco de Carcomo and a lover of Constanza
Sancho, a foolish gentleman and ward to don Pedro
Soto, a merry fellow, his man
Alvarez, and old lord disguised like the father of the gipsies
Claro and Antonio, two gentlemen disguised like gipsies
Maria, wife to don Pedro
Clara, their daughter
Guyamara, wife to Count Alvarez, and sister to Fernando, disguised like the mother of the gipsies, and called by the name of Eugenia
Constanza, daughter to Fernando, disguised like a young Spanish gipsy and called by the name of Pretiosa
Christiana, a gentlewoman, disguised like a gipsy
Cardochia, a young hostess to the gipsies
Servants

Synopsis

Act 1

Night time. Roderigo and his friends Lewys and Diego are on the outskirts of Madrid. Roderigo has seen a woman (Clara) with whom he is 'bewitched' and who is approaching them with her parents (Maria and Pedro). He persuades Lewys and Diego to help him abduct her and this they do. In the course of the abduction, Pedro calls out who he is – don Pedro de Cortes – and Lewys is horrified, because he realizes that the woman he has helped to kidnap is the woman whom he has been courting. Meanwhile, Roderigo has taken Clara to a house and raped her. He leaves her locked in a room, the features of which she memorizes and she also takes a crucifix which she finds there. Roderigo returns and Clara makes him repent of his actions. He swears never to reveal his crime, and to take her back to the place whence he abducted her. Lewys and Diego search for Roderigo. Diego follows don John, thinking him to be Roderigo, and realizes that he is in love with a gipsy girl. Lewys finds Roderigo and explains that they have abused the woman he hopes to marry; Roderigo praises the woman's virtue and asks Lewys never to reveal her identity to him. He will leave Madrid, to avoid her, and go to study in Salamanca. Diego meets them and tells them of don John's infatuation.

Act 2

The gipsies are lodging at the house, near Madrid, of Juanna Cardochia, where they are visited by Sancho, don Pedro's foolish ward, and his servant Soto; Sancho has brought verses for the famous gipsy girl, Pretiosa, and gives her money, as well as his cloak, hat, scarf and ruff. As he leaves, don John arrives: he wishes to marry Pretiosa, and she says that if he will serve for two years as a gipsy, then she will marry him.

Clara has told Maria and Pedro what has happened to her, and they advise discretion. Lewys continues his suit to Clara, but she is not interested. Lewys remains in conversation with Pedro, and discusses the fate of Alvarez, who had killed Lewys's father and had been in exile ever since. Don Fernando, Corregidor of Madrid, and Alvarez's brother-in-law, has been encouraging Lewys to have Alvarez brought back to Spain – if he is still alive.

Sancho and Soto return home, and are scolded by don Pedro for having lost Sancho's clothes. Outraged, they decide to turn gipsy.

Act 3

Roderigo is now disguised as an Italian and overcome with remorse. He meets Sancho and Soto, and goes with them to join the gipsies. They go with the troop to perform at the house of don Francisco de Carcomo (don John's father), where don Fernando, don Pedro, Maria, Lewys and Diego are also present, and tell fortunes. Don Francisco recognizes his son in disguise, but keeps quiet.

News comes that Clara has been injured in an accident, outside don Fernando's house, and he instructs that she should be cared for in his home: he will follow Pedro, Maria and Lewys to see her. Clara recognizes the room in which she is being nursed as the same as the room in which she was raped, and when her parents and don Fernando arrive, she asks him if he is married. Yes, he was, and he has a son Roderigo still alive; but his wife died in childbirth and the daughter to whom she gave birth was lost at sea with his sister. Clara gives don Fernando a note describing her rape. He is horrified, and vows revenge on his son.

Act 4

Don John goes through a betrothal ceremony with Pretiosa and adopts the gipsy-name of Andrew. But Juanna Cardochia also asks him to marry her, an offer which he refuses. She asks him to wear a token jewel of hers, which she gives him.

Don Fernando has had Alvarez's banishment repealed: don Francisco is lamenting the loss of his son don John who has left a letter saying he has gone to the wars. The gipsy troop arrives at don Fernando's house, and he commissions them to act a play which he has drafted, in which he wants their Italian poet to play the role of a son asked to marry a rich but ugly heiress, to restore the family's fortunes. The play proceeds, but is interrupted with the news that Diego has been wounded by the gipsy Andrew, whom he saw wearing a jewel belonging to his own mistress, Juanna Cardochia, and which Cardochia says was stolen. Andrew is arrested for theft and for assault. Don Fernando tells Roderigo that he has seen through his disguise, but that the play was in earnest and he must marry the ugly heiress. Roderigo pleads instead to be allowed to marry the beautiful woman who sat with his father during the play (i.e. Clara). His father agrees, as long as the woman is willing.

Act 5

Roderigo has married Clara, and don Fernando now tells him that his new wife is a wanton. Roderigo must, he says, have committed a dreadful sin in order to deserve such a punishment, and questions him until Roderigo finally breaks his vow and admits the rape. He wishes he had married the woman whom he violated. At this point, Clara, Maria and don Pedro emerge from behind an arras and all is explained.

Preciosa pleads for the release of her gipsy husband, Andrew, who is to be hanged. The mother of the gipsies reveals in private to don Fernando that Andrew is don John de Carcomo, and further that she herself is don Fernando's own sister and Alvarez's wife, whom he had believed drowned; Pretiosa is his daughter Constanza, and Alvarez is the leader of the gipsy troop. Alvarez offers Lewys the opportunity to kill him and expresses his remorse at the death of Lewys's father. Lewys finds himself unable to take revenge and they are reconciled. Don John and Constanza (Pretiosa) are to be married and Sancho and Soto see the error of their ways.

Works cited

Allen, J. J., '*El Cristo de la Vega* and *La fuerza de la sangre*', *MLN,* 83 (1968), 271–75.

Calcraft, R. P., 'Structure, Symbol and Meaning in Cervantes's *La fuerza de la sangre*', *BHS,* 58 (1981), 197–204.

Cervantes Saavedra, Miguel de, *Exemplary Novels / Novelas ejemplares*, ed. B. W. Ife, 4 vols (Warminster: Aris & Phillips, 1992).

Colley, Linda, *Captives* (London: Jonathan Cape, 2002).

Collinson, Patrick, *The Birthpangs of Protestant England. Religion and Cultural Change in the Sixteenth and Seventeenth Centuries* (Basingstoke: Macmillan, 1988).

Crooks, Esther J., *The Influence of Cervantes in France in the Seventeenth Century* (Baltimore, 1931).

Darby, Trudi Laura, 'Cervantes in England: the Influence of Golden-Age Prose Fiction on Jacobean Drama', *BHS*, 84 (1997), 425–41.

El Saffar, Ruth S., *Novel to Romance: A Study of Cervantes's 'Novelas ejemplares'* (Baltimore: Johns Hopkins University Press, 1974).

Forcione, Alban K., *Cervantes and the Humanist Vision* (Princeton NJ: Princeton University Press, 1982).

Howe, Elizabeth Teresa, 'The Power of Blood in Cervantes' *La fuerza de la sangre*', *FMLS*, 30 (1994), 64–76.

Humphrey Newcomb, Lori, *Reading Popular Romance in Early Modern England* (New York: Columbia University Press, 2002).

Ife, B. W., 'Miguel and the Detectives: Crimes and their Detection in the *Novelas ejemplares*', *Journal of Hispanic Research*, 2 (1993–94), 355–68.

Lewis-Smith, Paul, 'Fictionalizing God: Providence, Nature and the Significance of Rape in *La fuerza de la sangre*', *MLR*, 91 (1996), 886–97.

Middleton, Thomas, and William Rowley, *The Spanish Gipsie and All's Lost by Lust*, ed. Edgar C. Morris (Boston, USA: D. C. Heath, 1908).

Slaniceanu, Adriana, 'The Calculating Woman in Cervantes'*s La fuerza de la sangre*', *BHS*, 64 (1987), 101–10.

Welles, Marcia L., 'Violence Disguised: Representation of Rape in Cervantes' *La fuerza de la sangre*', *Journal of Hispanic Philology*, 13 (1989), 240–52.

9

Free-Thinking in *EL celoso extremeño*[1]

Paul Lewis-Smith
University of Bristol

In this essay I am resuming an enquiry into the theological reach of Cervantes's *Novelas* which I began in 1996 in a study of *La fuerza de la sangre* (The Power of Blood).[2] This novella, as I understand it, is a kind of Christian mystery tale which unfolds a warning against prejudiced and pessimistic perceptions of a world in which the innocent suffer and evil can seem to prevail. Its essential theme for a shrewd and not too squeamish reader is the hidden immanence of God. Behind it there lies a medieval Scholastic doctrine on the nature of divine sovereignty which was still accepted by seventeenth-century theologians. Pilloried by agnostic thinkers of the European Enlightenment, this doctrine declared that the whole of life is governed by two forms of providence, one of which is the God who wills what is good in life (*providentia approbationis*) and the second of which is the God who permits what is evil (*providentia concessionis*) whilst still intending good. Hence the *novela*'s explicit theme of a God who 'permits' an innocent child to suffer an accident which is instrumental in bringing about the marriage of his parents; and hence (in my interpretation) the darker and, as Cervantes knows, potentially offensive theme of a God who permits the rape of a virtuous woman with the same end in view. Presented in a form which allows a narrow-minded reader to bury his head in the sand, the theme of providential rape is an example of Cervantine free-thinking concerning the theoretical implications of a traditional religious doctrine. In this essay I wish to show how the same doctrine reappears in forms which I think are still more free-thinking in *El celoso extremeño.*[3]

1 This essay is based on the introduction to my critical edition of *'El viejo celoso' and 'El celoso extremeño'* (London: Bristol Classical Press, 2001) but contains important amplifications and revisions of the views expressed there. In quoting in Spanish from Cervantes's *novela* I use my own edition. For the translations I am indebted to Michael and Jonathan Thacker as translators in Miguel de Cervantes, *Novelas ejemplares / Exemplary Novels*, ed. B. W. Ife, 4 vols (Warminster: Aris & Phillips, 1992), III, pp. 8–55. Other translations are my own.

2 Paul Lewis-Smith, 'Fictionalizing God: Providence, Nature, and the Significance of Rape in *La fuerza de la sangre*', *MLR*, 91 (1996), 886–97.

3 The positioning of *El celoso extremeño* immediately after *La fuerza de la sangre* is evidently systematic. Schematically the second tale is an inversion of the first. Marriage is

Cervantine free-thinking is not specifically metaphysical and it is that of a man whose Christian core is undoubtedly fideist. It is nevertheless an attempt at thinking objectively which sometimes crosses the dividing line between safe thought and curiosity in theological matters. It naturally involves a habit of self-detachment. In the latter respect it is the kind of thinking that Cervantes espouses in the off-beat prologue of Part I of *Don Quijote* (1605) in an exemplary fashion when he refuses to pay his solemn regards to the traditional modesty *topos* ('I know, dear reader, that I am not God's gift to literature') whilst making a point of refusing to recommend his work in view of the fact that he is likely to be biased. Free-thinking when dealing with generalities is the opposite of bigotry, a habit of mind which is part of Don Quijote's comic make-up as an intelligent man who has taken leave of his senses. *El celoso extremeño* repeatedly alludes to the virtue of free-thinking. It does so in its many examples of what is true, probable, or possible in the particularities of daily life being misconstrued when appearances deceive people who are not mad, but whose judgement is prejudiced in some degree by their personal attributes. At the same time it extends an invitation to readers to practise free-thinking as Christians. What I think distinguishes it in this respect from the preceding *novela* is the greater space it provides for readers to think in an adventurous way about the nature of freedom itself in a providentially ordered world.

My main purpose in this essay is to reveal what I see as the space for heresy. I have to concede that I may be chasing illusions, but I do not think that I am being quixotic in my capacity as an intellectual researcher. My critical judgement tells me that what I see in the work is meaning the author has put into it for a receptive reader by triggering and remotely controlling, as it were, his intellectual potential. Cervantes purposely 'permits' his reader to think heretically. It is the appropriate method of communication for an author who is seeking objectivity in representing a world which is seen through the eye of the beholder, especially when he is writing under a system of censorship by whose standards his free-thinking is excessive.

On an explicit level *El celoso extremeño* is a cautionary tale for jealous men with young and attractive wives. Its essential message is that it is impossible for a jealous husband to safeguard himself against cuckoldry by placing his wife under virtual house arrest. The reason given is that one person cannot imprison another person's will. This is a shallow explanation of what might be called the first law of predestination: that all human beings are born to be morally tested. The jealous husband is bound to fail because no one can deprive another of the power of moral self-assertion in a fallen world where all are under judgement. The exemplarity of Cervantes's tale partly lies in its

now an evil as opposed to an elusive good, the hero is now a jealous old man instead of a libidinous youth, and the ending is a matrimonial breakdown followed by the hero's death and the heroine's retreat to a convent, as opposed to a happy wedding followed by procreation. Various partial forms of inversion surround this basic pattern.

fictionalization of this Christian understanding of life. What I wish to emphasize here is that it also contains an anatomy of human freedom which problematizes its own evocation of life as moral trial. There is a tension between this and the corresponding depiction of the freedom of the will. In a discreet way which requires the reader to understand and flesh out characters whom the narrator sees only in embryo, the *novela* offers a sceptical view of that idea of 'free will' which was defended by the Catholic Church against Protestant, neo-Stoic, and quasi-scientific forms of doubt and disbelief.

As it continues to do in the twenty-first century, the doctrine of *libre albedrío* (free will) meant that God, who foreknows how people are going to behave, does not actually predestine them to behave in the foreknown way by means which divest them of real responsibility for their lives. It meant especially that He did not in a deterministic sense predestine them to glory or damnation, even though He chose those souls who were destined for the former, according to the doctrine of 'election'. *El celoso extremeño* shows freedom in a limited sense, which we now might call 'autonomy', to be very real indeed. It emphatically shows that the choices made by individuals may not comply with laws, conventions, or norms: people will not necessarily do as they ought to do from the point of view of the social consensus, and they may not conform to moral stereotypes. It also shows that intellectual life is free in an autonomous sense, both within and independently of the sphere of human action. The imagination is not debarred from engaging in immoral thought (Leonora, for example, imagines herself committing adultery) and judgement can be wrong.[4] On the other hand it strongly hints to a receptive reader that such social and intellectual freedoms do not entail the kind of freedom which is necessarily a condition of moral trial from the logical viewpoint of Catholic 'natural' theology (Catholic rationalism). The fundamental suggestion is that behaviour in the moral realm is the outworking of disposition: it is a manifestation of a person's gender (male or female)[5] and of the nuanced form of disposition which in the text is called a person's *condición*. Disposition, moreover, as Cervantes depicts it, is not located just in the human passions. Moral behaviour may owe much to a person's innate intelligence. Thus, for example, Carrizales's behaviour is profoundly affected by the mental aspect of his 'plainness' or *llaneza* – the fact that he has a simple or straightforward intellect. What emerges is a Christian exploration of freedom which is discreetly slanted towards a determinist interpretation of the Scholastic doctrine of Providence and which replicates in more extreme and, as we shall see, more

4 Freedom of judgement is what Cervantes has in mind in the prologue of *Don Quijote*, Part I when he invests his readers with what he actually calls 'free will'. He means by this the freedom to form their own opinions of the quality of his work.

5 Cervantes, I think, does recognize that in exceptional cases the sexual instincts do not correspond with biological gender. The issue of homosexuality does not arise in *El celoso extremeño*, however.

morbid form a tendency of the preceding work, where predestination, moving towards a happier end, is identical in having a characterological basis.[6]

The key 'examples' are Carrizales and Leonora. In the case of Carrizales, the more sinister of the two, we are dealing with a Christian throwback to the heroes of Classical tragic drama of that poignantly ironic kind which Aristotle regarded as a model for the tragic genre and theorized in his *Poetics*. These were characters whose suffering was the convincing effect of their own fallibility. As Aristotle observed, the catastrophe sprang in a 'probable' or 'necessary' way from the hero's own 'error' or 'failure' (*hamartia*). In dramatic practice this was often predetermined by a supernatural curse: the hero was set up for his fall, as it were, by a malicious god or a supernatural Fate.[7] Carrizales's story is a novelistic

[6] I have yet to address this aspect of the preceding *novela* directly. However, the article to which I have referred above (n.2) provides a good idea of how I see it. Certain of Cervantes's works give limited credence to a politically very acceptable view according to which a person's 'blood' ('genes', we would say today) determines disposition. One such work is *La fuerza de la sangre*. Others reveal his belief in the importance of nurture. See, for example, his reasons for commending Jesuit teachers in *El coloquio de los perros* (The Dialogue of the Dogs). *El celoso extremeño* does not address the blood versus nurture question. In common with other Cervantine works, it does suggest that *condición* is formed at an early stage in life, and that it starts to appear when we begin to make choices which contribute towards some settled form or habit of existence. Of special importance in any sweeping consideration of Cervantes's position on human freedom is *El rufián dichoso* (The Fortunate Ruffian), which is one of his later plays. Based on the life of a real person whom he knew through religious biography, its hero is a young delinquent who lacks a coherent set of values (a precursor of the 'mixed-up kid'), undergoes a personal crisis in which he repents of his sins, takes holy orders, and develops into a Roman Catholic saint. His metamorphosis is the fulfilment of a special vocation which was hidden from him until he began to fulfil it. The virtues he shows as a saintly man are the positive attributes of the delinquent youth – private piety, humility, and other virtues – together with certain neutral qualities to which he has given delinquent form – crucially those of courage and a propensity for extremism – when these have been perfected by the interaction of grace with human nature. His decision to reform himself is prompted by his objective and therefore pained reflection on a depraved choice he had intended to make in a situation of desperation which did not in fact arise, and which, had he made it, would have turned him into a fully-fledged criminal. It denotes his virtual realization that to be a delinquent is not his calling in life. His *condición* is fully apparent when he has negotiated this crisis, though it was formed in his early years. He is probably called *dichoso* (fortunate) because of the high vocation he has been given. Arguably the key ingredient in his calling to Christian excellence is a deep-seated need to make a spectacular splash in life in order to make up for a false sense of inferiority which he derives from his humble background. If this is so, he is a Christian version of modern Man in one of the archetypal forms in which most of us believe. *El rufián dichoso* is a brilliant adventure in free-thinking character-study. Cervantists have paid little attention to it only because Cervantes's theatre was neglected in its own day and is very imperfect when judged by the modern consensual idea of good drama of the Golden Age, which has much in common with the consensual values of the Golden Age itself.

[7] Aristotle did not investigate the supernatural background of his favoured form of tragic drama but focused attention on the need for 'probability' or 'necessity' in the natural order of events. He noted their dependence on dramatic characterization: 'As in the arrangement of the incidents, so too in characterization one must always bear in mind what will be either necessary or probable; in other words, it should be necessary or probable that such and such

and Christian adaptation of this tragic genre in which the hero's failures are now multiple, they spring from sin, and his fall may be seen on the deepest level, not as the mortal delusion he suffers, but as the fulfilment of his natural vocation for failure in the trial of life.

God and the Devil are the powers at work in the supernatural background. Their relationship, though nowhere explained, is discernibly the Scholastic one which operates in *La fuerza de la sangre*. God decrees all things, but He only wills what is good; what is evil is willed by the Devil under God's authority. Hence we are told at first that it is the Devil, 'el sagaz perturbador del género humano' (p. 23) (crafty disturber of the human race), who wrecks Carrizales's marriage, yet are later told that it is God who decrees the natural event which triggers the catastrophe: 'Y en esto ordenó el cielo que a pesar del ungüento, Carrizales despertase' (p. 41) (At this point Heaven decreed that despite the ointment, Carrizales should wake up). The full implication of these remarks is that the early awakening from drugged sleep is willed by the Devil but occurs because an omnipotent God allows it to occur, wishing Carrizales to be tested.

Whilst Cervantes's *novela* shows faint support for the doctrine of *libre albedrío*, it strongly supports the corresponding belief that life puts Man on trial. The absurd marriage is itself the result of a moral trial which chiefly tests the hero's will to mortify his desires. He fails the test because age weakens his judgement (this explanation the narrator gives us) and because he views the choice before him from a thoroughly self-centred perspective.[8] Finding cause for ignoring his fears in his own self-centred reasoning, he succumbs to wishful thinking. This in its final form is the deluded assumption that to marry Leonora is to do the will of God: 'Alto, pues; echada está la suerte, y ésta es la que el cielo quiere que yo tenga' (p. 21) ('Enough now: the die is cast and this is the path that Heaven wants me to follow' [III, p. 13]). Here he is confusing what God wills with what He simply allows – is confusing God with the Devil, that is – because he believes that the thing he is strongly inclined to do must be what God wants.

As a married man he undergoes three further tests in each of which he maintains his record of failure. This series of matrimonial tests suggests two further laws of predestination: people must suffer for their moral mistakes, and failure will lead to further and more difficult testing. The first trial after the wedding is the instant attack of jealousy. It requires the hero to recognize the mistake he

a person should say or do such and such a thing' (*Classical Literary Criticism*, translated with an introduction by T. S. Dorsche [Harmondsworth: Penguin, 1965], p. 52).

[8] To put it in the language of Scholasticism: age is the secondary cause of Carrizales's error, whilst self-centredness is the first. A Scholastic would blame the man, not his age, and he would be right in doing so. Carrizales's error is the product of a self-centred outlook, operating in conditions (old age) which weaken his judgement, but only his judgement of what is best for himself. However one chops the logic, his essential problem is his disposition, not his old age. The effect of age is to increase the power of evil in his nature.

has made and to try to get the marriage annulled (which is possible until it is consummated) and failing that, to mortify his jealousy. He chooses instead to continue the marriage whilst eliminating risk. By doing so he merely ensures that his wife's temptation occurs in abnormally trying conditions which produce another crisis. The backlash is the shocking scene he witnesses in the duenna's room after God has decreed that the doped ointment should be less effective than its suppliers said it would be. This second matrimonial test is the equivalent in Carrizales's life of the destruction of his security measures in the life of Leonora. The latter event is inevitable, theologically, precisely because it exposed Leonora to temptation, thwarting what is effectively her husband's wish to interfere with the divine order of life. The early awakening from drugged sleep is a similar sort of event. It paves the way for another event which corners Carrizales in an inescapable trial of his will to conquer his jealousy, in conditions, of his own making, as extreme as those in which his wife has just been tested.

His failure of this second matrimonial test is more 'probable' still than his failure of the previous one. Of all the trials he undergoes, this is the one in which failure seems most 'necessary'. In order to succeed in it, he needs to exercise self-control, let the potentially dangerous Loaysa disappear from the scene, and then do one of two things. Either he must humbly forgive Leonora for presumed adultery, a step which would give her an opportunity to explain herself and thus help him to trust her in a marriage that would henceforth be more normal; or he must doubt that a well-bred wife who hitherto has doted on him could be utterly and maliciously disloyal to him, must check the evidence by talking to her, and must then forgive her, offering her his future trust, when he receives her explanation. In seeking a reconciliation by either of these two routes, however, he must be prepared to accept a disappointing outcome and to dismantle the marriage as all but a legal contract which protects his wife financially. (Though couples could not divorce each other, it was possible to arrange separations). None of this is possible for him unless he can find those very virtues which have eluded him so far. They are the cardinal virtues of Christianity: justice, temperance, fortitude, and prudence. But his predicament now is more difficult, for he also needs – in conditions which more than ever before are inimical to their acquisition – those higher and supernatural virtues of Christianity which, had Carrizales been blessed with them, would have inclined his will against marriage. The higher virtues are the three 'theological' virtues: faith (profound belief in the truth of Christian revelation, and not the shallow habitual belief whose foundation is human authority), which, if he possessed it in this its supernatural form, would make God the hub of his life; hope (faith-based optimism); and altruistic love, otherwise known as charity. Unfortunately for Carrizales, these higher virtues are gifts of supernatural grace which are accessible only to those whose wills are naturally inclined to receive them. He is therefore in a spiritual double bind. What he most needs – the intervention of grace – he needs in order to correct the very worst in his human nature – his capacity for murderous anger – in the moment of its excitement. His enraged response to the scene in the bedroom is a manifestation of sinfulness in what is almost certainly an utterly helpless form.

The third matrimonial trial begins when the hero's vengeful intentions have been thwarted by a heart attack and he has awakened from a faint, his energy drained and aware that he is dying. His exhaustion and premonition of death can be attributed in the supernatural order to *providentia approbationis*. They prompt him to repent, and a repentance does take place. This is not a healthy repentance involving the receipt of spiritual guidance, however. It is an autonomous form, closed to all external wills, whose central component, the act of penance, is essentially an act of self-reversal consistent with mental *llaneza*. It is reminiscent of the hero's repentance in earlier life as another Prodigal Son, 'un otro Pródigo' (p. 19), a phrase in which 'un otro' signals both circumstantial and moral difference from the biblical prototype. On the previous occasion he reversed himself out of prodigality into prodigious wealth-production. Now he does the same sort of thing in a form which is impious: he turns his jealous possessiveness back to front by willing his widow to marry the man with whom he thinks she has committed adultery. In doing so he ignores signs that he has in fact misjudged her. Probably the more significant ones are the concerned affection his wife displays when he says he is dying, and the goodwill, humility, and candour she displays when telling him that she has offended him only 'in thought' ('con el pensamiento' [p. 45]). It is impossible for a reader to know if such signs are the will of God asserting itself in a way that He knows will be ineffective, or if they are the will of the Devil, now intent on turning his knife in Carrizales's wounds. From Carrizales's point of view, they mean that his wife is a hypocrite. Misunderstood in this way, their sole effect is to re-confirm that his heart is closed to God's grace and that he is disposed to think the worst. Their only effect is to torture him as he premeditates his repentance.

His big speech (pp. 43–4), chiefly addressed to his parents-in-law, is the most delicate and significant example of direct-method characterization to be found anywhere in the text. For a shrewd reader it is shot through with tension and cant. Carrizales does not, in his heart, forgive Leonora for proving the marriage was wrong. He does not forgive her with real generosity of spirit. He still has feelings of tenderness towards her which are inspired by her prettiness, as he reveals, for example, when he refers to her as a gem (*joya*), but he bears her no spiritual love. To the extent that he has moral feelings at all towards Leonora as distinct from towards himself, he actually despises her. At the point at which he discloses how he found her, he spittingly calls her 'ésta' (literally: 'this', which has something like the pejorative force of 'this woman' in English) and not 'my wife' or 'Leonora'. Neither does he have an objective view of the past. Prejudiced by anger, self-pity, and pride, his recollection of it is a kind of sophistry. He virtually claims that the way in which he treated his wife could not have been more prudent or caring, and that her infidelity was ungrateful and unjust. His exculpation of Leonora is a twisted form of self-recrimination. It is driven by the anger he patently feels towards himself for getting himself into trouble. This anger appears in his self-accusing piety. He condemns himself, not for being the

Devil's agent in the life of Leonora, but for attracting the wrath of a jealous God who punishes truant Christians:

> Mas como no se puede prevenir con diligencia humana el castigo que la voluntad divina quiere dar a los que en ella no ponen del todo en todo sus deseos y esperanzas, no es mucho que yo quede defraudado en las mías. (p. 43)
>
> (But since human endeavour cannot prevent the punishment which Divine Will holds for those who fail to entrust their desires and hopes entirely to this Will, then it is not surprising that I should be disappointed in mine. [III, p. 51])

The idea that God has willed an adultery is as grotesque as Carrizales's suggestion later on in his speech that the arrangement of an adulterer's marriage can be counted as an *obra pía* ('pious' or 'good work'). The truth must be that God has simply let nature follow its course. He has allowed Carrizales to suffer the natural consequences of his jealousy, the most painful of which is a delusion. The God in whom Carrizales believes is really a refracted image of his own angry self.

Carrizales is not seeking God's forgiveness any more than he is genuinely forgiving his wife. In part he is coming to terms with his own conscience as a proud and self-reliant man who must deal with his guilt entirely on his own. He is expiating his own self-accusing anger by the *llano* means of reversing the basic mistake he made in marrying Leonora. He is lashing out at his past. Hence he calls his plan a 'vengeance' he is inflicting upon himself. He is also coping with humiliation and bitterness by seeing and representing himself as a responsible and loving husband who is magnanimous in death. At the same time he is courting posthumous fame. As he virtually says to his parents-in-law, he is planning to become a unique example to the outside world of altruism on the part of a dying husband.[9]

[9] He says that he is less hopeful of being remembered for goodness (*bondad*) than for extraordinary simplicity (*simplicidad*) (p. 44). The most important implication of this is that he is more interested in fame itself than in the quality of his fame, though he is not seeking notoriety. What exactly he has in mind is unclear. Carrizales here disappears into the recesses of his own mind, which, since Cervantes does not unlock it for us, challenges our comprehension. In my critical edition I offer two possible readings of his statement: either he suspects that his arrangement of his widow's future will seem harsh to a world that will not know that she is marrying her lover; or he suspects that he will be deemed an incompetent judge of character in choosing Loaysa as his successor. I now find the second reading to be inconsistent with his perception of Loaysa, whom he narrowly sees as the seductive youth who can satisfy Leonora, i.e. as no more and no less than the very inverse of himself. I also think that the first reading is incomplete unless we suppose that his foresight of fame as a 'simple' man entails assumptions about public sensibilities which are prejudiced by his own nature. These assumptions alone could account for his foresight of being remembered more for 'simplicity'. I therefore offer this further reading of his mind: he surmises that people will think less of the goodness of his last wishes (his concern for his wife's future) and more of the eccentric but logical form that it takes. The style of his goodness, so to speak, will impress them more than its quality. This is a reading which seems to me to fit the likely prejudices of

Although Cervantes does not speculate about the destiny of the hero's soul, there are grounds for the utmost pessimism. Carrizales renounces his jealousy only in the sense that he is generous in death. Furthermore his generosity is impious, for he plots a sacrilegious marriage which would unite a pair of adulterers; and his basic motives are bitterness, anger, and pride; not love for his wife, justice, or moral humility. All these failures are signs of a heart which has not received and is closed to saving grace. Their significance is reinforced by the hero's failure to seek spiritual guidance before he decides on a path of repentance, and is consistent with a concluding narrative where no reference is made to a priest attending Carrizales and administering the last rites. There is nothing in the account of his death to restrain a reader who is inclined to see him as irredeemably lost.

From a theological point of view Carrizales's failings are his own responsibility, but from the same point of view they are failings which God foresaw, and from the probing perspective I have taken here, they are 'probable' or 'necessary', as Aristotle would have put it. The fatalistic impression is reinforced when they are seen in the broader context of his life. Though Cervantes gives only a thumbnail sketch of Carrizales as he was in his bachelor years, the complete picture strongly hints that he was someone whose moral *condición* held no vocation for spiritual reunion with God, and that his whole life was the working out of a diabolical will which was virtually that of a supernatural Fate. Carrizales was always at heart a self-reliant materialist. To the extent that he became aware of God in the conduct of his private life, it was only when his life went wrong and it never led to any form of spiritual crisis in which he truly surrendered his will: he remained his own authority. The goods he sought were worldly; and even by worldly standards they were shallow: adventure and pleasure-seeking up to the age of forty-eight, when his money ran out; wealth-creation from forty-eight to sixty-eight; and then comfortable retirement, married to a pretty girl whom he hoped would bear him heirs. Although he was 'liberal' with his worldly wealth, he had no affinity with supernatural love. Returning to Spain as a millionaire, he had no desire to relieve the poverty of his native Extremadura,[10] and his lack of charity was the spiritual void

the man we are dealing with: a self-centred materialist who, in naturally thinking practically rather than morally, does so with a straightforward or *llano* intellect. With this sort of man, 'simplicity' could be the steely practicality which is normally associated with business, not private life. Carrizales is the kind of person who would be happy to be known for preparing for death in a business-like way, and inclined to think that such practical virtue, when shown to the world, overshadows pure goodness.

10 He saw it as a threat to his social tranquility (p. 20). Carrizales's industrious life in the Indies and his hoarding of the wealth he made reflect his idea of a suitable repentance for squandering his inheritance. This receipt of free money and the later reacquisition of wealth test his will to put money beyond need to good use, the last of the trials, built on his success in the Indies, not beginning till he returns to Spain as an old man. Whether the receipt and acquisition of wealth are works of God (*providentia approbationis*) or works of the Devil (*providentia concessionis*) is unclear. In Christian teaching money is a neutral thing and only does harm when it is loved, but Cervantes may have felt that the receipt or acquisition of money which well exceeded a person's individual needs was diabolical. Carrizales is not

which accommodated his marriage: he did not really want a wife; what he wanted was heirs (p. 20; III, p. 11). Neither did he show any genuine charity to his wife's impoverished parents. He did decide to shower them with gifts, but presumably in order to achieve the anaesthetic effects which this liberality so successfully produced (p. 23; III, p. 15). His decision to end his celibacy arose from his desire for heirs, his weakness for a pretty face, and a selfish and complacent view of his bride's immaturity. His greatest passion, his jealousy, was clearly rooted in 'self-love' (what Spaniards call *amor propio*) and was the nastier side of a deep-seated fear of being dispossessed of property, whose more acceptable side was his diligent care of his money. At the deepest level it was a manifestation of his possessiveness towards himself, of his stubborn will to control his own life.

On one level Carrizales is a mythic embodiment of the conflict between the essential demand of Christianity in all its forms – the surrender of the self, of the individual human will – and the egotism of human nature in its mass of fear and desire. On another level he is a particular example of egotism in an extreme form whereby someone who professes the Christian faith may be pathologically incapable of Christian self-surrender. What is the implied archetype? Someone, it seems, who is self-centred and stupid enough to trust his own unguarded judgements; someone who, for the same reasons, is incapable of resisting passions and engaging in self-sacrifice (as distinct from liberality or prodigality); and someone who at no point in life undergoes an adversity to which he or she – probably 'he', as a type conceived before women were socially liberated – cannot find some practical answer in which he finds satisfaction, if not necessarily happiness. It is also someone who fails the test of foreseeing his own death. Rather than focusing his mind on God and seeking an objective view of what his maker expects of him, he preoccupies himself as his life ebbs away with putting his private affairs in order, declaring his will for his dependants, and imagining – perhaps fashioning – his posthumous reputation.

Carrizales's wife is another character who is archetypal beneath the surface of her individuality. The Leonora type is the redeemable version of the Carrizales type, if we think fatalistically. The heroine is the immature but virtuous Christian who fully surrenders herself to God when weakness tells her that she can place no trust in the strength of her own will. Leonora represents this type in the contemporary guise of a young woman (who could also be a young man) whose fear of her own weakness drives her into a convent in search of moral safety. The difference between her and Carrizales is essentially very simple: she is a better-natured person.

guilty of loving money at any point, but he is certainly guilty of poor and abusive stewardship of it, and he should probably be seen as a man who lays up treasure on earth rather than in heaven. His Christian name, *Felipo* or *Filipo* (both forms occur in the first edition), which is an alternative form of the name *Felipe*, symbolically links him with money. A *filipo* was a silver coin minted during the reign of Philip II. It is defined as such by Covarrubias in his dictionary of 1611. See Maurice Molho, 'Aproximación al *Celoso extremeño*', *NRFH,* 38 (1990), 743–92 (p. 749).

It is very important to approach Leonora as an individual when judging her sexuality. Some of Cervantes's modern readers have derided the idea that a girl could refuse to have sexual intercourse having been taken to the brink of the sexual act. It is perfectly possible that Leonora's self-control appeared far-fetched to many of Cervantes's contemporaries, and especially to the men. Although there existed counter-traditions in which noble women and peasant women (but not women of the common urban class) were morally idealized, there still existed older misogynistic traditions which dispraised the female sex in general as morally weak and inferior to the male. What matters for my purposes here is that whatever Cervantes's readers may have thought, Leonora's behaviour could not be more 'probable' when the character is judged as Cervantes depicts her, and not in the light of prejudice. At this point his narrative method is pretty definitive except in dealing with the physical side of sex, and it is not as if he had portrayed Leonora as a woman in a sexual frenzy who suddenly acquires a conscience. The contrary is the case. She enters the seducer's lair only under extreme persuasion and in a zombie-like state of moral paralysis. This patently reflects a conflict between her sensual nature, which has been expertly stirred by Loaysa's procuress (we are told that she speaks the Devil's words), and her sense of obligation towards her husband. She goes where she is invited to go, but she goes there in tears, and with Marialonso almost having to drag her. What then happens is no more and no less than a resolution of her inner conflict which is consistent with both the weakness she showed and the strength which made it unacceptable to her conscience. She goes only as far as the brink of committing the sexual act because to go further would be to become an adulteress, and because that is the point at which her conscience necessarily rebels, revealing what Cervantes calls her *valor* (p. 41; III, p. 47).[11] This is a judgemental word which commends her moral strength. It combines the notions of 'valour' and 'merit', and is translatable as 'mettle'.

The affection Leonora later displays towards her husband in spite of having lost her innocence is entirely in keeping with the character as we already know her. It is the platonic love which she used to feel for him now revived by his suffering, which she registers through a thin skin (one of her traits is *terneza*: 'tenderness' or 'sensitivity': a childish impressionability) and possibly with a private sense of guilt (she does not know the cause of his suffering yet).[12]

When her husband presents his accusation against her, she says nothing in her own defence until she discovers that he wants her to marry Loaysa. At this point she claims that she has sinned against him only 'con el pensamiento' (p. 45)

[11] In the case of a wife, adultery is defined in a very biological way: she is not an adulteress until she has intercourse. Leonora's behaviour may be seen to validate this definition by showing it to be morally safe as an identification of women who are unworthy of being wives.

[12] It is worth remembering that her love for her husband was a 'first love' and that a young woman's first love is always her deepest love, according to Cervantes (p. 23; III, p. 17).

('in thought' [III, p. 53]). This is perfectly true in a technical or legalistic sense (she has not committed adultery) and it is probably true in an absolute moral sense. Considering that she entered the bedroom in a condition of moral paralysis, but that virtue eventually triumphed, it is a reasonable assumption that up to that point her will was uncommitted, and that Loaysa was the only active partner. Her claim, then, is likely to be an honest account of a 'probable' and forgivable sin which consisted only of putting herself in the way of sexual temptation, although it is, of course, at the extreme end of sexual venial sin. What Carrizales has failed to see is that his wife may be an exception to that rule of behaviour which shapes the stereotypical idea of the guilt of a woman whose husband finds her in bed with another man. In him we have another example of the prejudice which has caused some critics to judge Leonora an impossibly virtuous woman. They and Carrizales alike are closed to the idea of a woman who breaks the mould.

Leonora's changing responses to the prejudice shown by her husband – first passive acceptance of guilt as charged, then frantic protest when she discovers her husband's wish for her, followed by a fainting fit – have nothing to do with free will. These reactions do not mean that she is capable of making a moral decision which goes against prior inclination, and neither do they mean that prior inclination can be different from disposition. Leonora simply accepts the awful reality of her situation as she understands it, until she discovers something more on which she naturally chokes. In considering her passive acceptance of guilt, we should bear the following in mind: the fact that from her own point of view as a 'simple' person, she possesses not a shred of evidence to support a claim of innocence in all but thought, as she herself mistakenly says when she makes such a plea (because she is 'simple', it does not occur to her to cite her previous good character, as it were); her knowledge that her husband, by nature, distrusts her, because he is a very jealous man; and the tragic irony that pleading innocence to a disbeliever makes one a bare-faced liar. The change that suddenly comes over her when she learns of her husband's will for her merely refines her characterization as a young woman of superior quality who is vulnerable only when the source of temptation is expertly placed in her imagination (this was Marialonso's skill), or when the man in question is actually trying to seduce her. What her frantic protest shows is that she identifies Loaysa with guilt and depravity (probably with guilt on her own part, as the source of her husband's fatal distress, as well as guilt on Loaysa's part) and is morally horrified by the idea of marrying him. It also shows that she may have been thinking of widowhood in a convent. Prejudiced by her own inclinations, she may have expected Carrizales to be thinking on the same lines.

Though Cervantes feigns not to understand it, her failure to try harder to vindicate herself in her husband's eyes is well explained by the strength of the evidence that weighs against her and the opprobrium attached to lying. Together with her love for her stricken husband and his wish that she should marry the man with whom he thinks she has committed adultery, her disadvantaged position explains why her failure was also a disability – why she was, in fact, tongue-tied by emotion.

In withdrawing into convent life, she is seeking moral safety: she is rejecting a marriage which her conscience forbids but to which she is sexually attracted. Clues are the convent's extreme isolation (it may well belong to an enclosed order) and Cervantes's observation that Loaysa, having heard about the deceased's last wishes (presumably from Marialonso), looked forward to marrying Leonora and was angry when she retreated from the world. Loaysa must have wanted the marriage because the widow was not only beautiful but also very rich. Presumably she knew that he would. She saw the convent as a place of refuge from his sexual charm, his skills of deceit and trespass, and from the persistence he would undoubtedly show in pursuing a highly desirable woman whom he had nearly seduced already, despite the fact that she was married.

But the convent life is also Leonora's vocation. She saw it from the perspective of someone who was used to confinement and who during her childhood had been no stranger to poverty. Whether or not she also saw it as a place of future happiness is another matter entirely, but it is reasonable to suppose that it is in fact such a place. In choosing to become a bride of Christ rather than Loaysa's bride, Leonora has passed a test of conscience in accordance with the will of God that she should surrender herself to Him in Christ, and progress from a natural knowledge to a blessed supernatural knowledge of the truth of revelation – a faithful, loving, hopeful knowledge in the full 'theological' sense. If she has not acquired it in her final hours in the secular world, then certainly during her noviciate (when she will be under spiritual guidance) Leonora will develop a personal sense of community with Christ. Falsely accused, misunderstood, and suffering because of the sins of others, she resembles the historical Jesus. Her painful experience of worldly marriage should open up her heart to grace by helping her to identify with Him more viscerally than she can ever have done before. All that sets her apart from Him is her inability to face the nightmare which was bequeathed to her by her husband. Whilst Christ was granted the strength He needed to conquer His terror of crucifixion, Leonora finds no such strength when she looks forward to further battle against Loaysa. In this she resembles Carrizales, who could not cope with his jealousy as a married man. The difference is that Leonora's fear is a virtuous one which leads her towards her Saviour. Ensuring that she has no love for her money, sexuality, or life in the world, it is the crucial part of her calling. Though not in the lives of other women who have taken the vows of chastity, poverty, and obedience simply because a parent or guardian has ordered them to do so, in Leonora's life the convent is a legitimate place of enclosure. It is where God will bring her to full maturity as the person He means her to be; it is where she will be reborn.

From an intelligent Christian point of view, Leonora's story is no more tragic than that of Christ's passion. The real tragedy is protagonized by Carrizales as a man whose self-possessiveness cuts him off from God's love and who ends his life by imploding into his self-centredness, there to suffer a hell-on-earth which may well lead to perdition in the world to come. This is not a ritual tragedy offered up to a religious culture which the author considers enlightened. It is the more sinister part of an interrogation of Catholic spirituality which is hostile towards both secular Catholicism and Catholic systematic theology. The former, so Cervantes suggests, seldom involves profound conversion, whilst the latter is excessively influenced by Scholastic rationalism. The theologian is psychologically related to the distrustful Carrizales who would minimize his wife's sexuality. He is uncomfortable with a religion based on faith. Wishing to know in as rational a way as he possibly can that God is morally good, he does his best to minimize His mysterious otherness.

As a trial of faith – which is what it boils down to as a problematization of theology – *El celoso extremeño* is essentially an attack on a vision of God that is fearfully anthropomorphic. It reverses the theologian's effort to make God conform to human reason and particularly his effort to reconcile divine sovereignty with human ideas of justice. It does so most disturbingly in the hypothetical treatment of spiritual 'election' which is embedded in the interdependence of Carrizales's life and that of Leonora. Here we are dealing with a logic vacuum which makes the *novela* a Christian equivalent of Absurdist theatre and its author that of a spanner-throwing agnostic. Using the space that Cervantes gives us, let us suppose that Leonora is an 'elected' soul and that Carrizales is not. On this hypothesis God is the alpha and omega of an elective system whose only apparent justification is His own omnipotence. Try to understand its justice and you end up engaging in impious forms of thought. Carrizales was tested and he failed. God knew he would fail, had the power to stop him, but let him go ahead. At the same time He knew that, by delivering himself to the wrong address, Carrizales would ensure that Leonora did the converse. Logic now tells us that God predestined Carrizales to go to the Devil precisely in order that Leonora should surrender herself to Christ, along with her share of Carrizales's money. What would make the tale really bite for a contemporary reader is that neither of these two *ingénus* metaphysically created themselves (both originate in the mind of God, with subordinate help from the Devil) and they may not have possessed the kind of freedom which made them really responsible for their choices, despite the fact that God was continually putting them to the test.

What, then, is Providence? Is it old outrageous Fortune known by a different name? The answer must be no. But if the fiction gives plausible form to the question, to give that answer requires the reader to ignore the voice of autonomous reason and to survive on nothing but faith, whose plank must be the faithfulness of Christ. Whether or not he can do it is another matter. His actual response may be *angst*.

Cervantes narrates the concluding events in a superbly apposite style. Its sheer detachment, which is so inconsistent with the extraordinary nature of what is narrated, is a form of irony which powerfully hints at depth of meaning and at the same time is a plain assertion that the determination of deep meaning is entrusted to the reader. It is one of the strategies Cervantes employs to encourage his public to carry interpretation of the tale beyond the very simple level on which he himself positions it to a deeper level where paper characters become real people, significances are more important, conclusions are risky, and their formation individualizes the reader. It is a style which is both provocative and cautious, willing the reader to engage with the text in a speculative way, whilst technically absolving Cervantes from responsibility for whatever may be discovered. Its significance overlaps with that of his failure to comprehend his heroine when she yields to her husband's delusion. Amongst many other things, this is a veil which Cervantes casts over his curious interest in the doctrine of divine election (his feigned point of view is worldly: he regrets Leonora's silence) but which prompts a reader who has not yet done so to undertake the kind of research which could bring him into contact with that interest.

Considered as a form of caution, the deadpan style is a chip off the same block as the exemplary motif in which characters show us again and again that truth is not the same as perception, and always commit perceptual errors which in some degree are reflections of their qualities as judges. The cautionary implications of this motif are as relevant to how we read the fiction as to how we read real life; the literary-theoretical implications are positively enormous. In this essay I have offered readings of Cervantes's text which I think can be ascribed to the speculative mind of the author, considering the strength of the evidence, the cultural context in which he was writing, and his own awareness that he was anything but *llano.*[13] But such intentionalist interpretation transcends the spirit of the work; indeed, it is out of bounds – non-empathetic – to the point of conflicting with the clearer *ejemplaridad* of Cervantes's text when its meaning is judged by the examples set by deluded characters and a deadpan narrator. For readers who do what Cervantes actually wants them to do, the darker sense of *El celoso extremeño* is whatever sense they find in it by thinking as free agents. This does not mean that one reading is as good as any other, for Cervantes shows that truth exists independently of human judgement, that perception reflects the qualities of the perceiver, and that these may be sources of prejudice. It means rather that the reader is urged to seek what he himself believes and is capable of believing when he is doing his best to protect himself against prejudice in all its forms. A compliant reader endeavours to be a free-thinker.

The intentionalist critic on the other hand is faced with a task which is more difficult even than this: identifying those mechanisms of remote control which are designed to lead free-thinking readers to meanings which are preconceived. Needless to say, I have not hoped to convince the readers of this essay that what it says of Cervantes's thinking on human freedom is more or less true; I have hoped to convince them that what it says may be more or less true. Cervantes allows no higher aspirations.

[13] For example, in his late allegorical poem, the *Viaje del Parnaso* (Journey to Parnassus; Ch. 1), he singles out imagination and subtlety as his special artistic gifts. Mercury hails him as a 'rare inventor' and writer of 'subtle designs' ('sutil designio').

Works cited

Cervantes Saavedra, Miguel de, *Exemplary Novels / Novelas ejemplares*, ed. B. W. Ife, 4 vols (Warminster: Aris & Phillips, 1992), III, pp. 8–55.

———, *'El viejo celoso' and 'El celoso extremeño'*, ed. Paul Lewis-Smith (London: Bristol Classical Press, 2001).

Dorsche, T. S. (tr. and intro.), *Classical Literary Criticism* (Harmondsworth: Penguin, 1965).

Lewis-Smith, Paul, 'Fictionalizing God: Providence, Nature, and the Significance of Rape in *La fuerza de la sangre*', *MLR*, 91 (1996), 886–97.

Molho, Maurice, 'Aproximación al *Celoso extremeño*', *NRFH,* 38 (1990), 743–92.

10

Performances of Pastoral in *La ilustre fregona*: Games within the Game

D. Gareth Walters
University of Exeter

It is no surprise that pastoral has proved to be one of the more important areas of study for Cervantes scholars. Although it is not a dominant issue in *Don Quijote* the fact that his first book was a pastoral romance has tempted commentators to explore aspects of his later works by reference to the pastoral ethos, first incorporated in *La Galatea*. Such a consideration extends to those works, like *La ilustre fregona* (The Illustrious Kitchen Maid), that at first sight appear removed from sixteenth-century Spanish pastoral fiction. Two factors perhaps have been responsible for this probing for evidence of traces of the genre in unpromising settings. First, there is the nature of *La Galatea* itself and the way in which it has not yielded to a critical consensus. According to Mary Malcolm Gaylord some critics see it as 'too pastoral and insufficiently Cervantine', while others acknowledge that it is 'quite recognizably its author's work, but imperfectly pastoral'.[1] Little wonder then that Elizabeth Rhodes should refer to it as 'a text which is categorized as pastoral with some hesitancy'.[2] Secondly there is the protean quality of the term 'pastoral'. It ranges from the precisely delimiting, as when referring to the competing songs of shepherds, following a Theocritan or Virgilian model, to a definition such as 'any literature which deals with the complexities of human life against a background of simplicity'.[3] The image of Cervantes as a pioneer, as a 'modern' writer, readily encourages the broader acceptance of the term so that there is every reason for viewing works such as *La ilustre fregona* and *La gitanilla* (The Little Gypsy Girl) as, if not quite versions of pastoral, then certainly as texts that incorporate it. In the case of the former, the author himself provides the most blatant of nudges and winks at the

1 Mary Malcolm Gaylord, 'Cervantes' Other Fiction', in *The Cambridge Companion to Cervantes*, ed. Anthony J. Cascardi (Cambridge: Cambridge University Press, 2002), pp. 100–30 (p. 102).

2 Elizabeth Rhodes, 'Sixteenth-century Pastoral Books, Narrative Structure and *La Galatea* of Cervantes', *BHS*, 56 (1989), 351–60 (p. 351).

3 Peter V. Marinelli, *Pastoral*, The Critical Idiom 15 (London: Methuen, 1971), p. 3.

very start when Carriazo's experience of the picaresque life in the tunny fisheries is couched in terms of the *locus amoenus* of pastoral.[4] We might mistake the following sentence for a paraphrase of Garcilaso, the opening of such poems as his *Canción III* or *Égloga II*: 'ni el andar a pie le cansaba, ni el frío le ofendía, ni el calor le enfadaba. Para él todos los tiempos del año le eran dulce y templada primavera' ('nor did foot-slogging tire him, nor the cold bother him, nor the heat annoy him. All the seasons of the year were like a sweet, mild springtime to him').[5] When Cervantes later speaks of how this idyll is threatened by the sporadic attacks of Berber pirates on the Mediterranean coast of Spain, how 'esta dulzura que he pintado tiene un amargo acíbar que la amarga' (p. 375) ('the sweetness of this life that I have described has a bitter edge to it' [III, p. 65]), there is a reminiscence of Góngora's evocation in his famous *romance* 'En un pastoral albergue' of how the idyllic love of Ángelica and Medoro is ultimately menaced by the jealousy of Count Orlando. Less obviously, though plausibly in the light of the more generous understanding of pastoral, the inn where Avendaño and Carriazo stay while in Toldedo, according to Robert M. Johnston 'has similarities to a pastoral setting. It resembles the world of *La Galatea* in the way characters move freely in and out of its sphere'.[6] The inn, so others suggest, also represents a further trait of pastoral, that of a place apart: 'a sojourn in the pastoral oasis' (Hart, p. 287), and 'a stop-over on the excursions of life and identity'.[7]

William Clamurro, however, also draws attention to ways in which *La ilustre fregona* is not so easily recognizable as a pastoral. On the one hand, 'the quintessential thematic focus of conventional Renaissance pastoral – the discussion of the nature of love – is largely absent' (p. 194). On the other, 'it is clear that a version of pastoral discourse has been intertwined with elements of the picaresque and the familiar comedic discourse of loss and recovery, sin and restitution' (p. 195). These reservations are indicative of confusion or conflation, mainly because while Clamurro acknowledges, as have other commentators, the function of pastoral and the picaresque in the *novela*, he leaves out of the reckoning a third element which is better treated for the present purpose as separate from pastoral: the courtly. Accordingly my own understanding of *La ilustre fregona* has as its foundation (i) the precise nature of the relationship of the

[4] See Thomas R. Hart, 'Versions of Pastoral in Three *Novelas ejemplares*', *BHS*, 58 (1981), 283–91 (p. 285).

[5] Miguel de Cervantes, *Novelas ejemplares*, ed. Jorge García López (Barcelona: Crítica, 2001), p. 371. Translations are taken from Miguel de Cervantes, *Exemplary Novels / Novelas ejemplares*, ed. B. W. Ife, 4 vols (Warminster: Aris and Phillips, 1992), III (here p. 63). Further references are to these editions.

[6] Robert M. Johnston, 'Picaresque and Pastoral in *La ilustre fregona*', in *Cervantes and the Renaissance*, ed. Michael D. McGaha (Easton, PA: Juan de la Cuesta, 1980), pp. 167–77 (p. 172).

[7] William H. Clamurro, 'Identity, Discourse and Social Order: *La ilustre fregona*', in *Beneath the Fiction: The Contrary Worlds of Cervantes's 'Novelas ejemplares'* (New York: Peter Lang, 1997), pp. 191–209 (p. 208).

picaresque to the pastoral, and (ii) the distinctive significance of the courtly and its relationship to both of these.

The picaresque material of the *novela* is easily located. It centres on Carriazo and comprises his deeds past (the tunny fisheries) and present (the inn and the streets of Toledo), and the characters with whom he comes into contact both at the inn and while he plies his trade as a water-seller under the name of Lope Asturiano. He displays such hallmark characteristics of the *pícaro* as card-sharping skills and the successful use of physical violence. Yet graphic though the picaresque traits may be, commentators by and large have resisted accepting them without qualification. Whether this is due to fastidiousness about using a term that has such precise narrative implications – one that involves perspective, voice and attitude as well as subject-matter or content – is not clear. At one extreme is Joaquín Casalduero's outright dismissal of picaresque elements, but then he sees little evidence of pastoral in Cervantes either.[8] Other, more temperate approaches, postulate a fusion of the pastoral and the picaresque. Clamurro's idea of how they are 'intertwined' has already been cited (p. 195), while in similar vein Johnston suggests that Cervantes 'combines conventions from both pastoral and picaresque to produce something entirely new' (p. 167). That Cervantes's *novela* should be novel appears to me more than an etymological truism, but I believe that this quality is not dependent on either an 'intertwining' or a 'combination'. Rather it involves a separation of the two concepts. I do not, however, propose an understanding that implies antithesis, but one involving complementarity: the picaresque in apposition to the pastoral or, in other terms, as a sub-division – picaresque as a version of pastoral. The two have at first glance some features that can be seen to fit either genre, as we have already seen: the notion of escape or holiday, and the location, whether the tunny fisheries or the inn. What clarifies the nature of the relationship between the picaresque and the pastoral, however, is the third element – the courtly. Although commentators have been active in exploring the many avenues of pastoral and the manifestations of the picaresque they have hardly focused on the details of what is very appropriately designated courtly love in the *novela*. This is because the courtly can readily be considered synonymous with pastoral: the tribulations of the fictional shepherd are identical to those of his courtly counterpart. To distinguish between them, it could be argued, is to split hairs. Clamurro, in particular, understates the significance of the distinctiveness of the amatory aspiration entertained by Avendaño when he refers to 'the presence of the pastoral [. . .] in the conventional motif of courtship', and when he relegates 'romantic love' (and the choice of term is significant) to 'a necessary *given* of the story' and to merely 'a part in the text' (pp. 194–95).

Such an appraisal does not do justice to the wealth and precision of detail in Cervantes's portrayal of the stages of Avendaño's courtship of Costanza. Indeed,

[8] Joaquín Casalduero, 'Cervantes rechaza la pastoril y no acepta la picaresca', *BHS*, 61 (1984), 283–85.

the more this is examined the more the term 'courtly love' appears a necessary one, as both the plot and the protagonist's responses betray the classic features of the phenomenon as expressed in Renaissance poetry. Let us examine some of these in detail. It is through report and reputation that Avendaño falls in love, having overheard the discussion between the Andalusian muleteers about how beautiful Costanza is. His curiosity is sufficiently aroused for him to be receptive to love, imbued as he is with the 'intenso deseo de verla' (p. 383) ('eager desire to set eyes on her' [III, p. 71]). In Golden-Age poetry, the sight of the beloved, especially on a first meeting, was afforded a quasi-religious intensity. When the time comes, Avendaño is not to be disappointed:

> No puso Avendaño los ojos en el vestido y traje de la moza, sino en su rostro, que le parecía ver en él los que suelen pintar de los ángeles. Quedó suspenso y atónito de su hermosura, y no acertó a preguntarle nada, tal era su supensión y embelesamiento. (p. 384)
>
> (Avendaño was oblivious of the girl's dress but stared at her face, which to him looked like an angel's, just as in the paintings. He was awestruck by her beauty and could not think of anything to say to her, so stunned and entranced was he. [III, p. 73])

Cervantes does more than shape his narrative according to a literary amatory convention. He endows his love-struck hero with the kind of verbal wit that is surprising in one 'todo lleno de turbacion y sobresalto' (p. 384) ('in a complete daze, his mind in turmoil' [III, p. 73]), when he responds to Costanza's question:

> —¿Qué busca, hermano? ¿Es por ventura criado de alguno de los huéspedes de casa?
> —No soy criado de ninguno, sino vuestro- respondió Avendaño [. . .] (p. 384)[9]
>
> ('What are you looking for, brother? Are you by any chance the servant of one of the guests?' 'No, I am no man's servant but yours', answered Avendaño [. . .]' [III, p. 73])

Avendaño is totally smitten – wounded, as Carriazo perceptively discerns, by the 'amorosa pestilencia' ('plague of love' [III, p. 73]). Distinctively courtly, too, is the lover's blasphemous tone when Avendaño observes that it would be as impossible to separate him from Costanza's face 'como no es posible ir al cielo sin buenas obras' (p. 386) ('as impossible as to go to heaven without good works' [III, p. 75]). The jealousy that surfaces when he discovers that the Corregidor's son is a rival in love is often a requisite emotion in courtly love. Finally, the method

[9] A similar verbal subtlety involving double-meaning and a play on the literal and the metaphoric, albeit in a far less noble cause, characterizes the speech of Don Juan Tenorio in *El burlador de Sevilla*, notably in the scene where he is rescued from drowning by the fisher-girl Tisbea.

by which he eventually declares his passion through the stratagem of pretending to supply Costanza with a prayer to remedy her toothache when what she will read will be a confession of her suitor's ambitions constitutes a characteristic courtly-Petrarchist blend of timidity and daring, extremes at which the true lover perpetually seems to operate.

What confirms Avendaño's role as a courtly lover is the matching conception of Costanza as a courtly lady. When he blurts out that he serves her and no one else he is doing no more than pay her the appropriate homage. For there is nothing in her demeanour or conduct that gives the lie to her illustriousness of status – a condition that is as appropriate at this stage in the narrative, within the courtly play, as it is when her true identity is eventually confirmed. Ruth El Saffar does not accurately represent the distinctive roles of the two courtly lovers, therefore, when she states that Avendaño 'transforms himself into her image, becoming, like her, hard-working, patient and passive'.[10] Avendaño is hardly passive, except perhaps by comparison with Carriazo in his picaresque mode. As a decorous lover, however, he is inventive and probing. He can improvise, as when he lies to deceive the innkeeper, and he is imaginative in exploiting the circumstances of Costanza's toothache to advance his amatory cause.

Equally inapposite is the description of Costanza as 'un personaje pasivo que no manifiesta sus sentimientos ni influye en la acción' (a passive character who does not reveal her feelings or influence the action).[11] Cervantes, however, endows her not only with discretion but with verbal finesse, both in her cool-headed reply to Avendaño's initial compliment about being her servant and later when she skilfully deflects his written avowal of love in a way that rebukes but does not entirely discourage him. Such poise and initiative are signs of one who can play the courtly role to perfection, not of a hapless young woman who is at the mercy of circumstances. She is not then, as Berrenechea goes on to claim, 'un personaje en hueco, que el lector sólo conoce a través de los otros personajes por el influjo que ejerce en ellos' (p. 200) (a blank character, whom the reader only knows through the other characters and her effect on them). Furthermore, her reaction to Avendaño's letter is not so unexpected or out of character as to comprise a 'crucial but curious moment in the narrative' (Clamurro, pp. 204–5). Her role-play, unlike that of her suitor, may be unwittingly undertaken but her behaviour can only be properly assessed and understood in the context of a well-worn amatory literary convention.

Almost alone among those who have written on this *novela*, Karl-Ludwig Selig points to the philosophico-poetic conception of Costanza when he refers to 'the language, conventions, conceits, and images of love highly intellectualized,

[10] Ruth El Saffar, *Novel to Romance: A Study of Cervantes's 'Novelas ejemplares'* (Baltimore and London: Johns Hopkins University Press, 1974), p. 93.

[11] Ana María Berrenechea, '*La ilustre fregona* como ejemplo de estructura novelesca cervantina', in *Actas del Primer Congreso Internacional de Hispanistas celebrado en Oxford del 6 al 11 de septiembre de 1962*, ed. Frank Pierce and Cyril A. Jones (Oxford: Dolphin, 1964), pp. 199–206 (p. 199).

of neo-Platonism, and of certain aspects of Petrarchism'.[12] He also appreciates the consciously literary manner of Cervantes's presentation of his eponymous heroine: 'her descriptions reflect the aesthetic and artistic principles of idealized portraiture', so that 'her appearance is art itself' (p. 118). To illustrate this point he compares the depiction of her that includes the phrase 'una gargantilla de estrellas de azabache sobre un pedazo de una coluna de alabastro, que no era menos blanca su garganta' (p. 390) ('a necklace of jet-black stars on an alabaster column, for her throat was no less white' [III, p. 78]) to one from Garcilaso's *soneto* XXIII: 'por el hermoso cuello blanco, enhiesto' (on her lovely white neck held aloft) (Selig, p. 118).

That Costanza, like her counterpart in *La gitanilla*, should be able to preserve her honour in the unpromising setting of an inn is no less than what would be expected of one who plays the courtly part so well. Johnston correctly observes that she 'remains a symbol of virtue, and she encourages neither of her suitors' (p. 169). However, if we read the signs correctly – and the signs are there from the start – we will realize that Costanza's virtue is not going to be an issue, unlike for instance, Leonora's in *El celoso extremeño*. It is a given, a conventional and necessary quality, so we are not surprised that she should be neither threatened nor tempted. Consequently, the following explanations of Costanza's behaviour seem to me deficient in one important respect: 'Los cánones de la época imponían el ideal de la doncella que apenas osa levantar la vista para mirar a un hombre, que no habla si no la interrogan', and '[Costanza] está dentro de las reglas sociales y aún conviene que se extreme su recato como contraste con el tráfago que la rodea' (the social canons of the period imposed the ideal of the maiden who scarcely dares raise her eyes to look at a man, who does not speak unless she is spoken to; [Costanza] lives within the social conventions it is even necessary for her to exaggerate her reserve to offset the hustle and bustle that surrounds her) (Berrenechea, pp. 199–200). It is not social conventions that govern Costanza, however, as much as literary ones. If there are any rules involved they are those of courtly observance, not of contemporary morality. Such recognition makes her conduct more rather than less plausible in such unlikely surroundings, though it is opportune to recall how some commentators were disposed to interpret the inn at Toledo in terms of a pastoral location.

The separation of the courtly from the pastoral has enabled us to have a clearer view of the roles of the two male protagonists. Indeed the relationship of the courtly is, I believe, identical to that of the picaresque to pastoral: as a sub-division and, as I shall now explore, as a game within a game. Avendaño and Carriazo are participants in a game within the pastoral fiction, a game for two players: the *pícaro* ('rogue' or 'delinquent') and the courtly lover. The incorporation of double protagonists is common enough in Cervantes, as witness *Rinconete y Cortadillo*

[12] Karl-Ludwig Selig, 'The Metamorphosis of the *Ilustre fregona*', in *Filología y crítica hispánica. Homenaje al Prof. Federico Sánchez Escribano*, ed. Alberto Porqueras Mayo and Carlos Rojas (Madrid: Ediciones Alcalá, 1969), pp. 115–20 (p. 118).

and *El coloquio de los perros*. Commentators have justifiably drawn attention to the contrasts between the male leads of *La ilustre fregona*, but for some such an opposition appears a defect. In the opinion of William C. Atkinson the whole of the *novela* is less than the sum of its parts;[13] while Clamurro feels it to be 'somewhat disorganized and random' on an initial reading because 'the two young men whose adventures and desires dominate the narrative bring with them two very different kinds of action and hence two distinct generically determined tendencies of discourse' (p. 192). Such a conclusion is reinforced by the views of *cervantistas* such as Joaquín Casalduero, for whom Avendaño and Carriazo are 'amigos con una concepción opuesta del mundo' (friends with opposing views of the world),[14] and Harry Sieber, who believes that *La ilustre fregona* 'es una de las novelas ejemplares más curiosas' (one of the most intriguing of the Exemplary Novels), comprising as it does 'dos novelas de dos amigos' (two novels about two friends).[15] An even more extreme statement of this antithetical conception of the relationship is the one advocated by Berrenechea, in whose view the two protagonists partly resemble Don Quijote and Sancha Panza:

> Avendaño no come y no duerme perdido en sus pensamientos amorosos, mientras Carriazo come y duerme a su antojo. Al amor ideal del uno se oponen las metas más terrenas del otro (Costanza: Dulcinea; Almadrabas: Ínsula). [. . .] Avendaño es el héroe noble, mientras Carriazo despierta la risa, da y recibe golpes. (p. 202)
>
> (Lost in his amorous thoughts, Avendaño neither eats nor sleeps, while Carriazo eats and sleeps as he pleases. The more worldly goals of the one are set against the ideal love of the other [Costanza: Dulcinea; Tunny fisheries: Island]. [. . .] Avendaño is the noble hero, while Carriazo makes us laugh as he gives and takes hard knocks.)

I suggest, on the contrary, that there is more that unites the two protagonists than divides them. At the level of the plot they are bound together in friendship, as witness Carriazo's generous decision to stay with Avendaño rather than to go off to his beloved tunny fisheries. Such difference as there is can only be explained in terms of rivalry, but a rivalry that in both conception and realization is ludic in nature. It is moreover comprehensible as pastoral, as though they were two 'shepherds' further disguised as a *pícaro* and courtly lover respectively. In this connection it is pertinent to note that Cervantes thought of *La Galatea* as an eclogue and, as Rhodes reminds us, that he expressed 'a consciousness of having composed *poetry* when he penned *La Galatea*' (p. 352). Indeed, in the

13 William C. Atkinson, 'Cervantes, el Pinciano and the *Novelas ejemplares*', *HR*, 16 (1948), 189–208.

14 Joaquín Casalduero, *Sentido y forma de las 'Novelas ejemplares'* (Madrid: Gredos, 1962), p. 32.

15 Miguel de Cervantes, *Novelas ejemplares*, ed. Harry Sieber, 16th edn, 2 vols (Madrid: Cátedra, 1995), II, p. 21.

scrutiny undertaken of Don Quijote's library, Montemayor's *Diana* and its imitations are all called 'poetry'.

A classic feature of the eclogue is that of the 'desdoblamiento' (doubling): two shepherds vying with each other in song. The most famous example in Spanish literature is Garcilaso's *Égloga I*, where the shepherds Salicio and Nemoroso are allocated equal space for the articulation of their laments. The seriousness of the subject – betrayal versus bereavement – should not blind us to the playful origin of such a conception, as indeed Garcilaso himself implicitly reminds us through the reappearance of two shepherds in a more overtly ludic guise at the end of *Égloga III*. For instance, after Tirreno sings of fertility and the abundance of crops but how it will all change if his beloved, Flérida, abandons the place (ll. 337–44), Alcino in an alternating *octava* makes an opposite point, as he paints a picture of a sterile, harsh landscape that will come to bloom if his own mistress, Filis, were to return (ll. 345–52).[16] Such alternating or amoebean exchanges also characterize the repartee of the two 'shepherds' of *La ilustre fregona*. A mode of verbal parrying characterizes several of the discussions between Avendaño and Carriazo, notably when it comes to an argument about whether they should stay in Toledo or leave, as originally planned, for the tunny fisheries. Although the realization of the debate in the form of a prose dialogue approximates more to an *altercatio* than do the more rigidly structured dictates of the poetic form in Garcilaso there is nonetheless a reminiscence of the spirit of the game in the way in which one protagonist replies to the other in matching structures and similar syntactical patterning. Avendaño's riposte to Carriazo's jibe

> ¡Bien cuadra un don Tomás de Avendaño, hijo de don Juan de Avendaño, caballero lo que es bueno; rico lo que basta; mozo lo que alegra; discreto, lo que admira, con enamorado y perdido por una fregona que sirve en el mesón del Sevillano! (p. 386)
>
> (How fitting it is for one Don Tomás de Avendaño, son of Don Juan de Avendaño, every bit a gentleman, well off, a merry young man, eminently sensible, to fall head over heels in love with a serving-girl at the Sevillano Inn! [III, p. 75])

is:

> considerar un don Diego de Carriazo, hijo del mismo, caballero del hábito de Alcántara el padre, y el hijo a pique de heredarle con su mayorazgo [. . .] y [. . .] verle enamorado ¿de quién, si pensáis? ¿De la reina Ginebra? No, por cierto, sino de la almadraba de Zahara, que es más fea, a lo que creo, que un miedo de Santo Antón. (pp. 386–7)

16 Garcilaso de la Vega, *Poesías castellanas completas*, ed. Elias L. Rivers, 2nd edn (Madrid: Clásicos Castalia, 1972), pp. 206–7.

> (consider one Don Diego de Carriazo, son of a gentleman of the same name, the father a knight of the order of Alcántara, and the son [. . .] on the point of inheriting his *mayorazgo* [. . .] Witness him in love, and with Queen Guinevere? Certainly not, but with the tunny fisheries at Zahara, which are more repugnant, in my opinion, than the temptations of Saint Anthony. [III, p. 75])

The diction employed by Avendaño in his reply reinforces the case I am making for seeing both youths as shepherds. Rhodes asserts that 'shepherds are depicted as representative of the human condition [. . .] and are obsessed by love' (Rhodes, p. 352). Yet Carriazo, it will be objected, is not a lover and therefore can hardly be a shepherd to compete with the shepherd-cum-courtly lover that is Avendaño. Crucially, however, the nature of Carriazo's attachment to the picaresque life and to his beloved tunny fisheries is repeatedly envisaged as infatuation. Indeed, when Avendaño, in the extract quoted above, refers to him as 'enamorado [. . .] de la almadraba de Zahara' ('in love [. . .] with the tunny fisheries at Zahara'), he is doing no more than mimic the kind of language that Carriazo himself adopts or by which he is described. The very structuring of sentences has the effect of highlighting the directness of the contrasts between the two loves, as when Carriazo, losing patience with Avendaño, says: 'yo me iré con mi almadraba, y tú te quedarás con tu fregona' (p. 387) ('I'll go off to my tunny fisheries and you'll stay here with your kitchen-maid' [III, p. 75]). Even incidental turns of phrase bear the imprint of the lover's reasoning and diction. When he yearns for the tunny fisheries back in his parents' home we learn that 'en ellas [las almadrabas] tenía de contino puesta la imaginación' (p. 377) ('he had them [the tunny fisheries] on his mind continuously' [III, p. 65]). Such a formulation is a standard for the description of an unrequited lover, as indeed is Avendaño's view of him as 'melancólico e imaginativo' (p. 377) ('melancholy and pensive' [III, p. 65]). A similar lexicon is employed for Avendaño's own reactions after the initial encounter with Costanza: 'Carriazo cenó lo que le dieron y Avendaño lo que con él llevaba, que fueron pensamientos e imaginaciones' (p. 385) ('Carriazo dined on what they gave him and Avendaño on what he took with him, that is, thoughts and fancies' [III, p. 75]).

Having established the two guises of pastoral in the shape of our two protagonists united in friendly rivalry and sharing a common discourse it is now opportune to introduce a character who is anything but playful in the way that the two young men are: Carriazo's father. His function belongs very much in the past and he does not figure in the same settings as do the younger protagonists. Nonetheless, his behaviour invites assessment against theirs: like Avendaño he harboured a desire for a woman, and like his own son, 'a chip off the block' according to Barry Ife, he was impulsive.[17] Evidently he comes off worse in both comparisons. Whereas Avendaño pursues Costanza with an unerring decorum

17 B. W. Ife, 'From Salamanca to Brighton Rock: Names and Places in Cervantes' *La ilustre fregona*', in *Essays in Honour of Robert Brian Tate from his Colleagues and Pupils*, ed. Richard A. Cardwell (Nottingham: University of Nottingham, 1984), pp. 46–52 (p. 47).

within the courtly norms Carriazo senior had no compunction about raping her mother. There is perhaps a further connection between them. It is implied that the elder Carriazo had not seen Costanza's mother before the fateful meeting although the text is spare in ancillary detail and background at this point in the narrative. What we know is that one day, while out hunting, Carriazo senior decides to pay Costanza's mother a visit. He relates how on entering her bedroom, where she was taking a siesta, he is struck by her extreme beauty, even taken by surprise by it. His appraisal of the mother – 'Era por estremo hermosa' (p. 434) ('She was extraordinarily beautiful' [III, p. 129]) – is akin to that of Avendaño's when confronted by the daughter, so the presumption may well be that he, too, has got to know of her by reputation rather than prior acquaintanceship. While Avendaño immediately slips into the courtly role, however, the older man seeks instant gratification, with no thought of controlling or channelling his lust. The very wealth of detail of courtly observance that Cervantes bestows upon Avendaño serves only to throw into sharper relief the criminal recklessness of Carriazo's father.

Those commentators who are eager to point to similarities of character between the two generations of Carriazo run the risk of over-simplification. In the case of Ruth El Saffar the conclusion is erroneous, more than just over-stated: 'Don Diego de Carriazo, father and son, are redeemed from the effects of their aimlessness, lawlessness and lust by Costanza' (p. 107). This observation, tarring the two Carriazos with the same brush, scarcely does justice to Cervantes's subtle realization of the son's behaviour. For much of the *novela* he struggles with the demons of instinct whereas his father had not even entered this particular fray. More than that, he is ultimately successful, as a comparison of the outcome of the two principal picaresque episodes of the work reveals. In the encounter with the water-carrier his impetuosity gets the better of him and he returns the violence meted out to him with interest, as a result of which he is arrested and thrown into prison. In the second episode, too, the game of cards threatens to turn nasty after Carriazo's cunning at including the donkey's tail in the bet. When the other players start to object he backs up his devious strategy with a blatant threat of violence, of a kind picked up during his time at the tunny fisheries. However, on seeing the distress that his ruse provokes in his hapless victim he pulls back. In an act of surprising generosity he returns all the money he had won, aware that he is not so much playing a game of cards as playing the role of *pícaro*. The awareness that he is involved in such a game – a fiction – serves to check his violent instincts, for when one plays a game one subscribes – theoretically at the very least – to the rules. In a sense Carriazo ultimately demonstrates that he has learnt from Avendaño who, as we have seen, has been meticulously heeding the rules of his own game of love all the while.

Because these games are here rather more than just play they have obvious beneficial effects on the young men's behaviour at a social level. As well as guidance, they supply curbs, without which a life would be more prone to the uncertainties of fate. Indeed Carriazo senior prefaces his account of how he raped Costanza's mother with the phrase 'Ordenó la suerte' (p. 434) ('Fate decreed'

[III, p. 129]). He does not or cannot avail himself of corrective or deflective behavioural conventions. Consequently the conclusions of some commentators regarding the nature of such controls are open to question. They are not socially imposed; in fact the *novela*, if anything, implies the opposite. Theresa Ann Sears is correct in highlighting the dangers of desire as an important area of concern in the works of Cervantes. I do not, however, share her remedy of how desire can be controlled: by binding it to the 'social roles the participants play' or, more specifically 'to the familial roles he [Cervantes] associates with his protagonists', thereby distinguishing them 'from the substantial tradition of literary lovers'.[18] She concludes that 'what Cervantes gives us, in the end, is desire tamed, idealized yes, but more than that subjected to a controlling ideology' (p. 138). Yet there is nothing social, familial or overarchingly ideological about the methods to which Avendaño and Carriazo have recourse. That social life and its associated customs and pastimes cannot curb desire is surely borne out by the fact that Carriazo's father was engaged in the standard social pursuit of hunting prior to his assault. Again, the way in which the two young protagonists deceive their tutor and escape from him provides a clear sign of how 'social control' is rejected. When Avendaño and Carriazo set out on their adventure, under the pretence of going to study at Salamanca, the two fathers make due arrangements: 'proveyéronles de dineros y enviaron con ellos un ayo que los gobernase' (p. 378) ('having supplied them with money, they sent a tutor who would keep an eye on their behaviour' [III, p. 67]). Control is, rather, achieved through their own initiative – the adoption of guises and games – and not socially prescribed. In this way we could add to the various interpretations of pastoral in *La ilustre fregona* an understanding of it as a safety-valve. This does not, therefore, suggest a view of the protagonists' aspiration as 'a flight to the underworld of *pícaros*' motivated by a 'high-spirited desire for adventure and freedom' (El Saffar, p. 87). Rather it is nearer to the pastoral ideal of a movement 'through release to clarification' (Hart, p. 288) that produces an awareness and achievement of responsibility, not its abdication. In *La ilustre fregona* both the classical and modern understandings of pastoral are valid: through a version of the eclogue – essentially a poetic conception – Cervantes sets in motion the impetus towards self-knowledge that is a trademark objective of the genre in its more modern acceptance, and beyond that, he ultimately confirms the successful outcome of the games within the game.

No essay on any of the *Novelas ejemplares* would be complete without some consideration of what lesson may be learnt from it. I raise this issue especially because I share a view expressed by Sears:

> few critics [. . .] at least, until recently, have confronted the full complexity of Cervantes's involvement with the fictional ramifications of desire. In all too many cases, readers have distanced themselves from the very palpable

[18] Theresa Ann Sears, *A Marriage of Convenience: Ideal and Ideology in the 'Novelas ejemplares'* (New York: Peter Lang, 1993), pp. 136–7.

> atmosphere of anxiety, violence and uneasiness that pervades Cervantine texts by interposing philosophical, religious, and other symbolic systems between reader and literary text. (p. 131)

In particular it appears to me that the magnitude and the impact of the crime committed by Carriazo's father has been grossly understated. Whether this is because commentators have, as Sears implies, a particular agenda or *parti pris* that would simply wish away the grimmer edges in the stories or (to be more charitable) because the narrative itself is so matter-of-fact and downplayed at this juncture I cannot tell. Symptomatic of this tendency to gloss over the rape is Casalduero's failure even to mention the fact in his otherwise detailed summary of the plot, confining himself to how Carriazo's father recounts 'los sucesos que dieron lugar al nacimiento de Costanza' (the circumstances that led to Costanza's birth) (*Sentido y forma*, p. 192). Yet he is not alone in diluting the significance of this criminal act. Other commentators, as we have already seen, endeavour to stress the similarity of father and son as though their respective (mis)deeds were equally immoral. El Saffar's observation on how 'father and son are redeemed from the effects of their aimlessness, restlessness and lust by Costanza' (p. 107) has already been cited. Now we can appreciate how careless the enumeration is when applied to the two without distinction: the son may be aimless and restless, but he is not lustful, while the reverse is true of the father. Ife, likewise, is content to bracket the two together, thereby inviting a blanket judgement, when he speaks of the 'family curse' and 'the ghost of the Carriazo fecklessness' only being laid to rest with the third generation, that is when Carriazo junior's three sons actually do go to the University of Salamanca (p. 48). That this critic should seemingly equate rape with truancy is the more strange in view of the concluding paragraph he dedicates to the 'violated woman' in a more recent general study of Cervantes: 'Amid all the fluidity of Spanish society, Cervantes seems to argue, there are some things that never change. The violated woman has no value in the sexual economy of the time, and she can only be redeemed by marriage to the rapist, however implausibly this is brought about'.[19] Carriazo senior evidently had no thought of making amends until many years later and only when prompted by another event – the visit of the major-domo who had served Costanza's mother. Admittedly as a married man, marriage to the woman he had raped was not feasible, but what is striking about his account is the total lack of remorse. It is hard to see in his narrative any evidence of what Clamurro refers to as a 'guilt-driven conclusion' (p. 199). Yet this critic, unlike others, correctly perceives the differences between father and son: 'the wandering of the father's lust demonstrates the man's weaker, baser side, while the exuberant wanderlust of the son serves to underscore his virtue, as his noble character shows forth [. . .]' (p. 199). I would merely add to this that there is an irony in the fact that,

[19] B. W. Ife, 'The Historical and Social Context', in *The Cambridge Companion to Cervantes*, ed. Anthony J. Cascardi (Cambridge: Cambridge University Press, 2002), pp. 11–31 (p. 30).

though seemingly the rebel, it is the son who ultimately displays socially acceptable qualities, while the father, a nobleman and Knight of the Order of Alcántara, is the source and perpetrator of disorder and disruption.

What it is hard to see in the *novela* is that sense of redemption mentioned by Clamurro: 'The two youths' relatively innocent excursions and disguisings will correspond to and help redeem the previous and more grave moral detour of Carriazo senior' (p. 197). He is much nearer the mark when he alludes to 'the relative moral freedom of the elder Carriazo to sin and then, quite late, to make seemingly adequate restitution' (p. 208). The stock conclusion of the multiple marriages is a resolution at the level of the plot, but it would strain tolerance and generosity to interpret the mere acknowledgement of paternity as an act of penance or redemption.

In the last analysis, then, there is every reason to believe without demur or regret that *La ilustre fregona* lacks a satisfactory moral conclusion. Yet if this seems to sell Cervantes short then I would merely cite an analogy in another pastoral work. If the friendship and rivalry of Carriazo and Avendaño can be compared to the shepherds of Garcilaso's *Égloga III*, then the relationship between these two and Carriazo senior is akin to the process in the same poet's *Égloga II*.[20] This poem has a binary structure that vividly contrasts two lives and, significantly, two types of life. One, that of the Duke of Alba, a real-life figure, is exemplary, while the other, that of Albanio, a fictional shepherd driven mad by love, clearly embodies an example to be avoided, an *escarmiento*. Although the details in the analogy do not duplicate the situation in *La ilustre fregona* it is striking that in both the function of naming has an identical significance: Alba and the similarly-named Albanio, don Diego de Carriazo senior and junior. It is as though in both works we are shown the two possibilities of a single life in the sharing of the name but a divergence in the behaviour. Such a view suggests that just as critics have been unable to come up with a 'meaning' for the Garcilaso poem because there may not be one, so it appears to me that Cervantes is content to let the facts speak for themselves because he is a confident and honest enough writer to realize that not every crime has its explanation, that misdeeds are not always punished, and that miscreants will not invariably express remorse. If there is a lesson to be drawn from *La ilustre fregona*, then, let us be content with a modest one: an unregulated life may be an unruly one. In successfully avoiding this danger the watchword of our two 'shepherds' reflects a truth of the pastoral convention: 'part playing is a necessary part of all life, though a mind of puritanical cast will frequently see it as evidence of a lack of integrity' (Marinelli, p. 38).

[20] In Chapter 58 of the second part of *Don Quijote* some shepherdesses encountered by the eponymous hero refer to having learnt by heart two eclogues, one by Camões, the other by Garcilaso, for the purpose of performing them. Of the three Eclogues by Garcilaso it is the second that would best suit a dramatic representation, containing as it does indications of entrances and exits. See Pamela Waley, 'Garcilaso's Second Eclogue is a Play', *MLR*, 72 (1977), 585–96.

Works cited

Atkinson, William C., 'Cervantes, el Pinciano and the *Novelas ejemplares*', *HR*, 16 (1948), 189–208.

Berrenechea, Ana María, '*La ilustre fregona* como ejemplo de estructura novelesca cervantina', in *Actas del Primer Congreso Internacional de Hispanistas celebrado en Oxford del 6 al 11 de septiembre de 1962*, ed. Frank Pierce and Cyril A. Jones (Oxford: Dolphin, 1964), pp. 199–206.

Casalduero, Joaquín, *Sentido y forma de las 'Novelas ejemplares'* (Madrid: Gredos, 1962).

———, 'Cervantes rechaza la pastoril y no acepta la picaresca', *BHS*, 61 (1984), 283–5.

Cervantes Saavedra, Miguel de, *Exemplary Novels / Novelas ejemplares*, ed. B. W. Ife, 4 vols (Warminster: Aris & Phillips, 1992).

———, *Novelas ejemplares*, ed. Harry Sieber, 16th edn, 2 vols. (Madrid: Cátedra, 1995).

———, *Novelas ejemplares*, ed. Jorge García López (Barcelona: Crítica, 2001).

Clamurro, William H., 'Identity, Discourse and Social Order: *La ilustre fregona*', in *Beneath the Fiction: The Contrary Worlds of Cervantes's 'Novelas ejemplares'* (New York: Peter Lang, 1997), pp. 191–209.

El Saffar, Ruth, *Novel to Romance: A Study of Cervantes's 'Novelas ejemplares'* (Baltimore: Johns Hopkins University Press, 1974).

Gaylord, Mary Malcolm, 'Cervantes' Other Fiction', in *The Cambridge Companion to Cervantes*, ed. Anthony J. Cascardi (Cambridge: Cambridge University Press, 2002), pp. 100–30.

Hart, Thomas R., 'Versions of Pastoral in Three *Novelas ejemplares*', *BHS*, 58 (1981), 283–91.

Ife, B. W., 'From Salamanca to Brighton Rock: Names and Places in Cervantes' *La ilustre fregona*', in *Essays in Honour of Robert Brian Tate from his Colleagues and Pupils*, ed. Richard A. Cardwell (Nottingham: University of Nottingham, 1984), pp. 46–52.

———, 'The Historical and Social Context', in *The Cambridge Companion to Cervantes*, ed. Anthony J. Cascardi (Cambridge: Cambridge University Press, 2002), pp. 11–31.

Johnston, Robert M., 'Picaresque and Pastoral in *La ilustre fregona*', in *Cervantes and the Renaissance*, ed. Michael D. McGaha (Easton, PA: Juan de la Cuesta, 1980), pp.167–77.

Marinelli, Peter V., *Pastoral*, The Critical Idiom 15 (London: Methuen, 1971).

Rhodes, Elizabeth, 'Sixteenth-century Pastoral Books, Narrative Structure and *La Galatea* of Cervantes', *BHS*, 56 (1989), 351–60.

Sears, Theresa Ann, *A Marriage of Convenience: Ideal and Ideology in the 'Novelas ejemplares'* (New York: Peter Lang, 1993).

Selig, Karl-Ludwig, 'The Metamorphosis of the *Ilustre fregona*', in *Filología y crítica hispánica. Homenaje al Prof. Federico Sánchez Escribano*, ed. Alberto Porqueras Mayo and Carlos Rojas (Madrid: Ediciones Alcalá, 1969), pp. 115–20.

Vega, Garcilaso de la, *Poesías castellanas completas*, ed. Elias L. Rivers, 2nd edn (Madrid: Clásicos Castalia, 1972).

Waley, Pamela, 'Garcilaso's Second Eclogue is a Play', *MLR*, 72 (1977), 585–96.

11

Cervantine Traits in *Las dos doncellas* and *La señora Cornelia*

Idoya Puig
Manchester Metropolitan University

These two *novelas, La señora Cornelia* (Lady Cornelia) and *Las dos doncellas* (The Two Damsels), have often been relegated to a secondary place, and considered to be of less interest than the other stories in the collection of the *Novelas ejemplares* (Exemplary Novels).[1] However, when they are looked at closely, a number of interesting features can be identified which highlight Cervantes's personal and original traits in matters of content and style.

The two stories appear one after the other in the Cervantine collection and they share some general characteristics. They are included among the idealizing *novelas*. They are concerned with amorous relationships among the noble classes, and after a number of complicated and more or less plausible events, there is a happy ending with the reunion and marriage of the different protagonists of the stories. It is likely that they were written in the last years of Cervantes's life. There are a number of opinions on the chronology of the various *novelas*. Ruth El Saffar believes that Cervantes wrote them after 1606, when she identifies a change in attitude and style in subsequent works: the narrator dominates the narrative; the characters seek conformity with society; there is less social criticism; there are more adventures; there is a carefully planned structure, marriage is presented as salvation, etc., features which are certainly found in these two stories.[2]

[1] Caroline Schmauser includes a bibliographical summary of literary critics and their opinions about one of these short stories in her article 'Dynamism and Spatial Structure in *Las dos doncellas*', in *Cervantes's 'Exemplary Novels' and the Adventure of Writing*, ed. M. Nerlich and N. Spadiccini (Minneapolis: The Prisma Institute, 1989), pp. 175–203 (p. 175). In that same volume an article on the critical reception of the *Novelas* as a collection can also be found: see M. Nerlich, 'Juan Andrés to Alban Forcione: On the critical reception of the *Novelas ejemplares*', pp. 9–47.

[2] See *Novel to Romance. A Study of Cervantes' 'Novelas ejemplares'* (Baltimore: Johns Hopkins University Press, 1974), pp. 109–10 for a synthesis of the main opinions of critics on the subject of the chronology of the *Novelas ejemplares* and her own stand on this matter. Peter N. Dunn also summarizes the discussion in his article 'Las *Novelas ejemplares*', in *Suma cervantina,* ed. J. B. Avalle-Arce and E. C. Riley (London: Támesis, 1973), pp. 81–118 (p. 81).

Although they are generally classified as idealizing stories, Cervantes does not limit himself to following the conventions of a genre. He chooses to use a particular literary framework for his stories, but he goes beyond its boundaries and does not allow them to restrain him. He is able to play with the conventions and deploy his own ideas and style of writing within that framework.

This can be seen in these two stories, where Cervantes displays aspects of content and narrative technique that are very much his own. In that sense these *novelas* are exemplary, either because of the moral lessons and reflections they offer through the actions of the characters, or because of some innovation in narrative technique which makes the story an example of artistic originality.

Thus, in the two stories we are looking at, we have the theme of love and marriage as the central focus, which allows for a number of intricacies in the plot that permit Cervantes to explore some particularly problematic aspects of this theme: 'Marriage is a culminating dramatic and thematic recourse that unifies the action while it frames the *Novelas*.'[3]

Cervantes enjoys presenting human relationships as a reflection of human life in its complexity and variety. People depend on and influence one another, and a true characterization cannot ignore this essential interaction: 'He often pinpoints the complexities of human relationships, the way in which a person's behaviour depends upon that of people with whom he comes in contact.'[4]

Cervantes's predilection for paradox, irony and ambiguity is well known. The depiction of human relationships allows him to express more than one point of view, as he refuses to commit himself unambiguously to a particular judgement: 'La unicidad del punto de vista desvirtúa las inmensas riquezas de la realidad.' (The limitations of the single point of view distort the immense richness of reality.)[5]

In *Las dos doncellas* Cervantes tells the stories of two female characters, Teodosia and Leocadia, who act as vehicles for the presentation of a double *cuestión de amor* (enigma of love) and for an exploration of the intricacies of

[3] Thomas Pabón, 'Secular Resurrection through Marriage in Cervantes' *La señora Cornelia, Las dos doncellas* and *La fuerza de la sangre*', *AC*, 16 (1977), 109–24, (p. 109). Joaquín Casalduero states that love and marriage is one of the main themes of the *Novelas ejemplares* that appears in all the *novelas* and becomes a unifying element: *Sentido y forma de las 'Novelas ejemplares'* (Madrid: Gredos, 1962), p. 12. There are other studies that deal extensively with Cervantes's conception of love such as A. A. Parker's *The Philosophy of Love in Spanish Literature* (Edinburgh: University Press, 1985), or Robert V. Piluso, *Amor, matrimonio y honra en Cervantes* (New York: Las Americas, 1967).

[4] Jennifer Lowe, *Cervantes: Two 'Novelas ejemplares': 'La gitanilla' and 'La ilustre fregona'*, Critical Guides to Spanish Texts 2 (London: Grant & Cutler, 1971), p. 77.

[5] Miguel de Cervantes, *Novelas ejemplares,* ed. J. B. Avalle-Arce, 3 vols (Madrid: Castalia, 1987), I, p. 34 (Introduction). Translations of quotations from critical texts are my own. There has been great interest in Cervantes's concept of truth and reality. There are many contrasting views. The following studies may be considered representative: A. A. Parker, 'El concepto de la verdad en el *Quijote*', *Revista de Filología Española*, 32 (1948), 287–305 and Américo Castro, *El pensamiento de Cervantes* (Barcelona: Noguer, 1972).

marriage law because of the difficulties arising from their relationship with Marco Antonio:

> The whole *novela* is constructed round the *cuestiones de amor*, a technique commonly found in the pastoral novels and, in particular, in Cervantes's own *Galatea.* By his use of different stylistic devices, repetition of phrases and situations and special emphasis on various incidents in the story, Cervantes is able to create the framework for his *cuestiones* without making it too obvious. Moreover, he succeeds in bringing tension into what might otherwise have been a dull story by the way in which he shifts the emphasis at various stages of the narrative.[6]

This story is an example of Cervantes choosing a literary genre and adapting it to his own style. J. B. Avalle-Arce, in the introduction to his edition of this *novela* explains how Cervantes presents a *cuestión de amor,* characteristic of the pastoral novel, but his presentation does not really belong to that genre. The protagonists are human beings, with passions and failings, coming from a specific place in Andalusia and, in the case of Marco Antonio, from a family whose historical roots can be traced to Genoa. The characters are not shepherds and shepherdesses and, in many respects, they are far removed from the ideal world of the pastoral novel and neo-Platonic love. It is not so much that this *novela* is placed in a pastoral setting, but rather that Cervantes takes the pastoral model and brings it closer to the real world of human relationships:

> No se trata de una transmigración de Teodosia y Leocadia al mundo de la *Galatea*, sino el hecho mucho más sintomático y de más profundo significado de que el mundo de la *Galatea* ha trasmigrado al cortesano, concreto e histórico de Teodosia y Leocadia. Es en este pequeño intríngulis en que radica la absoluta novedad experimental de *Las dos doncellas*. (Cervantes, *Novelas*, III, p. 14)
>
> (It is not a migration of Teodosia and Leocadia to the world of the *Galatea* but, instead, something much more symptomatic and with a deeper meaning: the world of the *Galatea* migrating to the historically specific, courtly world of Teodosia and Leocadia. It is in this little twist that the whole experimental originality of *The Two Damsels* lies.)

Cervantes adds his own reflections on relationships as he presents the two protagonists with their passions and mistakes, their fears and disappointments, their jealousy and, finally their relief and joy at seeing their honour restored. They evince a great variety of feelings and inner conflicts that set them quite apart from the stereotypical characters associated with this genre. At the same time, Cervantes includes some pastoral features as, for example, the 'neo-Platonic'

[6] Jennifer Thompson, 'The Structure of Cervantes' *Las dos doncellas*', *BHS*, 40 (1963), 144–50 (p. 150).

account of the way in which both heroines fall madly in love just by seeing Marco Antonio:

> Digo, en fin, que él me vio una y muchas veces desde una ventana que frontero de otra mía estaba. Desde allí, a lo que me pareció, me envió el alma por los ojos, y los míos con otra manera de contento que el primero gustaron de mirarle, y aun me forzaron a que creyese que eran puras verdades cuanto en sus ademanes y en su rostro leía.
>
> (In short, let me tell you that he saw me time and again from a window which was opposite mine. From there, as it seemed to me, he sent me his soul through his eyes, and my eyes enjoyed looking at him with a pleasure different from at first, and even obliged me to believe that what I read in his expressions and in his face was absolutely true.)[7]

Cervantes presents the story of Teodosia first and then that of Leocadia. Their claims to be Marco Antonio's legitimate wife are very similar, making an 'intrincado laberinto' (III, p. 127) ('intricate labyrinth' [III, p. 147]) of the whole issue. The double promise of Marco Antonio raises the question of deciding who has the greater claim to marry him. Cervantes gives some clues to help the reader judge and decide. There are some factors that make it clear that it is Teodosia who deserves to marry Marco Antonio: she is the first to receive the promise of marriage from him and, unlike Leocadia's, her marriage to Marco Antonio has been consummated. All is resolved when the four protagonists (Teodosia's brother don Rafael being the fourth character) meet in the culminating scene in Barcelona where Marco Antonio has been wounded and is believed to be dying. Marco Antonio explains his position, giving the following two reasons in justification of his choice of Teodosia and his refusal of Leocadia:

> Porque antes que la firmase, con muchos días, tenía entregada mi voluntad y mi alma a otra doncella de mi mismo lugar, que vos bien conocéis, llamada Teodosia, hija de tan nobles padres como los vuestros; y si a vos os di cédula firmada de mi mano, a ella le di la mano firmada y acreditada con tales obras y testigos, que quedé imposibilitado de dar mi libertad a otra persona en el mundo. (III, p. 157)
>
> (For many days before I signed it, I had handed over my will and my soul to another damsel from my own town. Her name is Teodosia, the daughter of parents as noble as yours, and you know her well; and if I gave a document signed in my own hand to you, to her I firmly pledged that hand and guaranteed it with such deeds and witnesses that it became impossible for me to give my freedom to any other person in Christendom. [III, p. 179])

[7] Quotations from the text are taken from Cervantes, *Novelas*; here III, p. 130; the translations are from Miguel de Cervantes, *Exemplary Novels / Novelas ejemplares*, ed. B.W. Ife, 4 vols (Warminster: Aris & Phillips, 1992); here III, p. 148. For a fuller discussion of the Platonic influences on Cervantes's work, see Enrique Moreno Baez, 'Perfil ideológico de Cervantes', in *Suma cervantina*, ed. J. B. Avalle-Arce and E. C. Riley (London: Támesis, 1973), pp. 233–72.

It is true that some events in the story are not very plausible. Teodosia, for example, does not recognize her brother when they first meet in the inn. The equation of beauty and nobility is not particularly true-to-life either. But despite these conventional features, Cervantes succeeds in endowing his characters with a wealth of individualized reactions and offering some interesting psychological insights into them.

It is possible, for example, to discern some differences between the two heroines. Teodosia was convinced by Marco Antonio and acceded to his requests due to her youth and inexperience in love (III, p. 130; III, pp. 149, 151). Leocadia, however, is the one who takes the initiative and Marco Antonio eventually gives in to her, and promises to marry her. Leocadia is more responsible for her downfall than Teodosia. Leocadia says that: 'Me ofrecí a que hiciese de mí todo lo que quisiese' (III, p. 143) ('I gave myself to him to do as he wished' [III, p. 165]). And Marco Antonio explains that he committed himself: 'Más por cumplir con vuestro deseo que con el mío' (III, p. 157) ('More to satisfy your wishes than mine' [III, p. 179]). This is one more factor that makes Teodosia's claim stronger than Leocadia's.[8]

As a result, Teodosia and Leocadia will both have to try, although with different degrees of urgency, to find Marco Antonio: 'Cervantes's women are always acting in a way perfectly coordinated with their natures. Thus, because Leocadia and Teodosia wilfully loved Marco Antonio, they must actively seek him out' (Pabón, p. 116).

One more instance of Cervantes's own distinctive approach to love relationships can be found in his tolerant attitude toward some of the mistakes made by the characters in this story. Cervantes justifies his heroines' behaviour by reminding us that they were young and inexperienced in matters of love. Thus, don Rafael's reaction when he learns of his sister's dishonour is not one of vengefulness but rather of compassion and he finds an excuse for her mistake: 'Todavía quiero tomar por disculpa de vuestro yerro vuestros pocos años, en los cuales no cabe tener experiencia de los muchos engaños de los hombres' (III, p. 133) ('I am more inclined to accept your youth as an excuse for your error, for your few years cannot have provided experience of man's many deceits' [III, p. 153]).

Cervantes's narrator repeats this defence of the protagonists at the end of the story, although the name of the village they come from is withheld in order to protect their identity (III, p. 168; III, p. 189). As Michael and Jonathan Thacher point out: 'Cervantes asserts his own belief in forgiveness of human error and issues a warning to readers who make hasty moral judgements' (Cervantes, *Exemplary Novels*, III, p. 140).

Turning to *La señora Cornelia*, Cervantes presents another situation involving a secret relationship, which enables him to explore other problematic aspects of marriage and generate a number of adventures. The story is set in Italy, in

[8] For more details on the psychological differences between the two protagonists, see Ruth El Saffar, pp. 110–12. Schmauser also points to the development of individualized characters in this story as a feature which signals a departure from the Greco-Byzantine romances where characters do not develop (p. 198).

Bologna, and may to some extent be based on Cervantes's memories of the time he spent in that country, although it is unlikely that he lived in or knew that city in particular. Bologna was the only non-Spanish university where Spaniards were allowed to study. The Bentivoglio family from Bologna was well known, although Cervantes slightly changes the spelling. However, Lorenzo and Cornelia are Cervantes's creations and not historical characters.[9]

The Duke of Ferrara falls in love with the young and beautiful Cornelia. They make a mutual promise of marriage but they do not make their relationship public because the Duke's mother has arranged another match for him. Although their marriage is not blessed by the Church, their relationship is always seen in the framework of marriage and thus it is justified to a certain extent. Cervantes does not indicate when these events take place. He uses secret marriages in other stories too, always carefully explaining that the events happened before the Council of Trent, when such marriages were still permitted. The mutual consent of the partners was sufficient, without the need for a religious ceremony or public recognition. The Council declared this form of marriage invalid due to the number of abuses to which it led. The Council stipulated that banns were to be published, that the future marriage was to be publicly announced and that witnesses were to be present. Otherwise the marriage was not valid and had no sacramental value.[10] Cervantes uses secret marriage to add drama to his narrative and provoke thought on a topic that was a reality at that time. The sufferings and adventures in *La señora Cornelia* can be seen as the example that Cervantes puts forward to underline the dangers of this form of marriage.[11]

In the story, Cornelia's virtue is emphasized, and, once more, the love between her and the Duke is an idealized, platonic one. As in the case of Teodosia and Leocadia, this love is sparked off by her first sight of the Duke: 'Allí, finalmente, vi al duque y él me vio a mí, de cuya vista ha resultado verme ahora como me veo' (III, p. 185) ('There, finally, I saw the Duke and he saw me and, as a result, I find myself in my present plight' [IV, p. 21]).

At the same time, Cervantes broaches another issue, one which he explores in a number of his stories, and which seems to have particularly interested him: that of arranged marriages. This is the ultimate cause of action in this *novela*. The Duke refuses to obey his mother, who has somebody prepared for him to marry. Against his mother's will he marries Cornelia. Nevertheless, even when the characters are reunited and their relationship has become common knowledge, Cervantes postpones a public wedding until the Duke's mother dies, as if to mitigate the impact of a story of successful opposition to parental wishes: 'Y entre todos se dio traza que aquellos desposorios estuviesen secretos hasta ver en qué paraba la enfermedad

[9] Avalle-Arce provides historical information about the city of Bologna and the Bentivoglio family in his edition of this *novela* (III, p. 17 and p. 173, n. 10).

[10] See Paul Descouzis's study of the way in which some of the decrees of the Council of Trent are reflected in Cervantes's works: 'Cervantes, a nueva luz: 1. El *Quijote* y el Concilio de Trento, *Analecta Romanica*, Heft 19 (1966).

[11] Enrique Moreno Baez, p. 252.

que tenía muy al cabo a la duquesa su madre' (III, p. 218) ('And everyone agreed that the marriage should be kept secret until they should see the outcome of the illness which kept the Duchess, his mother, close to death' [IV, p. 53]).

In order to provide a counterweight to the couple's behaviour, Cervantes presents the exemplary Spaniards, don Antonio and don Juan, returning to Spain to marry the women their parents have chosen for them. They politely refuse the Duke's invitation to marry two of his cousins:

> Ellos dijeron que los caballeros de la nación vizcaína por la mayor parte se casaban en su patria; y que no por menosprecio, pues no era posible, sino por cumplir su loable costumbre y la voluntad de sus padres, que ya los debían de tener casados, no aceptaban tan ilustre ofrecimiento. (III, p. 218)
>
> (They replied that gentlemen from the Basque country usually married in their region, and that it was not out of contempt that they did not accept such a distinguished offer, for that was not possible, but in order to fulfill that laudable custom and comply with the wishes of their fathers, who felt their sons should be married already. [IV, p. 53])

It is interesting to note that in *Las dos doncellas,* the protagonists initially marry without their parents' consent. Nevertheless the story does not end until they return to their home-town and meet their parents. They find their respective fathers about to engage in a duel to defend their lost honours. Once everything is clarified, they all celebrate the double wedding together (III, p. 167; III, p. 189).

Cervantes, in his characteristic way, enjoys presenting two opposite points of view but does not side with either of them.[12]

Some critics have seen in these two stories a movement from disorder to harmony after a process of purification undergone by the characters. They learn from their mistakes after suffering the consequences. Eventually they achieve happiness in marriage. In *Las dos doncellas* the final pilgrimage to Santiago can be seen as a symbol of this reconciliation of the individual to society:

> The *intrincado laberinto* [complicated labyrinth] of *Las dos doncellas* serves to illustrate on a doctrinal level the teachings of the Council of Trent on the subject of Christian marriage, but more important is the novelistic artistry of Cervantes whose baroque trajectory leads us from chaos to order and from darkness to life. (Pabón, p. 118)[13]

Cervantes enjoys playing with characters and offering a variety of opinions. This allows him to present some themes with realism, displaying his characteristically

[12] Piluso explains that Cervantes defends the right of the children to choose their partner, but that he strongly recommends that they take into account their parents' advice on the matter. Children cannot be forced but they should obtain their parents' approval (p. 109).

[13] Schmauser's approach is similar: '*Las dos doncellas* presents the stages of a journey in order to show the importance of accepting the process of life and of keeping abreast of the constant dialogue with the world around us' (p. 200).

tolerant outlook on these matters. At the same time it must be remembered that Cervantes is writing works of fiction, not moral treatises. The two stories that we are looking at shed light on Cervantes's attitudes and thoughts concerning important themes without, however, losing their idealized character and their value as entertainment.[14]

Some other features of a more formal nature can be identified as characteristic of Cervantes in these two short tales. In *La señora Cornelia*, don Antonio and don Juan are good friends. They are Basque and it is not the only instance in the *Novelas ejemplares* where Cervantes chooses characters from that part of Spain. Once more, both friends appear to be similar but on closer inspection some contrasts can be found between them. Avalle-Arce has suggested that don Juan is more active than don Antonio:

> La pareja de protagonistas constituía casi una necesidad intelectual para Cervantes, y más de una de estas *Novelas ejemplares* lo ilustra ya desde el título, a partir de *Rinconete y Cortadillo* y terminando con el *Coloquio de los perros*. Esto, sin embargo, no implica en absoluto que un personaje sea la duplicación de otro, y el caso de don Antonio de Isunza y don Juan de Gamboa es un bucn cjcmplo. Dentro de un parecido fisonómico general, podemos decir que don Juan es más arrojado y don Antonio más contemplativo; en términos aun más generales podemos decir que don Juan inicia las acciones y don Antonio las remata. (III, p. 17)
>
> (The use of paired characters became almost an intellectual necessity for Cervantes. Even in their titles – from *Rinconete and Cortadillo* through to *The Dialogue of the Dogs* – more than a few of the *Exemplary Novels* illustrate this. This, however, does not imply that any one such character is the double of the other. The case of don Antonio of Isunza and don Juan of Gamboa is a good example: although they share a similar physiognomy it is clear that don Juan is more impulsive and don Antonio more contemplative; in even more general terms we can say that don Juan initiates actions and don Antonio brings them to their conclusion.)[15]

14 See, for example, Javier Herrero's remarks on *Don Quijote*, which could equally well be applied to the *Novelas ejemplares*: 'Against a sentimental and a Neoplatonic tradition which made of woman a goddess, Cervantes takes the side of the conjugal love presented by Erasmus and Vives as the Christian ideal which allows man not only to enjoy the legitimate pleasure of the sexual union, but to help each other to fight against the inevitable weakness and imperfection of the human condition. By emphasizing the social, civilizing aspects of marriage, Cervantes, as Bataillon and Márquez Villanueva have pointed out, was closer to the new doctrines of the reform than the Renaissance ideals of love': Javier Herrero, 'Sierra Morena as a Labyrinth: from Wildness to Christian Knighthood', in *Critical Essays on Cervantes*, ed. Ruth El Saffar (Boston: G. K. Hall, 1986), pp. 67–80 (p. 77).

15 Ruth El Saffar also affirms this diversity of roles, although she finds that in other respects the two friends are very similar to each other: 'Don Juan and don Antonio remain essentially undistinguished from beginning to end except in their role as mediators in the adventure of Cornelia' (p. 123).

Cervantes uses the two friends to hide himself from the reader, preferring to leave the task of narration to them. It is through them, therefore, that the different parts of the story are told, and it is left up to the reader to piece the various events together. The friendship of don Juan and don Antonio provides the instrument that allows the reader to amass the different pieces of information which amalgamate to form a picture of the love story of the Duke and Cornelia: don Juan is given a baby, don Antonio shelters a lady and don Juan, in his second outing, defends a man from some attackers. These stories are complemented by Cornelia's own account of events, which she relays to both of them.

A similar effect is obtained in *Las dos doncellas* where we also find out about previous events through confidences shared between the protagonists. Part of the excitement of the story lies in the gradual unfolding of the events that have caused the two female protagonists to end up dressed as men. The narrator does not tell us what has happened in chronological order. Thus, once again, friendship functions as the vehicle for a particular expository technique and provides an abundant source of dialogue.[16]

The use of paired characters is what makes the *cuestión de amor* harder to solve and unusual in its presentation. Cervantes stresses the similarities between the protagonists' reactions, but, as we have seen, he shows that their claims to be Marco Antonio's legitimate spouse are different and he also provides clues to help us discover whose claim is strongest. Yet again, Cervantes uses his paired characters to create a more sophisticated plot and achieve a carefully balanced structure:

> There is not an unnecessary duplication of roles. Each character is essential, either because, as in the case of the two girls, her story must form one aspect of the *cuestión de amor* or, as with Don Rafael because his fortunes are inextricably linked to those of the other characters in the story. (Thompson, p. 150)

In another scene, Cervantes's interest in providing contrasting views is achieved through the dialogue between the two apparently similar female protagonists. Leocadia imagines what Teodosia is likely to be doing, certain that she is with Marco Antonio. Teodosia herself is the listener, and tries to tell Leocadia how different her own present situation is to the one her rival has imagined. It is a lively game of perspectives and psychological nuances:

> Y estando juntos los que bien se quieren, ¿qué engaño puede haber? Ninguno por cierto; ellos están contentos, pues están juntos [. . .] Ella le goza, sin duda, sea donde fuere, y ella sola ha de pagar lo que he sentido hasta que le halle. —Podía ser que os engañásedes —replicó Teodosia—, que yo conozco muy bien a esa enemiga vuestra que decís y sé de su condición y recogimiento, que nunca ella se aventuraría a dejar la casa de sus padres ni acudir a la voluntad de Marco Antonio. (III, p. 146)

16 Marsha Collins explores this idea and states that Cervantes uses confessional discourse as an instrument to express love and bring about harmony and reconciliation: 'El poder del discurso confesional en *Las dos doncellas*', *Cervantes*, 22.2 (2002), 25–46.

> ('And when two people who love each other well are together, what deceit can there be? None, of course; they are happy because they are together [. . .] No doubt she is enjoying him, wherever it may be, and she alone must pay for what I have suffered when I find him.'
>
> 'It could be that you are mistaken,' replied Teodosia, 'for I am a very close acquaintance of the one you call your enemy and I know from her character and her reserve that she would never venture to leave her parents' house nor to accede to the will of Marco Antonio.' [III, p. 167])

The other effect produced by this Cervantine recourse to friends or pairs of characters is the creation of a certain suspense in the stories. It is another device that helps to maintain interest in the narrative and to delay the final outcome.

In *La señora Cornelia,* don Juan and Lorenzo Bentibolli go to meet the Duke. The encounter occurs on the road between Bologna and Ferrara. Cervantes describes the scene step by step. Don Juan approaches the Duke's party, while Lorenzo waits at a certain distance. Don Juan quickly gets off his horse to kiss the Duke's feet. The Duke also dismounts and they end up hugging each other. Lorenzo does not know what is actually happening because he is looking at the scene from afar, and so he thinks they are about to fight and runs towards them: 'El señor Lorenzo, que desde algo lejos miraba estas ceremonias, no pensando que lo eran de cortesía, sino de cólera, arremetió su caballo' (III, p. 202) ('Lord Lorenzo who was watching these ceremonious actions some distance away, thinking that they were not the result of courtesy but of anger, charged at them on his horse' [IV, p. 37]). When he gets closer he realizes that they are hugging each other and that there is no confrontation. The scene continues, and while they are talking, don Antonio now approaches the group from the road. He too is confused by what he sees. He does not recognise the Duke and does not know whether to come closer to them. He cautiously asks the servants who the third person is and he is alarmed when he finds out that it is the Duke. The confusion ends when don Juan sees don Antonio and he is introduced to the rest of the group: 'Fuele respondido ser el duque de Ferrara, con que quedó más confuso y menos sin saber qué hacerse; pero sacóle de sus perplejidad don Juan llamándole por su nombre' (III, p. 205) ('He was told in reply that he was the Duke of Ferrara, at which he was left more confused and less certain as to what to do, but Don Juan took him out of his bewilderment by calling out his name' [IV, p. 41]). Nothing important happens in this scene, but it creates a moment of suspense and enables Cervantes to engage in the description of feelings and reactions. This type of scene adds vividness to the story and is characteristic of the *Novelas* as a whole. The description of the characters' different reactions reinforces the central importance of the meeting of the Duke and don Juan. Without it the encounter would be very brief and the climactic effect would be considerably reduced.[17]

[17] Esther Lacadena y Calero offers an analysis of the story (based on Russian Formalism) that identifies the links between various elements in the story and the relevance of some of these scenes: '*La señora Cornelia* y su técnica narrativa', *AC*, 15 (1976), 199–210.

Cervantes furnishes further narrative tricks in his story, such as the disappearance of Cornelia and the Duke's final joke, in order to add to the suspense and create a more sophisticated novelistic structure.[18]

The way in which the structure of *Las dos doncellas* unfolds around the dialogues of the various protagonists also creates suspense. The story begins with a conversation between the people in the inn about the recently arrived traveller. This awakens the curiosity of the reader who, like the conversing friends, would like to know more about the traveller, although for the moment they have to be content with not knowing who he is: 'Quedáronse con la admiración de su gentileza' (III, p. 124) ('All they could do was to marvel at the fine appearance of the stranger' [III, p. 143]). In the course of the conversation, when several suggestions about the identity of the traveller are put forward, their interest and curiosity grow. As a result, when a second traveller arrives at the inn, they decide to let him spend the night in the same room with the first traveller, although he had asked for the room to himself. In this way, Teodosia, disguised as man, and don Rafael, her brother, end up together.

Teodosia and don Rafael's recognition of each other is presented in slow motion, adding suspense and excitement to the story. They remain with each other in the same room until daybreak. During the night, Teodosia has told don Rafael of her misfortunes and revealed that she is a woman. Don Rafael recognizes her as his sister. In the morning, don Rafael tells her to get up, and only when he opens the windows and the light fills the room does Teodosia realize that she has been talking to her brother. The narrator describes her reaction thus:

> Y diciendo esto abrió las ventanas y puertas del aposento. Estaba deseando Teodosia ver la claridad, para ver con la luz qué talle y parecer tenía aquel con quien había estado hablando toda la noche. Mas cuando le miró y le conoció quisiera que jamás hubiera amanecido, sino que allí en perpetua noche se le hubieran cerrado los ojos. (III, p. 134)
>
> (And saying this he opened the windows and doors of the room. Teodosia was keen to see the light of day in order to make out clearly the figure and appearance of the man with whom she had been talking throughout the night. But when she saw him and recognized him she wished that day had never dawned, but that her eyes had been closed there in everlasting night. [III, p. 153])[19]

Later in the story we have the climactic dialogue between Teodosia and Leocadia. At the very moment when Leocadia is about to reveal the most important part of

[18] Dunn (pp. 106–12) sees these polarities or symmetries as forming a pattern of reconciliation, which lies at the heart of the exemplary message of this short story.

[19] On the value and function of anagnorisis, see Miguel A. Tejeiro Fuentes, 'El recurso de la anagnórisis en algunas de las *Novelas ejemplares* de Cervantes', *AC*, 35 (1999).

her story, the narrative is interrupted. Teodosia (*alias* Teodoso) has become so tense that she stops Leocadia and begins to question her:

> Mas cuando llegó a decir: 'Llegó la noche por mí deseada', estuvo por perder la paciencia y, sin poder hacer otra cosa, le salteó la razón, diciendo:
>
> —Y bien, así como llegó esa felicísima noche, ¿qué hizo? ¿Entró por dicha? ¿Gozásteisle? (III, p. 144)
>
> (But when she came to say, 'the night I had longed for arrived,' his patience came to an end, and without being able to help it, he lost his self-control and said:
>
> 'I see, and so when this happiest of nights arrived, what did he do? Did he by any chance arrive? Did you enjoy him?' [III, p. 165])

Eventually, Leocadia reveals that Marco Antonio did not go back to meet her, and Teodosia breathes a sigh of relief, as does the reader, who begins to see the outline of the whole story emerging. It is a moment of great suspense and tension, which the dialogue between the two makes especially acute and palpable (Pabón, p. 117).

In the two stories we are considering, Cervantes chooses to begin *in medias res*. It is one more novelistic device which enables him to introduce the other parts of the story later on. Avalle-Arce has pointed out that in the case of *Las dos doncellas* it marks a deliberate move on Cervantes's part to distance himself from the pastoral novel, thus stressing his freedom to use the literary conventions to his own advantage rather than being subject to them:

> Es, por lo demás, algo totalmente ajeno a la técnica narrativa de la novela pastoril, como si Cervantes, al trasponer la *cuestión de amor* de lo pastoril a lo cortesano, buscase distanciarse en la medida de lo posible de la técnica narrativa asociada con dicho género. (III, p. 15)
>
> (In all other respects, it is something totally alien to the narrative technique of the pastoral novel, as if, in transposing the question of love from the pastoral to the courtly world, Cervantes was seeking to distance himself as much as possible from the narrative techniques associated with that genre.)

This type of beginning brings these stories closer to the tradition of the Byzantine novel of adventure which Cervantes attempted to emulate in his posthumously published final work, *Los trabajos de Persiles y Segismunda* (The Trials of Persiles and Sigismunda), but with which he also seems to be experimenting in some of these *novelas*.

As John Jones and John Macklin observe, *La señora Cornelia* presents a number of adventures which can clearly be associated with those of the Byzantine novel: '*Lady Cornelia,* with its duels, mistaken identities and misadventures, is in the tradition of the Byzantine or adventure novel in which the action, after a series of complications, is brought to a satisfactory resolution.' (Cervantes, *Exemplary Novels*, IV, p. 1)

I hope that the analysis of some of these examples has helped to show how Cervantes plays in his stories with content and form. He uses characters and their interaction as a means of exploring important themes, offering a uniquely humane perspective on them, something that typifies the outlook on life that emerges from his work as a whole. At the same time, these characters become instruments of his particular novelistic technique. They enable him to play with literary genres, create suspense and introduce structural devices which depart from the conventional norms and thus become personal and original. It is the presence of these elements that makes it possible for us to speak of characteristic traits of Cervantine style in these stories.

Works cited

Casalduero, Joaquín, *Sentido y forma de las 'Novelas ejemplares'* (Madrid: Gredos, 1962).

Castro, Américo, *El pensamiento de Cervantes* (Barcelona: Noguer, 1972).

Cervantes Saavedra, Miguel de, *Novelas ejemplares,* ed. J. B. Avalle-Arce, 3 vols (Madrid: Castalia, 1987).

———, *Exemplary Novels / Novelas ejemplares*, ed. B. W. Ife, 4 vols (Warminster: Aris & Phillips, 1992).

Collins, Marsha, 'El poder del discurso confesional en *Las dos doncellas*', *Cervantes*, 22.2 (2002), 25–46.

Descouzis, Paul, 'Cervantes, a nueva luz:1. El *Quijote* y el Concilio de Trento', *Analecta Romanica*, Heft 19 (1966).

Dunn, Peter N., 'Las *Novelas ejemplares*', in *Suma cervantina,* ed. J. B. Avalle-Arce and E. C. Riley (London: Támesis, 1973), pp. 81–118.

El Saffar, Ruth, *Novel to Romance. A Study of Cervantes' 'Novelas ejemplares'* (Baltimore: Johns Hopkins University Press, 1974).

Herrero, Javier, 'Sierra Morena as a Labyrinth: from Wildness to Christian Knighthood', in *Critical Essays on Cervantes*, ed. Ruth El Saffar (Boston: G. K. Hall, 1986), pp. 67–80.

Lacadena y Calero, Esther, '*La señora Cornelia* y su técnica narrativa', *AC*, 15 (1976), 199–210.

Lowe, Jennifer, *Cervantes: Two 'Novelas ejemplares': 'La gitanilla' and 'La ilustre fregona'*, Critical Guides to Spanish Texts 2 (London: Grant & Cutler, 1971).

Moreno Baez, Enrique, 'Perfil ideológico de Cervantes', in *Suma cervantina,* ed. J. B. Avalle-Arce and E. C. Riley (London: Támesis, 1973), pp. 233–72.

Nerlich, M., 'Juan Andrés to Alban Forcione: On the critical reception of the *Novelas ejemplares*', in *Cervantes's 'Exemplary Novels' and the Adventure of Writing*, ed. M. Nerlich and N. Spadiccini (Minneapolis: The Prisma Institute, 1989), pp. 9–47.

Pabón, Thomas, 'Secular Resurrection through Marriage in Cervantes' *La señora Cornelia, Las dos doncellas* and *La fuerza de la sangre*', *AC*, 16 (1977), 109–24.

Parker, A. A., 'El concepto de la verdad en el *Quijote*', *Revista de Filología Española*, 32 (1948), 287–305.

Parker, *The Philosophy of Love in Spanish Literature* (Edinburgh: University Press, 1985).

Piluso, Robert V., *Amor, matrimonio y honra en Cervantes* (New York: Las Americas, 1967).

Schmauser, Caroline, 'Dynamism and Spatial Structure in *Las dos doncellas*', in *Cervantes's 'Exemplary Novels' and the Adventure of Writing*, ed. M. Nerlich and N. Spadiccini (Minneapolis: The Prisma Institute, 1989), pp. 175–203.

Tejeiro Fuentes, Miguel A., 'El recurso de la anagnórisis en algunas de las *Novelas ejemplares* de Cervantes', *AC*, 35 (1999), 539–70.

Thompson, Jennifer, 'The Structure of Cervantes' *Las dos doncellas', BHS*, 40 (1963), 144–50.

12

The Peculiar Arrangement of *El casamiento engañoso* and *El coloquio de los perros*[1]

Edward Aylward
University of South Carolina

This essay will focus on the narrative strategies employed by Cervantes when he decided to fuse two completely independent stories into a single artistic unit that would close his collection of *Novelas ejemplares*. After providing a brief overview of the literary predecessors of the *Casamiento engañoso* (The Deceitful Marriage) and the *Coloquio de los perros* (The Dialogue of the Dogs), we will present a structural analysis of the two works in question, first as separate entities, then as complementary parts of a single hybrid text. The study closes by suggesting the artistic goal behind Cervantes's decision to meld what appear to be two very disparate entries: a concrete demonstration of how a talented writer might craft a plausible and entertaining literary work out of seemingly ridiculous subject-matter.

Classical Models for the 'Coloquio'

Any thorough examination of Cervantes's *El coloquio de los perros* should include a few words about the work's classical origins. Over the years many critics have noted certain similarities – particularly a common sense of irony – between Cervantes's unusual canine conversation and the satirical dialogues of the second-century Greek Cynic, Lucian of Samosata. Michael Zappala notes that some Hispanists thought it probable that Cervantes had become familiar with Lucian's writings through the works of a Renaissance intermediary such as Erasmus of Rotterdam.[2]

In 1953 Antonio Oliver commented on a number of possible classical influences on Cervantes, pointing to a clear parallel between what happens to

[1] An earlier and broader treatment of this subject was published in E. T. Aylward, *The Crucible Concept: Thematic and Narrative Patterns in Cervantes's 'Novelas ejemplares'* (Madison, NJ: Fairleigh Dickinson UP, 1999).

[2] Michael Zappala, 'Cervantes and Lucian', *Symposium*, 33.1 (Spring 1979), 65–82.

Cervantes's dogs and the protagonist of Apuleius's *Golden Ass*.[3] There is a clever inversion of the model, however, in that in the classical model Lucius loses, rather than gains, the power of speech when he is transformed into an ass, while Berganza and Cipión move in the opposite direction (Oliver, p. 296). At a later point Oliver goes on to discuss certain stylistic similarities between Lucian of Samosata and Cervantes, bolstering his argument by noting that the Cynic's translated writings enjoyed considerable popularity in Europe during the sixteenth century (Oliver, p. 301).

The same critic offers what he considers to be clear examples of Cynical satire in Cervantes's *Coloquio*, a feature most observable in the very specific kinds of social vermin that are targeted for criticism in that work. Oliver flatly declares Berganza and Cipión to be inverted symbols of the ancient Cynics: if the followers of Diogenes were formerly said to bark like dogs, in Cervantes's topsy-turvy literary rendition the philosophizing dogs are suddenly endowed with human speech (Oliver, p. 306). The key to understanding this symbolism, says Oliver, is the lantern the two dogs are reported to carry every night when they accompany the good Christian Mahudes on his charitable rounds; the lantern is designed to be an unmistakable reminder of the Cynic Diogenes' search for an honest man (Oliver, p. 307). In 1956 Agustín G. Amezúa y Mayo also noted the apparent influence of Lucian on Cervantes's prose dialogue, but he rejected the notion of any direct Cervantine knowledge of the Greek's work.[4]

The first stylistic comparison of the writings of Lucian and Cervantes was made by Michael Zappala in 1979. In Zappala's study these two literary figures are shown to share a number of characteristics. The first of these is a concern for the elusive nature of truth, which ultimately impels them to portray situations from more than a single perspective (p. 68). The subsequent ironic distance that Lucian and Cervantes manufacture in their works serves principally to separate the author from his characters and his reader, thereby generating the all-important illusion of fictional autonomy and the characters' 'freedom to function as co-agents of creation' (p. 71).

Zappala signals another point of convergence between these two writers in their sly use of lexical legerdemain. Both Lucian and Cervantes are masterful manipulators of insignificant information. They carefully feed the reader an abundance of small but realistic details, the intention being to distract the reader from the basic implausibility of their fictional creations. Another area of commonality between Lucian and Cervantes is their penchant for literary parody. In *Don Quijote* Cervantes parodies the novels of chivalry, just as Lucian previously burlesqued the excesses of the Greek romance and subjective (i.e. totally unreliable) historiography (p. 73). Yet another possible source of inspiration for Cervantes – and a much more contemporary one – could have been Erasmus of Rotterdam. In

[3] Antonio Oliver, 'La filosofía cínica y el *Coloquio de los perros*', *AC*, 3 (1953), 291–307.

[4] Agustín G. Amezúa y Mayo, *Cervantes, creador de la novela corta española*, 2 vols (Madrid: Consejo Superior de Investigaciones Científicas, 1956–58), I, p. 422.

Zappala's view, Lucian and Erasmus seemed to be authors in search of a genre. Their writings contained the raw materials needed for the creation of the narrative apparatus that would become the modern novel, but they never came upon the proper literary format for its development. It was left to Cervantes to elaborate and incorporate these elements – the appreciation of the direct style, the deft handling of irony, the awareness of the relationship between character, author and reader – into a viable new artistic form that would endure for centuries (Zappala, pp. 76–77).

A slightly different observation regarding the influence of the Cynics on Cervantes's thought is found in E. C. Riley's 1976 article on the *Coloquio* and *El licenciado Vidriera* (The Glass Graduate).[5] While both of these Cervantine *novellas* are judged to be steeped in Cynical pessimism, Riley prefers the 'light and ironical' musings of the two dogs to the more bitter judgments of the disillusioned Vidriera (p. 195). Berganza and Cipión are fully aware of the dangers of malicious gossip (*murmuración*) and the fact that such backbiting is frequently passed off by satirists as high-minded philosophy. This was precisely the charge that their critics levelled most often at the Cynics. In Riley's view, the vice of *murmuración* was precisely what Cervantes found objectionable about Mateo Alemán's *Guzmán de Alfarache* and its vituperative progeny (p. 196). To *murmurar* was to act like the vindictive and pessimistic Alemán; Cervantes believed that writers such as himself who had been attacked by bitter rivals needed to resist 'the temptation to lambaste others in kind' (Riley, p. 198). The result is a lighter, more tempered kind of social satire in the *Coloquio*, as when Berganza and Cipión imitate the Cynics' censure of the pursuit of useless knowledge in their comments on the four inmates they encounter at the Hospital: the poet, the alchemist, the mathematician and the crackpot *arbitrista* (professional consultant) (Riley, p. 199, n. 34).

Cervantes and the Picaresque

There can be no denying the affinity of Cervantes's *Coloquio* and the preceding *El casamiento engañoso* with the picaresque genre. When we consider the shady conduct of both Ensign Campuzano and his slippery bride, followed by the account Berganza renders of his adventures with a series of hypocritical masters, we cannot avoid the sense that Cervantes's stories are closely following the trail blazed by *Lazarillo de Tormes* (1554) and Mateo Alemán's *Guzmán de Alfarache* (1599). The scholar who has written the most complete and penetrating study of the *Casamiento* and *Coloquio*, Alban K. Forcione, leaves no doubt as to his belief that Cervantes had Alemán's work in mind as he designed and penned the dogs' colloquy.[6]

[5] E. C. Riley, 'Cervantes and the Cynics: *El licenciado Vidriera* and *El coloquio de los perros*', *BHS*, 53.3 (July 1976), 189–99.

[6] Alban K. Forcione, *Cervantes and the Mystery of Lawlessness: A Study of 'El casamiento engañoso y El coloquio de los perros'* (Princeton: Princeton University Press, 1984), p. 143, n. 34.

For his part, Juan Bautista Avalle-Arce calls the *Coloquio* 'the most revolutionary of Cervantes's approaches to the picaresque genre'.[7] Avalle-Arce proceeds to list some of the many parallels that can be drawn between the lives of Berganza and Guzmán: their birth in Seville, their early victimization at the hands of a scheming woman, a brief turn at procurement (*alcahuetería*), frequent moral or critical digressions that creep into their autobiographical account, and their eventual decision to repent and live a moral life (pp. 598–99). Nonetheless, Cervantes never viewed the picaresque as a polished literary form, says Avalle-Arce, but rather as a genre in development ('algo decididamente *haciéndose*' [decidedly something evolving], p. 600). This is not to say that Cervantes accepted every element of Alemán's model; among the factors in *Guzmán* that Avalle-Arce believes Cervantes rejected on ideological grounds was its strict adherence to the autobiographical format. Alemán's prototype saddled the protagonist with tainted blood lines that overpower all other social and cultural factors in determining his conduct as an adult. As Avalle-Arce reminds us, 'determinism was simply something unthinkable to the creator of Don Quixote' (p. 601).

In Avalle-Arce's view, *Lazarillo* established the autobiographical format – which the critic calls its systolic movement, the contraction of reality – as the norm for the picaresque genre. Alemán accepted *Lazarillo*'s canons and then proceeded to transgress them, particularly with regard to the sheer volume of material he chose to include in his narration. Cervantes, in turn, rejected *Guzmán*'s voluminous flamboyance in favour of *Lazarillo*'s original narrative economy, adding a diastolic movement by opening up his narration to accommodate more than a single point of view, e.g. Cipión's pithy interjections. It is indeed unfortunate, Avalle-Arce notes at the close of his argument, that posterity chose to follow Alemán's picaresque model, not Cervantes's (pp. 601–2).

Carlos Blanco Aguinaga also noticed the similarity of Cervantes's *Coloquio* to Alemán's masterpiece, but chose to emphasize the points on which they parted company. He makes special note of their distinct narrative techniques – a priori in *Guzmán*, a posteriori in the *Coloquio* – and the fact that the Cipión figure is unlike anything to be found in the picaresque.[8] The lack of a preamble, the forward-looking attitude of Berganza, and the open ending are other non-picaresque elements in the *Coloquio* that should be held up for praise (Blanco Aguinaga, pp. 334–35). The cumulative weight of all these non-picaresque elements in the *Coloquio* eventually leads this critic to wonder whether Cervantes might in fact have been parodying *Guzmán* in his canine colloquy (p. 333).

For Gonzalo Sobejano there is no doubt as to the picaresque nature of the *Coloquio*; Berganza is cut from the same mould as Guzmán, including his penchant for moralizing digressions. The major difference is found in their attitude

[7] Juan Bautista Avalle-Arce, 'Cervantes entre pícaros', *NRFH*, 38.2 (1990), 591–603 (p. 597).

[8] Carlos Blanco Aguinaga, 'Cervantes y la picaresca. Notas sobre dos tipos de realismo', *NRFH*, 11 (1957), 313–42.

toward evil: Berganza's reaction to the malefactors he encounters is always one of revulsion, while Guzmán's is not.[9] And finally, regarding the author's curious choice of the prose dialogue as the format for his most famous picaresque work, we have the observation made by Roberto González Echeverría about Cervantes's decision to enter the marginal literary field of the picaresque:

> Like the pícaro Cervantes accepted the values of society and pretended as best he could to live by them. The new novel, as it emerged then, was appropriately a marginal form of writing without substantial antecedents in the classical tradition. It was a combination of rhetorical moulds, a simulacrum of other texts with social acceptance. The picaresque lacked an official model; therefore it mimicked real, official documents to render effective its 'performance' of the functions of society's texts. Because it has no prescribed form, the novel often must pretend to be a non-literary document. It can appear as a *relación*, the report of a scientific expedition, as history, a correspondence, a police report, a chronicle, a memoir, and so on. One fruitful way to study the history of the novel and its relation to society would be to take notice of what it pretends to be throughout the centuries. Is not Cervantes suggesting [in the *Coloquio*] that the novel mimics whatever kind of text a given society invests with power at a certain point in history?[10]

General Structure

Critics had traditionally studied the *Casamiento* and the *Coloquio* as separate entries in Cervantes's collection of *Novelas ejemplares*. In the early 1960s Joaquín Casalduero broke new ground when he declared that the final two entries in the collection were in fact a single *novela*, not two.[11] At the same time Casalduero pointed out what he called a fugue-like movement in the *Coloquio* (p. 242). The latter concept was enhanced by Alban K. Forcione, who further defined the fugal technique as one which 'enunciates a dominant theme and restates it continually in innumerable episodic variations, all of which are held together by a recurrent narrative rhythm and a carefully patterned repetition of symbolic imagery' (p. 126).

When it comes to a discussion of structure, there is little agreement among the critics as to what the definitive arrangement is between the narrative *Casamiento* and the purely dialogic *Coloquio*. Aside from Casalduero's general observations about fugal movements, the first genuine attempt at a structural analysis of these stories is that of Oldrich Belic.[12] For this critic the key to understanding the

[9] Gonzalo Sobejano, 'El *Coloquio de los perros* en la picaresca y otros apuntes', *HR*, 43.1 (Winter 1975), 25–41.

[10] Roberto González Echeverría, 'The Life and Adventures of Cipión: Cervantes and the Picaresque', *Diacritics*, 10.3 (1980), 15–26.

[11] Joaquín Casalduero, *Sentido y forma de las 'Novelas ejemplares'* (Madrid: Gredos, 1962), p. 237.

[12] Oldrich Belic, 'La estructura de *El coloquio de los perros*', in *Acta Universitatis Carolinae; Philologica*, 4 (1966); *Romanistica Pragensia, IV* (Prague: Univ. Karlova, 1966), pp. 3–19.

Coloquio is to recognize that Cervantes's dialogic account of Berganza's psychological and moral evolution from a 'naïve puppy' to a 'mature philosopher' is artfully rendered through the principle of symmetry, both thematic and structural.[13]

With regard to the formal arrangement of episodes, Belic calls the first four adventures – which by his count make up 49.2 per cent of the story – Berganza's apprenticeship in what Belic terms 'la escuela de la vida' (the school of life). The central episode of Berganza's experiences with the witch Cañizares constitutes another 25.2 per cent of the dialogue and signals a profound attitudinal change in the protagonist; the final four episodes – the remaining 25.6 per cent – serve simply to confirm the lessons learned earlier (Belic, p. 10).

Figure 1

episodes 1–4	episode 5	episodes 6–9
49.2%	25.2%	25.6%

From a thematic standpoint, Belic again finds an antithetical symmetry in the arrangement of episodes: adventures one and nine are at opposite poles of the spectrum of evil and good, with all the intermediary episodes arranged according to the principle of gradation (p. 11). The first and fifth episodes are special landmarks on the road Berganza takes toward understanding the problem of evil in this world, the first portraying Berganza's initial experience with an evil master, the fifth representing the absolute nadir of his moral depravity. Episodes six through nine show him gradually ascending from the depths of despair to a kind of spiritual rebirth under Mahudes (Belic, p. 12).

Belic also considers the *Coloquio* a social satire. The various episodes are generally seen to alternate between the light 'cuadros de costumbres' (scenes of local colour) and more ponderous (and sometimes allegorical) condemnations of official governmental practices, a form which Belic calls 'sátira estatal' (satire of the state). According to Belic, episodes one (the butcher), three (the merchant), six (the Gypsies) and eight (the poet) are of the lighter variety; numbers two (the shepherds), four (the constable) and seven (the Morisco [Spaniard of Moorish descent]) are of the more serious type; adventures five (the drummer; the witch) and nine (the crazy inmates at the hospital; the government official who refuses to listen) are a mixture of the two.

For Vicente Cabrera the fundamental elements of the *Coloquio* are grouped in clusters of three. In his 1972 article Cabrera observes three distinct planes of

[13] In a 1992 article, M. J. Thacker disputes Belic's thesis. Thacker observes no noteworthy improvement or deterioration in either of the dogs during the *Coloquio*. This constancy, says Thacker, is precisely what makes Berganza and Cipión reliable witnesses. See M. J. Thacker, 'Cervantes' Exemplary *Pícaros*', in *Hispanic Studies in Honour of Geoffrey Ribbans*, ed. Ann L. Mackenzie and Dorothy S. Severin, *BHS Special Homage Volume* (1992), 47–53.

reality: (1) Cervantes facing Campuzano and Peralta, (2) the Ensign and the Licentiate facing the talking dogs, and (3) Berganza and Cipión against the world they critique.[14] Similarly, the combined stories, when viewed as a single entity, can be seen to consist of three major parts: a prologue (the *Casamiento*), a 'parte general' (main part) (the *Coloquio*) and an epilogue. Each of these sections, in turn, has a different theme: the first deals with deception among individuals, the second with deceit in human society as a whole, the third with literary trickery, as represented by Campuzano's manuscript (Cabrera, 'Nuevos valores', pp. 54–5). In a later study (1974) Cabrera observes yet another triad: the three stages through which Peralta, the reader of Campuzano's manuscript, is seen to pass. He moves from an absolute refusal to believe that two canines have had a conversation, through a period of vacillation between belief and incredulity, to a final stage in which he suspends all judgement in the matter.[15]

Cabrera also comments on what he considers the remarkable synchrony we observe in the behaviour of the two friends. He makes special note of a pair of occasions on which the lawyer and the soldier-turned-author are seen to act in perfectly complementary ways. At the precise moment when Peralta opens the manuscript to begin reading – i.e. the start of Campuzano's recovery and awakening to reality (*desengaño*) – we are told that the author goes off to take a nap on a nearby bench. His mind will be temporarily disconnected, so to speak, while his friend's is engaged in evaluating the document he has written. In the second instance the Ensign awakens at the very moment when his friend's reading (and moral disabusement) is completed: 'El acabar el *Coloquio* el licenciado y el despertar el Alférez fue todo a un tiempo' ('The Licentiate finished the Colloquy and the Ensign woke up at the same time').[16] Cervantes's point here, Cabrera says, is to show how and why the two friends are able to go off at the end united in their shared *desengaño*, not separated by it (Cabrera, 'El sueño', pp. 390–91).

Yet another analysis of the structure of the combined *Casamiento/Coloquio* was produced in 1981 by José María Pozuelo Yvancos. Borrowing heavily from the theories of Mikhail Bakhtin and Gérard Genette, Pozuelo Yvancos offered a very thorough examination of the combined stories and the five *registros* or narrative levels that he observes at work in them. This critic demonstrates convincingly that, contrary to what Casalduero and others have asserted over the years, the *Casamiento* is not simply a frame tale for the *Coloquio*, but rather a

[14] Vicente Cabrera, 'Nuevos valores de *El casamiento engañoso* y *El coloquio de los perros*', *Hispanófila*, 45 (1972), 49–58 (p. 51).

[15] Vicente Cabrera, 'El sueño del alférez Campuzano', *NRFH*, 23 (1974), 388–91.

[16] Miguel de Cervantes, *Novelas ejemplares*, ed. Harry Sieber, 2 vols (Madrid: Cátedra, 1980–81), II, p. 359. The English translation is from Miguel de Cervantes, *Exemplary Novels / Novelas ejemplares*, ed. B. W. Ife, 4 vols (Warminster: Aris & Phillips, 1992), IV; here p. 157. Further references are to these editions.

completely separate entity, with its own narrative frame.[17] Pozuelo Yvancos's design can be summarized in the following scheme:

Table 1

Narrator	**Medium**	**Narratee**
Cervantes	Register I: Frame for the *Casamiento* description and dialogue between Campuzano and Peralta at both extremes of the combined *Casamiento/Coloquio*	The Reader
Campuzano	Register II: The *Casamiento* oral and written versions of the story of his failed marriage	Peralta
Campuzano	Register III: Frame for the *Coloquio* introduction to the text of the overheard conversation between the two dogs	Peralta
Berganza	Register IV: The *Coloquio* oral and written versions of his life story	Cipión
Cañizares	Register V: Cañizares's Story the extraordinary experiences she had with Camacha[18]	Berganza

Later in this essay I shall offer my own outline of what I perceive to be Cervantes's plan for the *Casamiento/Coloquio*. It should be noted that my scheme will be based largely on Pozuelo Yvancos's design.

Narrative Style

Aside from the matter of the arrangement of the various narrative and dialogic parts of these combined stories, the fundamental critical question about the format of the combined *Casamiento/Coloquio*'s form has to do with the various narrative rhythms Cervantes employs in their telling. In Forcione's view, the *Coloquio* is told on two narrative planes, one (Berganza's life story) derived from the picaresque novel, the other (Berganza and Cipión's critical discussion and commentary) based on the Lucianic dialogue (Forcione, p. 24). Such a literary hybrid naturally requires him to include subject-matter and satirical techniques appropriate to each genre and 'to alter radically the rhythm of his narration, vary its tonalities, and endow its narrator with a protean capacity for shape-changing that goes well beyond the notorious powers of accommodation and disguise which one encounters in the picaresque hero' (Forcione, p. 26).

[17] José María Pozuelo Yvancos, 'Enunciación y recepción en el *Casamiento-Coloquio*', in *Cervantes: Su obra y su mundo: Actas del I Congreso Internacional sobre Cervantes*, ed. Manuel Criado de Val (Madrid: EDI-6, 1981), pp. 423–35.

[18] According to Genette, Registers I and III would be considered *heterodiegetic* narratives, i.e., told in the *third person*, from a point of view lying outside the actual story. Conversely, Registers II, IV and V, because they are autobiographical (told in the *first person* and focused from within the story), are called *homodiegetic* narratives.

The stylistic phenomenon that Forcione observes behind the satire of the *Coloquio* is an ingenious, if highly unusual, plan that the critic refers to as a 'deliberate cultivation of formlessness' (Forcione, p. 37). The reader is obliged to wade through a series of intrusive elements (constant interruptions, annoying repetitions, needless retrogressions and qualifications etc.) designed to interfere with his desire to arrive at some satisfactory explanation of Berganza and Cipión's sudden and miraculous acquisition of the power of human speech. Forcione states that Cervantes's intention was to make his reader experience a sense of narrative disintegration as he is confronted with 'an artistic creation that is outrageously and *self-consciously unartistic*' (p. 37; original emphasis preserved).

Forcione offers a memorable example of Cervantes's penchant for assembling disparate narrative rhythms. He describes Berganza's story of his life with the constable as being initially 'a quickly paced dramatic narrative which moves with no interference toward a climactic scene of farce' (p. 31). But then Cervantes abandons that fast-paced anecdotal technique in favour of the dramatic devices that he employed so successfully in the 1605 *Don Quijote* and his one-act comedies (*entremeses*). The episode of the constable (*alguacil*) ends with a tumultuous scene of confusion and mutual recrimination brought about by the sudden disappearance of the Breton's trousers. Chaos reigns as the criminal plot disintegrates into a torrent of abusive railing and bitter exclamations of mutual distrust. Here comic stereotypes abound, particularly in the inflated protestations of nobility and spotless blood lines from the innkeeper's wife; her rhetorical excesses are marked by her mutilation of the Spanish tongue and her hysterical invocation of certain Latin phrases in her certificate of nobility (*hidalguía*) (Forcione, p. 31).

What should be clear from all of the above is that in his coupling of the *Casamiento* with the *Coloquio* Cervantes was drawing upon a wide range of literary traditions and models for a work he intended to be a literary and critical *tour de force*. Let us now examine these two stories, first as separate entities, then as complementary parts of an ingenious plan.

'El casamiento engañoso'

One of the first things we note about *El casamiento engañoso* is that its basic structure differs remarkably from that of the other *Novelas ejemplares*. Rather than begin *in medias res* as many of the so-called idealistic *novelas* do, or at the beginning – as was the case with the three *novelas* with links to the Porras Manuscript: *Rinconete y Cortadillo*, *El celoso extremeño* and *El licenciado Vidriera* – this story opens at the very conclusion of the action, i.e. the moment when a weak and wobbly Ensign Campuzano stumbles out of the Hospital of the Resurrection in Valladolid and runs into his old friend, Peralta. The narration then leaps back in time while the Ensign reconstructs for Peralta the peculiar events that have conspired to bring him to such a gravely debilitated physical state. From the very title of the work and from the description of Campuzano's physical condition in the opening paragraph it would appear that the element of surprise is not of paramount importance in this story: 'un soldado que, por servirle su espada de báculo y por la flaqueza de sus piernas y amarillez de su rostro [. . .] Iba haciendo pinitos y dando traspiés, como convalesciente' (II, p. 281) ('a soldier using his sword as a walking stick [. . .] He staggered and stumbled as if not fully recovered from an illness' [IV, p. 67]).

No attempt is made to disguise the fact that the ailing Ensign has been devastated by a foolish marriage to some deceitful woman. This detail is revealed early on by Campuzano himself: 'salgo de aquel hospital, de sudar catorce cargas de bubas que me echó una mujer que escogí por mía, que non debiera' (II, p. 282) ('I have just come out of that hospital where I have sweated out a dozen or so sores from the clap given to me by a woman whom I took to be mine when I should not have done so' [IV, p. 67]). But even this apparent frankness on Campuzano's part is ultimately seen to be something quite different. Cervantes reserves one small but significant surprise for the very end, as we shall see. The narrative order of events in the *Casamiento* can be represented as follows:

A = Introduction.
B = Flashback narrative of Campuzano.
C = Moral commentary of Peralta and Campuzano.
D = Introduction to the *Coloquio*.[19]

Figure 3

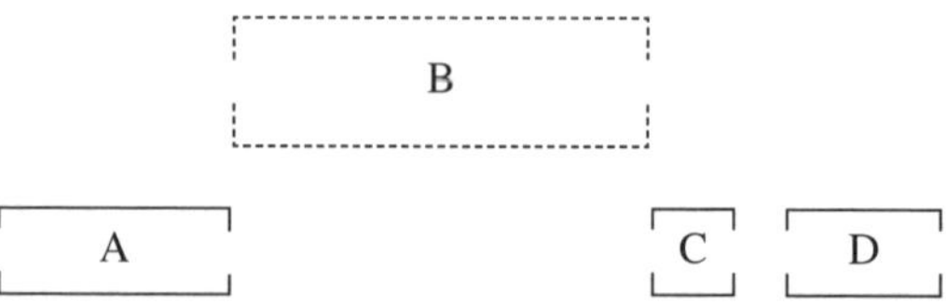

With regard to theme, this story deals with the closely related topics of hypocrisy, the universal conflict in human society between appearances and reality, and the general caution contained in the old saying about going out in search of wool and coming back shorn. The evidence of showy façades is present everywhere in this story; if the lady in question makes an initial grand display of her gaudy rings,

[19] In a purely chronological representation, however, sections A and B exchange places:

Figure 2

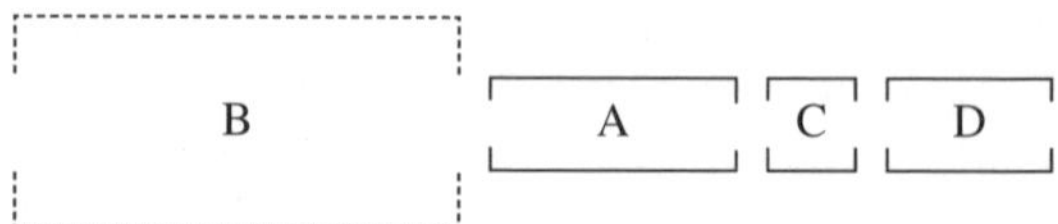

Campuzano himself plays the game with his colourful military uniform and gold chain:

> Estaba yo entonces bizarrísimo, con aquella gran cadena que vuesa merced debió de conocerme, el sombrero con plumas y cintillo, el vestido de colores, a fuer de soldado, y tan gallardo a los ojos de mi locura, que me daba a entender que las podía matar en el aire. (II, pp. 283–84)
>
> (At that time, I myself was rather flash, wearing that big chain that you have seen on me, a hat with feathers and hatbands, a coloured jacket, as befits a soldier, and so splendid was I in the eyes of my own delusion, that I believed I could have any woman I wanted. [IV, p. 69])

In a similar vein, the Ensign informs us that his lady friend's companion approaches another soldier under the pretext of asking him to carry certain letters to her 'cousin' in Flanders, but he realizes from the start that the intended recipient is her current lover. The Ensign's lady, whose name is Estefanía, baits the hook with her mysterious air (she refuses to uncover her face during their first encounter), the pale skin of her hands, and her soft, sensual voice: '[. . .] pues tenía un tono de habla tan suave que se entraba por los oídos en el alma' [II, p. 284] ('[. . .] for she had a tone of voice so soft that it entered the ear and reached the soul' [IV, p. 69]). After a courtship that lasts not much more than a week, the two are married and Campuzano moves with all his worldly possessions into the comfortable house that she has led him to believe is hers.

From all the clues Cervantes has scattered about the early pages of his narrative, the reader must realize that Estefanía's representation of herself and her financial situation is nothing but a great sham. The fragile tissue of her lies begins to disintegrate six days later when someone named doña Clementa suddenly appears at her door and claims the house belongs to her. Estefanía calms the fears of her new husband with a fairly flimsy explanation: she says doña Clementa is attempting to trick a certain suitor into proposing marriage to her by claiming that house as her own; things will return to normal as soon as Clementa convinces him to marry her, she asserts. What the reader surely suspects – and what the Ensign ought to realize – is that Estefanía is attributing to her friend the very same scam she has been perpetrating on him. Blinded by his own greed, Campuzano fails to recognize his own precarious situation in the scenario his wife has constructed. In the end he is left homeless, penniless, and afflicted with a venereal disease that will cause him to lose all of his hair and then have to undergo twenty days of treatment in a hospital. The Ensign can take consolation only from the fact that his deceitful bride will find herself equally embarrassed when she learns that all the flashy gold chains with which she has absconded are paste, virtually worthless. This final piece of information is the only real surprise that Cervantes has kept in reserve for the dénouement.

Ultimately, the story of Campuzano's 'Deceitful Marriage' turns out to be a deceitful narrative. The narrator pretends to reveal all in the opening pages, but such turns out to be not quite the case. The reader is seduced, in effect, just as Campuzano has been. We are deceived into believing that we are able to glimpse the objective reality of the situation from Campuzano's very subjective account of the events. But when the last piece of the picture finally falls into place, the reader realizes that he/she, too, has been duped. In the end, Campuzano's losses turn out to be not nearly so large as he had led Peralta to believe, nor has his character been quite so ingenuous as Cervantes had led his readers to suppose.

All in all, this is a masterful display of Cervantes's talents as a story-teller and manipulator of plot: the opening description of the pathetically enfeebled Ensign immediately draws us into the tale; Campuzano's carefully crafted account of his entrapment – with an abundance of verbal clues to add spice to the narration and deceive us into thinking we are more clever than the foolish protagonist – distracts the reader's attention while Cervantes sets up the final punch line. The *coup de grâce* is then administered painlessly, almost as an afterthought, a throw-away line to finish off the joke.

The characterization in this story is likewise very fine, which is sometimes difficult to achieve in a story overflowing with unsavoury types. In virtually every other *novela* in the collection we can find at least one morally upright character worthy of our admiration or sympathy, but the vast majority of critics believe this not to be the case here, although both Lloris and Rodríguez-Luis have attempted to make a case in defence of Estefanía.[20] What is remarkable is that in the *Casamiento*, a story that abounds in hypocrites and sleazy con artists, Cervantes somehow finds a way to temper the stinging social criticism he delivers. The self-deprecating humour with which Campuzano tells his tale renders him, if not quite lovable, perhaps somewhat less loathsome than he might have been in the hands of a less skilful narrator. He pays the full price for his stupidity, greed and short-sightedness, but he is seen to emerge a better man for the experience.

'El coloquio de los perros'

If one were to attempt a schematic representation of the chain of Berganza's adventures, one might profitably consider Belic's outline as a model:

Figure 4

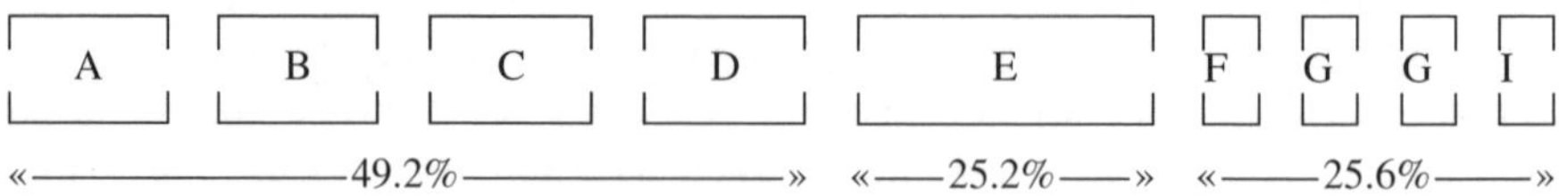

A = the butcher
B = the shepherds
C = the Sevillian merchant
D = the constable

[20] Manuel Lloris, 'El casamiento engañoso', *Hispanófila* 39 (May 1970), 15–20; Julio Rodríguez-Luis, *Novedad y ejemplo de las 'Novelas' de Cervantes*, 2 vols (Madrid: Porrúa-Turanzas, 1980–84), II, p. 49.

E = the drummer and the witch
F = the Gypsies
G = the Morisco farmer
H = the poet and theatre manager
I = with Mahudes at the hospital

A simpler and more accurate design for the *Coloquio* was suggested by Ruth El Saffar in her 1976 study of that work.[21] El Saffar depicts Berganza's story as consisting of 'clusters' of episodes, which can be grouped according to the following scheme:

Figure 5

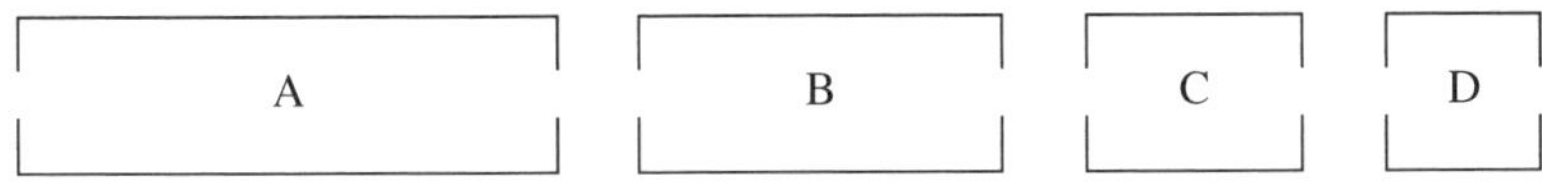

A. The Heart of Society: masters who 'contribute directly to the financial interests which dominate Seville':

1- the butcher [rural-outside]
2- the shepherds [rural-outside]
3- the rich merchant [urban-inside]
4- the constable [urban-inside]

B. Parasites: social types 'rejected by society and living off what they can take from it'; they demonstrate how deception and greed operate to undermine spiritual values both consciously (the drummer) and unconsciously (the witch):

5- the drummer [urban-inside]
6- the witch [rural-outside]

C. Outsiders: social groups who are excluded from the centre of commercial and social power:

7- the Gypsies [rural-outside]
8- the Moor [rural-outside]
9- the poet [urban-inside]
10- the theatre manager [urban-inside]

D. The Good Mahudes: he represents the spiritual order of reality, standing in contrast to the social/material order that dominates the first ten episodes. Here Berganza comes in contact with the following persons:

1- the idealists: a poet, an alchemist, a mathematician and an *arbitrista* (professional consultant)

2- the rich and powerful who lack spiritual values: the Chief Magistrate (*corregidor*) and the Rich Lady with a yapping lap-dog

[21] Ruth El Saffar, *Cervantes: A Critical Study of 'El casamiento engañoso' and 'El coloquio de los perros'*, Critical Guides 17 (London: Grant & Cutler, 1976), pp. 39–41.

In the first cluster Cervantes is attacking the hypocrisy of the most powerful members of Spanish society, including the Jesuits (episode three), regarding whom El Saffar says Berganza has an ambiguous attitude that renders any subsequent praise of them ironic (*A Critical Study*, pp. 46–9). I prefer to see the narrator's attitude as one of ambivalence, in the sense of displaying simultaneous conflicting feelings towards them. There can be no ambiguity or uncertainty about the praise that Cervantes, through Berganza, offers for the Jesuit order or their teaching methods. Any ambivalence attributed here would have to be found in Cervantes's reaction to the Jesuits' complicity in assisting wealthy New Christians to advance in certain delicate social areas. El Saffar notes that this episode could be a representation of the Jewish *converso* issue and the distasteful practice of investigating lineages that prevailed in sixteenth-century Spanish society (*A Critical Study*, p. 48). The Sevillian merchant in the *Coloquio* is probably a rich New Christian and the Jesuits are clearly helping him prepare his sons to ascend the socio-economic ladder. If we are looking for some symbolic meaning for the events that transpire at the school, the dog could be said to represent the tainted family blood lines that had to be kept under wraps (i.e. locked up at home) if the family hoped to avoid social embarrassment.[22]

In the first cluster, the structure of each succeeding episode is seen to be more complex than that of the previous one. With each new master Berganza becomes progressively more disillusioned, even as his moral stature seems to grow (El Saffar, *A Critical Study*, pp. 44–5). We observe Berganza moving steadily from the role of passive observer to that of active opponent of the hypocrisy he encounters in the world. With the butcher Berganza is simply an unwitting accomplice; with the shepherds he becomes a victim of their crooked scheme; with the African housekeeper he strives to expose her immoral sexual activities; and with the constable Berganza takes full charge of exposing his corrupt master's hypocritical – albeit profitable – subversion of the justice system in Seville (*A Critical Study*, pp. 55–6).

The second cluster, consisting of what El Saffar calls 'linking' episodes, represents the structural centre of Berganza's experiences, even though the adventures with the drummer and the witch Cañizares take place roughly three-quarters of the way through the *Coloquio*. As many have noted, Berganza's descent into the world of witchcraft and sorcery in these episodes represents the absolute low point of his moral and spiritual journey.

El Saffar observes that in the final cluster of adventures the episodes become progressively shorter (*A Critical Study*, p. 78). The Gypsies are said to represent

[22] Forcione observes that El Saffar's judgements here follow the lead of Maurice Molho in claiming that 'the Jesuits are subtly shown to be in collusion with the *converso* merchants in their efforts to "buy" clean genealogies' (Forcione, pp. 151–2, n. 12). El Saffar portrays Cervantes as an opponent of such subversive scheming on the part of the Jesuits, while Forcione casts him as a supporter of the order's efforts to foment greater social mobility in Spanish society. Considering Cervantes's well-known opposition to so many of the conventional beliefs of his contemporaries, Forcione's interpretation is the more plausible one, in my view.

the creative impulse that may be lacking in the rest of Spanish society; they are also thieves who honour neither Church nor King (*A critical study*, p. 71). The Moriscos, as represented by the Moorish farmer, are portrayed on the one hand as hard workers, but on the other as false Christians and miserly hoarders who are given to procreating at an unhealthy rate. All in all, says El Saffar, Cervantes seems to prefer the chaotic impulses of the Gypsies to those of the hard-working Moriscos (*A Critical Study*, pp. 73–4). In the episode of the poet Cervantes seizes the opportunity to satirize some contemporary notions of literary verisimilitude, and with the theatre manager he gets to vent some of his frustrations about the success of his rival, Lope de Vega (*A critical study*, p. 76).

The final cluster of Berganza's adventures, those taking place while he is in the employ of Mahudes, presents the reader with a series of indelible examples of mankind's misguided search for absolute truths. The poet is ignorant and ill-educated but dedicated to his craft, although he often mispronounces words and makes false attributions (*A Critical Study*, p. 80). We are also introduced in turn to an alchemist in search of the legendary Philosopher's Stone that is said to turn all base metals into gold, to a mathematician seeking the fixed point, and to an *arbitrista* or armchair politician with a wild scheme guaranteed to reduce the national debt. These, like Berganza, are persons in search of some absolute truth in a world that absolutely refuses to provide one (*A Critical Study*, pp. 80–1).

Cervantes is much less sanguine about the behaviour of political figures and the idle rich. The *corregidor* (Chief Magistrate) is deaf to Berganza's cries for reform. The official says he cannot understand Berganza's practical solution for dealing with the problem of venereal disease among prostitutes in Valladolid and has the complaining animal beaten and expelled (*A Critical Study*, pp. 81–2). Similarly, Berganza has to suffer the offensive yapping of a high-born woman's lap-dog, a poke at certain disagreeable loud-mouths who depend upon the power and position of their patrons to shield them from the retribution they would otherwise face from the victims of their verbal assaults (*A Critical Study*, p. 82).

As for the link between the *Casamiento* and the *Coloquio*, El Saffar's ultimate judgement is that the canine colloquy is simply a fantastic dream designed to reflect the real-life story that precedes it: the Ensign's futile search for a place in upper society (*A Critical Study*, p. 84).

The Combined Texts

Having studied the *Casamiento* and the *Coloquio* as separate entities, let us now examine how the combined *Casamiento/Coloquio* fits into Cervantes's overall artistic scheme for his *Novelas ejemplares*. Cervantes was fond of telling stories in sets of four modules. In Part I of *Don Quijote*, for example, in many instances a single story would be told from four different points of view (Marcela and Grisóstomo), in four distinct stages of development (Cardenio/Luscinda;

Fernando/Dorotea), or through an accumulation of plot reversals adding up to four separate actions (*El curioso impertinente*). In the second part of his masterwork Cervantes turned his attention to the device of telling stories in layers, usually four in number, each of which served as a commentary on the layer immediately below it. This is most noticeable in the episodes of the Cave of Montesinos and Maese Pedro's puppet show, as I have demonstrated elsewhere.[23] I find the same principle of quaternity at work in the combined *Casamiento/Coloquio*.

The structure of the *Coloquio* itself is quite simple: Berganza narrates the story of his life while Cipión comments on the content and style – mostly the latter – of the narration. However, the transcript of the dogs' conversation does not stand alone; it is joined to the preceding *Casamiento*, in what appears to have been a fortuitous late inspiration. At some point prior to publication Cervantes decided to join these two stories for what I perceive to be two different, though related, reasons. The first was a desire to provide a proper introduction for his prose dialogue; the second – an even more significant decision, as we shall see – was to add two new layers of commentary to the story's original pair of critical strata, thereby doubling the effect he was attempting to produce. Each layer of the *Coloquio* is designed to reflect critically on the style and content of the narrative presented in the section immediately below it. Cervantes's ultimate scheme for the *novela* was to produce a narrative spiral that first descends, then ascends, through four distinct planes of relation.

At the point of entry (Level A) there is the Licenciate Peralta, who in the frame tale reads and comments on the written narrative of Ensign Campuzano; immediately below that, on Level B, we have listener Campuzano recording the conversation of the miraculously gifted canines and also offering his own opinions regarding the verisimilitude of the events he has witnessed and recorded. Leaving the frame tale, we enter the text of the colloquy itself at Level C: here speaker/narrator Berganza recounts his picaresque adventures to listener/critic Cipión, who continually interrupts to interject his own critical opinions about the content of the narration and the manner in which it is delivered. The bottom stratum (Level D) is reached when the witch Cañizares, in the course of one of her reveries, relates to a somewhat incredulous Berganza a rather bizarre tale about a pair of children who were turned into dogs by a sorceress's incantation. In the following diagram we note that this strange tale of demonic forces and implied metempsychosis lies at the linear mid-point of Cervantes's *novela* and represents, literally and figuratively, the core of his labyrinthine narrative.[24]

23 E. T. Aylward, 'The Device of Layered Critical Commentary in *Don Quixote* and *El coloquio de los perros*', *Cervantes* 7.2 (1987), 57–69; see also E. T. Aylward, *Towards a Revaluation of Avellaneda's 'False Quixote'* (Newark, DE: Juan de la Cuesta, 1989), pp. 63–70.

24 It is worth noting that, from a purely chronological standpoint, the order of the various parts would reverse the order of the narrative sequence:

Figure 6

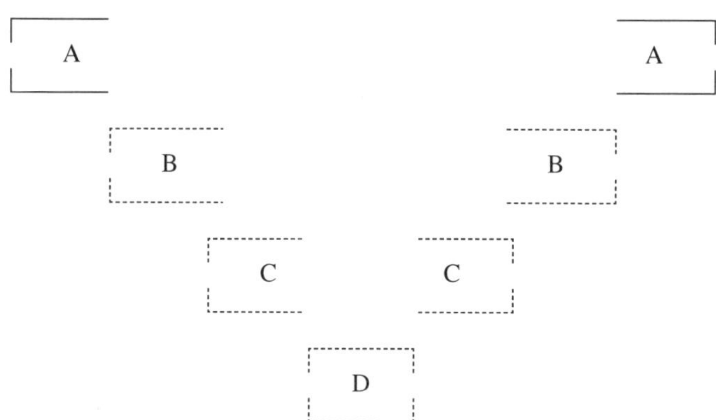

Furthermore, at each level Cervantes presents us with a different set of interacting characters, one serving as a narrator (N), the other as listener (L):

Level A = Peralta (L); Campuzano (N)
Level B = Campuzano (L); Berganza & Cipión (N)
Level C = Cipión (L); Berganza (N)
Level D = Berganza (L); Cañizares (N)

Having descended through three layers before reaching this core, the narration begins to ascend again after the witch has finished her incredible account. Back on level C Berganza comments as to whether Cañizares's strange prophecy may somehow be responsible for the faculty of speech with which he and Cipión have suddenly been blessed. He then continues with his life story and concludes his account by telling how he came to enter the service of the good Mahudes at the hospital in Valladolid and miraculously received there the power of speech. Cervantes brings the tale to a swift conclusion by returning the reader to the outside world, where Campuzano remarks about his own reaction to what he has overheard (Level B), and Peralta comments on the general verisimilitude of the Ensign's written account (Level A).[25]

Figure 7

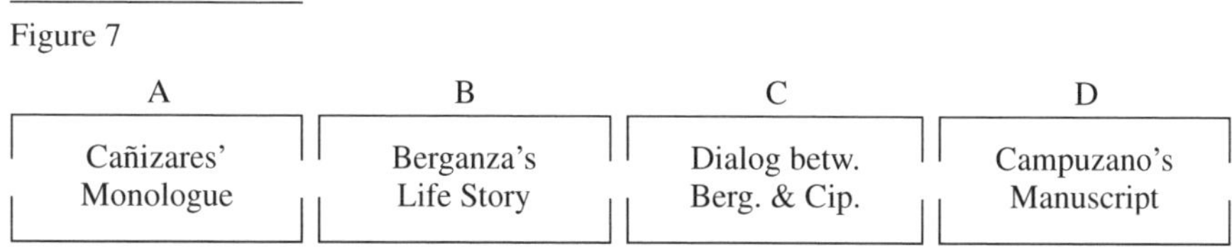

[25] George Haley was the first to comment on Cervantes's penchant for employing layered narrative structures in his prose fiction. Haley documented the existence of certain parallel narrative structures in selected episodes of the two parts of *Don Quijote* in his seminal article, 'The Narrator in *Don Quixote*: Maese Pedro's Puppet Show', *MLN*, 80 (1965), 145–65.

It is no mere coincidence that Cervantes should choose characters like Campuzano and Peralta to be his commentators on the *Coloquio*, or that the unfortunate Ensign should ultimately find himself in an untenable Quijote-like position. In the preceding frame story, the *Casamiento*, Campuzano tells a similarly incredible tale about a contrived counterfeit marriage that has inevitably backfired on him. At the end of Campuzano's narration Peralta demonstrates a reasonably sceptical attitude toward the Ensign's story. Asked now to read an even more fantastic tale about two talking dogs, Peralta declares that he is not prepared to believe anything from Campuzano's lips – or pen, for that matter. The Ensign is obliged to admit that this second story is also quite strange, that he himself had difficulty believing it, even as it was unfolding, and indeed had at first believed it to be a dream. Upon reflection, however, he has concluded that on his own he could not have imagined or invented such a voluminous amount of incredible dialogue, so he affirms that the dogs really did speak that night.

The compromise reached at the close of the *Coloquio* in many ways also echoes the treatment of the same themes in Part I of *Don Quijote* when both the Priest and don Fernando offer critical judgements regarding the written story of *El curioso impertinente* and the autobiographical oral history narrated by the Captain, respectively: history versus fiction, and the reliability of oral versus written accounts. At the close of the *Coloquio*, Peralta dismisses Campuzano's transcript of the dogs' colloquy as fiction ('fingido'), but praises it for being well composed and urges the Ensign to continue with the promised second part. Campuzano insists that the entire account is true (i.e. history), but the more sophisticated Peralta refuses to accept it as anything but fiction. In the end they decide not to dispute any further about whether the dogs' dialogue is history or fiction. Turning now to the thematic reason for Cervantes's linking the *Casamiento* to the *Coloquio*, let us consider the hypothesis advanced by Ruth El Saffar in 1973 when she proposed that the *Casamiento* is actually an after-the-fact reworking of the *Coloquio*, one which was intended to cast some light on the dogs' dialogue and transform its meaning, just as Part II of the *Quijote* represents a revaluation of Part I.[26] In El Saffar's view, the fusion of these two tales allows the lesser story, the dogs' colloquy, to become part of a greater and more meaningful whole. The process requires an otherwise implausible conversation to be incorporated into a broader and much more credible tale about the narrator's moral and physical recovery – or resurrection, if we consider the symbolic nature of the hospital's name – from the illness, alienation and disgrace that have recently plagued his life.[27]

[26] Ruth El Saffar, 'Montesinos' Cave and the *Casamiento engañoso* in the Development of Cervantes' Prose Fiction', *KRQ*, 20 (1973), 451–67 (p. 455).

[27] Forcione appears to concur with El Saffar at one point; he observes that the *Casamiento* is an independent confession framing and maintaining a subordinate one (i.e. the core episode of Cañizares's revelations about witchcraft). Forcione views the frame tale's elaborate set of imaginative correspondences as a link with the second story's episode of the Toledan witch (p. 135). At a later point he parts company with El Saffar, labelling the *Casamiento* a powerful counter force to the narrative movement of the *Coloquio*, which he declares to be the more dominant of the two stories (p. 146).

El Saffar points out that the Ensign, much like Don Quijote, is a suffering, alienated and intensely disoriented individual at the moment he enters the Hospital of the Resurrection ('Montesinos' Cave', p. 464). Consequently, Campuzano, like the mad Manchegan in the cave adventure, is obliged to descend in his dreams to a nether world where he is to undergo an intense spiritual transformation that will initiate his journey back to good physical and mental health.[28] Furthermore, each man's experience in these episodes is bipartite, consisting of one realistic and one fantastic encounter. Campuzano's ordeal opens with a clearly picaresque story about his disastrous courtship and marriage to the cunning Estefanía (leaving him both financially ruined and with a bad case of syphilis), then closes with his dream-like encounter with two chatty canines ('Montesinos' Cave', pp. 451–65).

Each narrator's strange experience seems to represent a fortuitous liberation from lingering patterns of action that have caused his intense feelings of failure and alienation ('Montesinos' Cave', p. 456). Moreover, through the process of verbalizing their hallucinatory adventures, both Don Quijote and Campuzano actually begin the long journey to recovery. The critic convincingly argues that Cervantes must have decided at some late point (*c.* 1612–13) to fuse the *Coloquio* to the *Casamiento* so as to replicate, thematically at least, the Cave of Montesinos episode ('Montesinos' Cave', p. 460). In this new arrangement, the Ensign's act of transcribing the dream-like colloquy is supposed to inspire his subsequent purgative confession to Peralta about his ill-conceived marriage.

There remains a nagging question about Cervantes's narrative technique: why has he opted to present the events of these two stories out of their normal chronological sequence? The answer can be found, I believe, by examining a special quirk in Cervantes's style and his marked preference for a particular story-telling strategy. What I have termed the device of layered critical commentary provides us with an important clue as to why Cervantes, upon deciding to combine these two tales, chose to begin *in medias res*, rather than simply narrate the events in their natural chronological order. The simplest linking arrangement would have dealt exclusively with Campuzano. Section A would have portrayed him in the painful process of courting, wedding and finally losing the shifty Estefanía. The action in the next section (B) would have taken place at the Hospital of the Resurrection, where the woeful Ensign would have experienced his hallucinatory descent into the realm of conversing canines. The final portion (C) would

[28] Forcione, disagreeing, prefers to interpret the Cave of Montesinos adventure as a parody of the romance conventions of anagnorisis, an ironic treatment of the descent and recognition themes so prevalent in the romantic tradition. These same conventions later reappear in the *Coloquio* during Berganza's grotesque encounter with Cañizares (pp. 48–9). In Forcione's view, the theme of Don Quijote's descent into the cave is man's adversarial relationship with time and its unpleasant consequences (e.g. mortality and decay). Quijote is confronted in his dream with the fact of man's inescapably transitory nature and the ultimate futility of his own dreams of immortality. The *Coloquio*, on the other hand, is said to deal with the moral theme of demonic powers in conflict with divine purposes (pp. 51–5).

have left the linking element (the transcription of the dialogue) for the very end, thereby vitiating the most artistic aspect of the undertaking.

Figure 8

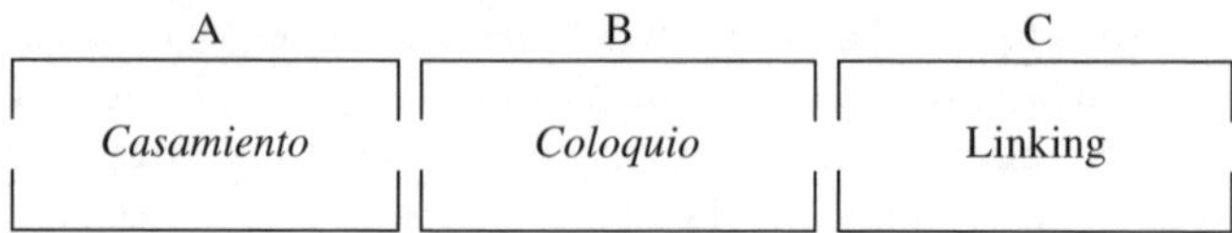

Moreover, such a bare-bones structure would have presented a *Coloquio* that featured only the bottom three narrative levels (Campuzano eavesdropping on the dogs' conversation, Cipión listening to Berganza's story, Berganza witnessing Cañizares's grotesque reverie). The topmost level, the role of the Licenciate Peralta as reader of and commentator on Campuzano's manuscript, would have been lost, which then would have made it difficult for Cervantes to point to the moral lesson that El Saffar says the Ensign and the reader were supposed to extract from these two closely related experiences. The all-important catalyst Cervantes designed to infuse moral exemplariness into this new arrangement is the sympathetic ear – and later, the acquiescing eyes – of Peralta. In the course of recounting to the Licenciate the bizarre particulars of these two unusual experiences, the narrating Ensign is forced to confront the unpleasant truth about his own previous comportment, draw the proper moral conclusions, and pledge himself to a serious reform of his personal conduct.

The decision to consider the *Casamiento* and the *Coloquio* as a single hybrid unit necessarily imposes new artistic roles upon them. While it is true that in such a scheme the largely descriptive *Casamiento* is transformed into a 'frame' for the purely dialogic *Coloquio*, there are other subtle changes that have not always been appreciated by the critics. Most notable among these is the fact that, while in their original form the two stories have occupied the narrative foreground in the reader's attention, the new arrangement forces both of them into the background, where their function now is to provide analeptic recapitulations or 'flashback' accounts of past events. In a purely structural sense, then, these two stories have moved from present to past narrative time. The new arrangement of these two major narrative blocks, along with the sections of text that connect them, is as follows:

Figure 9

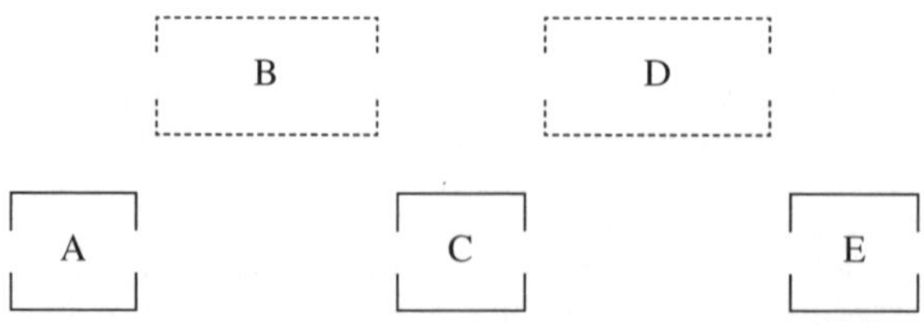

A = Campuzano meets Peralta outside the hospital.
B = Campuzano's story of his *Casamiento engañoso*.

C = Peralta begins to read the manuscript Campuzano has written.
D = Text of the *Coloquio de los perros*, as penned by Campuzano.
E = Peralta's comments.[29]

Thematic considerations aside, Cervantes's creation of the listening Licenciate is a sparkling demonstration of the author's technical virtuosity: Peralta's presence at the uppermost level as a commentator on all that is narrated below him illustrates Cervantes's intense commitment to greater technical sophistication and structural complexity in his *novelas*. Cervantes realized that by appending the dream-like dogs' colloquy to the more realistic account of Campuzano's deceitful marriage he could reproduce, thematically at least, a situation akin to the one Don Quijote faced in Montesinos's Cave.

But Cervantes also understood that certain technical adjustments would have to be made in order to maintain the four-tiered structure of his model(s) from the *Quijote*. Most notable was the need to invert the chronological order of some of the events in the combined stories. He would begin with the Ensign's emergence from the hospital (which comes very close to the end of the chronological sequence) and then fuse the overheard *Coloquio* to the previous *Casamiento* by means of the mediating figure of Peralta, who would hear the first story and read the other. To add the desired fourth level of critical commentary, Cervantes employed once again the analeptic 'flashback' device of which, to judge from the frequency with which he uses it in the other *Novelas ejemplares*, he was so obviously fond.

Cervantes's Plan

Generally speaking, it would have made perfect sense for Cervantes to fuse the *Casamiento* and the *Coloquio*, if only to provide a narrative frame for the second entry, which purports to be simply the transcript of a conversation between two canines. It also would have seemed appropriate, from a moral and thematic standpoint, to join these two stories because of their common theme: humankind's innate hypocrisy. From a psychological standpoint, moreover, the devastating embarrassment Campuzano suffers at the hands of Estefanía in the *Casamiento* certainly provides a plausible enough explanation for the strange reverie he subsequently experiences and records in the *Coloquio*. But there is yet

29 A strictly chronological ordering of these events would be quite different, however:

Figure 10

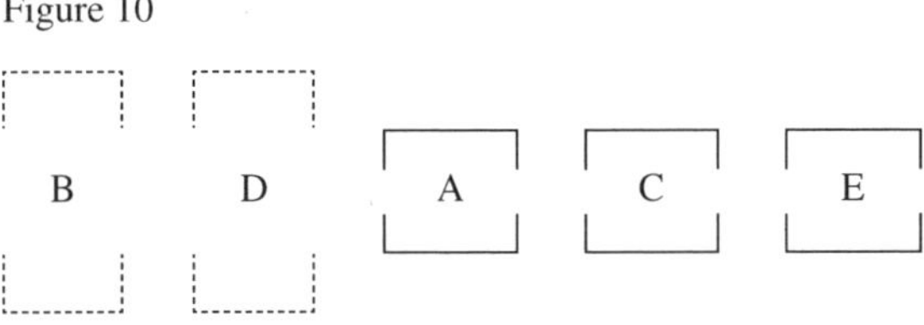

a deeper level of intention to be found here. The fusion of these two disparate elements also serves a critical/theoretical purpose in that it allows Cervantes to represent perfectly the complexity of artistic creation and the interdependence of the author and his reader.

In a 1974 study of Cervantes's *novelas*, Ruth El Saffar alludes to the theoretical implications of the combined *Casamiento/Coloquio*, pointing out that Campuzano represents the author while his friend Peralta assumes the role of the reader. Taken together, these two characters represent the two parts of the creative process, i.e. the cooperative effort that is required if works of fiction are to achieve the level of verisimilitude that neo-Aristotelian critics demanded of them.[30] El Saffar offers no comment at all about the role of the hypercritical Cipión in the process, but I would suggest that the second dog's role in the *Coloquio* is to give concrete form to the haunting voice of literary theorists who constrain the writer's creative instincts by trying to force him to work in accordance with established literary precepts.

The consensus of these conservative theorists, most notably Torquato Tasso, was that the plausibility of a fictional work depended entirely upon internal factors, i.e. whatever empirical data – usually of a historical, geographic or scientific nature – the author could provide to convince the sophisticated reader of the text's veracity. Cervantes, beginning with *Don Quijote*, dedicated much of his literary production to demonstrating a radically new notion: that verisimilitude depended upon both internal and external elements. For the Spanish writer, the quality of the artist's representation always works in conjunction with whatever the reader is willing to accept as believable; and the ultimate verisimilitude of a fictional work will perforce be determined by the 'cooperative effort' between the author and his reader that El Saffar signalled.

But even as Cervantes insists upon a harmonious effort on the part of the writer and his reader, he also appears to be doing everything in his power to discourage their cooperation. This is the observation made in 1992 by B. W. Ife when he notes that the fictional author Campuzano takes great pains to warn Peralta that the transcript he has provided is even more incredible than the bizarre story he has just told of his failed marriage. This unusual disclaimer is designed by Cervantes to call Peralta's attention – and ours – to the highly improbable nature of what is about to be recounted.[31] Had Cervantes's intention been to accentuate the verisimilitude of the *Coloquio*, the author might reasonably have made some reference to the long literary tradition of talking animals. The fact that he eschews this tactic indicates that Cervantes had some other purpose in mind (Ife, *Lectura y ficción*, p. 40).

To summarize Ife's observations, Cervantes prefaces the dialogue by having the author of the *Coloquio* impugn his own work's believability; then he presents

[30] Ruth El Saffar, *Novel to Romance: A Study of Cervantes' 'Novelas ejemplares'* (Baltimore: Johns Hopkins University Press, 1974), pp. 81–2.

[31] B. W. Ife, *Lectura y ficción en el Siglo de Oro: Las razones de la picaresca* (Barcelona: Edición Crítica, 1992), p. 39.

the dogs' conversation verbatim, with absolutely no authorial intrusion that might distract the reader from the protagonists' actual words. The next step is to remove the author entirely from the scene while Peralta reads the manuscript: Cervantes moves Campuzano off to a nearby bench where he slumbers long enough to allow his friend to absorb the text without any authorial interference. The purpose of all this, says Ife, is to confront Peralta with a pure, unadulterated text of the dogs' conversation. In short, the Licenciate is placed in the unique position of being able to function as both reader and critic – two very distinct roles – at the same time (*Lectura y ficción*, p. 41).

As any critic is expected to do, Peralta strives to suspend his scepticism about a canine conversation until he has read all of Campuzano's manuscript. Having completed his reading, Peralta proceeds to issue two apparently self-contradictory statements. First, he dismisses the colloquy as totally fictitious ('fingido'), but then praises the literary artefact as well written ('bien compuesto') and urges his friend to proceed with the second part, Cipión's story. Cervantes's point here, according to Ife, is that the credibility of a work of fiction has nothing to do with its internal verisimilitude. It is a matter of the author's skill and the willingness of the reader to be convinced (*Lectura y ficción*, p. 41).

Ife's analysis helps to explain two things: (1) why Cervantes wrote the *Coloquio* as a prose dialogue, without any authorial intervention; and (2) why he chose to combine it with the *Casamiento*. Cervantes needed a prefatory piece that would provide a critical level (or platform, if you will) from which to pass judgement on the dialogue that would follow. The *Casamiento* was also the perfect introduction to the *Coloquio* because the story of Campuzano's deceitful marriage was so bizarre that it would automatically cast him in the role of an unreliable narrator for the *Coloquio*. (This is not unlike Cervantes's earlier decision to make the source of *Don Quijote* a Moorish historian, i.e. a member of a notably mendacious and untrustworthy ethnic group.) The combined *Casamiento* and *Coloquio* provided Cervantes with the perfect vehicle to comment on the twin questions of credibility and verisimilitude.[32]

As for Cervantes's reasons for undertaking such a daunting task, we should consider the explanation offered by Edwin Williamson in 1989: that Cervantes disliked Alemán's narrative package and wished to offer the public an alternative to *Guzmán de Alfarache*. In Williamson's view, Alemán's novel is based on the assumption that the value of literature is dependent upon the virtue of the

[32] Fred Abrams, advocating an idea originally advanced by Émile Chasles in his work, *Michel de Cervantes, sa vie, son temps, son oeuvre politique et littéraire* (Paris: 1866), states that the name Berganza points to Cervantes himself. If we suppress the fourth and eighth letters of the dog's name ['g' and 'a'], says Abrams, we get the following anagrammatic sequence: Berganza » Beranz » Zerban » Cervan[tes]. The same process can be seen at work with Cipión's name: Cipión » Pincio » Pinci[an]o. If Abrams's theory is correct, it might be said that what Peralta is reading is a conversation between Cervantes and López Pinciano. See Fred Abrams, 'Cervantes' Berganza–Cipión Anagrams in *El coloquio de los perros*', *Names*, 24 (1976), 325–6.

implied author, the newly repentant Guzmán.[33] Any semblance of moral uprightness in the *Coloquio* is immediately compromised by the fact that its protagonists are canines and its author an unreliable scoundrel. Unlike Alemán, Cervantes has constructed his picaresque piece so as to leave his reader free to embrace or reject the story that Campuzano relates (Williamson, pp. 121–22).

In 1980 Robert V. Piluso proposed that the figure of the highly literate Licentiate was designed to represent the ideal critical reader not only for the *Coloquio*, but also for the entire collection of *Novelas ejemplares*.[34] Indeed, as he offers his final evaluation of Campuzano's text, Peralta can be viewed as a model critic because he wisely chooses to apply broad aesthetic norms (i.e. the quality of Campuzano's literary fabrication and the artful devices he employs) over narrow empirical, historical or scientific criteria: '—Señor Alférez, no volvamos más a esa disputa. Yo alcanzo el artificio del Coloquio y la invención, y basta' (II, p. 359). ('Ensign, sir, let's not get involved in that again. I see the art of the Colloquy and its invention and that is enough' [IV, p. 157]).

If there is some artistic purpose behind Cervantes's elaborate plan to fuse the *Casamiento* with the *Coloquio*, it is to demonstrate that a skilful author – as Campuzano in this case certainly is – will be able to create an interesting and plausible story out of virtually any subject-matter, even something as absurd as a conversation between two dogs.

Works cited

Abrams, Fred, 'Cervantes's Berganza–Cipión Anagrams in *El Coloquio de los perros', Names*, 24 (1976), 325–6.

Amezúa y Mayo, Agustín G., *Cervantes, creador de la novela corta española*, 2 vols (Madrid: Consejo Superior de Investigaciones Científicas, 1956–58).

Avalle-Arce, Juan Bautista, 'Cervantes entre pícaros', *NRFH*, 38.2 (1990), 591–603.

Aylward, E. T., 'The Device of Layered Critical Commentary in *Don Quixote* and *El Coloquio de los perros*', *Cervantes*, 7.2 (1987), 57–69.

———, '*Towards a Revaluation of Avellaneda's 'False Quixote'* (Newark, DE: Juan de la Cuesta, 1989).

———, *The Crucible Concept: Thematic and Narrative Patterns in Cervantes's 'Novelas ejemplares'* (Madison, NJ: Fairleigh Dickinson UP, 1999).

[33] Edwin Williamson, 'Cervantes as Moralist and Trickster: the Critique of Picaresque Autobiography in *El casamiento engañoso y El coloquio de los perros*', in *Essays on Hispanic Themes in Honour of Edward C. Riley*, ed. Jennifer Lowe and Philip Swanson (Edinburgh: Department of Hispanic Studies, University of Edinburgh, 1989), pp. 247–329 (p. 113).

[34] Robert V. Piluso, 'El papel mediador del narrador en dos *novelas ejemplares* de Cervantes', in *Actas del Sexto Congreso Internacional de Hispanistas celebrado en Toronto del 22 al 26 de agosto de 1977*, ed. Alan M. Gordon and Evelyn Rugg; foreword by Rafael Lapesa (Toronto: Department of Spanish and Portuguese, University of Toronto, 1980), pp. 571–74.

Belic, Oldrich, 'La estructura de *El Coloquio de los perros*', in *Acta Universitatis Carolinae*; *Philologica*, 4 (1966); *Romanistica Pragensia IV* (Prague: Univ. Karlova, 1966), pp. 3–19.

Blanco Aguinaga, Carlos, 'Cervantes y la picaresca. Notas sobre dos tipos de realismo', *NRFH*, 11 (1957), 313–42.

Cabrera, Vicente, 'Nuevos valores de *El casamiento engañoso* y *El coloquio de los perros*', *Hispanófila*, 45 (1972), 49–58.

———, El sueño del alférez Campuzano', *NRFH*, 23 (1974), 388–91.

Casalduero, Joaquín, *Sentido y forma de las 'Novelas ejemplares'* (Madrid: Gredos, 1962).

Cervantes Saavedra, Miguel de, *Novelas Ejemplares*, ed. Harry Sieber, 2 vols (Madrid: Cátedra, 1980–81).

———, *Exemplary Novels / Novelas ejemplares*, ed. B. W. Ife, 4 vols (Warminster: Aris & Phillips, 1992).

Chasles, Émile, *Michel de Cervantes, sa vie, son temps, son oeuvre politique et littéraire* (Paris: 1866).

El Saffar, Ruth, 'Montesinos' Cave and the *Casamiento engañoso* in the Development of Cervantes's Prose Fiction', *KRQ*, 20 (1973), 451–67.

———, *Novel to Romance: A Study of Cervantes' 'Novelas ejemplares'* (Baltimore: Johns Hopkins University Press, 1974).

———, *Cervantes: A Critical Study of 'El casamiento engañoso' and 'El Coloquio de los perros'*, Critical Guides 17 (London: Grant & Cutler, 1976).

Forcione, Alban K., *Cervantes and the Mystery of Lawlessness: A Study of 'El casamiento engañoso y El coloquio de los perros'* (Princeton: Princeton University Press, 1984).

González Echeverría, Roberto, 'The Life and Adventures of Cipión: Cervantes and the Picaresque', *Diacritics*, 10.3 (1980), 15–26.

Haley, George, 'The Narrator in *Don Quijote*: Maese Pedro's Puppet Show', *MLN*, 80 (1965), 145–65.

Ife, B. W., *Lectura y ficción en el Siglo de Oro: Las razones de la picaresca* (Barcelona: Edición Crítica, 1992).

Lloris, Manuel, 'El casamiento engañoso', *Hispanófila*, 39 (May 1970), 15–20.

Oliver, Antonio, 'La filosofía cínica y el *Coloquio de los perros*', *AC*, 3 (1953), 291–307.

Piluso, Robert V. 'El papel mediador del narrador en dos *novelas ejemplares* de Cervantes', in *Actas del Sexto Congreso Internacional de Hispanistas celebrado en Toronto del 22 al 26 de agosto de 1977*, ed. Alan M. Gordon and Evelyn Rugg; foreword by Rafael Lapesa (Toronto: Department of Spanish and Portuguese, University of Toronto, 1980), pp. 571–74.

Pozuelo Yvancos, José María, 'Enunciación y recepción en el *Casamiento-Coloquio*', in *Cervantes: Su obra y su mundo: Actas del I Congreso Internacional sobre Cervantes*, ed. Manuel Criado de Val (Madrid:EDI-6, 1981), pp. 423–35.

Riley, E. C., 'Cervantes and the Cynics: *El licenciado Vidriera* and *El Coloquio de los perros*', *BHS*, 53.3 (July 1976), 189–99.

Rodríguez-Luis, Julio, *Novedad y ejemplo de las 'Novelas' de Cervantes*, 2 vols (Madrid: Porrúa-Turanzas, 1980–84).

Sobejano, Gonzalo, 'El *Coloquio de los perros* en la picaresca y otros apuntes', *HR*, 43.1 (Winter 1975), 25–41.

Thacker, M. J., 'Cervantes' Exemplary Pícaros', in *Hispanic Studies in Honour of Geoffrey Ribbans*, ed. Ann L. Mackenzie and Dorothy S. Severin, *BHS Special Homage Volume* (1992), 47–53.

Williamson, Edwin, 'Cervantes as Moralist and Trickster: the Critique of Picaresque Autobiography in *El casamiento engañoso y El Coloquio de los perros*', in *Essays on Hispanic Themes in Honour of Edward C. Riley*, ed. Jennifer Lowe and Philip Swanson (Edinburgh: Department of Hispanic Studies, University of Edinburgh, 1989), pp. 104–26.

Zappala, Michael, 'Cervantes and Lucian', *Symposium*, 33.1 (Spring 1979), 65–82.

13

Eutrapelia and Exemplarity in the *Novelas ejemplares*

Colin Thompson
St Catherine's College, Oxford

In one of the four *aprobaciones* to the *Novelas ejemplares*, Fray Juan Bautista wrote:[1]

> [. . .] supuesto que es sentencia llana del angélico doctor Santo Tomás, que la eutropelia es virtud, la que consiste en un entretenimiento honesto, juzgo que la verdadera eutropelia está en estas *Novelas*, porque entretienen con su novedad, enseñan con sus ejemplos a huir vicios y seguir virtudes, y el autor cumple con su intento, con que da honra a nuestra lengua castellana, y avisa a las repúblicas de los daños que de algunos vicios se siguen.
>
> (Since it is the clear opinion of the angelic Doctor St Thomas that eutropelia, which consists of wholesome entertainment, is a virtue, I am of the view that true eutropelia is to be found in these *Novels*, because they entertain by their novelty, teach by their examples to eschew vice and follow virtue, and the author has fulfilled his intention, honouring thereby our Castilian tongue and warning of the harmful effects of certain vices for the public good.)[2]

In two articles from the 1980s, Wardropper and Jones brought the concept of eutrapelia back into critical debate about the *Novelas ejemplares*.[3] Hart, for example, mentions it in the following terms:

> Now forgotten by everyone except a handful of theologians, eutrapelia was well known to Cervantes' contemporaries. Eutrapelia is a wholesome recreation,

[1] *Aprobaciones* guaranteed that books were morally inoffensive.

[2] Spanish quotations are from Miguel de Cervantes, *Novelas ejemplares*, ed. Jorge García López (Barcelona: Crítica, 2001); here, pp. 5–6. Unless indicated, translations of other texts are mine, as here. The forms 'eutropelia' and 'eutrapelia' were both used in the seventeenth century.

[3] See Bruce Wardropper, 'La eutrapelia en las *Novelas ejemplares* de Cervantes' in *Actas del séptimo congreso de la Asociación Internacional de Hispanistas*, 2 vols (Roma: Bulzoni, 1982), I, pp. 153–69; Joseph R. Jones, 'Cervantes y la virtud de la eutrapelia: la moralidad de la literatura de esparcimiento', *AC*, 23 (1985), 19–30. Both critics refer to Hugo Rahner, SJ, *Man at Play: Or Did You Ever Practise Eutrapelia?* (London: Burns & Oates, 1965).

> *honesto entretenimiento*. It is both a temporary turning away from more serious concerns and a preparation for returning to them with renewed strength. The concept of eutrapelia thus dissolves the apparent opposition in the familiar Horatian doctrine that poetry should be both pleasant and morally beneficial: poetry is beneficial *because* it gives pleasure.[4]

The term, originally Aristotelian, was known in the Golden Age largely through its presence in discussions about the right use of leisure in the *Summa* of St Thomas Aquinas;[5] Covarrubias defines it in 1611 as 'un entretenimiento de burlas graciosas y sin perjuyzio' (harmless entertainment, consisting of amusing jests).[6] Wardropper and Jones confined themselves to the history of the term and its possible relevance to the *Novelas*, rather than attempting to show how it might shed light on their interpretation. Given the many different readings they have received, it is worth reflecting on how the theory of eutrapelia may illuminate the exemplarity Cervantes famously claims to be present, though hidden, in each story and across the whole collection.

Aquinas, the greatest of the medieval theologians, whose authority in the Roman Catholic Church was unequalled after the Council of Trent, defined eutrapelia as a form of relaxation necessary for human beings: 'ad eutrapeliam pertinet dicere aliquod leve convicium, non ad dehonorationem vel ad contristationem ejus in quem dicitur, sed magis causa delectationis et ioci. Et hoc potest esse sine peccato, si debitæ circunstantiæ observantur' ('playfulness includes making a light-hearted insult by way of entertainment and fun and not to discredit and upset the other. And this can be quite innocent, provided the circumstances are right').[7] He returns to the topic in q. 168, 'De modestia in exterioribus corporis motibus' (Good manners; XLIV, pp. 210–11), where he answers the objections of some of the Church Fathers to the pursuit of leisure by stating that the soul, like the body, requires rest after labour:

> Sicut autem fatigatio corporalis solvitur per corporis quietem, ita etiam oportet quod fatigatio animalis solvatur per animæ quietem. Quies autem animæ est delectatio [. . .] Et ideo oportet remedium contra fatigationem animalem adhiberi per aliquam delectationem, intermissa intentione ad insistendum studio rationis (XLIV, p. 216).
>
> (As bodily tiredness is eased by resting the body, so psychological tiredness is eased by resting the soul. Pleasure is rest for the soul [. . .] And therefore the

4 Thomas R. Hart, *Cervantes' Exemplary Fictions: A Study of the 'Novelas ejemplares'* (Lexington: The University Press of Kentucky, 1994), pp. 15–16.

5 The word occurs once in the New Testament (Ephesians 5: 4), but in a negative context.

6 Sebastián de Covarrubias Orozco, *Tesoro de la lengua castellana o española* (Madrid, 1611; repr. Barcelona: Alta Fulla, 1998), p. 574.

7 Latin and English texts from *St Thomas Aquinas: Summa Theologiae*, ed. Thomas Gilby and others, 61 vols (London: Eyre & Spottiswode, 1964–80); here, from 'De contumelia' ('Defamation'), 2a2ae q.72 a.2; XXXVIII, pp. 162–3. This translation renders 'eutrapelia' as 'playfulness'.

remedy for weariness of soul lies in slackening the tension of mental study and taking some pleasure. [XLIV, p. 217])

At this point he inserts an anecdote taken from the *Collationes Patrum* by the monastic writer St John Cassian (*c.* 360–*c.* 430).[8] Someone was shocked one day to discover that St John the Evangelist was playing a game with his disciples. St John called over one of the young men, who had a bow in his hand, and asked him to shoot it. When he had done so several times, St John asked him if this could be repeated continuously. He replied that if he did, the bow would break: 'Unde beatus Ioannes subintulit quod similiter animus hominis frangeretur, si nunquam a sua intentione relaxaretur' ('whereupon the blessed John pointed the moral that so, too, would the human spirit snap were it never unbent' [XLIV, pp. 216–17]). In other words, spiritual exercises, however important and necessary, cannot be practised uninterruptedly without damaging consequences for the soul. This does not lessen their importance; on the contrary, it enables them to be performed more effectively, because it acknowledges the constraints of human weakness, which requires periods of rest before it can return to its labours with renewed strength.

The topic of harmless recreation in Cervantes is not limited to the *Novelas ejemplares*: in *Don Quijote*, I, 48, the canon of Toledo says:

> Y si se diese cargo a otro [. . .] que examinase los libros de caballerías que de nuevo se compusiesen, sin duda podrían salir algunos con la perfección que vuestra merced ha dicho, enriqueciendo nuestra lengua del agradable y precioso tesoro de la elocuencia, dando ocasión que los libros viejos se escureciesen a la luz de los nuevos que saliesen, para honesto pasatiempo, no solamente de los ociosos, sino de los más ocupados, pues no es posible que esté continuo el arco armado, ni la condición y flaqueza humana se pueda sustentar sin alguna lícita recreación.
>
> (And if another person [. . .] were given the job of scrutinizing any new books of chivalry that were written, some of these might well show the perfection that you've specified, enriching our language with the delightful, precious treasure of eloquence, eclipsing old books in the light of the new ones published for the innocent amusement not only of the idle but also of the busy, because the bow can't always be bent, nor can our frail human nature subsist without some honest recreation.[9]

[8] For Cassian, see *Patrologia Latina*, ed. J. P. Migne, 221 vols (Tournai, 1844–64), XLIX, pp. 1312–15.

[9] Miguel de Cervantes, *Don Quijote de la Mancha*, ed. Francisco Rico, 2 vols (Barcelona: Crítica, 1998), I, p. 556. Translation from *Cervantes: Don Quixote*, tr. John Rutherford, Penguin Classics (Harmondsworth: Penguin, 2000), p. 446. In the 'Notas' (II, p. 408), Joaquín Forradellas attributes the image of the armed bow to St Gregory the Great, noting that 'la metáfora se convirtió en imagen literaria tópica' (the metaphor became a commonplace literary image) in the Golden Age. But Aquinas attributes it to Cassian, who wrote almost two centuries before Gregory.

The image of the bow may have become a literary commonplace, and its presence here does not prove that Cervantes had read the texts of Aquinas or Cassian. But it does suggest that he was familiar with the concept of eutrapelia, and that this enabled him to reflect on the two poles of Horatian literary theory, *prodesse* and *delectare*, instruction and entertainment, with a frequency and a depth rare in Golden-Age writing. The therapeutic value of literature written for times of leisure is central to the practice of Cervantes, and failure to grasp this risks misunderstanding the nature of exemplarity in his *Novelas*. As Riley observed: 'He takes the business of entertainment very seriously indeed'.[10]

Cervantes's version of this wise and humane concept occupies a significant place in the 'Prólogo' to the *Novelas*: 'Sí que no siempre se está en los templos; no siempre se ocupan los oratorios; no siempre se asiste a los negocios, por calificados que sean. Horas hay de recreación, donde el afligido espíritu descanse' (p. 18) ('After all, we cannot always be in church; the oratories are not always occupied; we cannot always be doing business, no matter how important it is. There is time for recreation, when the tormented spirit can rest').[11] Religion, prayer, the world of business – all the serious and important activities of human life, sacred and secular – cannot possibly occupy every hour of the day and night; it is essential for human beings to enjoy times of recreation. Cervantes locates the moral and spiritual significance of his stories in their ability to restore to the soul its capacity to resume its serious duties once it has rested from the weariness which is the inevitable consequence of any form of labour. By comparing the reading of his tales to the pleasures of gardening – 'para este efeto se plantan las alamedas, se buscan las fuentes, se allanan las cuestas y se cultivan con curiosidad los jardines' (p. 18) ('That is why poplar groves are planted, springs are made into fountains, slopes are levelled and gardens created in wonderful designs' [I, p. 5]) – he draws a parallel between mental and physical pleasures, repeated at the end of the collection, when the Licenciado says to Campuzano: 'Vámonos al Espolón a recrear los ojos del cuerpo, pues ya he recreado los del entendimiento' (p. 623) ('Let's repair to the Espolón to entertain our eyes for we have already entertained our minds' [IV, p. 157]; the verb 'recrear' should perhaps be read in the double sense of 'recreation' and 're-creation'). Literature of entertainment does not expect the mind to cease to function. Such entertainment continues as they leave to enjoy a walk through the gardens by the riverside, where art has co-operated with nature to bring pleasure to the eyes. At the moment of closure, therefore, Cervantes returns to the synthesis of the Horatian categories of instruction and entertainment first announced in the prologue, with its recognition that wholesome entertainment is a necessary good for humans and therefore has its own moral value. To take the concept of eutrapelia seriously in reading the *Novelas* liberates critics from having to make an inappropriate choice between a serious or a comic reading, and enables them

[10] E. C. Riley, *Cervantes's Theory of the Novel* (Oxford: Clarendon, 1962), p. 83.

[11] Translations from Miguel de Cervantes, *Exemplary Novels / Novelas ejemplares*, ed. B. W. Ife, 4 vols (Warminster: Aris & Phillips, 1992); here, I, p. 5.

to reconcile the entertainment of the *novela* with the presence of exemplarity – 'enseñar deleitando', 'deleitar enseñando' (to instruct by entertaining, to entertain by instructing).

Aquinas stresses that eutrapelia requires excesses like obscenity or slander to be avoided, and a certain decorum to be in place with respect to person, time and place. He proposes that 'ludus est necessarius ad conversationem humanae vitae' ('playing is necessary for human intercourse' [XLIV, pp. 222–23]), and that those who make such play possible do not sin. For example, 'officium histrionum, quod ordinatur ad solatium hominibus exhibendum, non est secundum se illicitum: nec sunt in statu peccati, dummodo moderate ludo utantur' ('the acting profession, the purpose of which is to put on shows for our enjoyment, is not unlawful in itself. Nor are actors in a state of sin, provided their art is temperate' [XLIV, pp. 222–23]). This apologia, unexpected, perhaps, from the greatest of the medieval theologians, became important in sixteenth-century defences of the theatre, particularly in the *Introduction à la vie dévote* of St François de Sales and, according to Jones (p. 22), in the response of a notable Carmelite preacher (Fray José de Jesús María) to those who demanded the definitive closing of theatres in Spain when Philip II died in 1598.[12]

The scholastic evaluation of recreation as beneficial, subject to the limits of moderation and decency, points towards a reconsideration of the nature of exemplarity in the *Novelas*. The prologue, with its variations on the theme that all the stories contain 'ejemplos' and 'algún misterio [. . .] escondido que las levanta' (p. 20) ('some hidden mystery which elevates them' [I, p. 5]) can be read as one of the many jokes Cervantes plays on the reader, with a sideways glance, perhaps, in the direction of the censors. But whatever problems it raises, it does not read like a conventional, let alone hypocritical piece of writing, if only because of the self-portrait with which it begins, and the proud reference to the wound Cervantes suffered at the battle of Lepanto, 'herida que, aunque parece fea, él la tiene por hermosa, por haberla cobrado en la más memorable y alta ocasión que vieron los pasados siglos, ni esperan ver los venideros' (p. 17) ('a [. . .] wound, which, although it looks ugly, he considers beautiful, since he collected it in the greatest and most memorable event that past centuries have ever seen or those to come may hope to see' [I, p. 3]) – suggesting perhaps that stories like *El casamiento engañoso* (The Deceitful Marriage) and *El coloquio de los perros* (The Dialogue of the Dogs), which deal with the darker side of human nature may contain a deeper, more positive truth.

Eutrapelia enables the synthesis of *prodesse* and *delectare*, teaching and entertaining, exemplarity and pleasure, so that the act of reading a story the art and inventiveness of which attract us ('el artificio' and 'la invención' [*Coloquio*, p. 623]; 'art' and 'invention' [The Dialogue, II, p. 157]) also 'nos podría enseñar' (*La española inglesa*, p. 263) ('can teach us' [The English

[12] It would be taken up again in the anonymous *La eutrapelia. Medio, que deben tener los juegos, Divertimientos, y Comedias, para que no aya en ellas pecado* (Valencia: Benito Macè, 1683).

Spanish Girl, II, p. 57]) a range of moral lessons to be pondered without the direct sermonizing which might lead the attention of readers to stray. Even if they simply take the *Novelas* as entertainment and fail to respond to their indirect and allusive exemplarity, they will at least have spent their time harmlessly, as the prologue suggests, 'sin daño de barras' (p. 18) ('without snookering anyone else' [I, p. 5]). The comments by the dogs in the *Coloquio* (e.g. pp. 552–53, 558, 562–63, 566–70) about 'murmurar' on the one hand and 'predicar' or 'filosofar' on the other ('gossip', 'preaching', 'philosophizing', e.g. IV, pp. 93, 97, 101, 105, 107, 109) offer an interesting reflection on this: each is apparently rejected, though neither can be avoided, and in some sense act as equivalents of 'deleitar' ('entertaining') and 'enseñar' ('teaching') respectively. It is a common assumption of our own time that comic art can have no moral content: the fourteenth-century *Libro de buen amor* (Book of Good Love) is another outstanding work which has suffered from a tendency to expect readers to choose between a serious or a light-hearted reading. Perhaps the most effective means of demonstrating human fallibility is for authors to appear to be laughing at themselves, offering readers examples their own failures, so they not only laugh with the author/protagonist but are reminded in a gentle way of how similar to him or her they are. Humour and laughter – except, perhaps, when they have a satirical twist – are the best allies of moralist and preacher alike, because they enable a lesson to be learnt almost unconsciously, and more effectively than when preacher or satirist awaken only a negative sense of guilt. Sometimes, when teaching the *Novelas* (or the *Libro*) I ask students what they would prefer if they had committed a serious mistake: have a sermon preached at them to correct it, or be told a story, perhaps about how I once did the same? The reply is always the same: the latter. And when I ask them why that should be, they reply that if they have to work out the moral point for themselves, it is more likely that they will grasp it than if it is served up to them on a plate.

Cervantes may be saying something similar in his prologue and throughout the *Novelas*. Their capacity to entertain us increases the more their author hints at or disguises the *exemplum* he wishes readers to consider through the words and actions of his characters. In order to explore this further, I look at two of them, *La gitanilla* (The Little Gipsy Girl) and *La fuerza de la sangre* (The Power of Blood), to show how a reading which takes eutrapelia into account can hold together the exemplary sense to which they point and the pleasure derived from a story well told. I then consider another, *Rinconete y Cortadillo* (Rinconete and Cortadillo), in which language itself becomes the principal thematic protagonist, in the sense that the exemplarity Cervantes has in mind depends on our responding to a series of linguistic errors which reveal, comically and indirectly, the false morality of the world of the eponymous protagonists and Monipodio's guild.

In his study of the close relationship he sees between the fundamental themes of the *Novelas* and the important issues of the age, Joseph Ricapito writes of *La gitanilla*: 'la larga descripción de la vida gitana por parte del viejo gitano representa la tentativa de Cervantes de ofrecer una imagen simpática de los valores que rigen la sociedad gitana' (the long description of gipsy life by the old gipsy represents Cervantes's attempt to offer a sympathetic picture of values which govern gipsy society); and later: 'La oración del viejo gitano es un panegírico a una sociedad ajena a preocupaciones como la honra' (the old gipsy's speech is a panegyric of a society free of concerns like honour).[13] Such a conclusion surely misses the point. In fact, in his evocation of the innocence and purity of gipsy life, the old man unwittingly condemns out of his own mouth the moral basis of the society he is intending to praise, by revealing how deeply flawed it is. It is easy to be seduced by the idyllic picture he paints of gipsy life, with its emphasis on friendship, freedom, and the absence of jealousy. But a closer look at what he actually says reveals a quite different picture, which does not seem to concern him:

> Nosotros guardamos inviolablemente la ley de la amistad: ninguno solicita la prenda del otro; libres vivimos de la amarga pestilencia de los celos. Entre nosotros, aunque hay muchos incestos, no hay ningún adulterio; y cuando le hay en la mujer propia, o alguna bellaquería en la amiga, no vamos a la justicia a pedir castigo; nosotros somos los jueces y los verdugos de nuestras esposas o amigas; con la misma facilidad las matamos y las enterramos por las montañas y desiertos como si fueran animales nocivos; no hay pariente que las vengue ni padres que nos pidan su muerte. (p. 71)
>
> (We keep strictly to the rules of friendship: nobody hunts after someone else's prize; we live free from the bitter pestilence of jealousy. Among us, although there us a lot of incest, there is no adultery; and if there is any with one's wife or any naughty behaviour in a mistress, we do not complain to the law; we are the judges and the executioners of our wives or our mistresses; we kill them or bury them in the mountains or the deserts as if they were harmful animals; there are no relations to avenge them, nor parents to charge us with their deaths. [I, pp. 57, 59])

Some panegyric! The passage raises many questions. The gipsy community may obey the tenth commandment ('Thou shalt not covet'), but this is scarcely praiseworthy, since they live by breaking the eighth ('Thou shalt not steal'): there is no need to covet if you can help yourself to the desired object. Jealousy – a constant theme of Cervantes's fictions, symbolizing that lack of trust between lovers which, unless overcome, will destroy their love – is absent only because gipsy males kill any female who does not behave according to their rules. The men are allowed to divorce their wives or abandon their women whenever they wish, in order to 'escoger otra que corresponda al gusto de sus años' (p. 71) ('choose another who suits the taste of his years' [I, p. 59]). More outrageous are the remarks the old man slips into his speech so casually that we risk overlooking their significance: 'Entre nosotros, aunque hay muchos incestos, no hay

[13] *Cervantes's 'Novelas ejemplares': Between History and Creativity* (West Lafayette, Indiana: Purdue University Press, 1996), pp. 13, 33.

ningún adulterio' (p. 71) ('Among us, although there is a lot of incest, there is no adultery' [I, p. 59]). He claims that they abide by the seventh commandment, only to contradict this in the next breath: 'y cuando le hay en la mujer propia' ('and if there is any with one's wife'). There is no adultery among the men, but when the women commit it (with whom? one wonders), they are brutally murdered, in contravention of the sixth commandment ('Thou shalt not kill'). Worse still, he seems to think that the frequency of incest in the community, a taboo which does not even figure among the Ten Commandments (though it occasionally occurs as a motif in the Old Testament) is scarcely worth mentioning. The old man believes he is commending gipsy life to its newest recruit, Andrés, but in so doing reveals its true nature. It may have many attractive features, but the alert reader will set these against the fact that three of the Ten Commandments, theft, adultery and murder, are integral to gipsy life, while incest is disregarded. It is hardly surprising that Preciosa rejects gipsy law in favour of 'la ley de mi voluntad, que es la más fuerte de todas' ('the law of my will, which is the strongest law of all'): 'estos señores bien pueden entregarte mi cuerpo, pero no mi alma, que es libre y nació libre, y ha de ser libre en tanto que yo quisiere' (p. 74) ('these gentlemen can indeed hand my body over to you; but not my soul, which is free and was born free' [I, p. 61]). Her virginity, so highly prized by her, is the physical symbol of her personal integrity and the spiritual freedom which governs her behaviour, in contrast to the harsh dictates of gipsy law with regard to women.

Only a hasty reading of the old gipsy's speech can blind the critic, as it blinds its speaker, to the fact that it subverts the very idyll it is claiming to portray. Far from representing gipsy life as ideal, it reveals it to be shot through with serious moral faults. Although the speaker believes he is portraying a society the ideals of which are superior to those of the city or the court, or is trying to persuade Andrés and the reader that this is so, closer attention to its actual nature may reasonably lead one to suppose that Cervantes is condemning a male society which devotes itself with bestial ferocity to the oppression of women, casting them aside when they are no longer of use and murdering them if they commit a sin the menfolk apparently do not. Of course gipsy society is also painted with other, attractive features, but its representation is fundamentally ambiguous. Here, in line with the prologue's reference to the mystery hidden in the text, we must learn to mistrust rhetoric. Nor does courtly rhetoric fare any better. Preciosa's analysis of Andrés's offer of marriage (pp. 74–5; I, p. 61) goes straight to the point: such rhetoric often masks a baser desire, to possess and then to abandon the woman to whom it is addressed once the pleasures of sex have been satisfied. If Andrés means what he says, he will have to prove it with his deeds.

A further example of the need to attend carefully to apparently unimportant elements in the narrative comes from *La fuerza de la sangre*, perhaps the most theatrical and symbolic of the *Novelas*. It remains a controversial work, appearing to condone rape as long as the perpetrator marries the victim. The presence of repeated images of darkness, blood, fall, and crucifix lend it a strong Christian resonance. Its binary structure sets the abduction and rape of Leocadia at the beginning against the restoration of her honour through marriage to her rapist at the end, and turns on the axis of the accident suffered by Luisico, the son conceived by Leocadia in the act of rape, who providentially recovers from an apparently near-fatal accident halfway through the tale, on the very bed where his mother had been violated.[14] The modern reader's reaction must depend on how the character of Rodolfo, the rapist, is interpreted. It seems abhorrent that so violent and sensual a man should end up marrying his victim, without showing any remorse for his crime. Is it anything more than a convenient, conventional ending, more suitable for a seventeenth-century reader than for one at the beginning of the twenty-first?[15] Are we meant to believe that it provides an exemplary solution? Leocadia has been forced to bring up her son secretly in the family home lest her private dishonour become public, while her selfish assailant abandons her once his lust is satisfied and goes off to the wars in Italy, unconcerned about any possible consequences of his actions.

The difficulties of interpretation are well summed up by Jeremy Robbins:

> 1) Leocadia loves her rapist by the end of the story; 2) Rodolfo fails utterly to repent; 3) Rodolfo demands proof, once he has married Leocadia [. . .] that Leocadia is indeed the woman he raped, despite claiming that he does not doubt her identity [. . .]; and 4) for all the talk of critics that Rodolfo has been redeemed and has transcended his earlier behaviour, he is motivated by sexual desire still – he has married Leocadia simply because of her beauty, and once married we are told of his impatience to sleep with her.[16]

A more careful reading, however, indicates that Cervantes has provided readers with clues, especially during the dramatic dénouement, which may suggest a less cynical interpretation. A series of apparently casual remarks in the text suggests that although Rodolfo does not openly repent, he has acquired a more morally appropriate attitude towards his sexual needs, because he has come to see how the physical and spiritual aspects of love must work together, in contrast to the sheer brutality of the rape scene. This change, the result, perhaps, of increasing maturity in the years spent abroad (though Cervantes is not explicit about this), is first revealed when his mother, having learnt that Luisico is her grandson, puts into action a plan intended to right the wrong committed by Rodolfo against Leocadia.

[14] Compare San Juan de la Cruz, 'Cántico espiritual', where the Bridegroom tells the Bride: 'y fuiste reparada | donde tu madre fuera violada'(and you were restored | where your mother was violated), and their biblical inspiration (Song 8: 5); see *San Juan de la Cruz: Poesía*, ed. Domingo Ynduráin (Madrid: Cátedra, 1989), p. 254. However, I am not proposing a typological interpretation of the *novela* here.

[15] Calderón's *El alcalde de Zalamea* (*The Mayor of Zalamea*; *c.* 1644), in which Pedro Crespo pleads unsuccessfully with the Captain who has raped his daughter to marry her, suggests that Golden-Age readers would have found such a solution less shocking than modern ones may.

[16] Jeremy Robbins, *The Challenges of Uncertainty: An Introduction to Seventeenth-Century Spanish Literature* (London: Duckworth, 1998), p. 93.

The narrator is not neutral. In terms of language, comment and analysis it is made clear that Rodolfo's action is cruel, blind and selfish. At the start, Rodolfo and his friends are presented in negative terms, 'lobos' (wolves) who act 'con deshonesta desenvoltura' ('with lewd insolence'), 'cubiertos los rostros' (p. 304) ('covering their faces' [II, p. 103]); he has 'un deseo de gozarla' (p. 305) ('the desire to enjoy her' [II, p. 103]), overcome by 'los ímpetus no castos de la mocedad' (p. 306) ('the lewd impulses of youth' [II, p. 105]). In a dark room, with Leocadia lying unconscious on his bed, Rodolfo, 'ciego de la luz del entendimiento, a escuras robó la mejor prenda de Leocadia' (p. 306) ('totally blind to the light of his own intelligence [. . .] robbed Leocadia of her greatest treasure' [II, p. 105]). Once his carnal desires have been satisfied, 'quisiera luego Rodolfo que de allí desapareciera Leocadia' (p. 306) ('he then wished she would disappear from the place' [II, p. 105]) – an allusion, perhaps, to the disgust felt by Amnon after he has raped his half-sister Tamar (II Kings 13: 15), and reminiscent of Preciosa's response to the declaration of love by Andrés: 'Si alcanza lo que desea, mengua el deseo con la posesión de la cosa deseada, y quizá abriéndose entonces los ojos del entendimiento, se ve ser bien que se aborrezca lo que antes se adoraba' (p. 54) ('If the will attains what it desires, that desire diminishes with possession, and if perhaps the eyes of reason open at that time, it sees that it should properly loathe what it previously adored' [I, p. 39]). When Leocadia awakens from her swoon, Rodolfo attempts to rape her again, aroused by 'las discretas razones de la lastimada Leocadia' (p. 308) ('the prudent words of the injured girl' [II, p. 107]). But when she defends herself:

> [. . .] los deseos de Rodolfo se enflaquecieron; y como la insolencia que con Leocadia había usado no tuvo otro principio que de un ímpetu lascivo, del cual nunca nace el verdadero amor, que permanece, en lugar del ímpetu, que se pasa, queda, si no el arrepentimiento, a lo menos una tibia voluntad de segundalle. (p. 308)
>
> (The strength and desire of Rodolfo weakened; and since the insolence he had shown to Leocadia had its beginning only in a lascivious impulse [from which true enduring love is never born], in place of that transient impulse there remains, if not repentance, at least less inclination towards repeating the action. [II, p. 109])

To underline the point, the ardent and sensual Rodolfo quickly turns 'frío' (indifferent) and 'cansado' (wearied). His lust has exhausted itself; he feels only disgust for its recent object.

This psychological analysis of the mechanism of lust should be borne in mind in the dénouement, if we are to capture the sense of what we are being told. Rodolfo was carried away by the power of his instincts, like an animal; his sexual desires entirely eclipsed reason and morality. Once satisfied, he loses interest in repeating his empty triumph. The only reference to love rules out its having any connection with the rapist's action ('un ímpetu lascivo, del cual nunca nace el verdadero amor' ('a lascivious impulse from which true enduring love is never born'); the only reference to the soul is equally negative, when Leocadia accuses him of being a 'desalmado hombre' (p. 308) ('cruel man' [literally: 'bereft of soul'] [II, p. 107]).

When the marriage at the end of the story is read against the language and imagery of the rape at the beginning, it becomes clear that Rodolfo is no longer quite the same person. The fact that sexual love remains essential to him does not call this change into question, as we shall see. He has come to appreciate the presence of 'alma' (soul), the spiritual quality of love, in sexual relationships. When his mother shows him the portrait of the wife she claims has been selected for him, he reacts with consternation: painters tend to exaggerate the beauty of their subject and this is the portrait of a woman who is distinctly plain. His reply shows that he is still a man of flesh and blood, but aware of the dangers to their marriage if his wife is not attractive:

> Mozo soy, pero bien se me entiende que se compadece con el sacramento de matrimonio el justo y debido deleite que los casados gozan, y que si él falta, cojea el matrimonio y desdice de su segunda intención [. . .] La hermosura busco, la belleza quiero, no con otra dote que con la de la honestidad y buenas costumbres. (pp. 318–19)
>
> (I am a young man, but I am sure that the holy sacrament of marriage is also consonant with the just and proper delight which married people enjoy, and that if that is lacking, then the marriage is lame, and denies its secondary intention [. . .] beauty is what I seek and desire, and no other dowry than that of chastity and good morals. [II, p. 121])

Is Rodolfo simply being hypocritical? If that were so, it is hard to see why he resists his mother's wishes, since marriage to a plain wife would give him all the opportunities he needs to deceive her and find more interesting outlets for his physical needs. In fact, his words suggest that he appreciates marriage as the locus for the fulfilment of both physical and spiritual desires. Instead of being aroused to possess Leocadia because of 'la mucha hermosura del rostro' (p. 304) ('the great beauty of the face'[II, p. 103]) and 'a pesar de todos los inconvenientes que sucederle pudiesen' (p. 305) ('despite all the consequences there might be' [II, p. 103]), as before, Rodolfo now makes a series of observations consistent with traditional Christian teaching about the appropriate, if secondary, place of sexual pleasure within the sacrament of marriage. He is aware of his potential to become an adulterer if he is married to a woman he does not find physically attractive, and of the consequent threat to the relationship which ought to exist between husband and wife. That is why on hearing his response to the portrait, 'contentísima quedó su madre' (p. 319) ('Rodolfo's mother was very happy to hear his words' [II, p. 121]).

In Rodolfo's psychological development during the dénouement, the word 'alma' (soul) is used three times to suggest the change he has undergone. The narrator tells us that everyone bows to Leocadia as she appears, 'como si fuera alguna cosa del cielo que allí milagrosamente se había aparecido' (p. 320) ('as if she were something divine which had miraculously come among them' [II, p. 123]). Rodolfo's reaction confirms this: '¿Es por ventura algún ángel humano?' (p. 320) ('Am I looking at some human angel?' [II, p. 123]). These expressions may be hyperbolic, but they introduce the observation that Rodolfo's desire for her is not purely physical: 'Y en esto se le iba entrando por los ojos, a tomar posesión de su alma, la hermosa imagen de Leocadia' (p. 320) ('And at once the beautiful image of Leocadia entered, by his eyes, into his soul and took possession of it' [II, p. 123]). This time, when Leocadia faints, as she had when she was abducted at the beginning, Rodolfo no longer acts violently, but, 'juntando su boca con la della, estaba como esperando que se le saliese el alma para darle acogida en la suya' (p. 321) ('as if he expected her soul to come out of her mouth, he put his mouth close to hers, in order to receive her soul into his own' [II, p. 125]). Finally, Leocadia 'quisiera con honesta fuerza desasirse dellos [los brazos de Rodolfo]; pero él le dijo: —No, señora [. . .] no es bien que punéis por apartaros de los brazos de aquel que os tiene en el alma' (pp. 321–22) ('wished modestly to free herself from them [Rodolfo's arms], but he said: "No, lady, it cannot be so; you should not struggle to free yourself from the arms of a man who cherishes you in his soul"' [II, p. 125]). Again, the contrast with the earlier rape needs noting. This time Leocadia recovers from her swoon in the arms of her rapist, but surrounded by witnesses and about to be married to him. The fact that he insists on confirming her identity is perhaps a narrative device intended to conclude the symbolism of the story: the crucifix Leocadia had removed from the scene of her dishonour as the silent witness of her shame is the supreme example, in Christian terms, of the redemptive power of blood. These repeated references to the spiritual dimension of love, and the clear allusions to the neo-Platonic *topos* of love as a relationship between souls rather than bodies, should not be overlooked. Cervantes, especially in the *Persiles*, is an inveterate commentator on love in all its forms, from the abductions and attempted rapes of the barbarians to the pure spiritual love which animates the relationship between Persiles and Sigismunda.

The problems outlined by Robbins become less acute when we respond to the presence of words like 'alma' in the text, and to the structure of the work, in which the violence and bloodshed of rape bring about a descent into suffering, while the bloodshed of the son conceived in that act initiates a sequence of events in which that pattern is reversed, so that good comes out of evil. Such a reading shows – 'si bien lo miras' (p. 18) ('if you look closely' [I, p. 3]) – that Rodolfo has become more morally aware. He may wish to 'verse a solas con su querida esposa' (p. 323) ('to be alone with his beloved wife' [II, p. 127]), but whereas his lust at the start led to abduction and rape, his love must now wait, at least for a while. The rape one summer's night is answered by marriage one night in winter. Cervantes does not make this obvious because he does not wish to moralize explicitly; he wants the reader to enjoy and to respond to the story without it turning into a form of didactic treatise. Eutrapelia requires a more indirect form of moral discourse: 'horas hay de recreación, donde el afligido espíritu descanse' (p. 18) ('there is time for recreation, when the tormented spirit can rest' [I, p. 5]). Hence the *ejemplo* (lesson) insinuates itself into the text, ready to be discovered by readers who are prepared to respond to the hints provided. Having so responded, they may remember it with greater pleasure, and consequently effect, than if the author had preached them a sermon on the question 'can anything good ever come out of anything evil?' Even if readers do not react in this way, they will at least have spent a pleasant hour or two in a world in which a positive answer can be given to the question. Modern readers may wish for some acknowledgement of the problematic nature of the solution, but I believe that there is sufficient evidence in the text to warrant the kind of reading I have proposed. The symbolism of the story and its antithetical structure in any case suggest that any realistic interpretation is inappropriate.

Whereas *La fuerza de la sangre* does not invite us to laughter, *Rinconete y Cortadillo* presents the exemplary elements of the *novela* above all through linguistic comedy, even though it deals with a world of criminals and hypocrites who might otherwise be the butt of the moralist's denunciations. The comedy begins with linguistic affectation and error, which reveal an almost complete disjunction between word and deed in the picaresque world of the eponymous protagonists and Monipodio's guild. Readers, made aware of this disjunction, laugh at the ignorance and pretensions of the characters, are on the verge of passing judgement on them, as Rinconete will in the final paragraph, before wondering if they are any more in a position to do so than he is. But it is all done with a smile, in accordance with the dictates of eutrapelia; never with the severe frown of the moralist.

Three forms of linguistic usage in the story can be described as false, because they hide or attempt to pervert the truth. They are located in the use of register, *germanía* (thieves' slang) and malapropism. At the same time as we laugh at the characters' linguistic evasions and distortions, we sense that these are symptomatic of an underlying series of moral errors, which point us towards the exemplarity of the *novela*.

In the first paragraph we are introduced to Rincón and Cortado, two lads who are 'muy descosidos, rotos y maltratados' (p. 161) ('shabbily dressed [. . .] their clothes [. . .] in tatters and shreds' [I, p. 175]). Their first exchange is comic and ironical, because the register is inappropriate to the very different social stratum to which the boys have been shown to belong:

> —¿De qué tierra es vuesa merced, señor gentilhombre, y para adónde bueno camina?
> —Mi tierra, señor caballero —respondió el preguntado, —no la sé, ni para dónde camino, tampoco. (p. 164)
>
> ('Where is your home town, good Sir, and whereabouts are you heading?'
> 'Look, Sir, I've no idea where I'm from, nor where I'm going,' replied the younger one. [I, p. 175])

Both are shown to be fully aware of this. At the end of this first meeting Rincón says to his new friend: 'pues ya nos conocemos, no hay para qué aquesas grandezas ni altiveces: confesemos llanamente que no teníamos blanca, ni aun zapatos' (p. 168) ('for now you know me and I know you, and there's no need to put on any airs or graces; let's just admit it; we haven't a penny to rub together between us, let alone a pair of shoes' [I, p. 179]). Once the formalities are concluded, each gives a brief account of his parentage and life. Cortado's father 'por la misericordia del cielo, es sastre y calcetero' (p. 164) ('mercy be to heaven above, is a tailor and makes stockings' [I, p. 177]); Rincón's, 'persona de calidad, porque es ministro de la Santa Cruzada, quiero decir, que es bulero, o buldero, como los llama el vulgo' (pp. 165–66) ('a person of some standing, because he is an officer of the Holy Crusade. In other words, he is a seller of indulgences or pardoner, as such people are commonly called' [I, p. 177]). These are the first of several indications in the story that they understand the difference between appearance and reality, couched here in terms of the invention of a myth of a noble and honourable origin, and the reality of poverty, deception and theft to which they have devoted themselves. The disguise is transparent: they have created it but do not believe in it, because they know it is as false as the life they have chosen for themselves is immoral. Early seventeenth-century readers would have needed no reminder, as we may, that tailors and pardoners were traditional butts of satire for their deceptive practices and (in the case of the latter) their manipulation of language to fleece their gullible audiences (see 'Tratado quinto' of *Lazarillo de Tormes* and, of course, Chaucer's description of the Pardoner in the Prologue to his *Canterbury Tales*).[17]

Soon we see them in action, cheating at cards a muleteer taken in by their youth and apparent innocence, and repaying the kindness of some travellers who give them a lift to Seville by robbing them of their possessions. When they enter the city a narratorial comment shows exactly how aware they are of the possible outcome of their crimes:

> admiróles la grandeza y suntuosidad de su mayor iglesia, el gran concurso de gente del río, porque era un tiempo de cargazón de flota y había en él seis galeras, cuya vista les hizo suspirar, y aun temer el día que sus culpas les habían de traer a morar en ellas de por vida (pp. 170–71).
>
> (They were amazed by the size and magnificence of its cathedral, and by the vast crowds gathered at the river because the fleet was being loaded up. Seeing the six galleys moored alongside sent a nasty shiver down their spines and they were filled with dread at the prospect that there would come a day when their crimes would catch up with them and they would be sent to the galleys for life. [I, p. 183])

[17] Lines 669–714; particularly lines 710–14: 'But alderbest he song an offertorie; | For wel he wiste, whan that song was songe, | He moste preche and wel affile his tongue | To wynne silver, as he ful wel koude; | Therefore he song the murierly and loude': Geoffrey Chaucer, *Canterbury Tales*, ed. A. C. Cawley, Everyman's Library (London: Dent, 1958), p. 22.

They learn their new trade as basket-boys 'por parecerles que venía como de molde para poder usar el suyo con cubierta y seguridad, por la comodidad que ofrecía de entrar en todas las casas' (p. 171) ('for they thought that being a basket-carrier would be a perfect foil for their own activities, giving them freedom of access into everyone's houses' [I, p. 183]), that is, as a cover for their stealing. They rob a student of money which is 'dinero sagrado y bendito' (p. 175) ('money that is holy and sanctified' [I, p. 187]) because it belongs to the Church, and when the victim asks Cortado if he has seen it, the latter replies 'con extraño disimulo, sin alterarse ni mudarse en nada' ('without changing his expression in the slightest'), in words which are simultaneously sententious, ironical and hypocritical: 'podría ser que, con el tiempo, el que llevó la bolsa se viniese a arrepentir y se la volviese a vuesa merced sahumada' (p. 174) ('perhaps in time, the person who stole your purse will come to his senses and restore it to you, duly sanctified by perfume' [i.e. in a better condition than when it was stolen] [I, p. 185]).

We may deduce from this first part of the narrative that the boys are perfectly aware of what they are doing, but that neither stealing from those who have helped them or from the Church, nor the sight of the cathedral, nor the threat of being condemned to the galleys, make any difference to their determination to continue deceiving as many people as they can. On the other hand, the story is meant to entertain, and will not, therefore, moralize overtly. The lads are presented to us as lively, humorous, and clever; we admire their cheek, excusing them, perhaps, on the grounds that they come from families whose exemplarity leaves a lot to be desired.

The arrival of a young basket-boy introduces the second part of the story and a new set of linguistic errors and abuses which prolong the comedy and the theme of deceit until the end. The two young rogues know that they cannot ply their new trade as freely as they had thought, 'sin alcabala y fianzas' (p. 200) ('untaxed, with no duty paid on it' [I, p. 189]) because Monipodio controls the criminal sector of this part of the city. From this point, the comedy of language begins to acquire a more explicitly religious tone, underlining the hypocrisy of Monipodio's brotherhood and offering through linguistic evasion and error a verbal analogy to the false morality on which it is founded. The boys are sharp enough to sense at once that if they persist in acting as independent agents and do not embrace Monipodio's protection there will be trouble. Hence Cortado returns to the comedy of false register: 'Y así, puede vuesa merced guiarnos donde está ese caballero que dice, que ya yo tengo barruntos, según lo que he oído decir, que es muy calificado y generoso, y además hábil en el oficio' (p. 178) ('As that's the case, you can take us to where this gentleman is, for I am already getting the message, from what I've heard, that he is very well qualified, generous and the sharpest brain in the business' [I, p. 189]). A further ironic twist comes when Rincón asks the boy '¿Es vuesa merced, por ventura, ladrón?' ('Are you, by chance, a thief yourself?'). His conventionally polite response, 'Sí, [. . .] para servir a Dios y a la buena gente' ('You bet! [. . .] to serve God and the fellowship of man'), provokes a further ironical comment from Rincón, who demonstrates his full awareness of the sordid reality which such courteous expressions are masking: 'Cosa nueva es para mí que haya ladrones en el mundo para servir a Dios y a la buena gente' ('It is a new one on me that thieves are in the world to serve God and man'). The ironies multiply: the lad protests that 'yo no me meto en tologías' ('I don't know about theology nor any other ologies') – the first example of many of a word wrongly articulated, in this case an important one. If he cannot pronounce the word 'teología' (theology) it is not surprising that he has little idea as to its significance. Indeed, he continues in sententious vein: 'lo que sé es que cada uno en su oficio puede alabar a Dios, y más con la orden que tiene dada Monipodio a todos sus ahijados' (p. 179) ('what I do know is that each man in his own calling can praise God, and do it better under the regime which Monipodio has instituted for all his adopted children' [I, p. 189]), to which Rincón, knowing as ever, replies: 'Sin duda [. . .] debe de ser buena y santa, pues hace que los ladrones sirvan a Dios' (p. 179) ('Without a doubt [. . .] there must be something special and saintly about the régime, since it makes thieves serve God' [I, p. 191]). The lad is oblivious to any irony and carries on, praising the goodness and sanctity of Monipodio and attributing miracles to a holy image to the upkeep of which members of the brotherhood are required to pay a tithe from their ill-gotten gains. The boy appears overly impressed by the effectiveness of the protection Monipodio offers to his gang, since the number of those caught and punished seems high: four hung, thirty whipped, sixty-two condemned to the galleys, while the only miracle adduced is that a livestock thief endured torture without cracking.

The boy also begins to initiate Rincón and Cortado into *germanía* (thieves' slang), a private language, but one which uses learned euphemisms – *finibusterrae* for the scaffold – and words only intelligible to initiates, to make the punishments visited on them by the law sound less fearsome than they actually are. He praises the religious practices of the community in ridiculous terms: 'rezamos nuestro rosario repartido en toda la semana, y muchos de nosotros no hurtamos el día del viernes, ni tenemos conversación con mujer que se llame María el día del sábado' (p. 180) ('we pray with our rosary, spread over the entire week, and many of us [evidently not all] do not steal on Fridays, and we don't talk to anyone called María on Saturdays' [I, p. 191]). The parody of a religious community intensifies when we learn than they never go to confession, and that letters of excommunication 'jamás llegan a nuestra noticia, porque jamás vamos a la iglesia al tiempo que se leen, si no es los días de jubileo, por la ganancia que nos ofrece el concurso de la mucha gente' (p. 180) ('we never get to know about them, because we never go to church when they are proclaimed, unless of course they are read out on jubilee days [. . .] because a large gathering of people offers rich pickings' [I, p. 191]). When Cortado asks him if this is a good and holy life, the boy condemns himself out of his own mouth: 'Pues ¿qué tiene de malo? [. . .] ¿No es peor ser hereje o renegado, o matar a su padre y madre, o ser solomico?', an error for 'sodomita', as Rincón observes (p. 181) ('Well, what's so wrong about it? [. . .] Surely it's worse to be a heretic or a renegade, or a patricide or a matricide or to be a solomile?' [I, p. 191]). 'Todo es malo' ('It's all bad'), Cortado replies. One simply cannot overlook the density of religious expression, the verbal confusions and evasions, the false logic which treats crime as a profession and justifies theft on the grounds that there are offences deserving greater condemnation. But conscious of the fact that this is meant to be a story offering innocent diversion, Cervantes makes sure that we judge the behaviour of the characters light-heartedly, through laughing at their mistakes.

The entry of Rincón and Cortado into Monipodio's guild marks a tightening of the web of linguistic games and evasions. Instead of offering an implied contrast between the opposing perspectives of virtue and vice, the narrator shows us an encounter between two types of criminal, the *pícaro* ('rogue' or 'delinquent') and the gang, the former acting as moral commentator on the latter, as if he represented the objective and trustworthy voice of the moralist. If we fail to notice how Cervantes is playing with the reader, with all his usual skill, we shall lose the exemplary thread of the text: the voice of the moral expert belongs to a pair of thieves who are quite prepared to judge the conduct of Monipodio's community but who seem to be blind to the fact that they too are implicated in the life they are condemning, as if they could emerge unscathed by maintaining their distance and using their intelligence to correct their leader's malapropisms and to point out the gang's religious hypocrisy. The voice of the narrator accompanies the observations of Rinconete and Cortadillo, now ironical, with its reference to 'toda aquella virtuosa compañía' (pp. 183–84) ('all that worthy company of people' [I, p. 195]), now critical, describing Monipodio as 'el más rústico y disforme bárbaro del mundo' (p. 184) ('the world's most uncouth and ugliest barbarian' [I, p. 195]).

The language of the gang is characterized by a religious register which presents the community as the ironic antithesis of a spiritual one and which reveals the hypocrisy which runs like a fault-line through it, in terms reminiscent of the satirical writings of Erasmus.[18] The two lads 'son dignos de entrar en nuestra congregación' (p. 184) ('the right sort to join our community' [I, p. 195]); when they enter, they 'hicieron una profunda y larga reverencia' ('bowed long and deeply'), before they receive 'algún hábito honroso' (p. 185) ('the robes of some holy order' [I, p. 195]); Monipodio gives them new names; he explains that 'tenemos de costumbre de hacer decir cada año ciertas misas por las ánimas de nuestros difuntos y bienhechores, sacando el estupendo para la limosna de quien las dice de alguna parte de lo que se garbea' (p. 186) ('it is one of our customs to have certain Masses said each year for the souls of our deceased members and for our patrons, when we use a share of what we have "borrowed" as the "stupendous" payment for the officiating priest' [I, p. 197]) – 'estupendo' (stupendous) in error for 'estipendio' (stipend), 'garbear' (to borrow) the thieves' slang for 'robar' (to steal). Since they are already experienced, Monipodio initiates

[18] Ricapito (p. 7) denies any Erasmian influence, which Alban K. Forcione stresses in *Cervantes and the Humanist Vision: A Study of Four 'Exemplary Novels'* (Princeton: Princeton University Press, 1982).

them as 'cofrades mayores' (p. 189) ('elders' [I, p. 199]), without their needing to spend a year in the novitiate. His attempts to impose his authority by use of Latin terms or learned words are highlighted; his lack of education becomes clear every time he makes mistakes in usage. The absurd devotions of old Pipota are also ridiculed. The elderly *abispones* (hornets), whose job is to act as spies in the city, are, according to Monipodio, 'hombres de mucha verdad, y muy honrados, y de buena vida y fama, temerosos de Dios y de sus conciencias, y cada día oían misa con estraña devoción' (p. 200) ('fine, upstanding, clean-living, God-fearing men with unsullied reputations, who each day went to Mass with a clear conscience, and with a show of great piety' [I, p. 213]).

These confusions and errors represent in linguistic terms the deformed morality of the community, with Rinconete acting variously as witness, participant and commentator. This process reaches its climax in the final paragraph, in which the playful art of Cervantes presents a series of cutting moral judgements in an otherwise comic wrapping. Readers laugh at the community with Rinconete, they assent to his astonishment at its hypocrisy, they look down on Monipodio, they applaud Rinconete's intention to leave behind so vice-ridden a life – and may be lulled into forgetting that he presents himself as the arbiter of something in which he is himself fatally implicated. Meanwhile, the narrator's voice maintains its ambiguous, ironic, indignant but always good-humoured stance.

'Era Rinconete, aunque muchacho, de muy buen entendimiento, y tenía un buen natural' (pp. 214–15) ('Rinconete, although still a juvenile, was a pretty sharp lad, and had all his wits about him' [I, p. 229]). We agree. He is an attractive character, clever in a street-wise sense, though we know he is capable of deceiving even those who help him. The narrator further informs us: 'Y como había andado con su padre en el ejercicio de las bulas, sabía algo de buen lenguaje' (p. 215) ('As he had trolled around with his father in the papal bull business, he knew a thing or two about correct language' [I, p. 229]) – an ironic comment, as we have already seen, since this 'buen lenguaje' (correct language) exists purely in order to con people. Like his father, Rinconete has learnt long before he joins Monipodio how to exploit language and its multiple deceits for his own advantage. As a linguistic expert, 'dábale gran risa pensar en los vocablos que había oído a Monipodio y a los demás de su compañía y bendita comunidad' ('he was mightily amused at the words he had heard spoken by Monipodio, and by others around him and belonging to that godly community'), and he recapitulates some of them: 'cuando por decir *per modum sufragii*, había dicho *per modo de naufragio*' (p. 215) ('when he heard Monipodio say "salvage operation" instead of "suffrage"' [I, p. 229]). But the list of comic misuses of language is at once followed by an observation which goes straight for the moral jugular: 'y, sobre todo, le admiraba la seguridad que tenían y la confianza de irse al cielo con no faltar a sus devociones, estando tan llenos de hurtos y de homicidios, y de ofensas de Dios' (p. 215) ('more than anything else, he was astonished that they were all certain and confident that they had their tickets booked to heaven, provided always that they did not fall down on their devotions, when they spent all their time in robbery and murder and in crimes against God'

[I, p. 229]). Rinconete appears to grasp what the community cannot: breaking at least three of the Commandments (theft, murder, blasphemy) cannot be bought off with a handful of superstitious devotions. He is quick to unmask religious hypocrisy: 'Y reíase de la otra buena vieja de la Pipota, que dejaba la canasta de colar hurtada, guardada en su casa, y se iba a poner las candelillas de cera a las imágenes, y con ello pensaba irse al cielo calzada y vestida' (p. 215) ('He also smiled when he thought of that old biddy, Pipota, who had left the stolen wash-tub safe at home, whilst she went to place wax candles in front of sacred images, believing that that was the way to get to Heaven with shoes on her feet and clothes on her back' [I, p. 229]): once more, that same combination of laughter and serious moral observation. Rinconete is astonished by 'la obediencia y respeto que todos tenían a Monipodio, siendo un hombre bárbaro, rústico y desalmado' (p. 215) ('the obedience and respect that they all showed towards Monipodio, since he was such an uncouth, heartless barbarian' [I, p. 229]), although he seems to forget that he too is bound to him. The lack of effective justice in the city seems to attract his opprobrium because of its failure to deal with this 'gente tan perniciosa y tan contraria a la misma naturaleza' (p. 215) ('people who were so obnoxious and whose behaviour so contradicted the laws of nature' [I, p. 229]), even though he belongs to them.

Rinconete's reactions contain a series of apparent contradictions which are important to grasp if we are to uncover the playful exemplarity of Cervantes. Rinconete shows himself to be a severe critic of the crimes, hypocrisy and leadership of the community, using harsh terms reminiscent of the voice of the moralist or preacher. But his criticisms are accompanied by laughter – not the bitter and cruel laughter of the satirist, but of a young man of apparently good judgement and possessed of a strong moral sense, who is not disposed towards taking what he has seen too seriously, rather as an entertaining kind of game. The contradiction between the serious and the funny elements in his observations produces an ambivalent response on the part of readers. Is Rinconete an innocent lamb among wolves, as his attitude towards the brotherhood's values seems to imply, or is he as hypocritical, or even more so, than they are? That is the nub of the problem. As we have noted, Rinconete is very aware of the criminal life he and his companion have adopted. The story ends with his making of a series of accusations against other people, notably the criminal community of which he is himself now a member. Hence he both participates in its sins and is presented as their judge.

It is precisely this contradictory role which enables Cervantes to amuse us and offer us an *ejemplo*, as long as we are prepared to respond to what we are being told. Rinconete's decision is a case in point. Seeing all the faults of Monipodio's world:

> propuso en sí de aconsejar a su compañero no durasen mucho en aquella vida tan perdida y tan mala, tan inquieta, y tan libre y disoluta. Pero, con todo esto, llevado de sus pocos años y de su poca experiencia, pasó con ella adelante algunos meses (p. 215).

> (He made up his mind that he would advise his companion that they should not stay long living in that God-forsaken way of life, which was so evil, so precarious, so libertine and so corrupt. Nonetheless, despite all this, since he was not very old and still wet behind the ears, he went on to spend several months living like that. [I, p. 229])

If this life were truly as terrible as the five adjectives imply, he would surely escape from it as soon as he could. But the truth of the matter is that he enjoys it, just as we have enjoyed reading about the story of the two lads and of their entry into the comically immoral world of Monipodio and his gang. The enjoyment we experience represents the pleasure, the wholesome entertainment the author promises and prizes. Were there no laughter, were the moral commentary deprived of its subtlety, its indirect, almost casual character, the 'afligido espíritu' ('tormented spirit') of the reader would be weighed down even more. The world Cervantes creates is one of comic distortions of language alongside the shifting perspectives of objective observations and subjective value-judgement; a world which brings the comic and the serious, the ironical and the straightforward, into a happy coexistence in the final paragraph of the *novela*.

I have tried to underline the importance of a reading of this *novela* which is alert and open to the witty techniques of its creator, who draws our attention to the gap between what his characters say and do, through the coexistence of the ludic and the serious, especially at its climactic point, where one might naturally expect a statement of the *ejemplo*.[19] How, then, are we to interpret the ending of *Rinconete y Cortadillo*, so lacking in any definitive conclusion, let alone exemplarity? Everything we have learnt about Rinconete leads me to suppose that the justification offered by the narrator for the boy's failure to leave the community is another Cervantine joke, because it is simply untrue: 'llevado de sus pocos años y de su poca experiencia' ('since he was not very old and still wet behind the ears'). Rinconete is seventeen (two years older than Preciosa), and, like all *pícaros*, wise beyond his years. What lack of experience, one might ask? I do not believe the explanation, and I do not believe Cervantes expects me to. Nor do I believe that Rinconete is in a position to make moral observations as if he were the detached observer of what he is criticizing. Although he is not taken in by the false logic and the false religion of Monipodio's world, he too, as an experienced thief, reveals himself to be a hypocrite, because he sees the mote in his brother's eye and not the beam in his own (Matthew 7: 1–5). He lacks moral conviction, because he cannot connect theory with practice. He knows what he ought to do, but has not the courage to do it: 'propuso en sí de aconsejar a su compañero no durasen mucho en aquella vida [. . .] Pero [. . .] pasó con ella adelante

[19] Cervantes is notoriously reluctant to fulfil such an expectation, though two of the *Novelas, La española inglesa* (The English Spanish Girl) and *El celoso extremeño* (The Jealous Old Man from Extremadura) hint at or openly make reference to *ejemplos* at their conclusion.

algunos meses' (p. 215) ('he made up his mind that he would advise his companion that they should not stay long living in that way of life [. . .] Nonetheless [. . .] he went on to spend several months living like that' [I, p. 229]). He is presented as morally superior to the gang only because he can use language more accurately. He makes fun of Monipodio's linguistic errors, expresses horror at his moral failings, but cannot find the will-power to free himself from the community, not for some months, at least, during which, the narrator informs us, many other things concerning their 'vida y milagros' (p. 215) ('life and wondrous doings' [I, p. 229]) could be told, were there time. He knows the attraction of the criminal life, although it does not offer the freedom he and Cortado sought from it, a life which the *novela*, faithful to the concept of eutrapelia, presents to us as more amusing than worthy of censure. As a fiction, it needs to entertain us, but that does not mean it cannot touch on important issues. We too find the linguistic errors of Monipodio and his followers amusing, but we also recall that before their initiation the two boys had themselves practised a different form of linguistic deceit, addressing each other as if they were gentlemen. They have, as it were, appropriated words which properly belong to a different social context, just as they have played with a naïve comment about thieves serving God and good people.

Inappropriate language reveals the world of *Rinconete y Cortadillo* to be a world of inverted moral values. This receives a fundamentally comic treatment because Cervantes believes that there are lessons better learnt through laughter than through explicit moral comment. We laugh with Rinconete and Cortadillo at the absurd religion of the community, at the slang which protects them from articulating the reality of the punishments they face, at the ridiculous attempts of Monipodio to impose his authority by his superior intellect. But perhaps in the end, Cervantes is asking us to laugh at ourselves: at our own duplicity, our moral evasions, our false justifications. Is it not easier (and more entertaining) to point out the errors of others than to correct our own? Or, like Rinconete and the witch la Cañizares in *El coloquio de los perros*, to know what we ought to do than to find the will to do it? If Cervantes disguises or hides his *ejemplos*, hints at them in apparently unimportant phrases, it is perhaps because he is inviting us to see ourselves as we are and our world as it is, and offering to undeceive us with the light touch of eutrapelia, an effective, entertaining and refreshing form of therapy.

Works cited

Anon. *La eutrapelia. Medio, que deben tener los juegos, Divertimientos, y Comedias, para que no aya en ellas pecado* (Valencia: Benito Macè, 1683).

Calderón de la Barca, Pedro, *El alcalde de Zalamea*, ed. A. Valbuena Briones (Madrid: Cátedra, 1999).

Cervantes Saavedra, Miguel de, *Exemplary Novels / Novelas ejemplares*, ed. B. W. Ife, 4 vols (Warminster: Aris & Phillips, 1992).

———, *Don Quijote de la Mancha*, ed. Francisco Rico, 2 vols (Barcelona: Crítica, 1998).

Cervantes Saavedra, Miguel de, *Cervantes: Don Quixote*, tr. John Rutherford, Penguin Classics (Harmondsworth: Penguin, 2000).

———, *Novelas ejemplares*, ed. Jorge García López (Barcelona: Crítica, 2001).

Chaucer, Geoffrey, *Canterbury Tales*, ed. A. C. Cawley, Everyman's Library (London: Dent, 1958).

Covarrubias Orozco, Sebastián de, *Tesoro de la lengua castellana o española* (Madrid, 1611; repr. Barcelona: Alta Fulla, 1998).

Forcione, Alban K., *Cervantes and the Humanist Vision: A Study of Four 'Exemplary Novels'* (Princeton: Princeton University Press, 1982).

Hart, Thomas R., *Cervantes' Exemplary Fictions: A Study of the 'Novelas ejemplares'* (Lexington: The University Press of Kentucky, 1994).

Jones, Joseph R., 'Cervantes y la virtud de la eutrapelia: la moralidad de la literatura de esparcimiento', *AC*, 23 (1985), 19–30.

Patrologia Latina, ed. J. P. Migne, 221 vols (Tournai, 1844–64).

Rahner, Hugo, SJ, *Man at Play: Or Did You Ever Practise Eutrapelia?* (London: Burns & Oates, 1965).

Ricapito, Joseph, *Cervantes's 'Novelas ejemplares': Between History and Creativity* (West Lafayette, Indiana: Purdue University Press, 1996).

Riley, E. C., *Cervantes's Theory of the Novel* (Oxford: Clarendon, 1962).

Robbins, Jeremy, *The Challenges of Uncertainty: An Introduction to Seventeenth-Century Spanish Literature* (London: Duckworth, 1998).

San Juan de la Cruz: Poesía, ed. Domingo Ynduráin (Madrid: Cátedra, 1989).

St Thomas Aquinas: Summa Theologiae, ed. Thomas Gilby and others, 61 vols (London: Eyre & Spottiswode, 1964–80).

Wardropper, Bruce, 'La eutrapelia en las *Novelas ejemplares* de Cervantes', in *Actas del séptimo congreso de la Asociación Internacional de Hispanistas*, 2 vols (Rome: Bulzoni, 1982), I, pp. 153–69.

14

'Entre parejas anda el juego' / 'All a Matter of Pairs': Reflections on some Characters in the *Novelas ejemplares**[1]

In Memoriam E. C. Riley

José Montero Reguera
Universidad de Vigo

It has not gone unnoticed by students of Cervantes's literary production that a great many of his characters appear in pairs, something that is frequently the case not only in the *Novelas ejemplares* but also in other Cervantine texts.[2] I am referring to characters who either appear together from the very start, or who, in the course of events, become an inseparable pair, difficult to disassociate from each other. The following are some examples of such characters: Don Quijote and Sancho, the priest and the barber, the housekeeper and niece, Marcela and Grisóstomo, the two Benedictine monks who appear in Chapter 8 of *Don*

* The original Spanish title is: ' "Entre parejas anda el juego": Reflexiones sobre algunos personajes de las *Novelas ejemplares*'. Translation by the editor.

1 All quotations from texts by Cervantes are taken from the following editions: Miguel de Cervantes, *Don Quijote de la Mancha*, ed. Francisco Rico, Instituto Cervantes, 2 vols (Barcelona: Crítica, 1998); *Novelas ejemplares*, ed. Jorge García López (Barcelona: Crítica, 2001). English translations of the *Novelas* are taken from Miguel de Cervantes, *Exemplary Novels / Novelas ejemplares*, ed. B. W. Ife, 4 vols (Warminster: Aris & Philips, 1992). Henceforth only chapter numbers (if required) and page numbers will be indicated.

2 The following is an example: '[. . .] otro lector bien podría darse cuenta de que, con harta frecuencia, los personajes forman pareja, como Carriazo y Avendaño (*Fregona*), Ricardo y Mahamut (*El amante*), Campuzano y Peralta (*Casamiento*), Isunza y Gamboa (*Cornelia*), Teodosia y Leocadia (*Doncellas*) [. . .]' ([. . .] another reader might well realize that the characters very often form pairs, for example: Carriazo and Avendaño [Illustrious Kitchen Maid], Rincón and Cortado [Rinconete], Cipión and Berganza [Dialogue], Ricardo and Mahamut [Generous Lover], Campuzano and Peralta [Deceitful Marriage], Isunza and Gamboa [Lady Cornelia], Teodosia and Leocadia [Damsels] [. . .]): Antonio Rey Hazas, '*Novelas ejemplares*', in *Cervantes*, ed. Anthony Close and others (Alcalá de Henares: Centro de Estudios Cervantinos, 1995), pp. 173–209 (pp. 98–9).

Quijote, Part I; Persiles and Sigismunda, etc. In the *Novelas ejemplares*, as is immediately obvious, the list is extensive and, on occasion, anticipated by the very titles of the stories themselves (*Rinconete y Cortadillo* [Rinconete and Cortadillo], *Las dos doncellas* [The Two Damsels], *Novela y coloquio que pasó entre Cipión y Berganza* [Novel and Dialogue that Took Place Between Cipión and Berganza]) but, most significantly, this phenomenon is present in almost all of them: Ricardo and Mahamut, Carriazo and Avendaño, don Juan de Gamboa and don Antonio de Isunza. . . This kind of character presentation extends right down to some very minor figures who are not even given names and whose role in the *novelas* is sometimes quite insignificant. This preference for duality, which is clearly evidenced in the way in which many of the characters are presented, is also visible in other aspects of the *novelas*, such as the structure, as is the case in *La señora Cornelia* (Lady Cornelia) whose central monologues – those of Cornelia and Lorenzo –, as Peter Dunn has shown,[3] divide the action into two parts, and whose dénouement is complicated by a final obstacle resulting from the division in the action: don Juan, don Antonio and don Lorenzo journey towards Ferrara, while doña Cornelia and the housekeeper (*ama*) make their way to Piova. It is even more obvious in *Las dos doncellas*.[4] On another level, the use of the number two in expressions of time is very striking, so much so that, in the words of Isabel Lobazo Renieblas, it becomes 'una suerte de aritmética formulística' (kind of formulaic arithmetic):

> [. . .] es digno nuestro gallardo Quijote de continuas y memorables alabanzas, y aun a mí no se me deben negar, por el trabajo y diligencia que puse en buscar el fin desta agradable historia; aunque bien sé que si el cielo, el caso y la fortuna no me ayudan, el mundo quedará falto y sin el pasatiempo y gusto que bien casi dos horas podrá tener el que con atención la leyere. (*Don Quijote*, I, 9, p. 107)
>
> ([. . .] our gallant Quijote is worthy of continuous and enduring praise, which even I am not to be denied, because of the work and effort I put into finding the end of this pleasant history; although I know very well that if heaven, circumstances and fortune do not assist me, the world will be left wanting and without the entertainment and pleasure that anyone who reads its attentively can have for nigh on two hours.)

In *Los trabajos de Persiles y Sigismunda* (The Trials of Persiles and Sigismunda), Leonora makes Manuel de Sosa Coutiño wait for two years before accepting his proposal of marriage; Mauricio knows from the stars that he and his daughter will meet once again in two years' time, and Ambrosia Agustina is condemned to the galleys for two years. Going back to the *Novelas ejemplares*,

3 Peter N. Dunn, 'Las *Novelas ejemplares*', in *Suma cervantina*, ed. J. B. Avalle-Arce and E. C. Riley, (London: Támesis, 1973), pp. 81–118 (pp. 107–9).

4 See also the remarks by Florencio Sevilla Arroyo and Antonio Rey Hazas in the Preface to their edition of this *novela* (Madrid: Alianza Editorial, 1997), pp. lxv–lxvi.

the period of waiting that Isabel imposes on Ricaredo is the same; similarly, Andrés Caballero must spend two years living with the gypsies before being finally accepted by Preciosa; Tomás Rodaja's period of madness as the Licenciado Vidriera (Glass Graduate) lasts the same length of time; in *La ilustre fregona* (The Illustrious Kitchen Maid) the period of time stipulated by the mother for waiting to collect the daughter she leaves in custody is two years, etc.[5]

In this essay I intend first to present a taxonomy of these characters who are presented as pairs, before going on to offer some reflections on the presence and function of a number of them in the *Novelas ejemplares*.

An Extensive List: Numbers and Possible Classifications

One simple classification is that which allows the paired characters to be grouped into three major categories according to their gender: man/woman, man/man, and woman/woman. Beyond that, I do not think that it is necessary to consider the dogs Cipión and Berganza under a separate heading since they are really the child victims of a spell cast at birth.

1. Man – Woman

1a. Gentleman – Lady Here we are dealing with pairs who most probably feature because of the *comedia* (drama of the Golden Age) or the Byzantine roots of the *novelas* in which they appear: Preciosa and Andrés (*La gitanilla*) (The Little Gypsy Girl), Ricardo and Leonisa (*El amante liberal*) (The Generous Lover), Isabela and Recaredo (*La española inglesa*) (The English Spanish Girl), Leocadia and Rodolfo (*La fuerza de la sangre*) (The Power of Blood); Avendaño and Constanza, la Argüello and Carriazo – although in this case we are dealing with a comic pair – (*La ilustre fregona*) (The Illustrious Kitchen Maid); Cornelia Bentibolli and The Duke of Ferrara (*La señora Cornelia*) (Lady Cornelia); and the Ensign Campuzano and Estefanía Caicedo (*El casamiento engañoso*) (The Deceitful Marriage).

Two unlikely pairs, formed quickly and unexpectedly, and, no doubt in accordance with the eminently theatrical principle of 'birds of a feather. . .' are Leocadia and Rafael de Villavicencio (*Las dos doncellas*) and Mahamut and Halima (*El amante liberal*). One must also point to two love triangles: Carrizales, Loaysa and Leonora (*El celoso extremeño*) (The Jealous Old Man from Extremadura) and, with the reverse structure (two women and a man), the group formed by Teodosia, Leocadia and Marco Antonio (*Las dos doncellas*).

1b. Siblings Teodosia and Rafael de Villavicencio (*Las dos doncellas*); the orphaned Cornelia and Lorenzo Bentibolli (*La señora Cornelia*).

[5] See Isabel Lozano Renieblas, *Cervantes y el mundo del 'Persiles'* (Alcalá de Henares: Centro de Estudios Cervantinos, 1998), p. 51.

1c. Pícaros (Rogues) In this case we are dealing with characters who form a partnership in order to deceive someone, even though this relationship is only revealed *a posteriori*. Thus, doña Estefanía Caicedo and her cousin have come together to deceive the Ensign Campuzano in *El casamiento engañoso* (The Deceitful Marriage): '[. . .] digo que supe que se había llevado a doña Estefanía el primo que dije que se halló en nuestros desposorios, el cual de luengos tiempos atrás era su amigo a todo ruedo' (p. 533) ('[. . .] I discovered that Doña Estefanía had been taken away by the cousin I told you was at our wedding, who had stuck with her through thick and thin' [IV, p. 79]).

1d. Parents (Father and Mother) Isabela's parents, although their names are not given, and Ricaredo's, Catalina and Clotaldo (*La española inglesa*) (The English Spanish Girl); the parents of Isabela and Rodolfo although their names are not specified either (*La fuerza de la sangre*) (The Power of Blood); and Leonora's parents (*El celoso extremeño*).

1e. Secondary Characters Clementa Bueso and don Lope de Meléndez de Almendárez (*El casamiento engañoso*) (The Deceitful Marriage): through them the Ensign Campuzano finds out about the trick that has been played on him. The pair of black servants belonging to the Sevillian merchant (*El coloquio de los perros*) (The Dialogue of the Dogs), who bring about a sudden change in Berganza's fortunes. As one can appreciate, these are very much secondary characters, but they play a decisive role at certain points in the *novelas*.

2. Man – Man

2a. Characters of Similar Age who do not know each other but who end up forming close friendships. In *La gitanilla* (The Little Gypsy Girl) we find Juan de Cárcamo (Andrés Caballero) and the page (Clemente); in their case the social difference is worthy of note, since one is noble and the other a mere page; even so, it should be remembered that on one occasion Clemente defines himself as '[. . .] entre paje y caballero' (p. 83) ('[. . .] partly page and partly a gentleman' [I, p.71]). Pedro Rincón and Diego Cortado (*Rinconete y Cortadillo*) are social equals, but from the lowest stratum of society. The possible permutations – from the point of view of social class – are rounded off by Diego Carriazo and Tomás de Avendaño (*La ilustre fregona*), where no social difference is involved since both belong to the highest class.

2b. Characters of similar age who have known each other since childhood and who behave almost as though they were brothers: Ricardo and Mahamut in *El amante liberal*; don Antonio de Isunza and don Juan de Gamboa in *La señora Cornelia*.

2c. Characters of similar age who have been friends for a long time and who meet up again: Campuzano (the Ensign) and Peralta (the Licenciate) in *El casamiento engañoso*.

2d. Characters of similar age who are rivals in love: Juan de Cárcamo and the page –although the rivalry is only apparent – in *La gitanilla*; Ricardo and Cornelio, in *El amante liberal*; Ricaredo and Count Arnesto in *La española inglesa*; and Avendaño and don Periquito, the son of the *corregidor* (Chief

Magistrate), in *La ilustre fregona*. Although very different in age and involved in a love rivalry that is quite *sui generis*, one could also include Carrizales and Loaysa (*El celoso extremeño*) under this heading.

2e. Characters of similar age who are rivals because a point of honour: Rafael de Villavicencio and Marco Antonio Adorno in *Las dos doncellas*.

2f. Brothers Cipión and Berganza in *El coloquio de los perros* are the sons of la Montiela turned into dogs because of the envy of another witch, la Camacha:

> [. . .] la Camacha su maestra, de invidia que la tuvo, porque se le iba subiendo a las barbas en saber tanto como ella [. . .], estando tu madre preñada y llegándose la hora del parto, fue su comadre la Camacaha, la cual recibió en sus manos lo que tu madre parió, y mostróle que había parido dos perritos [. . .] (p. 593).
>
> ([. . .] her mentor, Camacha, was jealous of her because she was getting to know as much as she did [. . .], when your mother was pregnant and about to give birth [. . .] Camacha was the mid-wife, and took into her hands what your mother gave birth to, and showed her that she had given birth to two pups. [IV, p. 129])

2g. Father/s The father of don Juan de Cárcamo in *La gitanilla*; Diego Carriazo and Juan de Avendaño who are presented as a virtually inseparable pair in *La ilustre fregona*; the fathers of Teodosia and Leocadia who act jointly in opposition to Marco Antonio Adorno's father in *Las dos doncellas*.

2h. Secondary Characters These appear to be of similar age, practise the same or related professions and, although set on a lower plane, can occasionally be of exceptional importance as, for example, the two young Andalusian muleteers overheard by Carriazo and Avendaño in *La ilustre fregona*. Among those of minimal importance– on occasion their names are not even mentioned – one may include Tomás Rodaja's first masters, who are merely two gentlemen studying at Salamanca: Tomás Rodaja will remain in their service until he goes off to follow Captain Valdivia. Also to be included in this category are the two servants who accompany doña Clementa Bueso and don Lope Meléndez de Almendárez and the two friends who act as witnesses for the Ensign in his marriage to doña Estefanía (*El casamiento engañoso*); two of the shepherds (p. 557; IV, p. 97), the two sons of the Sevillian merchant (p. 560; IV, p. 101), the *alguacil* (police officer) in league with the *escribano* (notary), both, in their turn, cohabiting with two *mujercillas* (little bits of women) 'que tenían [. . .] mucho de desenfado y taimería putesca' (p. 573) ('who [. . .] had all the brashness and slyness that one associates with tarts' [IV, p. 113]); two *corchetes* (constables) (p. 574; IV, p. 113) and two thieves (p. 581; IV, p. 119) in *El coloquio de los perros*.

3. Woman – woman

3a. Main characters of similar age and circumstances and with no previous relationship between them: Teodosia and Leocadia in the *Las dos doncellas*.

3b. Secondary characters la Argüello and la Gallega (inn wenches) in *La ilustre fregona*, 'two perfect anti-heroines' as Ana María Barrenechea so aptly calls them; the child's two nurses in *La señora Cornelia*, one perhaps (like la Argüello with respect to la Gallega) with a more defined role than the other since she makes Cornelia vary her route at the end of the *novela*; two women and two maids (p. 524; IV, p. 69) in *El casamiento engañoso*; and la Cañizares and la Montiela, both pupils of la Camacha, and the two *mujercillas* cohabiting with the police officer (*alguacil*) and the notary in *El coloquio de los perros.*

Similarly, it is worth remembering that a good many of the paired characters (although not only these) change their names in the course of the *novelas*, especially depending on the place or circumstances in which they happen to live:

Juanico (to his family) → Juan de Cárcamo (in Madrid) →Andrés Caballero (among the gypsies); the Page (to Preciosa) → Sancho (in Madrid) → Clemente (among the gypsies) in *La gitanilla.*

Ricardo → Mario in *El amante liberal.*

Pedro Rincón → Rinconete; Diego Cortado → Cortadillo (courtesy of Monipodio, who re-christens them, throwing in for good measure the surname *El bueno* [The Good], applied – possibly through an oversight – to both) in *Rinconete y Cortadillo.*

Tomás Rodaja → Licenciado Vidriera (Glass Graduate) → Señor Redoma → Licenciado Rueda in *El licenciado Vidriera.*

Diego Carriazo → Urdiales → Lope Asturiano; Tomás de Avendaño → Tomás Pedro; don Periquito (to his family) → don Pedro → the Corregidor's son (to others) in *La ilustre fregona.*

Teodosia →Teodoro, Leocadia → Francisco in the *Las dos doncellas.*

Finally, Berganza → *perro sabio* (wise dog) → Barcino (with the shepherds) → Gavilán (in the service of the drummer) → Montiel (to la Cañizares) in the *Coloquio de los perros.*

The classification that I have outlined is, as I have already indicated, simple but very useful, revealing besides: (a) the multiple interconnections between the *Novelas ejemplares*;[6] (b) how, based on a quite simple scheme built around the pairing of characters (man/woman, man/man, and woman/woman), Cervantes achieves the *variatio* required of prose fiction by the literary theory of the period, by means of minimal variations in the pairings; (c) the conspicuously small number of pairs constituted by women compared to those made up of men, or those that are mixed; and (d) how the number of pairings increases as the collection of *novelas* unfolds, and is particularly evident in *El casamiento engañoso y El coloquio de los perros.*

About Some of the Characters

In *La gitanilla* we encounter the pair formed by Preciosa and Juan de Cárcamo, but I am more interested in the relationship between don Juan and the page.

[6] See Rey Hazas, '*Novelas ejemplares*', pp. 196–209.

These are characters who are not introduced together but who end up as inseparable friends:

> En fin, Andrés y Clemente eran camaradas y grandes amigos, asegurándolo todo la buena intención de Clemente y el recato y prudencia de Preciosa, que jamás dio ocasión a que Andrés tuviese celos de ella. (p. 60)
>
> (Finally Andrés and Clemente became comrades and great friends; the good will of Clemente and the modesty and prudence of Preciosa assured this, because she never gave Andrés any occasion to feel jealous about her. [I, pp. 79, 81])

One must assume that they are more or less the same age, and at the start they are differentiated not only by their social class but also because they are presented as apparent rivals for the favours of Preciosa. Don Juan is a nobleman of considerable wealth who, out of love for Preciosa, agrees to live with the gypsy tribe for two years and become one of them, taking the name of Andrés Caballero. The page is presented as having a very good appearance ('muy bien aderezado' [p. 39]) ('very well turned-out' [I, p. 25]); he is called Sancho in Madrid, and Clemente among the gypsies. These characters end up becoming a virtually inseparable pair and, in addition, share a double identity according to whether they are in Madrid or among the gypsies, as Preciosa explicitly states: '[. . .] pensando que como había don Juanes en el mundo y que se mudasen en Andreses, así podia haber don Sanchos que se mudasen en otros nombres' (p. 89) ('[. . .] thinking that since there were don Juans in the world who changed themselves into Andreses, there might also be don Sanchos who might also change their names' [I, p. 79]). That is, each has two names that correspond to the two worlds in which the action is developed: that of Madrid, with its rules and regulations, and that of the gypsies, which is devoid of them; and it is in this latter world, that of the open countryside and its freedom, that two characters of different social backgrounds can not only speak, but form a very close bond of friendship, which is, in a sense, what happens to Don Quijote and Sancho,[7] or, from a complementary point of view, to Sancho and the Duchess in Part II of Cervantes's classic novel.[8] We have, then, two characters who did not know each other beforehand and who form an almost indissoluble pair in the context of the new life they lead as gypsies: something that would be impossible in the convention-bound world of Madrid can happen in the haven of gypsy life – one of continual wandering and total freedom; it must not be forgotten, despite the effort at bridging the gap between the two characters that we have just been mentioning, that while one may be 'bien aderezado' ('well turned-out') and a poet he still remains a page, while the other is a titled gentleman and heir to a 'razonable mayorazgo' (p. 53) ('reasonable estate' [I, p. 37]). This is why don Juan always

7 See Pablo Jauralde Pou, 'El *Quijote*, II, 9', *AC*, 25–26 (1987–1988), 177–91.

8 See Elias L. Rivers, 'Sancho y la duquesa: una nota socioliteraria', *Cervantes*, 11.2 (1991), 35–42.

sees things from the view point of a social superior, as the following passage illustrates:

> [. . .] quiso Andrés que fuese Clemente su camarada, y Clemente tuvo esa amistad por gran favor que se le hacía. Andaban siempre juntos, gastaban largo, llovían escudos, corrían, saltaban, bailaban y tiraban la barra mejor que ninguno de los gitanos, y eran de la gitanas más que medianamente queridos, y de los gitanos en todo extremo respetados. (p. 89).
>
> ([. . .] Andrés asked Clemente to be his comrade, and Clemente took this friendship as a great favour. They went about together, they spent a lot of money, they rained gold coins about, and they raced and jumped and danced and threw the bar better than any of the gypsies, and were more than moderately liked by the gypsy girls and extremely respected by the gypsy men. [I, p. 77])

Even so, they are not presented together from the beginning, probably due to the theatrical way in which *La gitanilla* is conceived (it is like a three-act play), so that the page is initially presented to us as an apparent rival to don Juan. This is also, of course, don Juan's first impression: '—¿Qué puedes imaginar, Preciosa? —respondió Andrés —Ninguna otra cosa, sino la misma fuerza que a mí me ha hecho gitano le ha hecho a él parecer molinero y venir a buscarte' (p. 86) (' "What can you think, Preciosa?" answered Andrés, "nothing else but the power that made me a gypsy has made him dress up like a miller to come to look for you" ' [I, p. 69]), and it is also Preciosa's. She warns Clemente about how he must now behave among the gypsies:

> [. . .] no afees a Andrés la bajeza de su intento, ni le pintes cuán mal le está preseverar en este estado; que, puesto que yo imagino que debajo de los candados de mi voluntad está la suya, todavía me pesaría de verle dar muestras, por mínimas que fuesen, de algún arrepentimiento. (pp. 89–90)[9]
>
> ([. . .] [do not reproach] Andrés for the lowliness of his aims, and [or point] out to him how bad it is for him to persist in this state; for although I imagine that his will is locked up by mine, it would still grieve me to see him reveal even the smallest indications of repentance. [I, p. 79])

A final reflection now on the page and on Juana Carducha, the female character who appears towards the very end as the last obstacle to the fulfilment of the relationship between Preciosa and Andrés Caballero: they appear to be purely ancillary characters, and even, to a certain extent, expendable ones. The page serves to awaken don Juan's jealousy (and therefore to prompt the mistakes that

[9] On the possible influence of the theatre on *La gitanilla*, see José Montero Reguera, '*La gitanilla*, de novela a comedia', in *El mundo como escritura. Estudios sobre Cervantes y su época*, ed. Inés Carrasco de Santos, anejo 48, Analecta Malacitana, (Málaga, Universidad de Málaga, 2003), pp. 123–38.

are so characteristic of comedy and with which Cervantes bestrews the *Novelas ejemplares*), but also to create for don Juan a sporting companion, who, even though he does not belong to the same social class, is close enough to it because of his profession as a page. He also becomes the means by which don Juan is helped not to forget his former life in Madrid and, indeed, to avoid feeling lonely in a world – that of the gypsies – which, however welcoming, is completely different from the one he is used to. For her part, Juana Carducha is used to precipitate the ending of the story. Although it is true that the page is more fully developed with a greater and earlier-established role, what is striking about these characters is that once they have served their function, they are then cast aside so that the page disappears almost without the reader noticing: he had left the scene at a certain point and he only reappears considerably later to provide information about his disappearance and its causes ('[. . .] pero no le hallaron ni supieron dél, hasta que desde allí a cuatro días tuvo nuevas ciertas que se había embarcado en una de las dos galeras de Génova que estaban en el puerto de Cartagena, y ya se habían partido' [p. 107]) ('[. . .] but they did not find him or hear anything of him, until four days later when he received reliable news that he had gone on board one of the Genoese galleys which were in the port of Cartagena, and which had already sailed' [I, pp. 99, 101]). This is even more obvious in the case of Juana Carducha: Cervantes had forgotten about her – her story is left hanging as a loose end – and when everything is over the narrator has to add a final postscript, like a patch which could almost have been omitted without any harm being done:

> Olvidábaseme de decir cómo la enamorada mesonera descubrió a la justicia no ser verdad lo del hurto de Andrés el gitano, y confesó su amor y su culpa, a quien no respondió pena alguna, porque en la alegría del hallazgo de los desposados se enterró la venganza y resucitó la clemencia. (p. 108)
>
> (I forgot to say that the girl from the inn who had fallen in love with Andrés revealed to the police that the theft he was accused of was not true; she confessed her love and her guilt, and was not punished, because in the happiness surrounding the discovery of Andrés and Preciosa, vengeance was buried and clemency triumphed. [I, p. 101])

Within the parameters typical of a Byzantine novel, *El amante liberal* tells the story of yet another love relationship (Ricardo–Leonisa) obstructed by a third party (Cornelio), but also by the many accidents of fortune that befall the lovers. However, for the purposes of this study, it is the relationship between Ricardo and Mahamut that holds more interest.

At the start of the *novela* two characters are introduced: a captive, bitterly complaining of his lot, and a Turk. They have been brought up together: ('[. . .] por lo que te obliga el ser entrambos de una misma patria y habernos criado en nuestra niñez juntos [. . .]' [p. 111]) ('[. . .]for the sake of [. . .] the obligation laid upon you by the fact that we are both of the same country and were brought up together during childhood [. . .]' [I, p. 111]). The captive is called Ricardo and we only find out the name of the Turk a little later (p. 112) (I, p. 113), while his true origins will not be revealed until a very late stage in the story ('[. . .] natural de Palermo, que por varios accidentes estoy en este traje y vestido diferente del que yo solía traer' [p. 134]) ('[. . .] a native of Palermo, who as a result of various unforeseen events wear these clothes which I would not normally wear' [I, p. 137]). They are of similar age and background. Cervantes slowly and skilfully selects the information he supplies to the reader (a process easily observable in other *novelas*) so that the facts relating to the two characters are proffered little by little, drop by drop, as it were.[10] First, we hear the complaints of Ricardo, but it is only later that the true nature of these complaints becomes apparent. We are told initially about the origin of the other man (a Turk), but only later is his name (Mahamut) revealed, and the fact that he has renounced his faith, and the details of the way in which he is dressed, all of these elements leading us to suspect that under the outward appearance of a Turk lurks someone who is not a Turk at all. His character is immediately relegated to a secondary position while Ricardo tells his story at length, something made possible by the secrecy and silence that surrounds them in circumstances very similar to those that facilitate the conversation between Cipión and Berganza in the last of the *Novelas ejemplares*: '[. . .] es menester que me la cuentes, como ha menester el médico la relación del enfermo, asegurándote que la depositaré en lo más escondido del silencio' (pp. 111–12) ('[. . .] it is necessary for you to give me an account of it just as a doctor needs an account from his patient. I assure you that I shall keep it all in the strictest confidence' [I, p. 113]). His function now – and throughout the whole *novela* – is to corroborate Ricardo's statements, to guide and supervise the narrative so that the person relaying it does not stray into talking about things of no importance ('—Bien lo sé —dijo Mahamut; —pasa adelante, Ricardo, que más de cuatro días tuve en él, cuando Dios quiso, más de cuatro buenos ratos' [p. 115]) (' "I know it well," said Mahamut. "Please continue, Ricardo, for on several occasions, when it pleased God, I have enjoyed more than a few pleasurable moments in it" ' [I, p. 117]), ensuring that the story is kept going. Mahamut serves as a catalyst of the narrative, loosening Ricardo's tongue, as it were; a close friend and virtual brother to Ricardo, he becomes his confidante and adviser, to the extent that Ricardo does nothing without first consulting him: 'Antes que Ricardo respondiese a su amo, se aconsejó con Mahamut de qué le respondiera' (p. 146) ('Before he replied to his master, Ricardo took counsel with Mahamut over how he should reply' [I, p. 155]). The first and, I think, the only time that Ricardo acts on his own initiative is after he has regained his freedom ('Diéronse luego todos, por consejo de Ricardo [. . .]' [p. 153]) ('On Ricardo's advice, they all then agreed [. . .]' [I, p. 161]) almost at the end of the *novela*. Mahamut is his informant and – since he is largely responsible for Leonisa's forming a favourable opinion of Ricardo and an unfavourable

[10] See the article by Aurora Egido, 'El silencio de los perros y otros silencios *ejemplares*', *Voz y letra*, 6.1 (1995), 5–23.

one of Cornelio – even the intermediary and facilitator of the love between Ricardo and Leonisa,:

> Mahamut se volvió a las tiendas a contar a Ricardo lo que con Leonisa había pasado; y hallándose, se lo contó todo punto por punto, y, cuando llegó al del sentimiento que Leonisa había hecho cuando le dijo que era muerto, casi se le vinieron las lágrimas a los ojos. Díjole cómo había fingido el cuento del cautiverio de Cornelio, por ver lo que ella sentía; advirtióle la tibieza y malicia con que de Cornelio había hablado [. . .] (p. 136)
>
> (Mahamut meanwhile returned to the tents in order to tell Ricardo how he had fared with Leonisa and, having found him, he proceeded to tell him everything, sparing no detail and when he reached the part where Leonisa had displayed such emotion on hearing that Ricardo was dead, tears almost came to his eyes. He told how he had invented the story of Cornelio's captivity so as to discover what Leonisa felt and described the coolness and contempt with which she had spoken of Cornelio. [I, p. 141])

Cervantes uses the device of offering a variety of opinions in order to move his characters towards one decision or another in other *novelas*, such as *La ilustre fregona*.[11] To a large extent, this pair consists of a character who tells a story and is the protagonist of the action, and another who, from another (one might say 'superior') point of view, watches over and directs the narration, while at the same time offering advice to the first, becoming in the process his confidante and closest friend. Yet, at certain points, this first character (Ricardo) also relinquishes this role and comes to behave like Mahamut, a concrete example of the exchange of defining characteristics between the main protagonists – something that happens on other occasions, as we shall see.

The presence and function of this pair (Ricardo and Mahamut) must be seen in relation to other characters in the *novelas,* as we shall now demonstrate.

La ilustre fregona also furnishes examples of various characters who appear in pairs: Diego Carriazo and Juan de Avendaño (fathers), Diego Carriazo and Tomás de Avendaño (sons), la Argüello and la Gallega (inn wenches), the two Andalusian muleteers, etc. Of all these pairs, the one that especially interests me is that formed by the two sons. They are neighbours, of the same age, and both eldest sons, and when Diego Carriazo returns from the tunny fisheries they become inseparable friends.

Carriazo has a prehistory (his life as a *pícaro*) which is recounted in detail, while all that is said of Avendaño, with no further detail, is that for three years he had studied Latin and Greek 'por su gusto' (for pleasure). Therefore, from the reader's point of view, when the two boys meet and decide to set off together, there is one character (Carriazo) who is much more rounded out, and another

11 See Ana María Barrenechea, '*La ilustre fregona* como ejemplo de estructura novelesca cervantina', *Filología*, 7 (1961), 13–32 (*Actas*, pp. 198–206); and also José Montero Reguera, 'Cervantes y la verosimiltud: *La ilustre fregona*', *Revista de Filología Románica*, 10 (1993), 335–57.

(Avendaño) whom the *novela* will only gradually develop. To a large extent, Carriazo does not change his personality in the course of the *novela* – he merely offers to help out his friend, distracting him from his desire to return to the tunny fisheries. Avendaño, on the other hand, is a character who is progressively developed through his actions as the story advances, unlike Carriazo whose personality has been constructed through the narrator's account, in accordance with a very similar pattern found in *El celoso extremeño*, where the narrative that serves to relay Carrizales's story gives way to dialogue through which we are informed of all that happens in the jealous Extremaduran's house.

The two boys set off together on their journey, deceiving their parents (who think that they are going to study at Salamanca) and making a fool out of a tutor ('más hombre de bien que de discreto' [p. 378]) ('more a man of honour than of good sense' [III, p. 67]) sent to accompany them. This character, called Pedro Alonso, appears only briefly, but a few brush strokes suffice to characterize him and explain why the boys are able to make their escape so easily. The *pícaros* (as they are now) follow a well-known route (Burgos → Valladolid → Mojados → Madrid → Illescas) until, in Illescas, they encounter the two muleteers who will bring about an unexpected change in their plans. So far, the *novela* has been shaping up as a travel narrative and it is Carriazo who has had the leading role, so clearly so that Avendaño appears to have a mere supporting role: it is Carriazo who leads and channels the narration and also, of course, his companion in adventure. Avendaño insists on going to the Sevillano Inn, while Carriazo would prefer to go to another lodging: 'Desesperábase Carriazo, y Avendaño se estaba quedo' (p. 383) ('Carriazo was in despair but Avendaño would not move' [III, pp. 71, 73]). It seems, then, that until they reach Illescas, the picaresque story (first that of Carriazo, then that of both boys) has served as a frame for Avendaño's story. In this sense one could speak of a new framing structure, similar to the one we find in the *Coloquio de los perros*, or in *El celoso extremeño*, whereby the story of Carrizales serves as a frame for the adventures that occur in his house – and even in *Rinconete y Cortadillo* where the picaresque life of Rincón and Cortado functions as a frame for the interlude in Monipodio's house.

Diego Carriazo is presented to us as a virtuous *pícaro* who, after a certain period spent leading a picaresque life, returns to Burgos from where he originally set out and where his family, one of the noblest and wealthiest in the city, lives. But the aristocratic life is not to his taste – quite the opposite: he misses his tunny fisheries, so much so that he has started to look somewhat 'meláncolico e imaginativo' (p. 377) ('melancholy and pensive' [III, p. 65]). This leads him to persuade Avendaño to take up the picaresque life also. He undergoes quite a number of transformations that involve corresponding changes of name:

1: gentleman to *pícaro* (Urdiales).

2: *pícaro* to gentleman (he goes back to being Diego Carriazo: 'Estúvose allí [Valladolid] quince días para reformar la color del rostro, sacándola de mulata a flamenca, y para trastejarse y sacarse del borrador de pícaro y ponerse en limpio de caballero' [p. 376] ['There (Valladolid) he stopped for a couple of weeks to let his face change from a dark brown to a ruddy colour, and to put himself straight by losing the outward signs of a *pícaro* and turning himself into a gentleman again' (III, p. 65)]).

3: gentleman to peasant ('vistiéronse a lo payo' [pp. 379–80]) ('They donned peasant outfits' [III, p. 69]).

4: peasant to water-carrier (Lope Asturiano).

5: water-carrier to gentleman ('gentilhombre' [p. 439]) ('gentleman' [III, p. 135]).

Carriazo carries the burden of the story, which develops as a journey narrative, until they reach Toledo, following the change of plan imposed by Avendaño, who had decided in Illescas to modify their intended route. In Toledo, Carriazo's role shifts to that of a supporting character for Avendaño, whom he helps (in as much as he can) to win the love of Costanza. The contrasting characters of the two boys are clearly expressed through their reactions to Constanza: while for Avendaño she is an 'angel', Carriazo is rather less impressed: 'No digo más sino que a Carriazo le pareció tan bien como a su compañero, pero enamoróle mucho menos, y tan menos que quisiera no anochecer en la posada, sino partirse luego para sus almadrabas' (p. 390) ('All I will say is that she seemed as beautiful to Carriazo as to his companion, but that she aroused less passionate feelings in him. So much less that he did not want to spend another night at the inn but to set off for the tunny fisheries there and then' [III, p. 79]). Carriazo goes along with him since '[. . .] consideró el gran gusto que haría a Avendaño si le seguía el humor [. . .]' (p. 392) ('[. . .] he was thinking of the pleasure he would give Avendaño if he conformed to his mood' [III, p. 81]) and becomes in his turn a water-carrier with the name of Lope Asturiano. But he continues to long for the tunny fisheries, where he has learned the lessons that account for the talents he displays in the inn: he plays the guitar, is the life and soul of the party, sings the song of the *chacona* (chaconne) and in a sense it is he who brings a sense of life and fun to the sojourn in the Sevillano Inn. He was possessed, we are told, of 'presto, fácil y lindo ingenio' (p. 402) ('a quick, easy, sharp wit' [III, p. 91]). While Avendaño sticks close to his beloved Costanza, Carriazo buys an ass (for his new job as a water-carrier), loses all his money at cards, which is perfectly understandable in the light of what has already been remarked of him: 'era de propiedad del azúcar, que jamás gastó menestra' (p. 419) ('was of the nature of sugar, which never spoiled the soup' [III, p. 111]), which amounts to saying that he was ready for anything. He even loses the ass, but his quick wits and the lessons learned from his time as a *pícaro* – his knowing, for example, that there were such things as asses with five quarters is undoubtedly down to his acquaintance with daily life in the tunny fisheries – allow him to win back the ass and part of the money. Not content with this, he is capable, besides, of displaying generosity and compassion, managing to win the affection of the city's water-carriers, so that the dash and generosity of the 'Asturiano' become famous throughout the city. But fame plays a dirty trick on him: what people remember is the story of the ass's tail ('Daca la cola, Asturiano, daca la cola[. . .]' [p. 422]) ('Give us the tail, Asturiano! Give us the tail!' [III, p. 135]) not his generosity and good nature. This leads him to change his lodgings and to venture forth about the city only at night. Such is the perverse injustice of fame in a *novela* which, amongst other things, is about reputation and the diversity of opinions.

Avendaño, for his part, has been a student of Latin and Greek at Salamanca for three years. At the start of the *novela* he is presented as the friend and confidante of Carriazo, thanks to which he learns of his picaresque adventures, which seem to attract him, for 'antes alabó que vituperó su gusto' (p. 377) ('[he] was of a mind to applaud rather than condemn his taste' [III, p. 67]). It seems, then, that his curiosity – one of the traits that most typifies this character – has been aroused: it is curiosity that leads him to accompany Carriazo and experience the picaresque life; likewise, having overheard what the Andalusian muleteers say, it is curiosity that makes him decide to go and see Costanza in the Sevillano Inn. Like Carriazo, he too undergoes a number of transformations:

1: gentleman → *pícaro*

2: *pícaro* → stable-boy (called Tomás Pedro).

3: stable-boy → gentleman ('Vieron al mozo de la cebada, Tomás Pedro, vuelto en don Tomás de Avendaño y vestido como señor', [p. 439] ('They saw the stable-boy, Tomás Pedro turned into Don Tomás de Avendaño and dressed as a gentleman' [III, p. 135]).

This character, who is in a supporting role to Carriazo until he falls in love with Costanza just by hearing about her, then goes on to carry the burden of the action in Toledo. His first encounter with Costanza impels Avendaño to try by all possible means to remain in the Sevillano Inn, something that he manages to achieve by means of a lie: is he now starting to behave like a *pícaro*? One would have to say that, in this sense, the two protagonists have exchanged character traits. The stay in Toledo is the subject of mutual reproach between the two boys, but even so they go on living together in the inn: Avendaño becomes a stable-boy, while Carriazo is transformed into a water-carrier. The new stable-boy – with the name of Tomás Pedro – manages to make himself indispensable in the hostelry: '[. . .] el mozo sirve de manera que sería conciencia despedille' (p. 415) ('[. . .] the lad is a good worker so it would be a pity to dismiss him' [III, p. 107]); he writes chaste love poems and reveals his true origins to Costanza, something that Carriazo would never do.

There is an abundance of paired characters in *El casamiento engañoso*: Campuzano (the Ensign) and Peralta (the Licentiate), who are friends of almost the same age; doña Estefanía Caicedo and her cousin, who collaborate in deceiving the Ensign ('[. . .] digo que supe que se había llevado a doña Estefanía el primo que dije que se halló a nuestros desposorios, el cual de luengos tiempos atrás era su amigo a todo ruedo', [p. 533]) ('[. . .] I discovered that Doña Estefanía had been taken away by the cousin I told you was at our wedding, who had stuck with her through thick and thin' [IV, p. 79]); 'dos amigos míos' (p. 527) ('two friends of mine' [IV, p. 71]), who act as witnesses for the Ensign in his marriage to doña Estefanía; two women and two servants: 'Es mi señora doña Clementa Bueso, y viene con ella el señor don Lope Meléndez de Almendárez, con otros dos criados, y Hortigosa, la dueña que llevó consigo' (p. 528) (' "My lady Doña Clementa Bueso, and she's accompanied by Don Lope Meléndez de Almendárez, and Hortigosa, the lady-in-waiting she took with her' " [IV, p. 73]). Furthermore, this plethora of paired characters corresponds to the fact that there are two stories that Campuzano has to tell (Cipión's and Berganza's), although only one is told, over two nights, which, once again, are reduced to one.

Remaining with the kind of pairings that I am attempting to analyze in detail, the one that I want to look at now is that formed by Campuzano and Peralta. The Ensign tells his story in response to the Licentiate's questions. The latter's interventions are brief, but they serve to direct, develop, and channel the conversation; they have the effect of making the Ensign's account more enjoyable. These are double characters in the tradition of some humanist dialogues, especially of those inscribed within the Lucianic tradition: *El crotalón* (a dialogue between a cobbler called Micilus and Pythagoras in the form of a cock); the *Dream* or *The Cockerel* by Lucian, etc. With respect to the dogs in the Hospital of the Resurrection in Valladolid, Sevilla Arroyo and Rey Hazas have said: '[. . .] tanto en Cervantes como en *El crotalón* hay un dialogante (Berganza, Gallo) que cuenta sus lances, y otro (Cipión, Micilo) que escucha e interviene menos desde una posición de superioridad reconocida siempre' ([. . .] in both Cervantes and *El crotalón* there is a participant (Berganza, the Cockerel) who recounts his adventures, and another (Cipión, Micilus) who listens, intervening less, and always from an acknowledged position of superiority).[12] This could certainly be applied to some of the characters I am analyzing. What is particularly remarkable in some cases is the way in which the first character (the one telling the story) gradually acquires some of the traits of the second (the one in the superior position) and, finally, even reproaches and advises him. This happens above all in the *Coloquio*, but also in other *novelas*. Thus, the generic mould, which is the source of the dialogic form, is reformulated, and, at the same time, in the course of the *novela*, the characters acquire greater shading and are more fully rounded out.

In *El coloquio de los perros* we encounter two characters who converse throughout the whole work. Cipión is the one who organizes and apportions the narrative material:

> Sea desta manera, Berganza amigo: que esta noche me cuentes tu vida y los trances por donde has venido al punto en que ahora te hallas, y si mañana en la noche estuviéremos con habla, yo te contaré la mía. (p. 545)
>
> (Let's make an agreement, Berganza my friend, that tonight you will tell me the story of your life and the events that led you to the point here you are now, and if tomorrow night we still have speech, I will tell you mine. [IV, p. 87])

12 See their edition of this *novela* (Madrid: Alianza Editorial, 1997), p. xxvii.

Sometimes he seriously reproaches Berganza:

> Si en contar las condiciones de los amos que has tenido y las faltas de sus oficios te has de estar, amigo Berganza, tanto como esta vez, menestar será pedir al cielo nos conceda la habla siquiera por un año, y aun temo que, al paso que llevas, no llegarás a la mitad de tu historia (pp. 547–48)
>
> (Berganza, my friend, if you are going to take as long telling me about the circumstances of the masters you have had and the defects of their occupations as you have done this time, it will be necessary to ask heaven to give us the power of speech for a year, and even then I fear that, given the pace at which you are going, you will not get halfway through your story [IV, p. 89]);
>
> Basta; adelante, Berganza, que ya estás entendido (p. 560)
>
> (That's enough. Get on with it, Berganza, for we get your point [IV, p. 99]);

and

> ¿Al murmurar llamas filosofar? ¡Así va ello! ¡Canoniza, canoniza, Berganza, a la maldita plaga de la murmuración!, y dale el nombre que quisieres, que ella dará a nosotros el de cínicos, que quiere decir perros murmuradores; y por tu vida, que calles ya y sigas tu historia. (p. 566)
>
> (You call gossiping philosophy? That's great! Dress up the accursed plague known as gossiping and give it whatever name you like, it will call us cynics, which means gossiping dogs; for heaven's sake keep quiet and carry on with your story. [IV, p. 107])

He is discreet, a friend, an adviser: '[. . .] y no se te olvide este advertimiento, para aprovecharte dél en lo que te queda por decir' (p. 548) ('[. . .] don't forget this and bear it in mind for the remainder of what you have to say' [IV, p. 89]); 'Berganza. —Yo tomaré tu consejo' (p. 552) ('Berganza: "I shall take your advice"' [IV, p. 93]). He always speaks from a position of superiority: '[. . .] Hiciste muy bien' (p. 549) ('[. . .] You did well' [IV, p. 91]); expectations are therefore created about his story, although it will never be heard. He expresses his opinion at every turn, confirming or denying what Berganza says; always wise and sometimes with a very noticeable touch of the moralizer about him, he is strongly reminiscent of the character of Valdés in the *Diálogo de la lengua* (Dialogue on Language). He always has the lead role, but there are also moments when Berganza appears to rebel and succeeds in correcting Cipión:

> CIPIÓN. —Así es verdad, y yo confieso mi yerro, y quiero que me le perdones, pues te he perdonado tantos: echemos pellilos a la mar, como dicen los muchachos, y no murmuremos de aquí adelante; y sigue tu cuento [. . .] (p. 562)
>
> (CIPIÓN: 'That's true, and I confess my error and ask you to forgive me mine as I have forgiven many of yours. Pax, as children say, and let us not gossip from here on; continue your story' [IV, p. 101]);
>
> BERGANZA. —Habla con propiedad: que no llaman colas las del pulpo (p. 568)

> (BERGANZA: 'Speak properly: you don't talk of an octopus having tails.' [IV, p. 107])

He even goes so far as to censor what he himself is about to say:

> ¡Oh Cipión, quién te pudiera contar lo que vi en ésta y en otras dos compañías de comediantes en que anduve! Mas, por no ser posible reducirlo a narración sucinta y breve, lo habré de dejar para otro día, si es que ha de haber otro día en que nos comuniquemos. ¿Ves cuán larga ha sido mi plática? ¿Ves mis muchos y diversos sucesos? ¿Consideras mis caminos y mis amos tantos? Pues todo lo que has oído es nada, comparado a lo que te pudiera contar de lo que noté, averigüé y vi desta gente [. . .] (pp. 615–16).
>
> (Oh, Cipión, I wish I could tell what I saw in this and another two actors' companies that I joined! But since I cannot cut it down to a brief and succinct account, I will leave it for another occasion, if indeed there is to be another occasion on which we can communicate with each other. Do you see how long my discourse has been? Do you see my many and diverse experiences? Do you see the many masters I've had and the many paths I've walked? Well, all that you have heard is nothing compared to what I could tell you of what I noted, ascertained, and saw of these people [. . .] [IV, pp. 149, 151])

Thus the roles have been reversed and Berganza has acquired traits that are characteristic of Cipión. This is, I believe, exactly what happens with Carriazo and Avendaño.

Rinconete and Cortadillo could be included in this same group of characters: one of them apparently dominates the other, although in reality, I believe, a perfect balance is achieved. We encounter two *pícaros* of more or less the same age and circumstances. Rincón is a little older than the other boy and serves as his teacher in the art of card playing. Their prehistory – although we are not provided with many details of it – is very similar: their fathers are respectively a pardoner and a tailor, but there is no hint of their having the lowly background typical of the *pícaro*. Until their names are mentioned, the narrator refers to them as the older (Rincón) and the younger (Cortado). Theirs is a relationship born of necessity: they are two *pícaros* with their backs to the wall, 'sin blanca' (without a penny to their name). Besides this, they share similar circumstances: they are both more or less the same age, separated from their families, surviving on the basis of petty (or not so petty) theft, living in exile (from Madrid; from Toledo), leading a life on the run. They follow a common destiny by heading south to Seville, which is what brings them into contact with each other at the Molinillo Inn. All of this is detailed in their first, lively, fast-moving conversation. They form an association, pooling their criminal skills, which enables them to engage in new scams. Immediately there follow the thefts in Seville, their shared, typically picaresque job as basket carriers, and the conversation with Monipodio's *confrère*. It is clear that they lead absolutely parallel lives up to the point when they meet at the inn and even more so afterwards for, until they reach Monipodio's house, they do everything jointly. If Rinconete's role in Monipodio's house is perhaps of greater weight than that of Cortado, who practically disappears – it is Riconete who answers Monipodio's initial questions and it is he who reads the *memorial* (list) – the differences in their roles are minimal. In fact, when the interruptions from outside the house begin, the two virtually disappear and both react in concert as if they were a single person: 'Espantáronse Rinconete y Cortadillo de la nueva invención de la escoba [. . .]', (p. 204) ('Rinconete and Cortadillo were astonished by the novel use to which the broom was being put [. . .]' [I, p. 217]); 'Los dos novicios, Rinconete y Cortadillo, no sabían qué hacerse, y estuviérónse quedos, esperando en qué paraba aquella repentina borrasca [. . .]', (p. 206) ('Rinconete and Cortadillo, the two postulants, had no idea what to do and kept still waiting to see how the storm would end' [I, p. 219]). Of the two, it is, perhaps, Rinconete who seems to show a more rounded personality, since the portrait of him that Cervantes gives us is not just physical, but is more detailed with respect to his origins and is also a psychological and behavioural one: Rinconete is 'de suyo curioso' (p. 200) ('by nature an inquisitive individual' [I, p. 213]) and 'de muy bien entendimiento, y tenía un buen natural' (pp. 214–15) ('a pretty sharp lad, and had all his wits about him' [I, p. 229]). So much is this the case that the narrator's moral reflection – this is one of the few *Novelas ejemplares* in which the moral of the tale is made explicit – is conveyed through Rinconete. This gives the impression that the whole story might have been told about only one *pícaro*, but because there are two the narrative is enlivened and made more enjoyable through the use of dialogue. This allows Cervantes to play his characteristic games of perspective and it also ensures that, as Rey Hazas puts it, the *novela* succeeds in 'evitar el realismo dogmático de la picaresca alemaniana y ampliar los puntos de vista de la narración, a la búsqueda de una mayor fiabilidad y objetividad de la misma' (avoiding the dogmatic realism of Alemán's picaresque fiction and expanding the narrative perspective in search of greater credibility and objectivity).[13]

Conclusion

The generic models that Cervantes had in mind when he came to present a good number of the characters in the *Novelas ejemplares* as pairs are, therefore, various: the Byzantine novel, the *comedia de capa y espada* ('cloak-and-dagger' plays) (and also, perhaps, other sub-genres of Golden-Age theatre), the *cuestiones de amor* (love debates) and the humanist dialogue along with its Lucianic antecedents. On this occasion I have been principally concerned with pairs of characters who, I believe, may best be understood in relation to this latter generic source. In the humanist dialogue Cervantes found a way of avoiding the awkward repetition of the *dicendi* verbs ('El coloquio traigo en el seno; púselo en forma de coloquio por ahorrar de "dijo Cipión", "respondió Berganza", que suele alargar la escritura' (p. 537) ('I am carrying the colloquy on my person;

[13] Rey Hazas, '*Novelas ejemplares*', pp. 198–99.

I wrote it in the form of a dialogue to avoid having to write "Cipión said", "Berganza replied", which tends to lengthen the account' [IV, p. 83]), a rationale certainly not exclusive to Cervantes but belonging to a longstanding tradition'[14] a way of making the narration of events more enjoyable and attractive, especially when these are particularly complex or dry (Riley, p. 242), and a way of achieving suspense and entertainment.[15] Similarly, in dialogue, Cervantes found a tool whereby characters could be allowed to mould themselves, add shadings, gradually round themselves out, modify and reformulate previous versions of themselves, especially in cases where the defining traits of paired protagonists are interchanged, and so achieve a balance between them. It is also worth pointing out that this happens not only in the *novelas* that are obviously influenced by humanist dialogue – hence the high incidence of paired characters in *El casamiento engañoso y El coloquio de los perros* – but also in others with little or no relationship to that genre: *El amante liberal*, *La ilustre fregona*, and perhaps even *Rinconete y Cortadillo*.

Works cited

Barrenechea, Ana María, '*La ilustre fregona* como ejemplo de estructura novelesca cervantina', *Filología*, 7 (1961), 13–32; also in *Actas del Primer Congreso Internacional de Hispanistas celebrado en Oxford del 6 al 11 de septiembre de 1962*, ed. Frank Pierce and Cyril A. Jones (Oxford: Dolphin, 1964), pp. 198–206.

Cervantes Saavedra, Miguel de, *Exemplary Novels / Novelas ejemplares*, ed. B. W. Ife, 4 vols (Warminster: Aris & Philips, 1992).

———, *Las dos doncellas*, ed. Florencio Sevilla Arroyo and Antonio Rey Hazas (Madrid: Alianza Editorial, 1997).

———, *Don Quijote de la Mancha*, ed. Francisco Rico, 2 vols (Barcelona: Crítica, 1998).

———, *Novelas ejemplares*, ed. Jorge García López (Barcelona: Crítica, 2001).

Dunn, Peter N., 'Las *Novelas ejemplares*', in *Suma cervantina,* ed. J. B. Avalle-Arce and E. C. Riley (London: Támesis, 1973), pp. 81–118.

Egido, Aurora, 'El silencio de los perros y otros silencios *ejemplares*', *Voz y letra*, 6, 1 (1995), 5–23.

Jauralde Pou, Pablo, 'El *Quijote*, II, 9', *AC*, 25–26 (1987–1988), 177–91.

Lozano Renieblas, Isabel, *Cervantes y el mundo del 'Persiles'* (Alcalá de Henares: Centro de Estudios Cervantinos, 1998).

Montero Reguera, José, 'Cervantes y la verosimiltud: *La ilustre fregona*', *Revista de Filología Románica*, 10 (1993), 335–57.

14 See Edward C. Riley, 'Los antecedentes del *Coloquio de los perros*', in *La rara invención. Estudios sobre Cervantes y su posteridad literaria* (Barcelona: Crítica, 2001), pp. 239–53 (pp. 241–42).

15 See Isabel Lozano Renieblas, *Cervantes y el mundo del 'Persiles'* (Alcalá de Henares: Centro de Estudios Cervantinos, 1998), pp. 70–1.

Montero Reguera, '*La gitanilla*, de novela a comedia', in *El mundo como escritura. Estudios sobre Cervantes y su época*, ed Inés Carrasco de Santos, anejo 48, Analecta Malacitana (Málaga, Universidad de Málaga, 2003), pp. 123–38.

Rey Hazas, Antonio,'*Novelas ejemplares*', in *Cervantes*, ed. Anthony Close and others (Alcalá de Henares: Centro de Estudios Cervantinos, 1995), pp. 173–209.

Riley, Edward C., 'Los antecedentes del *Coloquio de los perros*', in *La rara invención. Estudios sobre Cervantes y su posteridad literaria* (Barcelona: Crítica, 2001), pp. 239–53.

Rivers, Elias L., 'Sancho y la duquesa: una nota socioliteraria', *Cervantes*, 11.2 (Fall, 1991), 35–42.

Appendix I: Synopses

1. La gitanilla (The Little Gypsy Girl)

The extraordinary beauty and virtue of Preciosa, a young gypsy dancer living in Madrid, attract the particular attention of two young men: Clemente, a page, dedicates poems to her, while don Juan de Cárcamo, a handsome young nobleman, agrees to prove the sincerity of his love for her by living among the gypsies for two years, assuming the name of Andrés Caballero (literally: Andrew Gentleman). When Clemente turns up in the gypsy camp, claiming to be in difficulties with the law, Andrés is convinced that he is a serious rival for Preciosa's love. Eventually, persuaded by Preciosa, Andrés learns to conquer his jealousy and to accept Clemente as a friend. In a small town near Murcia, an innkeeper's daughter, Juana Carducha, offers herself to Andrés, and then takes revenge for his refusal of her by planting 'stolen' silver plate in his baggage. While being arrested, Andrés kills a young soldier, the nephew of the local mayor, who had insulted him as a thieving gypsy. He is imprisoned in Murcia to await trial for theft and murder. Meanwhile Preciosa and her grandmother are lodged in the home of the Corregidor (chief magistrate). Preciosa pleads with him to save her fiancé, Andrés. Her grandmother now reveals that she had stolen Preciosa as a very young child from this same house. In proof, she produces some trinkets and a note recording the date of the theft and the real name of the child: doña Constanza de Azevedo y de Meneses. Preciosa's new-found parents are finally convinced that she is their daughter when they see the mole under her left breast and her webbed toe, the only blemishes on their baby girl's body. They are not displeased when Preciosa reveals the true identity of her 'gypsy' fiancé: he comes from just the right social background, and indeed his parents are friends of theirs. The Corregidor visits Andrés in prison and, without revealing that he knows his true identity, tells him that, if he really loves her – and as a special concession – he may marry his young gypsy girl before being executed the following day. That night Andrés is brought to the Corregidor's house, but because the proper procedures have not been observed the priest refuses to perform the ceremony. The Corregidor now reveals the whole truth to Andrés, uses his wealth to dissuade the dead man's relatives from pressing charges, and his influence with the Archbishop of Murcia to have the normal period of banns reduced. The young couple are married and their story becomes famous throughout the whole area and is celebrated in verse by local poets. Clemente, in the meantime, has slipped away to take ship for Genoa, while Juana Carducha confesses her misdeed, but is pardoned in the atmosphere of goodwill and forgiveness generated by the wedding.

2. *El amante liberal (The Generous Lover)*

Standing in front of the ruined walls of Nicosia, Ricardo, a native of Trapani in Sicily, and now a captive of the Turks, who have taken control of Cyprus, is bitterly lamenting his fate. He explains to his renegade (Christian-turned-Muslim) friend and compatriot, Mahamut, that he is sad, not so much because he is a captive, but because Leonisa, the woman he loved back at home, is dead. Leonisa, however, had had eyes only for another, effeminately handsome young man called Cornelio. One day, in a jealous rage, while Leonisa and Cornelio were picnicing in a garden overlooking the sea, he had attacked Cornelio with his sword. Cornelio ran off, but just then a Turkish raiding party came ashore and took Ricardo and Leonisa captive. Ricardo passed into the hands of a man called Fetala, and Leonisa into those of a Greek-born renegade called Yzuf. As the Turks made their way to the coast of Africa, he witnessed Leonisa's ship perish in a storm. Shortly afterwards, when Fetala died, Ricardo became the property of Hazan Pasha, the incoming Turkish viceroy of Cyprus. As Ricardo and Mahamut observe the ceremony during which the outgoing viceroy, Ali Pasha, hands over power to Hazan, a Jewish merchant appears, offering for sale an extraordinarily beautiful girl in Moorish dress. Ricardo realizes with astonishment that she is Leonisa, but must remain silent. Both Ali and Hazan want to buy Leonisa, each pretending that he wants to present her to the Great Turk in Constantinople. Mahamut's master, the Cadi (Civil Magistrate) of Nicosia, who is equally interested in Leonisa, hypocritically offers a solution: each can pay half the asking price and he will take her to the Great Turk on their behalf. Ali and Hazan reluctantly accept, and Leonisa is taken off to the home of the Cadi and his wife, Halima. Mahamut uses his good standing with the Cadi to persuade him to buy Ricardo. Halima takes as strong a fancy to Ricardo (now called Mario) as her husband had to Leonisa, and both use the young Sicilians as go-betweens, enabling them to speak freely to each other. Leonisa describes how she survived the shipwreck and eventually came into the hands of the Jewish merchant. They decide that they will try to escape. Ricardo and Mahamut persuade the Cadi to secure Leonisa for himself by purchasing another female Christian captive. During the voyage to Constantinople, Leonisa will pretend to die of a serious illness; the body of the other Christian woman will be publicly thrown overboard, allowing the Cadi to inform the Grand Turk of Leonisa's 'death' and keep her for himself. The Cadi accepts the plan, but announces his intention to substitute his wife, Halima, for the second Christian woman. Halima (who is a renegade) plans, in turn, to use the journey as an opportunity to escape with Ricardo, reconvert to Christianity and marry him. During the trip the Cadi's ship is attacked by two other ships, commanded respectively by Hazan and Ali, both still set upon on seizing Leonisa. In the resulting battle they are killed, and, although the Cadi is wounded, he eventually reaches Constantinople, determined to lodge an official complaint about their behaviour. Ricardo, Leonisa, Mahamut, and Halima (whose plans have not changed) are able to make their way back to Sicily. Believing that he has overcome his jealous possessiveness, Ricardo now offers Leonisa to Cornelio, but then realizes that his act of generosity is just another manifestation of that same possessiveness. Leonisa, however, freely chooses to marry Ricardo, while Mahamut and Halima are reconciled with the Church and marry each other. Ricardo becomes famous as 'the generous lover' and enjoys a happy and fruitful married life with Leonisa.

3. Rinconete y Cortadillo (Rinconete and Cortadillo)

One summer's day, two badly dressed boys in their mid-teens meet each other at the Molinillo inn on the road from Castile to Andalusia. Initially affecting the language of gentlemen, they exchange information about their backgrounds. The older boy, Pedro del Rincón, had worked as an assistant pardoner (a seller of papal indulgences), but had absconded to Madrid with the money he had collected. He was soon caught, severely punished, and banished from the city, and now earns his living as a professional card player. The other, Diego Cortado, had trained as a tailor but prefers cutting purses to cutting cloth. Openly admitting that they are penniless drifters, they agree to pool their talents. They clean out a muleteer at cards and viciously assault him when he tries to take his money back by force. A group of men making their way to Seville help to break up the brawl, and offer to take the boys with them. Just at the entrance to Seville, the boys steal a few personal belongings from one of their benefactors, which they then promptly sell off. They explore the city, and are impressed by its grandeur, although momentarily disheartened by the premonitory sight of six galleys (ships rowed by convicted criminals) moored alongside the quays. They begin to work as basket-carriers, delivering foodstuffs bought at the market to the homes of the purchasers – a perfect cover for their thieving. Their first customers are a soldier and a student who is also a sacristan. Cortado steals the student's purse and then manages to filch his handkerchief as well. The boys are warned that they need to register themselves with Monipodio, the city's crime boss. Having been taken to his house, they wait in its central courtyard and watch it fill up with members of the city's criminal community returning from their day's work. Monipodio, an uncouth, hairy-chested giant of a man, explains the life-style and laws of his brotherhood to the boys in comically incorrect Spanish, interviews them about their skills, admits them to the community (waiving the customary period of probation), and gives them the new names of Rinconete and Cortadillo. A constable appears in search of a purse stolen that morning from a student relative of his. Rinocente admits what happened and Cortadillo hands over the purse to Monipodio, who is anxious to return it to the constable, a man who has done him many favours. Some prostitutes arrive, one of them, called Juliana la Cariharta, in great distress. She has been assaulted by her pimp and lover, Repolido, and demands justice from Monipodio. Eventually, when Repolido turns up, the two are reconciled. An impromptu party gets underway, but everyone (except

Rinconete and Cortadillo) scarpers when they hear that the magistrate with two policemen is making his way down the street. However, he simply passes by, and the community reassembles. Now a gentleman appears, complaining that a face-slashing he had commissioned has not been carried out on the right person. When he has been successfully mollified, duped into paying a supplement to have the job done properly, and sent on his way, Monipodio (who is clearly illiterate) asks Rinconete to read out a list of 'jobs pending' from the community's order book. These include beatings, stabbings, and multifarious acts of physical and verbal humiliation and intimidation. Finally, Rinconete's reactions to what he has witnessed are described: on the one hand, he is amused by the uneducated speech of various members of the community (Monipodio's in particular), and by their firm conviction that despite everything they are good Catholics, and, on the other, he is so appalled by their violent, godless way of life that he decides to persuade Cortadillo that they should not stay much longer. Even so, we are told that he goes on living with Monipodio's group for several more months and that a lot more could be written about his adventures during that time.

4. La española inglesa (The English Spanish Girl)

During the English raid on Cádiz in 1596, a young girl of about six years of age, called Isabel, is carried off to London by Clotaldo, a nobleman and a secret Catholic. Isabel is brought up by him and his wife Catalina in the company of their son, Ricaredo, who later falls in love with her, so much so, that he becomes ill when his parents arrange a marriage for him with a Scottish noblewoman. He proposes marriage to Isabela (as she is called in England), and she declares her love for him. Informed of the situation, his parents agree to withdraw from the existing marriage arrangement. Now aged fifteen, Isabela is presented at court to Queen Elizabeth I, who takes a great liking to her, and agrees that she may marry Ricaredo if he proves his worth in a sea-borne raiding expedition. Relieved not to have had to attack fellow Catholics, Ricaredo helps to capture a large, treasure-laden vessel previously taken from the Portuguese by the Turks. Among the Christian prisoners released are Isabela's parents, who tell the story of her abduction and ask to be brought to England. Ricaredo obliges without revealing his own identity. Arousing some criticism for doing so, he presents himself fully armed at court to recount his exploits. The Queen now fully approves his marriage, and in the royal presence Ricaredo reintroduces Isabela to her overjoyed parents. A complication arises when the Queen's chief lady-in-waiting tries to persuade her to marry off Isabela to her son, Count Arnesto. The Queen refuses and has Arnesto arrested when he tries to fight a duel with Ricaredo. When Arnesto's mother's suggestion that Isabela, as a secret Catholic, should be sent back to Spain is also rejected, she has Isabela secretly poisoned. Although Isabela does not die, she suffers a severe reaction, losing all her hair and becoming hideously disfigured. Ricaredo still wishes to marry her but his parents insist on reopening negotiations with Clisterna, the Scottish noblewoman. He arranges with Isabela, who has already begun to recover some of her beauty, that, if she returns to Spain with her parents, he will come for her in two years' time. He avoids marrying Clisterna by telling his parents that he must first make a pilgrimage to Rome. Almost at the end of the agreed period of waiting, Isabela, now living in Seville, is informed that Ricaredo has been murdered by Count Arnesto in Italy. She decides to enter the convent of Santa Paula and is just about to make her profession on the very day she should have been reunited with Ricaredo when the ceremony is interrupted by Ricaredo himself. He explains that he had been badly, but not fatally, wounded by the Count's servants; then, having taken ship for Spain, he had been captured by Turkish pirates and held captive in Algiers. Eventually ransomed by Trinitarian friars, he had made his way to Spain, and had just arrived that day in Seville. A week later, amidst general rejoicing, Ricaredo and Isabela are married and are said to be still living happily in Seville in a house facing the convent church of Santa Paula. Their story is presented as an illustration of the power of love and beauty, and of the mysterious workings of Divine Providence.

5. El licenciado Vidriera (The Glass Graduate)

One day as they are out riding in the countryside near the university city of Salamanca, two gentlemen students come across a young boy of about eleven asleep beneath a tree. Curious to know what he is doing all alone in such a solitary place, they have their servants wake him up. The boy tells them that his name is Tomás Rodaja, and that he intends to become famous and bring honour to his home town and his parents (whose names he refuses to disclose) through his studies. The gentlemen students like his spirit and offer to pay his fees at Salamanca if he will become their servant. Tomás agrees, serves his new masters loyally, and becomes a well-liked figure in the city; and famous in university circles for his extraordinarily quick mind and prodigious memory. When he and his masters have finished their studies, they invite him to come and spend some time with them in their native Andalusia. He accepts the invitation, but soon finds himself itching to return to Salamanca to pursue further studies. His masters generously offer to help him pay for these, and he sets off to return to the university. On the way, he falls into conversation with an army officer, Captain Valdivia, who is conducting a recruiting drive in the Salamanca area. He sings the praises of the soldier's life in Italy (much of which was then a Spanish possession); Tomás is persuaded by this eulogy to go along with him and his company of soldiers as they cross from Cartagena to Genoa, but without putting himself under any obligation to join the army. He then makes an extensive round trip of all the major cities of Italy and Sicily, visiting both Rome and the famous shrine of the Blessed Virgin at Loreto. Eventually he meets up with Valdivia's company once again and goes with them to Flanders (then also a Spanish possession). Finally, he makes his way back to Salamanca and successfully pursues a degree in Law. Some friends take him to visit a famous courtesan, who claims to have met him previously. She becomes attracted to him and declares her feelings. Furious and frustrated at his lack of interest in her, she gives him some quince jelly, which she has doctored with a love potion. Tomás contracts a serious physical illness, from which he recovers, and then begins to suffer the delusion that he is made of glass. He cannot bear anyone to come near him; he can only wear the lightest of clothes, and will only sleep in a hay barn. He wanders the streets of Salamanca offering acidly critical comments on almost all groups in society to anyone who will listen to him, becoming famous as 'the glass graduate'. After two years, he is restored to sanity by the charity and skill of a Hieronymite friar with a reputation for helping those with physical and mental afflictions. Now calling himself the Licentiate Rueda, Tomás attempts to set himself up as a lawyer, but has difficulty finding clients since no one can quite forget his madness or believe that he has recovered. In disillusioned despair, Tomás joins the army, and dies fighting in Flanders alongside his former friend, Captain Valdivia, leaving behind him a reputation for loyal friendship and courage on the battlefield.

6. La fuerza de la sangre (The Power of Blood)

While enjoying an evening stroll with her family along the banks of the Tagus just outside Toledo, a young girl called Leocadia is abducted by one of a group of rowdy young men who have been harassing them. The young man, whose name is Rodolfo, brings her back to his private room in his parents' house where he rapes her and then, having blindfolded her, leaves her in the street near the Cathedral. Leocadia makes her way home and tells her parents what has happened to her. She does not know who the young man was or where his house is, but when he left her alone in the room for a while, she had time to study it carefully and to remove a silver crucifix as a 'witness' to her misfortune. The rich furnishings of the room indicate that the young man belongs to a wealthy, aristocratic family. Leocadia's father reminds her that her own family, although noble, is poor, making it inadvisable for them, even if they knew the identity of her assailant, to seek revenge; also, since a woman who had been raped was considered to have been dishonoured, Leocadia's misfortune must remain a secret. Leocadia accepts her father's advice and is comforted by his assurance that God will eventually put everything right. Shortly afterwards she discovers that she is pregnant. When her child, a little boy, named Luis, is born, he is immediately sent to be fostered, before being brought back to the family and passed off as a nephew. One day, when he is seven years old, he is trampled in the street by a careering horse. An old man, who has witnessed the accident, and fancies that the little boy looks like his own grown-up son, has him brought back to his house and given medical attention. Leocadia and her parents arrive, and Leocadia recognizes that her child is lying in the same room and on the same bed where she had been raped. She maintains a discreet silence and in the course of Luis's recovery becomes friendly with Rodolfo's parents, managing to find out from them that he is away in Italy. At last she reveals the truth to Rodolfo's mother, showing her the crucifix she had kept as proof of her bona fides. Rodolfo's mother is sympathetic, and writes telling her son to come home because she wants to introduce him to a beautiful woman whom she and his father have chosen to be his wife. On Rodolfo's return she shows him a miniature 'portrait' of her: she is much too plain-looking for Rodolfo's taste, and he refuses to consider marrying her. His mother agrees to withdraw from the marriage negotiations. When the family have assembled for the evening meal, a special guest is introduced. It is Leocadia, who enters the room leading Luis by the hand and flanked by two female servants carrying silver candlesticks. Rodolfo is overwhelmed by her beauty and cannot take his eyes off her. When Leocadia, overcome by her emotions, suffers a fainting fit, Rodolfo rushes forward to help her, and also faints. When he revives, he is very happy to be told that this is the woman his parents have actually chosen to be his wife. When Leocadia comes to, she and Rodolfo are immediately married by the parish priest, who had been waiting outside the room with her parents. Leocadia's identity is then revealed and proven to Rodolfo, who is happy to confirm his commitment to her. Although Rodolfo is not shown to express any sorrow for his act of rape, the tale ends announcing that he and Leocadia had a happy life together in Toledo and left many children and grandchildren after them.

7. El celoso extremeño (The Jealous Old Man from Extremadura)

Like the Prodigal Son, Felipo de Carrizales, the son of a noble family from Extremadura, squanders his inheritance on wild living in Spain, Italy, and Flanders, eventually ending up destitute in Seville. In despair, he decides to emigrate to the New World, vowing to be more careful with money and women in future. He keeps his promise, and after twenty years in Peru, aged sixty-eight, and a very wealthy man, he returns to Seville. All his friends and relatives are dead. Rejecting the idea of retiring to Extremadura, and wondering what to do with his fortune, he toys with the idea of marriage, but, because he is 'the most jealous man in the world' and cannot bear even the thought of a wife being unfaithful, this option is also discarded. One day, walking along the street, he looks up and sees a very beautiful young girl of about thirteen or fourteen sitting at an upper window. From the look of the house, he calculates that her family is not well off and that, should he marry her, she is young enough for him to control. He decides to ask her parents for her hand. Although noble, they are poor, and quite willing to entrust their daughter, Leonora, to such a wealthy suitor. Carrizales buys a house and reconditions it to ensure that his wife will neither see or be seen by any man except himself: the windows overlooking the street are blocked up; the parapet is raised; supplies will be delivered through a revolving hatch; the only male servant (the doorkeeper) will be a black eunuch; no male animals will be admitted; and no males, human or animal, will be represented in the paintings and tapestries. Carrizales's and Leonora's married life quickly settles into safe, predictable routine: he attends to business in the mornings, while Leonora amuses herself playing with dolls and making sweetmeats in the company of her maids and slaves. Then, an inquisitive young layabout, called Loaysa, discovers that the strange house contains a beautiful young woman. As a challenge, he decides to breach its defences and catch a glimpse of her. Using his (limited) skills as a musician to charm, first Luis, and then the female servants, he gets as far as the inner courtyard. By this time Leonora has become implicated and agrees to administer a sleeping ointment to her husband so that all the women of the household can safely enjoy a nocturnal musical party. Leonora's duenna, Marialonso, makes a private bargain with Loaysa: if she can get her mistress to go to bed with him, he must go to bed with her. Marialosno succeeds in cajoling Leonora into bed with Loaysa, but once there, she resists his efforts to make love to her, and they both fall asleep. The ointment applied to Carrizales does not work properly and he wakes up to find his wife and the master-key of the house missing. He searches for her, and eventually discovers her lying asleep in Loaysa's arms. Assuming the worst, he returns to his bedroom to fetch a sword and wipe out the stain on his honour with the blood of every member of the household, but, overwrought with emotion, he suffers a stroke and collapses on the bed. At dawn, Leonora returns to the bedroom and finds her husband apparently still asleep. She shakes him and is surprised to find that he wakes up and stares fixedly at her. Without explanation, he orders her to summon her parents. When they arrive, he reminds them of his generosity to their daughter, and then reveals her supposed betrayal, causing her to faint. He admits that hc is to blamc for marrying a woman so very much younger than himself. Declaring that he has not long to live, he announces the terms of his will: Leonora will inherit virtually all of his wealth, and is requested to marry the young man she slept with. Leonora attempts to explain her innocence but suffers another fainting fit. Carrizales dies within a week. Leonora enters a strictly enclosed convent; the servants are paid off; the slaves are freed; and Loaysa, in great dejection, abandons Spain for the New World.

8. La ilustre fregona (The Illustrious Kitchen Maid)

Two aristocratic teenagers from Burgos, Diego de Carriazo and Tomás de Avendaño, leave home, ostensibly to study in Salamanca, but actually to enjoy the free life-style of the tunny fisheries of Zahara in Andalusia, the gathering place for *pícaros* (delinquents or petty criminals) from all over Spain. Carriazo has only recently returned home after spending three years living such a life, a period which Avendaño has spent studying Greek and Latin at Salamanca. In Valladolid they slip away from their tutor, make off for Madrid, and don rough clothes before heading south. A conversation overheard between two real *pícaros* about a very beautiful kitchen maid working at the Sevillano inn in Toledo makes Avendaño is anxious to see her. Having done so, he falls in love with her, and persuades his reluctant companion to stay at the inn. Assuming the name of Tomás Pedro, he becomes a stable-boy, and Carriazo (now Lope Asturiano) works as water-carrier. While Avendaño adores the extremely reserved kitchen maid, Costanza, from afar, finding that he has a (not very serious) rival in the son of the Corregidor (chief magistrate), Carriazo is arrested for brawling with an older water-seller. Avendaño, however, uses their parents' money to secure his release. In the meantime, two middle-aged inn-prostitutes, la Gallega and la Argüello, take an (unrequited) fancy to the boys. Avendaño writes poems addressed to Costanza in the stable ledger-book, and eventually declares his love for her, and his real identity, in a letter, which she tears to shreds. Carriazo buys a donkey from a water-seller, then loses it, a quarter at a time over four card games, but refuses to surrender it, claiming that the tail is a fifth quarter which he did not stake. Over more card games, he wins back the animal and some money, but magnanimously hands back the money and the price of the donkey. The story of the tail spreads all over Toledo, and Carriazo is followed everywhere by young boys shouting 'Asturiano, give us the tail! Give us the tail, Asturiano!'[1] The Corregidor comes to have a look at the kitchen maid who so obsesses his son. He is told by the innkeeper that fifteen years earlier, an aristocratic lady on her way to the shrine of Our Lady of Guadalupe had spent a night in the inn and given birth to a child (Costanza); that she had asked that the child be brought up locally for two years, after which she would send for her; that she left behind, as a sign, some links of a gold chain, and half of a document containing the alternate letters of its one sentence, THIS IS THE TRUE SIGN; that the lady had never returned; and that he and his wife had brought up Costanza as their own child. Next day the boys' fathers, don Diego de Carriazo (Senior) and don Juan de Avendaño, arrive at the inn on a special mission. Don Diego brings with him the other links of the gold chain and the missing half of the document mentioned by the innkeeper, and explains that he is Costanza's father: many years before he had raped a noblewoman, with whom he had had no further contact. Just before his recent death, her steward told him about the birth of the child conceived as result of the rape, and surrendered the money entrusted to him by his now long-dead mistress as a dowry for her daughter, money which he had greedily kept for himself. Just then, Carriazo is dragged into the inn, and into his father's presence, under arrest for almost killing a boy who shouted after him in the streets. A shamefaced Avendaño is also reunited with his father. The charges against Carriazo (Junior) are dropped – the Corregidor is don Juan de Avendaño's cousin – and all ends happily: Tomás marries Costanza; Carriazo marries the Corregidor's daughter; and the Corregidor's son, marries one of Tomás's sisters. We are told that now Carriazo's three well-behaved sons are studying in Salamanca, and that all that troubles his respectable maturity is the fear that one day he may hear someone call after him in the street, 'Asturiano, give us the tail!' (III, p. 135).

9. Las dos doncellas (The Two Damsels)

A young traveller faints on arrival at an inn in Andalusia. Having recovered, he pays double to ensure that he does not have to share his room. His extraordinary good looks and extreme reserve arouse such curiosity among other visitors to the

[1] Translations are taken from Miguel de Cervantes, *Exemplary Novels / Novelas ejemplares*, ed. B. W. Ife, 4 vols (Warminster: Aris & Phillips, 1992); here, III, p. 113.

inn that they hatch a plot to trick him into letting another recently arrived guest (equally handsome but slightly older) into his room for the night. This second young man is awoken by the sobs of the first who begins talking to himself about a disaster that has befallen him. The newcomer offers his help and encourages his companion to share his story. In fact, the first guest turns out to be a woman called Teodosia, who has been abandoned by the young man (Marco Antonio Adorno) with whom she has had an intimate relationship based on the promise of marriage. Dressed as a man, she has gone in search of him in order to make him keep his promise, or avenge her dishonour by killing him. In the morning, Teodosia recognizes the person she has confided in as her brother, don Rafael de Villavicencio. Despite her pleas, he refuses to kill her and insists on helping her to find Marco Antonio. With Teodosia still dressed as a man and calling herself Teodoro, they set out for Barcelona, having heard that Marco Antonio is aboard a ship that will call there. Outside Barcelona they meet a young man who has recently been robbed by bandits. Teodosia finds out that this is, in fact, another woman in disguise. Her name is Leocadia, and she is searching for a young man called Marco Antonio who had given her a written promise of marriage but then failed to turn up for their first sexual assignation. He has absconded, she believes, with another woman called Teodosia. Without revealing their identities, Teodosia and don Rafael (who has started to fall in love with Leocadia) offer to assist her. In Barcelona they spy Marco Antonio involved in a fracas between the locals and people from one of the ships in the harbour. Although they assist him, he is badly wounded. They arrange for him to be brought to the house of don Sancho de Cardona, a Catalan gentleman whom they have befriended. When it looks as though he will die, Leocadia pleads with him to marry her, but he tells her that his obligation to Teodosia must take precedence on two grounds: although he had only given a verbal promise of marriage to Teodosia, he had made love to her, and does love her; although he had made a written promise of marriage to Leocadia (which has been stolen from her by the bandits), he had never made love to her, and does not love her. To Leocadia's great disappointment, he now renews his vows to Teodosia. Shortly afterwards, however, Leocadia accepts a proposal of marriage from don Rafael. Marco Antonio recovers from his illness, and they all set out on a pilgrimage to the shrine of Santiago de Compostela, helping Marco Antonio to fulfil a vow that he had made when he thought he was dying. Later, as they approach their native town in Andalusia, they see three men engaged in knightly combat. It turns out that they are the fathers of Teodosia and Leocadia, who have sought to avenge their daughters' dishonour by jousting with the father of Marco Antonio. The four young people are able to resolve the quarrel; marriage ceremonies take place on the following day, and both couples enjoy long and happy lives. They are succeeded by many distinguished descendants, some of whom, it is said, are still alive to this day.

10. La señora Cornelia (Lady Cornelia)

While studying in Italy, two young Spanish gentlemen, don Juan de Gamboa and don Antonio de Isunza, help Lady Cornelia Bentibolli, a Bolognese noblewoman finally to marry Alonso de Este, Duke of Ferrara, the man with whom she has been having a relationship, who has promised to marry her, and by whom she has had a child, but from whom she has become separated on the eve of their elopement to France by a complicated series of accidents. That night, the newly-born child is placed into the hands of don Juan by someone who thinks that he is the Duke's servant, Fabio; later the same night, don Juan unwittingly helps the Duke in a sword-fight against Cornelia's bother, Lorenzo, who has sought to avenge what he believes to be her dishonour, and then returns home to find that don Antonio has given refuge there to a beautiful woman, who turns out to be Cornelia. She tells them her story and is reunited with her child. Don Lorenzo then appears and, unaware of his sister's presence in the house, persuades don Juan to accompany him to Ferrara to confront the Duke. They are secretly followed by don Antonio. Meanwhile, the Spanish gentlemen's housekeeper goes with Cornelia and her child to seek refuge with a priest in a village near Ferrara. The Duke explains to don Lorenzo that his intention to marry Cornelia is sincere; if he had not done so previously, it is because he did not want to upset his mother – now very ill and expected to die – who had wanted him to marry the daughter of the Duke of Mantua. The Duke returns to Bologna with don Lorenzo, don Juan, and don Antonio. Not seeing Lady Cornelia immediately, they are told that she is in a page's room, but it is merely another woman of the same name in bed with the page; informed that she is upstairs, they find another Cornelia in bed with another page. The Duke returns to Ferrara and, on the way calls on an old friend who is a priest, the same priest who has given refuge to Cornelia. Don Lorenzo and the two Spaniards are summoned. When they arrive, they are told that the Duke cannot marry Cornelia because he must honour a previous promise to a peasant girl. The other men are about to kill the Duke, when it is revealed that the whole thing is just a jest: the peasant woman is, of course, Cornelia. The Duke and Cornelia are unofficially married, a fact is kept secret until the death of the Duke's mother, which happens shortly afterwards. Cornelia's maid, Sulpicia, marries the Duke's man, Fabio. Don Juan and don Antonio stay in Italy long enough to see Cornelia have two more children, and, on their return to Spain, marry 'wealthy, noble and beautiful ladies' (IV, p. 55).

11. El casamiento engañoso (The Deceitful Marriage)

The Ensign Campuzano, who has just emerged in an enfeebled state from the Hospital of the Resurrection in Valladolid where he has been undergoing a course of treatment for syphilis, meets his friend, the Licentiate Peralta, and explains how he ended up there. Pretending to be a man of substance, he had married a woman called doña Estefanía, who, in turn, had made herself out to be a wealthy woman. They had gone to live in doña Estefanía's very comfortable home, but when a woman called doña Clementa Bueso, accompanied by a don López Meléndez de Almendárez, arrived, claiming the house as theirs, doña Estefanía explained that she had arranged to loan it to doña Clementa for the purpose of playing a trick on don Lope. Campuzano and Estefanía had then moved into cramped lodgings with another friend of Estefanía's. After a week, the friend had confided to Campuzano that doña Estefanía had deceived him, and that doña Clementa was the real owner of the house. When he had gone to confront her, he found that she had absconded with his gold chains, which, as Campuzano, informs Peralta, were not made of real gold. The whole affair had been a classic case of 'tit for tat'. All he got out of the marriage was a dose of syphilis, and a very strange experience: on the last two nights of his stay in hospital, he claims that he overheard two long conversations between the guard dogs, Cipión and Berganza. He had transcribed the first conversation from memory, and he now offers it to Peralta to read. Despite his openly expressed incredulity about its truthfulness, Peralta begins to read the 'Dialogue of the Dogs' while Campuzano settles back in his chair to sleep.

12. El coloquio de los perros (The Dialogue of the Dogs)

The dogs Cipión and Berganza, finding themselves miraculously endowed with the gift of speech, agree to extract the maximum benefit from it by telling each other their life stories over two successive nights. Berganza goes first. In a manner reminiscent of picaresque autobiography he tells of his experiences with a number of different masters representing the whole spectrum of society. He believes that he was born in Seville, and recalls that his first owner worked in the slaughterhouse there. When he was unfairly beaten for something he did not do, he moved away to work for some shepherds in the countryside, but found them to be even crueller than his first master. He also worked in Seville for a merchant and a constable (*alguacil*), then as a performing dog for an army drummer he encountered in Mairena. His most unusual experience was an encounter in Montilla with a witch, la Cañizares, who informed him that she remembered seeing both him Cipión and being born as the human children of a fellow witch, la Montiela, before being transformed into dogs by their jealous teacher, the great witch, la Camacha. She told him of a prophecy, which seemed to promise that when they saw the mighty cast down and the humble raised up by a mysteriously powerful hand, they would eventually recover their original human form. Berganza then spent short periods with some gypsies; a Morisco (Baptized Moor) in Granada; a poet-playwright; and a company of actors. Finally, having seen Cipión out collecting alms with Mahudes (a historical personage) for the Hosptital of the Resurrection in Valladolid, and attracted by the goodness they represented, he decided to join them. As a dog, he has been able to observe the whole gamut of human failings – pride, greed, hypocrisy, deception – in their unmasked form, and so his observations add up to a devastating and depressing critique of human nature in general and of Spanish society in particular. In the hospital itself he has witnessed the derangement produced by intellectual pride in four inmates – a poet, an alchemist, a mathematician, and a political theorist (*arbitrista*) – and had brief encounters with the Corregidor (magistrate), and with a noble lady and her lap-dog, that have confirmed his experience that power and rank will always take precedence over truth. Throughout, Berganza's narration is frequently interrupted by Cipión's critical comments on its form and content, and by both dogs' reflections on a whole range of subjects, including literature, philosophy, and morality. As soon as Peralta finishes reading the transcript of the dogs' dialogue, Campuzano wakes up. They agree to disagree about the literal truth of the dogs' conversation, but Peralta expresses his appreciation of what he calls its 'art' and 'invention' (IV, p. 157). They decide that, since they have given enough exercise to their minds, they will now take some physical recreation in the form of a stroll around the Espolón, a famous square in Valladolid overlooking the river.

Appendix II: Further Reading

General

Avalle-Arce, J. B., and E. C. Riley (ed.), *Suma cervantina* (London: Támesis, 1973).

Cascardi, Anthony J. (ed.), *The Cambridge Companion to Cervantes* (Cambridge: Cambridge University Press, 2002).

Close, Anthony, and others (ed.), *Cervantes* (Alcalá de Henares: Centro de Estudios Cervantinos, 1995).

Forcione, Alban K., *Cervantes, Aristotle, and the 'Persiles'* (Princeton, NJ: Princeton University Press, 1970).

Riley, E. C., *Cervantes's Theory of the Novel* (Oxford: Clarendon Press, 1962).

———, 'Cervantes: A Question of Genre', in *Medieval and Renaissance Studies on Spain and Portugal in Honour of P. E. Russell*, ed. F. W. Hodcroft and others (Oxford: Society for the Study of Mediaeval Languages and Literature, 1981), pp. 69–85.

———, *La rara invención: estudios sobre Cervantes y su posteridad literaria*, tr. Mari Carmen Llerena (Barcelona: Crítica, 2001).

Urbina, Edward (dr.), 'Cervantes Project 2001': <http://www.csdl.tamu.edu/cervantes/english/>.

Williamson, Edwin (ed.), *Cervantes and the Modernists: The Question of Influence* (London: Támesis, 1994).

The *Novelas ejemplares*

a. Editions

Avalle-Arce, Juan Bautista, *Novelas ejemplares*, 3 vols (Madrid: Clásicos Castalia, 1982, 1987).

García López, Jorge, *Novelas ejemplares* (Barcelona: Crítica, 2001).

Sieber, Harry, *Novelas ejemplares*, 2 vols (Madrid: Cátedra, 1984).

Schevill, Rodolfo, and Adolfo Bonilla, *Novelas ejemplares*, 3 vols (Madrid: Gráficas Reunidas, 1921–25).

b. English Translations

Ife, B. W. (ed.), *Exemplary Novels / Novelas ejemplares*, 4 vols (Warminster: Aris & Phillips, 1992).

Jones, C. A., *Exemplary Stories* (Harmondsworth: Penguin, 1972).

Mabbe, James, *Exemplary Novels by Cervantes*, ed. S. W. Orson, 2 vols (London, 1640; London: Gibbings; Philadelphia: J. B. Lippincott, 1900).

Onís, Harriet de, *Six Exemplary Tales* (Woodbury, NY: Barron's, 1961).

c. Critical Studies

Amezúa y Mayo, Agustín G. de, *Cervantes creador de la novela corta española*, 2 vols (Madrid: Consejo Superior de Investigaciones Científicas, 1956–58).

Atkinson, William C., 'Cervantes, El Pinciano and the *Novelas ejemplares*', *HR*, 16 (1948), 189–208.

Aylward, E. T., *Cervantes: Pioneer and Plagiarist* (London: Támesis, 1982).

———, *The Crucible Concept: Thematic and Narrative Patterns in Cervantes's 'Novelas ejemplares'* (Madison, NJ: Associated University Press, 1999).

Bustos Tovar, José Jesús de, *Lenguaje, ideología y organización textual en las 'Novelas ejemplares'* (Madrid: Universidad Complutense; Toulouse: Université de Toulouse-Le Mirail, 1983).

Casalduero, Joaquín, *Sentido y forma de las 'Novelas ejemplares'* (Madrid: Gredos, 1974).

Clamurro, William H., *Beneath the Fiction: The Contrary Worlds of Cervantes's 'Novelas ejemplares'* (New York: Peter Lang, 1997).

Dunn, Peter N., 'Las *Novelas ejemplares*', in *Suma cervantina*, ed. J. B. Avalle-Arce and E. C. Riley (London: Támesis, 1973), pp. 81–118.

El Saffar, Ruth S., *Novel to Romance: A Study of Cervantes's 'Novelas ejemplares'* (Baltimore: The Johns Hopkins University Press, 1974).

Forcione, Alban K., *Cervantes and the Humanist Vision: A Study of Four 'Exemplary Novels'* (Princeton, NJ: Princeton University Press, 1984).

———, *Cervantes and the Mystery of Lawlessness: A Study of 'El casamiento engañoso' and 'El coloquio de los perros*' (Princeton, NJ: Princeton University Press, 1984).

Gaylord, Mary Malcolm, 'Cervantes' Other Fiction', in *The Cambridge Companion to Cervantes*, ed. Anthony J. Cascardi (Cambridge: Cambridge University Press, 2002).

Hart, Thomas R., *Cervantes's Exemplary Fictions: A Study of the 'Novelas ejemplares'* (Lexington, KY: University Press of Kentucky, 1994).

Nerlich, Michael, and Nicholas Spadaccini (eds), *Cervantes's 'Exemplary Novels' and the Adventure of Writing* (Minneapolis: The Prisma Institute, 1989).

Pierce, Frank, 'Reality and Realism in the *Exemplary Novels*', *BHS*, 30 (1953), 134–42.

Rabell, Carmen R., *Rewriting the Italian Novella in Counter-Reformation Spain* (London: Támesis, 2003).

Rey Hazas, Antonio, '*Novelas ejemplares*', in *Cervantes*, ed. Anthony Close and others (Alcalá de Henares: Centro de Estudios Cervantinos, 1995), pp. 173–209.

Ricapito, Joseph V., *Cervantes's 'Novelas ejemplares': Between History and Creativity* (West Lafayette, IN: Purdue University Press, 1996).

———, *Formalistic Aspects of Cervantes's 'Novelas ejemplares*' (Lewinton, NJ: Mellen Press, 1997).

Rodríguez-Luis, Julio, *Novedad y ejemplo de las 'Novelas' de Cervantes*, 2 vols (Madrid: Porrúa Turanzas, 1980).

Sánchez, Francisco J., *Lectura y representación: Análisis cultural de las 'Novelas ejemplares' de Cervantes* (New York: Peter Lang, 1993).

Sears, Theresa A., *A Marriage of Convenience: Ideal and Ideology in the 'Novelas ejemplares*' (New York: Peter Lang, 1993).

Zimic, Stanislav, *Las 'Novelas ejemplares' de Cervantes* (Madrid: Siglo Veintiuno, 1996).

Index